Forbidden Federalism

Secret Diplomacy
and the Struggle for a
Danubian Confederation
1918–1921

Zoltán Bécsi

Helena History Press

Copyright 2020 © Zoltán Bécsi
All rights reserved
Published in the United States by:

Helena History Press LLC
A division of KKL Publications LLC, Reno, Nevada USA
www.helenahistorypress.com
Publishing scholarship about and from Central and East Europe

ISBN 978-1-943596-11-9

Order from:
UK: *orders@nbni.uk*
USA: *orders@hfs.com*
Hungary: *ceupress@press.ceu.edu* or *editor@helenahistorypress.com*

Copy Editor: Jill Hannum, Krisztina Kós
Graphic Designer: Sebastian Stachowski

Printed In Hungary by Prime Rate Kft., Budapest

To my parents

Table of Contents

Acknowledgements ix
A Note on the Spelling of Names xi
Preface xiii
Introduction 1

CHAPTER I
Danubian Confederation and Legitimism 11

CHAPTER II
Karl Tries Britain and France 57

CHAPTER III
The New Centre of Danubian Europe? 95

CHAPTER IV
The Croatians' Struggle for Autonomy 131

CHAPTER V
Slovaks: The Unwilling Czechoslovaks 171

CHAPTER VI
Habsburg or Little Entente? August 1920–November 1921
and What Followed 211

Epilogue 257
Postface 273
Bibliography 275
Index 289

Acknowledgements

This book is a somewhat adapted version of my doctoral dissertation presented at the Graduate Institute of International Studies of the University of Geneva and supervised by professors at both Oxford and Geneva. I haven't space to mention all the people who have helped and supported me during almost a decade of research, but I wish to convey my special thanks to some of the most important contributors to, and facilitators of this enterprise. I'll start by thanking Marianne de Szeoczy (+), Count and Countess László and Erzsébet Károlyi for their special support. Thanks also to László's aunt, Princess Erzsébet Windischgraetz (Prince Lajos Windischgraetz's daughter), and Archdukes Rudolph (+) and Lorenz of Habsburg-Lorraine for having opened their private libraries, family archives and remembrances. I owe much to academics such as Prof. Szabolcs de Vajay (+) and his inspiring unpublished dissertation, Prof. André Reszler, Lieut.-Col. F. Guelton (Director of Research of the SHAT in Vincennes), Prof. Dénes Sokcsevits (Dinko Šokčević) (University of Pécs). Thanks also to my colleagues at the Teleki László Institute's Centre for Foreign Affairs, who received me as their guest, among them Professors György Granasztói (+), Tamás Magyarics, László Kiss J. and their very helpful and efficient librarian, Anna-Mária Sándor.

I am also grateful to my mentors and supervisors from Oxford, Paris and Geneva: Regius Professor R.J.W. Evans, Professors Jean-Paul Bled, Bruno Arcidiacono and, last, but not least, André Liebich for advising and assisting me with all their expertise and knowledge during my research and writing phases. Very special thanks to the sharp-eyed Jill Hannum for copy editing and correcting the final manuscript. My thanks also go to all the kind

Acknowledgements

archivists in Paris, London, Oxford, Budapest, Vienna, the Vatican, and the Hoover Institution for their assistance and useful advice. Also, for the extraordinary support, kindness and friendship I thank my editor, the historian Katalin Kádár Lynn, and her husband Douglas Lynn, without whom this book could not have been published. And finally, I owe much to my family for their enduring support and patience.

A Note on the Spelling of Names

It can be rather confusing to the reader to encounter many different spellings of the same name. First, with regard to Karl/Charles: I use "Karl", as he is known throughout historiography by that name. However, when quoting French- or English-language sources, I have retained their original use of "Charles". In Austria-Hungary there were many spellings of personal names and places depending on the language used. Some villages and towns had more than three names, such as today's Bratislava, capital of Slovakia, called Pozsony in Hungarian, Pressburg in German, Prešporok in Slovak (before 1918) and Possonium in Latin. It even had a French name: Presbourg. The same goes for the town, today in Slovakia, of Košice/Kassa/Kaschau, Cassovie in French, and Cassovia in Latin. For the names of persons, a similar problem can appear. An individual's name can have many spellings. The Slovak politician František Jehlička's name would be spelled thus in Bratislava, but in Budapest he would be called Ferenc Jehlicska and in Vienna, Franz Jehlitschka. I have chosen to use the Slovak and Croatian spellings of the Slovak and Southern Slav (Croatian, Serbian, and Bosnian) names respectively. For Hungarian names, I use Hungarian spelling. In some cases I use the German, Hungarian or even Italian (for Dalmatian towns) version for the simple reason that they appear as such in the primary sources I studied. I will often mention in brackets the Hungarian or German names and surnames when required, because before 1918 they were often used as such, especially in Hungary, where the national language was Hungarian. In the case of Slovak and Croatian localities, I sometimes indicate the version used with a letter in backets; e.g., H for Hungarian, D for German, I for Italian, or SK for Slovak.

Preface

History lingers on. Historians and their readers like specific dates: 11 November 1918 for the end of the First World War; 9 November 1989 for the fall of the Berlin Wall. As Zoltán Bécsi shows, however, history has an after-life. Empires in particular do not disappear in a single day. From 1918 to 1921, the Austro-Hungarian Empire lived on in the minds of many, as a terrifying scarecrow for some, as a not-yet-completely lost ideal for others.

It is these others whom Zoltán Bécsi looks at in this book. The key concept of his title is that of federalism, understood as a unifying factor for the peoples of the former Austro-Hungarian Empire. During the First World War, even those resolutely in favour of dismantling Austria-Hungary, such as those who put out *The New Europe*, an influential weekly publication based in London to which not only Wickham Steed and R.W. Seton-Watson but also the future Czechoslovak president, T.G. Masaryk, contributed, recognized that the Danubian area required some sort of federal unity, if only for economic reasons. They may not have realized it then, but it became clear soon thereafter, that the fragmentation of this part of Europe would play into the hands of German ambitions and would soon subject the region to overwhelming German influence. Zoltán Bécsi makes much of this danger, looking ahead to the 1930s, and adding, for good measure, Soviet domination at a later date.

Why did federalist plans, acknowledged at least with lip service by all concerned, come to naught? This is the question that Zoltán Bécsi tackles and answers ably in this book. He reminds the reader that Anglo-French rivalry, until recently conveniently forgotten, was the dominant diplomatic reality in the aftermath of the First World War. We have seen how this rivalry played out in the Near East, where Anglo-French jockeying over Palestine, Syria and Iraq has attracted scholarly attention. Zoltán Bécsi shows that a similar dynamic operated in Central Europe. French support for Hungarian-based confederation schemes was half-hearted and self-contradictory; British lip-service to confederal plans even more so. Zoltán Bécsi does well to point out that the Little Entente was not the creation of France, and even less so that of Great Britain. Its creator was Eduard Beneš, the wily and ever-present foreign minister and, after the death of T.G. Masaryk in 1937, president of a Czechoslovakia, doomed, the author of this book would agree, by an excess of Machiavellian intransigence. Indeed, the villain of this book is Czechoslovakia, the most single-mindedly anti-Habsburg of the successor states and the one which took the lead in opposing federalist schemes which would have revived the shadow of the defunct empire.

A term which does not appear in the title of this book, but is present throughout, is that of "legitimism", the ideology of a Habsburg restoration promoted by the deposed emperor-king, Charles I or Károly IV, and by his numerous, if ineffective, supporters. Many of these supporters had other priorities. Some Croats, including former Austro-Hungarian officers who figure largely in this account, thought of a Habsburg restoration to counter Serb hegemony. Slovaks found that they preferred Hungarian to Czech domination. Zoltán Bécsi enlightens us on the division within royalist Hungary itself between "legitimists" who wished Charles back and "free electors" who wanted to choose their king. He does not conceal the fact, though he might have insisted much more, that a Habsburg restoration was a red flag to the Entente powers and the governments of the successor states.

What comes out most clearly is the extent to which emperor-king Charles contributed, innocently and almost unknowingly, to the fear and repugnance aroused by plans of a Habsburg restoration. His correspondence with the pope, cited extensively here, demonstrates his almost complete detachment from the hard realities created in post-war Central Europe. None of the successor states would give anything up to further Charles' plans. Even in Hungary, territorial revisionism took pride of place to federal or confederal schemes, thus guaranteeing the enmity of its neighbours and the failure of Charles' generous projects. His abhorrence of bloodletting was one of the factors that won him canonization in the Roman Catholic Church, to which he remained perfectly faithful throughout his life. It did not further his political ambitions. Zoltán Bécsi makes a strong case for Charles' Francophilia, an important factor in the emperor-king's rejection of a German-Austrian Anschluss. It is not surprising, however, that within the Entente military men, mindful of how closely Austria-Hungary had followed German leadership throughout the First World War, proved sceptical about this reorientation. Had Charles chosen to break with Germany before the Central Powers had suffered defeat, his place in history may well have been different. The Entente Powers were astonishingly well-disposed to Austria-Hungary and it was only very late in the War that they accepted its dissolution. Once the War was over, their hands were tied and their sympathy for the deposed, and demonstrably weak, monarch petered out.

Bécsi's book is a study in virtual history, what might have been, and reading it one is tempted to follow this line of thought as well. The shadowy figures that cross its pages—the Marquis de Castellane who sought to win over the Foreign Office to Charles' plans, the better-known Stepan Radić who played with federal schemes in an effort to advance the Croatian cause, or the obscure swindler Karol Bulissa—all failed in their attempts. However, history is an account of failures as it is of successes and the former deserve their place in historical narrative.

Success, and with it, failure, may be fleeting. Zoltán Bécsi's book is riding on the current Habsburg nostalgia, a sentiment that has, surprisingly, even reached Hungary. Historians of a quite different bent from that of Bécsi, such as Eric Hobsbawm, have stated, somewhat inelegantly that "the chickens of World War I have come home to roost". The present configuration in Central Europe, with the emergence of the Visegrad bloc and disintegration in the Balkans, would seem to confirm Hobsbawm's intuition and to make Zoltán Bécsi's work more relevant than ever. This book remains a story of failure. It is a failure that we would do well to reflect upon.

Andre Liebich
Honorary Professor of International History and Politics
The Graduate Institute, Geneva

Introduction

There were many misunderstandings, differences, and conflicts within the Habsburg Monarchy, but when the anthem was intoned, all subjects of the monarch, from Bregenz to Czernowitz and from Krakow to Dubrovnik, Christians, Jews, and Muslims alike would sing: "Gott Erhalte …". There is something fascinating about the centripetal forces of this multiethnic state that made me wonder why historians have written so much about the decline and fall, the destruction and the non-viability of Austria-Hungary instead of concentrating on what was successful, common and viable in the so-called "prison of peoples". What made some ethnic groups or nationalities want to remain members of it, in its new form as a Danubian Confederation, even after the bloodshed, famine, and misery of World War I?

I will endeavor to present a history that ran parallel with the official one. It is about diplomacy, often secret, that happened behind the scenes. This diplomacy was the opposite of what was then the official policy of the Entente, with sympathisers—on both the Entente and the Central European sides—who had a different idea of Central Europe.

In the following pages I study these sympathisers and often their shared vision for Central Europe. I briefly look at two concepts, Federalism and Legitimism,[1] and two categories of political actors, federalists and legitimists. These political actors and thinkers made plans, often vague, or suggestions for the reorganisation of the region of the former Habsburg Mon-

---

1   Legitimists were monarchists that supported legal continuity—interrupted after World War I—and the reestablishment of Karl IV, the crowned king of Hungary, and his descendants.

archy. My first hypothesis is that no matter whether these political actors were federalists, legitimists[2] or both—or many other things such as autonomists, separatists, nationalists, etc.—they had one thing in common: they did not want to belong to a nation state that would crush their will for autonomy or independence. My second hypothesis—which is the reason I connect the two groups—is that federalists were often legitimists or at least had legitimist feelings because they wanted to keep some sort of link to their old, larger homeland, the Habsburg Monarchy. In some cases, they were still fascinated by that entity, in other cases, they missed its mere existence, which procured for them a feeling of security in a postwar world full of uncertainties and threats. One should not forget that the war happened mainly outside of the monarchy's borders, and when it ended, turmoil, revolutions, conflicts, occupations, hunger, and hardship caught up with its former inhabitants. For many of his subjects, the monarch held a position which was above the different nationalities, and they could turn to him if they felt that they were not treated equitably or that their rights were being menaced. This was particularly the case for the Muslim Bosnians and the Jews of the monarchy in general. They felt that the emperor-king was their protector and their objective judge against arbitrary treatment. There were probably many other reasons why the monarch was an archetypal father figure representing stability for the different ethnic groups. For those who felt threatened by internal or external menaces, his person was an obviously important and reassuring figure to look up to.

Most of the legitimist federalists, including the main person concerned, Emperor-King Karl of Austria-Hungary (Karl I in Austria, Károly IV in Hungary)[3] himself, wished to see Austria-Hungary reformed into a federation before the end of the war or recreated on a federal basis after 1918. But in what form—a confederation or a federation,[4] a monarchy or a republic

---

2   As I will show, on one hand, some Hungarian legitimists recognised autonomy for Slovaks but not the transformation of Hungary into a Federation. On the other, they were not against a form of confederation with other nation states of the region.
3   When putting the title "king" before the name of the king, I will use the Hungarian version of his name: "King Károly" or Károly IV.
4   I use the words "confederation" or "Danubian Confederation" as general terminology for most of the projects, as they were called by their authors, which were often different in content than the definition of a confederation. I will come back to the exact definitions later.

or both, or perhaps little republics federalised around the Habsburg monarch? Or was it to be a sort of Habsburg commonwealth, or a military alliance to protect the little nations and nationalities from the gluttony of neighbouring states with imperialistic designs on other nations (Serbia, Germany, Soviet Russia etc.) and from Panslavism and Pangermanism; and to protect them as well from internal nationalisms and the designs of small nations regarding even smaller ones, as in the case of the Czech domination over the Slovaks?

This leads us to the principal question, which is to understand whether the nations of the Habsburg Monarchy had any chance of reappearing in a federal/confederal structure in the years following World War I. And its corollary: was a Danubian Confederation a feasible alternative to the Versailles System in Central Europe? I will also try to answer the question whether it was possible to recreate it with or without the Habsburgs and to look at the role of French foreign policy in support of a Danubian Confederation.

One of the challenges of this work has been to identify what the federalists and legitimists really fought for. It would be, however, far fetched to claim that all persons involved in questioning the geographical status quo were part of one these two groups or both. Some were opportunists and claimed to be one or the other or even both. Others were openly or secretly independentists, hence it is difficult to claim with certainty that they were federalists. To achieve their aims, some would only instrumentalise these notions without really believing in them. These observations obliged me to widen the scope and describe many groups of resistance and, when sources enable me to do so, I have tried to identify their real convictions and aims.

As a result, my research is limited not only to the study of confederal or federal projects, but also to projects that tended to evolve towards these two solutions, such as national autonomies granted by Hungary. I also present the links these plans have to the Legitimist movement or to legitimist individuals, if they exist. In other words, I describe the different plans, confederal or federal structures and autonomies, and the efforts, be they military or peaceful, to realise them.

Introduction

The Period Studied

In choosing the period studied, 1918–1921, two events were considered: the first date (16 October 1918) was the federalisation of the Austrian Empire (Cisleithania) by Karl I; the terminus was the law of dethronement of the Habsburgs in the Kingdom of Hungary (November 1921).

Though the federalisation attempt of 1918 would only affect the structure of the Austrian Empire (Cisleithania) and not the Kingdom of Hungary (Transleithania), it still gave a signal to all the ethnic groups, even the ones in Hungary, the effect of which would hasten the disintegration of the Dual Monarchy.[5]

Practically, all the present day histories that treat the end of the Habsburg Monarchy finish with 1918, and very few of them extend into subsequent years. It is an omission not to mention the attempts at restoration in Hungary (1921)—and the consequence of their failure: the dethronement in 1921—as part of the phenomenon of integration or disintegration of the Habsburg Monarchy, as Robert Kann would phrase it.[6] By showing how important these years were for the future of Central Europe, I hope to contribute to a new interpretation of the end of the Dual Monarchy. Indeed, these few years represent a concentration of some of the major problems that survived up to the 1990s.

But why stop in 1921? Three arguments can legitimise such a limitation:

(1) 1921 is the year of the dethronement by the Hungarian Parliament—under Entente pressure—of King Károly, which would exclude the possibility of any Habsburg again sitting on the throne of Hungary.

(2) Even though a parliamentary decision could be changed in the future, dethronement proved to be a *point de non retour*, as Hungary never re-estab-

---

5   In the sources presented in this book the authors often call Austria-Hungary the Austrian or Habsburg Empire, or just the Empire. For the sake of being precise, I have opted to call it Austria-Hungary, the Empire-Kingdom or the Dual Monarchy and only use the word "Empire" when specifically speaking of Austria, unless of course I am mentioning the Empire before 1867, the year of the creation of the Dual Monarchy, or in a broader period of history.
6   Kann, Robert, *The Habsburg Empire, A Study of Integration and Disintegration*, Octagon Books, New York, 1979.

lished the Habsburgs. This was due to the victors' policy of establishing the new order of Versailles and its by-product, the Little Entente, this made a Central European monarchy or even a Danubian Confederation hardly possible, as it isolated Hungary. The death of the Habsburg monarch in 1922 only added to the difficulty of a return to the monarchy. The Entente chose to recognise the Little Entente, and by doing so it put into the grave any possibility of uniting the nations of this region. The Little Entente, as the new by product of the Versailles system, was truly confirmed in 1921, during the attempts to return Karl IV to Hungary; and no change could be made without its deconstruction, due to the fierce opposition between its members and, mainly, Hungary. Eventually, in 1938, under pressure from the revisionist powers, a change did come that definitively meant the end of the system, though this change did not bring federalism but war. Eventually, no country in Central Europe gained a real victory in Saint-Germain and Trianon, since the treaties signed there soon resulted in minority problems, fascisms, communism, and Soviet occupation. All nations were losers at the end of the game, even if some enlarged their territory or gained a state after 1918.

(3) The last reason to close in 1921 is to show that the Habsburg Monarchy terminated, in Hungary's point of view, in November 1921; and this is another hypothesis that I hope to prove in this work. As no possibility was provided to recreate the Austro-Hungarian Monarchy, the distant watcher of history can confirm that for the Monarchy's admirers, this date truly was fatal. It was also fatal for some in the camp opposing the Habsburgs, such as Sir Anthony Eden, Churchill's Foreign Minister, who went as far as to say retrospectively in the *New York Times* of October 6, 1950: "The collapse of the Austro-Hungarian Empire was a calamity for the peace of Europe."

The Nations Studied

This study is limited to three Danubian states of the former Austro-Hungarian Monarchy: Hungary, SHS (Serb, Croatian, and Slovene) or the Yugoslav Kingdom, and Czechoslovakia. Among these countries, I only look at regions that were part of the Kingdom of Hungary (Transleithania)—Hungary, Croatia, and Slovakia—and therefore do not include Austria (Cisleithania). The other half of the former Monarchy, Cisleithania (Austria), is incorporated in this work only as the home or refuge of legitimists and federalists, for during this period German Austria was preoccupied mainly with joining Germany, and not by reverting to monarchy. I concentrate on the Hungarian, Croat, and Slovak federalists and legitimists and do not cover, for practical reasons, ethnic groups such as the Sub-Carpathian Ruthenians (representing a small ethnic minority in pre-1918) or the Serbs of the former Hungarian region of Vojvodina.

Though Romania had occupied a very important region of Hungary, Transylvania, I do not look at minorities (Hungarian and German) in Romania for three reasons: first, after the establishment of the interwar Horthy regime (1920), the Hungarian government was trying, briefly, to establish an alliance with Romania; second, Karl IV was maintaining rather good relations with his cousin, the Hohenzollern King of Romania; third, the main non-Romanian ethnic groups of the old region of Transylvania (Hungarians and Germans)—which were already a minority in the region before the break up of Hungary—were integrated into the nation state of the Kingdom of Romania. Consequently, both Hungarians and Germans became even smaller ethnic groups of the newly enlarged Kingdom of Romania.

The choice of limiting the study to only two peoples apart from the Hungarians, the Slovaks and the Croatians, is justified by their similarities: their homelands were part of the Kingdom of Hungary before 1918 and did not exist as independent states and would only become such under the protectorate of Nazi Germany; they were both distinctive ethnic groups and considered themselves as such; and they both were refused autonomy, or simply independence, first by Hungary and then by the governments of their respective Successor States (the Czechs and Serbs claimed that Slovaks and Croatians respectively were the same people). Finally, they did not have some of their population living outside of the borders of the Dual Monarchy, as in the example of Transylvanian Romanians, who had a nation state motherland, the Kingdom of Romania. The differences were fewer in number: Croatia benefited from a form of autonomy—though not very generous—and was represented in the Budapest Parliament; Croatians were considered a "historical nation" by the German Austrian literature and Slovaks were not. The Slovaks of Upper Hungary (later to be called Slovakia) did not benefit from such advantages and privileges.

These questions on autonomy lead us to the choice of this work's title: federalism as a political idea forbidden or outlawed by the Successor States of the Habsburg Monarchy. I will try to address how this could happen once the Slovaks and Croatians were liberated from Austria-Hungary, called "the prison of peoples".

The Place of the Work in Historiography

The most prominent protagonist among the old school of historians, who claimed that the Habsburg Monarchy was brought down by the nationalities problem and that it was doomed, was Oszkár Jászi, himself involved in the process of keeping the non-Magyar nationalities in Hungary as minister of minorities of Hungary (1918–19).[7] The first, Anglo-Saxon historian (of Austrian origin) to bring countering elements on the period was Robert Kann, who used the same method as Jászi, which consisted of studying the centripetal and centrifugal, integrating and disintegrating forces in order to see whether or not the Dual Monarchy was still viable.[8] British historiography had to wait until Alan Sked's *The Decline and Fall of the Habsburg Empire, 1815–1918* (1989), which revised the old historiography and claimed that Austria-Hungary was not doomed because there was no decline until 1914 (in fact, it had been ascending since 1867); the nationality problem was not so acute as to bring it down, since the nationalities fought in the k. u. k. army until the end of the war; it was mainly the war that made it fall.[9] Pieter Judson's recently published revisionist account of the Habsburg Empire also goes in this direction and points out that the end of it was brought about by the war and the Allies.[10] French historians developed a similar revisionist school, led by François Fejtö with his *Requiem pour un Empire*

---

7 Jászi, Oszkár, *The Dissolution of the Habsburg Monarchy*, University of Chicago Press, Chicago, 1929.
8 Kann claimed that the catalyst for disintegration was the war, *op. cit.*, mostly 135–41, 153–67.
9 Sked, Alan, *The Decline and Fall of the Habsburg Empire 1815–1918*, Longman, London, 1989, 258–69.
10 Judson, Pieter M., *The Habsburg Empire, A New History*, The Belknap Press of Harvard University Press, Cambridge, MA, 2016.

défunt (1988), who inspired Jean Bérenger (1993) and Pierre Béhar (1999).[11] Bérenger claimed again that the Empire-Kingdom did not fall because of the nationalities, but he added that neither was it caused by "the formidable tensions created by the world conflict".[12] It was the Entente, and especially France, that decided to pull it down in an effort to "extirpate from Europe the last remains of clericalism and monarchism", even if Austria had introduced universal suffrage in 1907, and even if it was, with Hungary, one of the most liberal states of Europe and one of the most advanced states of law on the continent.[13] This brought Fejtö to say, "la Première Guerre mondiale a commencé comme une guerre classique (impérialiste) et a fini comme une guerre idéologique."[14] In other words not only to defeat but to destroy, and Bérenger goes as far as to say that it was the fault of the anti-Habsburg French left, which had listened to Tomáš Garrigue Masaryk's[15] ideas to reorganise the map of Europe in the belief that it would secure peace and bar German imperialism instead of allowing the development of the federalist project of empire elaborated by the Habsburgs.[16] However, one cannot neglect to mention that public opinion in France was far from unanimous in its aim of destroying the Habsburg Monarchy. Even the zealous republican and anticleric Georges Clemenceau, prime minister of France during the second half of the Great War, would send his natural son, Paul Dutasta, to Bern as a diplomat in order to continue talks with the Austro-Hungarian emissaries until October 1918, just a few weeks before the armistice.[17]

This interpretation puts the question of the destruction of the Habsburg Monarchy into a new perspective, and this work is, to a certain extent,

---

11   Especially in his book inspired by François Fejtö's *Requiem pour un Empire défunt*. Béhar, Pierre, *Vestiges d'Empire, La décomposition de l'Europe centrale et balkanique*, Editions Desjonquères, Paris, 1999.
12   Bérenger, Jean, *Histoire de l'Empire des Habsburg, 1273–1918*, Fayard, Paris, 1993, 736.
13   Bérenger quoting Fejtö: Bérenger, *op. cit.*, 734.
14   Fejtö, François, *Requiem pour un Empire défunt, Histoire de la destruction de l'Autriche-Hongrie*, Edima/Lieu Commun [1988], Paris, 1992, 306.
15   President of the Czechoslovak National Council, with headquarters in Paris during World War I, and recognised as the head of the Provisional Czechoslovak Government by the Allies, he became the first president of Czechoslovakia.
16   Bérenger, *op. cit.*, 737.
17   Laroche, Louis-Pierre, "L'Affaire Dutasta: Les dernières conversations diplomatiques pour sauver l'Empire des Habsbourg", *Revue d'Histoire diplomatique*, Editions A. Pedone, Paris, 1994, 51–76.

a continuation of this school of thought, though I will be more nuanced on the issue. As no work has ventured to understand whether, after 1918, the nationality problem was a possible factor in reconstruction after being a factor of destruction, I can claim to fill a gap in both chronological (1918–1921) and methodological perspectives. An enquiry based on these premises entitles me to ask whether a Danubian Confederation was possible just after World War I, and if so, it can only help to reinforce the above-mentioned English and French historiographies. With this question, I bring an element of uchronia to this book. Uchronia was invented by the French philosopher Charles Renouvier;[18] which we call Virtual History today, and it is practiced in the Anglo-Saxon world by former Oxford scholars such as Naill Ferguron and Mark Almond. I present my own uchronistic interpretation of how the events would have unfolded only towards the end of this book, after having solidly analysed the archival material and other primary sources available, which tend to project a different outcome for Central Europe in the interwar period.

The Research and the Archives

My research has taken me to Paris, Budapest, London, the Hoover Institution at Stanford University, Vienna and the Vatican, and the interpretation of the problems studied will be viewed mainly through French archives and the eyes of French politicians, diplomats, members of the military and observers. This choice was made due to the rich material found there (in the Archives du Quai d'Orsay, Archives de l'Armée de Terre and Archives Nationales de France) and because France created the Czech army and had a prominent role in the creation of the Republic of Czechoslovakia and the Yugoslav Kingdom. The National Archives of Hungary opened its files on the Foreign Ministry and the Ministry of National Minorities, which dealt with the separatist nationality groups. British archives are a good complement to this, but they have no military intelligence archives that are pres-

---

18 Renouvier, Charles, *L'Uchronie, l'Utopie dans l'histoire*, Bureau de la Critique philosophique, Paris, 1876.

ently accessible to the public. The other complementary research done in Vienna (Staatsarchiv) and the Vatican (Secretariat of State Archives) offered information on federalists and legitimists who operated in the region treated and who fought internationally for their concept of Central Europe. The aim of my work is not to present a history of "Entente" diplomacy in the region but to unveil the mainly diplomatic activities of federalists, autonomists and legitimists whose aim was to create a form of Danubian Confederation, to show the diplomatic interactions that they triggered, and to concentrate mainly on French efforts to create such a confederation.

The Structure of the Opus

In order to clarify the different notions studied in this work, I introduce the reader to a certain number of concepts and define the principle notions in their meaning of the day. One of the main actors of the narrative is Karl of Habsburg-Lorraine, the last Emperor-King of Austria-Hungary. As soon as Austria-Hungary fell apart, Karl started actively to try to reconstruct his empire by writing a plan for a new con/federal monarchy and by contacting the pope and the leaders of the Entente regarding this plan.

Karl's efforts were first directed towards Britain and then more and more towards France. For this reason, I concentrate mostly on France's own plans for Central Europe but also because Hungary became a main concern of French foreign policy in the region.

I then briefly present French-British rivalry in the region and at the treaty of Trianon and move on to two other nationalities, the Croats and the Slovaks, and their struggle for autonomy or independence from Yugoslavia and Czechoslovakia respectively.

Finally, I address the final attempts of Karl to return to Hungary and reclaim his thrown, which ended with his arrest, deportation to Madera and eventual death. As a result, the prospects of restoration and of the creation of a Danubian confederation were halted and postponed to a later date by the legitimists. Eventually I explain the reasons why France failed in its attempt to consolidate the region with a larger confederal structure.

CHAPTER I

Danubian Confederation and Legitimism

The End of World War I and Its Aftermath

October 1918: The Belated Federalising of the Empire

President Woodrow Wilson presented to Congress his Fourteen Points program for peace in Europe in January 1918. The tenth point said: "The people of Austria-Hungary, whose place among the nations we wish to see safeguarded and assured, should be accorded the freest opportunity to autonomous development."[19] This was the condition of the Habsburg Monarchy's survival after the war. On the advice of the Austrian cabinet, Karl belatedly proclaimed Cisleithania a federation of national member states. As Hungary had refused any such project to be applied in Transdanubia in the past and underlined that any change to the Austrian Constitution would be a violation of the *Ausgleich*, its parliament and government used this *fait accompli* as a pretext to declare the dual state severed, and this in spite of the fact that the manifesto would not have had an effect on the constitutional setup and the *Ausgleich*.

As Austrian-American historian Robert Kann explained, the Magyars agreed on one point:

> The independent Magyar national state, even a truncated one, was preferable to a feeble union. [...] Owing to the interdependence of the nationality problems, no constitutional reform program affecting only one part of the empire could be acceptable to the national groups in the other. This was true in peacetime and it proved all the more true under wartime conditions, which were in fact already semi-revolutionary war-end conditions.[20]

---

19   http://avalon.law.yale.edu/20th_century/wilson14.asp (11.09.2018)
20   Kann, Robert, *op. cit.*, 162.

Emperor Karl was hoping that his Declaration, inspired by the Fourteen Points, would save the monarchy, but Wilson replied that he was no longer willing to accept the simple autonomies of peoples as the prerequisite of peace, since the United States had recognised the Czechoslovak National Council as a co-belligerent and would accept the aspirations of the Yugoslavs.[21]

The different national movements considered the emperor's manifesto as confirmation of their will to separate, and it acted as the signal that precipitated the implosion of the Dual Monarchy. From the Allied point of view, one could only observe that the Declaration not only came late but also only concerned Austria. A declaration federalizing the whole of Austria-Hungary in early 1918 would have been a more convincing sign to the Entente, to President Wilson and to the different nationalities in Transleithania. The Allies would have given greater credit to Karl's decision, since it would have been applied to both Cisleithania and Transleithania. The emperor's failure to sign a separate peace with the Entente in 1917, his lack of decision to act earlier in federalising Austria, and his failure to convince Hungary of the necessity of federalism all contributed greatly to the fall of the Dual Monarchy. Though we should not imply that Karl could have implemented federalism with a stroke of the pen. The reason he delayed such a manifesto until October 1918 was the firm opposition of his own establishment.

But as Kann claims: "The fact [that] setting up a great eastern Central European federation scheme was impossible in 1918 does not mean that such a solution must be discarded for ever."[22] Thus, the Danubian Confederation remained an idea for the future.

The International Situation after the War

Following the war, the situation in the Duplice (the German Reich and Austria-Hungary) and former Triplice (the two former with Italy) states was rather explosive. While the general armed conflict had ended, local skirmishes and conflicts continued in many places, not to mention revolutions.

---

21 Bogdan, Henry, *Histoire des Habsbourg, Des origines à nos jours*, Perrin, Paris, 2002, 362–63.
22 Kann, *op cit.*, 167.

The German Revolution (November 1918–August 1919) that broke out with the end of the war transformed the Reich into a democratic parliamentary republic known as the Weimar Republic. This new situation did not mean that it was the end of turmoil. There were both communist and right wing coups coming up in Germany: the Spartakist uprising was crushed in Berlin (January 1919); in Munich a Bavarian Republic of Councils was proclaimed and existed for about a month (April–May), followed by a right wing putsch in Berlin to overthrow the Weimar Republic, called the Kapp Putsch, which ended after a general strike (March 1920).

In Central Europe the situation was as bad as it could be. Not only did famine strike the region but the chaos that prevailed made room in 1919 for strikes, communist revolution and take-over in Hungary (March–July), and a foiled communist uprising in Vienna (June 1919).

Following the declaration of the Hungarian Republic and the dismantling of the Honvéd (the Hungarian Army), Hungary became the prey of most of the armed forces that had been in conflict with Austria-Hungary during the war, comprising the new Czechoslovak army, whose members were once part of the united (k.u.k.) and Honvéd armies, not metionning the Czech legions that had joined the Allied armies during War. Conflicts between Hungarian and Romanian forces, and Hungarian and Czechoslovakian forces were appearing: first, the Székely Hadosztály (the Transylvanian Székely regiment made of Hungarian officers and their Transylvanian soldiers) did not accept the occupation of Transylvania by the Romanian army; then came the Hungarian Commune's military resistance against the Czechoslovak forces that occupied upper Hungary (now called Slovakia) and against Romanian forces occupying Transylvania a part of Hungary as well.

Owing to French support, a national government was founded in 1919 in Szeged (Southern Hungary). Its objective was the return of order and the old regime. After the Hundred Days Commune (133 days), which fell when Romanian forces entered Budapest, it was the turn of the National Army—created by the Szeged Government and headed by Admiral Miklós Horthy de Nagybánya, the last commander-in-chief of the Austro-Hungarian fleet and former aide-de-camp of Franz Joseph—to enter the capital. A counter-revolutionary government was set up in Budapest and was working to restore the old order. Soon, with the support of Britain, Horthy was elected regent of Hungary.[23]

To the south the situation was no better. Though allied to Germany and Austria-Hungary during the war, the Italian government signed the secret Treaty of London (1915) in exchange for territories belonging to Austrian-Hungary once the war was over. It had asked for Istria, the Dalmatian cost, Gorizia and Gradisca, and the Trentino as a condition of it entering the war. On November 4, 1918, the Italian National Council of Fiume declared the union of Fiume with Italy though this town and harbour, which belonged to Hungary, were not part of the 1915 deal. After brief military occupation by the new SHS Kingdom, Italian and allied forces jointly occupied the town. After skirmishes between the French and Italian occupying forces, the Italian army left. The Italian writer, war hero and irredentist Gabriele D'Annunzio was asked by a Fiumese delegation led by the head of the Italian National Council of Fiume, the Austrian Antonio Grossich, to accept the challenge of leading the Fiumese resistance.[24]

D'Annunzio occupied Fiume (September 1919) with a small army of legionaries called the Arditi and in August 1920 declared it a sovereign state (called the Italian Regency of Carnaro) under his control as head of state with the title of *Primo Rettore*. It was only in November 1920 that the problem of Fiume could be settled between Italy and the SHS Kingdom, as a result of the 1st Treaty of Rapallo (November 12, 1920). The Italian navy bombed Fiume and removed D'Annunzio in December 1920. The Free State of Fiume was created on December 31, 1920, before the state was eventually partitioned between Italy and the SHS Kingdom in 1924.[25] It is in this unstable European post-war climate that federalists and legitimists were going to flourish and form into resistance against the new Successor States of Austria-Hungary.

---

23 Admiral Miklós Horthy was called *kormányzó*, "governor" in Hungarian, but was, in fact, regent of Hungary, since he was elected to rule after the restoration of the monarchical system and to save the throne for the king until it was the right time for him to return, but this situation became permanent.
24 Kilinger, William, "Antonio Grossich e la nascita dei movimenti nazionali a Fiume", *Quaderni*, vol. XII, Centro ricerche storiche Rovigno, 1999, 139–41.
25 Ledeen, Michael Arthur, *The First Duce, D'Annunzio at Fiume*, Johns Hopkins University Press, Baltimore, London, 1977, 182–83.

The Roots of a Danubian Confederation

In the history of political thought, the Danubian Confederation first appears in the nineteenth century. It was part of a process of discovering or rediscovering national identities among the central European ethnic groups. This meant that they were fighting for recognition through the acceptance of their rights to a certain level of autonomy or to be part of a federation or sovereign members of a confederation. Hence the concept of a Danubian Confederation is the heritage of the nineteenth century.

Prince Adam Czartoryski, a Polish anti-Habsburg revolutionary is considered to be one of the fathers of this political idea. Czartoryski based it on a union of Central European republics. In 1849, during the *Printemps des peuples* revolutions that was surging over Europe, Czartoryski invited to his home in Paris—the famous Hôtel Lambert on Ile Saint-Louis—revolutionary leaders from Hungary and Bohemia to plan the new Confederation. Among them was the envoy to Paris of the short-lived revolutionary Hungary, Count László Teleki. For its creation it was necessary to establish an alliance with Turkey against Austria and Russia, which, in the name of Panslavism, had designs on all Slavonic nations. The revolutions and insurrections were crushed by the Habsburgs, and, in the case of the Hungarian war of independence, with the help of the Tsar.[26]

Lajos Kossuth, the leader of the Hungarian war of independence (1848–1849), went into exile in Turkey and then Italy, where his first concept of Danubian Confederation was published in the review *Alleanza* of Torino in 1861.[27] It was presented as an alliance of three sovereign states: Hungary, Romania and Serbia. He proposed a system constructed on cultural and not territorial autonomies such as Czartoryski had proposed. The three states would allow autonomous communities to administer their own affairs without creating autonomous territories. This idea was to prevent cutting up Hungary into autonomous regions. His plan was revolutionary, though never realised, and would inspire many other political thinkers—except that

---

26 Kiss Gy., Csaba, *Közép Európa, nemzetek, kissebségek*, Pesti Szalon, Budapest, 1993, 114–15; Droz, J., *L'Europe Centrale, l'évolution historique de l'idée de "Mitteleuropa"*, Payot, Paris 1960, 63–64.
27 Because of this publication many consider him as the father of Danubian federalism.

Kossuth owed some of his inspiration to the "Hungarian Tocqueville", Baron József Eötvös, who established the concept of "historical-political individualities".

This brings us to the second concept, much older than the idea of a Danubian Confederation, which is the cohabitation of nations in a multinational state inspired by the concept of a *Schicksalsgemeinschaft*[28] based on unity and pluralism at the same time. As Central Europe specialist Jean-Paul Bled was to say: "Depuis des siècles, l'histoire de l'Europe centrale s'est développée autour du rapport dialectique entre ces deux principes: une unité nourrie de ce pluralisme, mais un pluralisme également générateur de conflits."[29] In other words: "L'originalité de cette communauté de destin, *Schicksalsgemeinschaft*, tient à la pluralité des peuples qui s'adossent au Danube, qui constitua lui-même leur principe d'unité politique, longtemps incarné par la monarchie des Habsbourg."[30]

It is, indeed, the mixture of the idea of the confederation of nation states with that of the multi-nation (unity in plurality) that gave way to the seemingly-new idea of personal autonomy, which already existed, in medieval Hungary, in the form of the right of self-administration and the recognition of a nation—such as the Saxons in Transylvania—without allotting it a territory.[31] It was Baron Eötvös who took a significant step by admitting that like the choice of a religion, the choice of nationality is an individual decision. The question of nationality became a fundamental right.[32]

After the *Augsleich* (compromise) between the Hungarians and their sovereign Franz Joseph I in 1867, the Habsburg Empire became a dual state: the Dual Monarchy. Franz Joseph was emperor in Austria and king in Hungary, uniting the two states in his person: the concept of *Personalunion* (personal union). As a result, the Austrian Empire was from then on called Aus-

---

28 German word for a shared common destiny.
29 "For centuries, the history of Central Europe has developed around the dialectic relationship between these two principles: a unity nourished by this pluralism, but a pluralism that likewise generates conflict." Bled, Jean-Paul, "Avant-propos", in *Revue d'Europe centrale*, no. 1, 1993, 2.
30 "The originality of this community of destiny is attached to the plurality of the peoples who depend on the Danube, which itself constituted their principle of political unity, long embodied by the monarchy of the Habsburgs." Pierré-Caps, Stéphane, *La Multination*, Ed. Odile Jacob, Paris, 1995, 256.
31 King Matthias Corvinus (born Hunyadi) gave the Saxons of Transylvania this privilege. Ibid., 258.
32 Ibid., 261.

tria-Hungary. This new structure was de facto a type of two-state federalism with three common ministries: foreign, finance and defence. All other administrations were specific to each of the two states. Whether this form was a federation or a confederation is a question I answer later when treating the definitions of these terms.

The development of federalist ideas was different in the two parts of the Habsburg Monarchy, Cisleithania and Transleithania (Hungary). In Transleithania the idea of the French nation state prevailed and was the result of the French-inspired 1789 and 1848 revolutions that did not suit Hungary with its many nationalities. The same was true for Cisleithania, except that in the Austrian part of the Dual Monarchy, the development went towards giving more autonomy to some regions, such as Galicia, which was the Polish, Ukrainian and Jewish-inhabited region.

Two political thinkers are representative of the two different parts of the Dual Monarchy. Both wanted to respond to the nationality problem but each in his own state: in Austria it was Karl Renner, later the chancellor of Austria, and in Hungary Oszkár Jászi, a member of the Károlyi government (1919).

Renner developed the idea of personal autonomy in *Struggle of the Nations of Austria for their State* (1902) and *The Crisis of Dualism* (1904). This idea was strongly inspired by Eötvös and Kossuth. Personal autonomy was just a step further from Kossuth's cultural autonomy. He proposed to attach the notion of nationality to the person and not to a territory: "Nationality has no essential connexion with territory; Nations are unions of autonomous persons."[33] Each person had the right to choose his nationality and register himself on national registries. As it was for religion, each citizen had the right to choose his national belonging. The community formed by the persons of like nationality would be represented by a national council, and the system would be the same at each level of the state: Kreis (old Austrian administrative division), district and commune. But Renner separated cultural from political and economic questions. In ethnically mixed regions, each nationality would administer its own cultural affairs in an au-

---

33   Droz, *op. cit.*, 183.

tonomous way. But for political and economic questions of common interest there would be territorial mixed councils with proportional representation.³⁴ This model was only realised in some parts of Moravia.

In his book *The Future of the Monarchy* (1918) Jászi imagined the creation of a federation of five nations: Austria, Hungary, Bohemia, Poland and Illyria (Southern Slavs). For those remaining, he thought that he could give them cultural and linguistic rights "in the spirit of [Ferenc] Deák and Eötvös and transform Transylvania into a system of cantons."³⁵

Both Renner and Jászi wished to federalise Austria-Hungary in the framework of the Habsburg Monarchy. After the war they buried their ideas of creating a federalised monarchy and moved on to defend the idea of republicanism. Thus, they cannot be considered as legitimists after 1918.

There were other political thinkers, called the Belvedere Group, who gravitated around the Belvedere Palace in Vienna, residence of the heir to the throne, Archduke Franz Ferdinand. Franz Ferdinand himself was preparing the Trialism project, in which he would recognise the southern Slavs as a third state of the monarchy. Other plans were prepared by collaborators of the Archduke such as the Romanian Aurel Popovici. All these projects had one aim: to continue the federalisation of Austria-Hungary and give to other nationalities rights similar to those given to the Hungarians, which meant the federalisation of both Austria and Hungary into autonomous regions.

The common denominator of these projects was that they tried to avoid the different nations' secession from the Monarchy. It was to be an internal federalisation, and, evidently, a way of avoiding the splitting Austria-Hungary into Successor States.

The idea of personal autonomy survived the war. On February 20, 1920, the Hungarian delegation at the peace negotiations—led by the legitimist Count Albert Apponyi—submitted a project based on personal autonomy regarding minorities such as Serbs, Croatians, Slovenes, Romanians, Austrians and Slovaks. The Hungarian citizens belonging to these ethnic mi-

---

34 Ibid., 182–84. Renner, Karl, *La Nation, Mythe et Réalité* [1964], Presse Universitaire de Nancy, Nancy, 1998, 104.
35 Jászi, O., *A Monarchia Jövője*, (reprint of 1918 ed.), AKV-MAECENAS, Budapest, 1988, 129. Ferenc Deák, called the "wiseman of the nation", was the father of the compromise with Austria.

norities would form a moral person in possession of cultural autonomy. The Hungarians were truly hoping that the Successor States would do the same with their Hungarian minorities. The desired result was not attained, not only because Hungary was a loser in the war but also because the concept of national autonomy frightened the "experts" at the peace treaties, who saw in it the road to chaos in the region.[36] This form of autonomy cannot truly be called federalism and even less confederalism, which are territorial concepts. In other words, the development of this idea is not relevant to this work. Moreover, this idea was only realised in the 1990s, in Hungary after the fall of the Iron Curtain. Autonomies (be they personal or territorial) are a step towards a Federal State and therefore are often viewed with suspicion by unitary nation states.

Definitions

Before examining further the problem of confederal or federal Central European plans, it is important to understand the differences between these two notions.

In international law a confederation is an association of sovereign states. The cooperation is based on the principle of equality among members, which keep their sovereign (*régalien*) rights, such as defence, currency finances and police, and decisions are taken unanimously.[37] It should be noted that the member-states delegate only a part of their international competencies and keep their partial independence and right to secede. A confederation is, in general, an intermediary phase towards or away from a federation.[38]

A federation is an association of states in which there are shared competencies between the central authorities (federal authority) and its members (the federal states), which are distinct from each other. Although the members accept to give away part of their sovereignty, they keep control of cer-

---

36 Pierré-Caps, *op. cit.*, 273–74.
37 Chaigneau, Pascal (ed.), *Dictionnaire des relations internationales*, Ed. Economico, Paris, 1998. (Entry: *Confédération*, 190).
38 Boniface, Pascal (ed.), Lexique des Relations internationales, Ellipses, Paris, 1995 (no pages: refer to entry: *Confédération*).

tain aspects: in general, territorial administration, social affairs, education and police. The federal state is competent at least for diplomacy, and sometimes currency and defence.[39] The central authority is thus the holder of sovereign rights. Members normally have no right to secede.[40] A federation is an entity other than its components and is superior to them. Decisions can be taken against the will of a component and imposed on all components. The core difference between the two is that in a confederation, a member state "delegates" and in a federation it "renounces" certain competencies.

It is rare for a confederation to result from a process initiated by a unitary state, since by definition it is an alliance of sovereign states.[41] I would consequently opt for the Dual Monarchy to qualify as a type of federation, because it was negotiated between the monarch and the Hungarians, which led to two states with internal sovereignty but having three common ministries, and most importantly a common foreign policy (external sovereignty). Since the Foreign Ministry was in Vienna and was common, foreign policy and representation had the characteristics of a federal state.

Austria-Hungary had the original concept of a dual (double headed and double crowned) monarchy uniting two states. The head of both states was the emperor-king, but the Hungarian prime minister was very influential in some of the decision-making. A good example is that when Franz Joseph proposed sending the ultimatum to Serbia in 1914, Hungarian Prime Minister Count István Tisza refused to sign it. He only agreed the second time, which means that in common affairs, Hungary had its say. It makes one wonder whether Austria-Hungary was not more of a confederation with unanimous decision-making, since in important decisions, such as war, both states (the emperor-king and the Hungarian prime minister) had to agree. However, in the end, it was the sovereign who took the final decision to declare war.

---

39 There is no consensus on the exact number of common ministries to achieve a federation, but in general terms a common foreign ministry is necessary to achieve one. A confederation is not subject to international law as it doesn't have a common foreign ministry. Boniface, *op. cit.*, (entry: *Fédération*).
40 Chaigneau, *op. cit.*, 191–93, (entry: *Fédération*).
41 Internal confederalisation is also possible. There is the example of canton Vaud in Switzerland, which was a region annexed by canton Bern in the sixteenth century. It was elevated to the rank of sovereign canton in 1803 and made part of the Confederation thanks to Napoléon's intervention.

Some might claim that a confederation can only be an association of republics. It is true that Switzerland was a confederation (until 1848, when it became a federal state) of republics that mainly dated back to the Middle Ages. The Germanic Confederation of 1815 was a union of both republics and monarchies. There is little doubt that in certain cases monarchy seems necessary to guarantee cohesion. The contemporary case of Belgium is a good example. In recent times, Belgium's unity was saved by federalizing the country into Flanders and Wallonia—and not to forget the less important German region—and it is only the king who can guarantee its unity. His role, today, is, in a way, similar to the concept of *Personalunion* but with only one crown. As an analogy, those who defended the necessity of maintaining the Habsburg Monarchy thought that without a unifying imperial dynasty it wouldn't have survived for so many centuries. The emperor was the linchpin who held the monarchy, with so many nationalities, together. Whether it was in a dualist, trialist or a federal system of many nationalities, the federative role of the monarch was crucial for its survival.

The idea of a Danubian Union had evolved since the nineteenth century, and the Habsburg monarch's perception of his place in *Mitteleuropa* had evolved as well. The evolution of the Habsburg Monarchy from Francis I to Karl I (1804–1918) had been an interesting process. Francis I took the new title of Emperor of Austria in 1804 and abandoned the title of German Emperor, which had lost its value, in 1806. He then went on to head the German Confederation in 1815. Franz Joseph would see his privileges as *primus inter pares* disappear after the battle of Sadowa. As a young man, he was still a *deutscher Fürst*, before truly becoming Emperor of Austria and turning more and more towards the East and the Balkans. The shift was significant and had important consequences, since by becoming the ruler of southern Slav Orthodox populations the Habsburgs entered into competition with Tsarist Russia, the protector of the Orthodox Slavs and leader of Panslavism. In 1914, Franz Joseph was the ally of Germany against Russia. With the arrival of Karl I and the end of Tsarist Russia, the secret enemy became Germany. Karl was Francophile and was envisaging a betrayal of his German ally, Kaiser Wilhelm. Franz Joseph could have never imagined this. At the death of Franz Joseph in 1916, a new monarch with a new conception was crowned, and a new direction was taken.

Chapter I

Hungarian Legitimism and Legitimists

Who were the legitimists? This is the first question the reader is entitled to ask. One would also inquire whether Habsburg Legitimism was a strictly Hungarian phenomenon, or an Austrian one, or more a Central European one. Only after having explained what Hungarian Legitimism was will I be able to clarify whether there was Legitimism in the other Successor States of the Austro-Hungarian monarchy. There are two notions to understand: the evolution of the ideas of inheritance or election of the Crown and the constitutional aspect.

The Hungarian legitimists supported the restoration of the crowned king of Hungary, that is, Karl IV. When the king died in 1922, the legitimists were also supportive of the heir to the throne, Archduke Otto. Facing them were the free-electors of a national king, called simply "free electors". They were also monarchists but wanted to have the choice to elect their "national", and therefore Magyar, king.

To gain a global understanding of the matters that were at stake, it is important to have an overview of the principal problems facing the Hungarian monarchy.

There was long-standing discord between the supporters of a gentry democracy[42] in the Polish style, with a king elected *inter pares*, and the disciples of a hereditary monarchy. In the Arpadian period (eleventh to fourteenth centuries), the kings were not, as in Western Europe, crowned based on the standard of *hereditas*, the primogenitary right to rule, but based on the eastern (Constantinople) standard of *idoneitas*, the capacity to rule among the heirs of the same (Arpadian) family. It was only after the extinction of the Árpád dynasty and later of its collateral branches with Ladislas Postumus (+1457)— a Habsburg with some Árpád blood in his veins—that the crown truly became elective, and persons and families which did not have the royal and sacred blood of the Árpáds[43] were elected. Eventually the Habsburgs got the

---

42 At the beginning of the nineteenth century at least 6 percent of the Hungarian population was noble, and they all had the right to be represented at the *Dieta*. Therefore, it was a limited democracy but much more vast than on oligarchy. E.g., in France the nobility represented only about 1 percent of the population.

43 Two canonised kings (Stephan and László) and many other canonised members (Saint Elisabeth, Saint Margaret, Saint Imre, Saint Kunigunda and Blessed Hedvig of Poland, among others).

crown again in the sixteenth century (Ferdinand I in 1526) and were due to keep it when Hungary was divided into three parts: the Kingdom of Hungary under Habsburg rule, Ottoman Hungary and independent Transylvania, an Ottoman protectorate. The Habsburgs managed to regain the lost parts under Leopold I, and in recognition, the Hungarian Diet decided (1687) that the crown would be assured to the Austrian dynasty. The Pragmatic Sanction of 1723 confirmed this right definitively in Hungary and guaranteed the crown of Saint Stephen to a female member of the Habsburg family lack of males: Maria Theresia. After the Insurrection of 1848, the hereditary right was reinforced by the Austro-Hungarian Compromise of 1867.

The other important element for the comprehension of Legitimism is its constitutional aspect. The Hungarian constitution was founded by the union of king and nation. The symbol of this community was the Holy Crown of Hungary. This object was not only the holy reliquary that empowers the heir to the throne to be king but also the symbol of the State itself. It represented a shared power which could make law only if there was symbiosis between the public body, as exercised by the Parliament, and the king, which together expressed the will of the nation. Thus no law could be created without these two bodies. This is what the Hungarian legislators called the Doctrine of the Holy Crown.[44]

This doctrine was the guarantee of the continuity of law, and it was confirmed in the *Opus Tripartitum* of 1514, which predated Habsburg rule in Hungary. The *Opus* was the basis of the system of *ancien régime* in Hungary, which could be changed only by the dual agreement of Parliament and king.

It was on this continuity of heredity and the doctrine of the Holy Crown that the legitimists based their beliefs. The opponents of Legitimism, the so-called free electors, believed that the crown was always elective and that the Habsburgs had imposed hereditary succession to insure their power in Hungary, and in so doing had violated the ancient law.

In the sixteenth century, most of the Hungarian nobles differentiated themselves from their monarch by embracing the Geneva confession (Cal-

---

44 József Kardos explained the doctrine in depth in medieval and modern times, with the necessary Marxist rhetoric, in his introductory chapter of *A Szentkorona-tan története (1919–1944)*, Akadémia Kiadó, Budapest, 1985, 11–37.

vinism) as a protest against their autocratic king. But this Protestant period was doomed to be short, for Jesuits were soon sent to Hungary to activate the Counter-Reformation and re-Catholicise 80 percent of the nobility. The emperor eventually managed to reconvert most of Hungary, except for Transylvania and some other less important regions, where Protestants successfully resisted with the support of the Ottomans, who offered their protection to Transylvania without occupying it or intervening in its internal policy. After World War I, in Trianon Hungary, some 24–27 percent of the population was still Protestant (Calvinist and Lutheran alike), and it was the Hungarian Calvinist commoners (non-nobles) and minor nobility (untitled nobles or gentry) that most resisted the idea of a legitimate restoration.

During the years studied, the aristocracy, or titled nobility, was naturally legitimist, as they were the guardians of tradition and continuity. If some were anti-legitimists, they chose to be so because of international pressure, and there were very few free electors among them. Even many Protestant members of the aristocracy served the Habsburgs faithfully.[45] But there was a tendency among Protestant families, many of them from Transylvania, to be free electors or just to accept the status quo of Miklós Horthy as regent.

When in 1920 Admiral Horthy was elected regent by the Parliament, a true scission appeared within the population between Habsburg loyalists and free electors. The former wanted the return of the legitimate king and did not want a regent or a new elected king, because the one and only crowned king was still alive and well in exile. Regency did exist in Hungarian history, but only when the heir to the throne was still a minor, thus in their view there was no reason to elect a regent. The legitimists feared, with reason, that Horthy would acquire too much power and that eventually the free electors would take over power.[46] The free electors had their pretenders,

---

45 It should not be forgotten that almost all the titles in Hungary were given by the Habsburgs. Titles did not exist in medieval Hungary, and there was only one nobility—*unam et eademque nobilitas* an untitled one, as defined by the great Hungarian legislator of the sixteenth century Werbőczy. So titles were, in fact, a Western import of prestige and domination. In exchange, the emperor expected fidelity from those of his servants elevated to titled nobility.

46 Ránki, György (ed.), *Magyarország Története, 1918–1919*, vol. 8/1, Budapest, 433; Bangha, Ernö, *A Magyar Királyi Testörség 1920–1944*, Europa, Budapest, 1990, 18.

persons they wanted to convince to accept the crown, including the regent himself. Horthy, even if flattered, never accepted such an idea. The attempts at restoration were to worsen the row between the two sides, and a third side as well, which chose to wait for a better moment to decide about the question of kingship. Among the legitimists were Karlists, who wanted to put Karl back into power as soon as possible and who were unconditional legitimists. The more moderate legitimists—represented by Count Pál Teleki and Count István Bethlen (who openly chose the legitimist camp for a short while in 1921), both consecutively prime ministers in 1920–1921—were putting the nation's interests first and would only accept Karl's restoration if it was advantageous for their conception of an independent Nation State of Hungary, without Austria. The aim was to revise the Trianon treaty and rebuild Saint Stephen's Hungary (pre-1918 Hungary). Their policy was also characterised by the concept of "wait and see" and prudence.

Not only the aristocracy but other groups as well represented the leadership of Legitimism. The high clergy of the Catholic Church, the higher bourgeoisie, the Jewish upper-class—made up of industrialists, bankers and landowners—were also mainly legitimists, as were many military officers, especially those from the united army of Austria-Hungary, as opposed to the Honvéd (Hungarian National Army) officers.[47] It was patent that these groups were defending their interests and their position in society. They were also anxious about the White Terror that had followed the Red Terror of the Communists. During this White Terror, often uncontrolled detachments of the Hungarian Army were organising reprisals on the communists, among which there were quite a few Jewish victims who feared this new regime and its evolution.[48]

These elites were present in different political parties, the most important of which was the Keresztény Nemzeti Párt (Christian National Party) founded in 1919, which was conservative and had a Legitimist programme. It was the largest party in the Hungarian Parliament. In the opposition was the Nemzeti Demokrata Polgári Párt (National Democratic Civic Party), a

---

47 *Documents on British Foreign Policy* (henceforth *DBFP*), vol. XII, no. 268, 324–25, Athelstan-Johnson (High-Com. to Budapest) to Curzon, Budapest, November 7, 1920.
48 Horel, Catherine, *L'Admiral Horthy: le regent de Hongrie*, Perrin, Paris, 2014, 110.

liberal party founded in 1919, which also shared legitimist feelings, like its Jewish leader Vilmos Vázsonyi.[49]

There were no actual legitimist parties, as Legitimism was not a party issue but a legal one. Legitimist clubs and associations would appear after 1922 to conserve the memory of King Karl and keep up the faith in a future restoration. On a popular level there was no real legitimist grouping, but in fact, the Catholic Church played this role, as the Hungarian clergy, like the Vatican, was traditionally on the monarch's side.[50]

Legitimism had a special role in Hungary because it existed as an opposition to the theory of free election. Legitimism was a way of interpreting Hungarian law to defend the necessity of continuity. The theory of free election was also once a Hungarian law, in existence for 300 years, commencing in 1387 when Sigismund of Luxemburg was elected king of Hungary and ending in 1687 when the Hungarian Nation (the Orders) enabled the Habsburgs to continuously inherit the crown in gratitude for the dynasty's contribution to liberating Hungary from Turkish occupation. In other words, the free electors were referencing a law that had been inactive for more than 200 years.

It was, in fact, the disaster following World War I and the absence of the king that made possible such a discussion. However, many of the other nations of the former Habsburg Monarchy used the word legitimist to describe themselves as faithful to the crowned emperor or king and his successor. That is why people calling themselves legitimists were not limited to Hungary. There were also Austrian, Czech, Slovak, Romanian, Croatian, Slovene, Bosnian and even Serb legitimists.

Just after the war, only Hungary had strong legitimist support from the population. In Austria, which had become a republic, legitimist feelings had a much smaller base of support, and the Austrian government was preoccupied with its attachment to Germany. In other words, Hungary remained the

---

49 Gergely, Jenö, Ferenc Glatz, Ferenc Pölöskei (ed.), *Magyarországi pártprogramok 1919–1944*, Kossuth Kiadó, Budapest, 1991, 31–34, 86–87.
50 The Hungarian monarchy and state was traditionally a papal creation. The original crown—which was lost and replaced by a second one, located today in the Hungarian Parliament and venerated as the Holy Crown—was sent directly from Rome for the coronation of the first king of Hungary, Vajk, baptised Stephen, with the title of Apostolic King of Hungary, one of the most prestigious titles of Europe. The Apostolic King was more than a usual king, he was *Rex Sacerdotes*, which gave him the right to elect bishops.

ideal country that could become the refuge for legitimists and the headquarters of legitimist activity, but with little prospect of exporting it.

It remains, however, to ask whether behind Legitimism and the legitimists there was some sort of political content apart from the legal one. Aside from the conservative feelings of tradition, stability and continuity, it had neither a party nor a programme to campaign for—both of which appeared only after the death of the Emperor-King. Only after 1929—the coming of age of the heir to the throne, Archduke Otto—did legitimism develop beyond a legal row into a political programme that would be of Christian social inspiration and appear as opposition to conservative authoritarianism as well as Fascist and Nazi influences.

Relating to the question of Legitimism vis-à-vis federalism, a famous Hungarian legitimist journalist and historian, Sándor Pethő, founder of the respected *Magyar Nemzet* newspaper, which survived even through communism, wrote that the only way to realise a confederation of Danubian nations was with the Habsburg Monarchy. He was also able to summarise in the early 1930s the importance of legitimism in a multi-ethnic Hungary and how it could serve Hungary:

> The regime of Danubian autonomies is not in accordance with the psychology of the peace of nationalities in a republican form of state. The state is neither independent nor objective nor impersonal, and at each election the battle for hegemony would renew, as a consequence of which, the confederation could not resist the attraction of Pangerman and Panslav solidarities.[51]

The legitimate monarch would offer a power as solid as a republic but above and respectful of the autonomy of the different nations of this big territory.

Hungarian Legitimist Activity during the Commune

On November 2, 1918, the armistice was signed by General Weber in the name of the Austro-Hungarian Monarchy in front of the Entente officials.

---

51 Pethő, Sándor, *A Magyar Capitoliumon, A Magyar királyeszme a Duna völgyében*, Budapest, 1932, 53.

A week earlier a National Council was formed in Budapest, which dissolved the parliament and proclaimed a republic, choosing Count Mihály Károlyi as prime minister. This government was dragged into a Republic of Councils by agents sent from the Soviet Union, such as Béla Kun, the leader of the revolution, the consequence of which was the Hundred Days Commune, a communist regime of terror.

During the short-lived communist regime in Hungary, in order to set up a conservative government, many opponents of the regime moved to Vienna and later to Szeged, southeast of Budapest, which was occupied by the French garrison of General Franchet d'Espérey.

Having been one of the centres of the Habsburg Monarchy, Vienna was the natural setting for malcontent émigrés fleeing not only Budapest but all the Successor States. Many nationality groups gathered in Vienna and formed committees or groups, for example, the Croatians. The Hungarian one was the first committee to be set up, on April 12, 1919. It was named the Hungarian National Committee of Vienna, or the ABC, the Antibolsevista Comité, (Anti-Bolshevik Committee). A wide political spectrum was represented in the ABC, an anti-communist gathering of politicians and diplomats in exile. The parties represented were the Nép Párt (People's Party) of György Szmrecsányi and the Alkotmány Párt (Constitution Party) of Marquis György Pallavicini,[52] which were allies and had the common feature of being legitimists. Another group, consisting of the founders of the Nemzeti Egyesülés Pártja (National Unity Party), recognised Count István Bethlen, the future prime minister of Hungary, as their leader. Many persons who were legitimists were in this group as well, such as Gusztáv Gratz and Count Antal Sigray.

Gusztáv Gratz was a lawyer and liberal politician. In 1917, he was chief of section in the common Foreign Ministry, and the same year he became Hungarian minister of finance in the Esterházy government. Then in 1918 he returned to the Foreign Ministry until November, before joining the ABC. Count Antal Sigray was one of the most faithful legitimists. Internationally educated and wed—having been to the Jesuit public school Stonyhurst in England and hav-

---

52 Marquis György Pallavicini was a lawyer and MP. In 1917 he became state secretary to the Hungarian prime minister, Count Móric Esterházy, and continued as an independent MP throughout the interwar period.

ing married a rich American from the New York aristocracy—he was a champion of the pre-war democratic reforms in Hungary. After 1918 he tried to use his impressive international network to help his country after the war.[53]

There were also some staunch enemies of Karl IV in the ABC, among them Captain Gyula Gömbös and Count Gedeon Ráday. Both of them were prominent anti-Habsburgs and free electors in the 1920s.

The third group was made up of independent politicians who had seceded from Count Mihály Károlyi's Independence Party, such as the liberal Count Tivadar Batthyány. Even moderate social democrats had showed up in Vienna, such as Ernő Garami, who had had to flee Hungary as well.[54] The aim of the ABC was to overthrow the Republic of Councils in Hungary with the help of the Entente forces and their own.

The ABC was dissolved at the end of May because of a number of factors, among them Chancellor Renner's irritation—he had not reacted to a note from Béla Kun asking him to halt the committee's activity but he did not want Vienna to become an "Hungarian Koblenz"—and because of the creation of a counterrevolutionary government in Arad (today Arad, Romania) by Count Gyula Károlyi.[55] The ABC recognised Gyula Károlyi's government in Arad before the government moved to Szeged when the Romanian troops occupied Arad.[56]

There was another small group of Hungarian legitimists, in Switzerland, that was close to the ABC of Vienna: Count Gyula Andrássy Jr., Prince Lajos Windischgraetz and Vilmos Vázsonyi. After having met their monarch in exile in Prangins, they addressed the task of setting up a legitimist propaganda office in Switzerland and commuted from time to time to Vienna to be in touch with the ABC and other dissidents.[57] Gyula Andrássy Jr., the son of the famous foreign minister of the Dual Monarchy, himself became foreign

---

53 Borbándi, Gyula, *Magyar politikai pályaképek 1938–1948*, Európa, Budapest, 1997, 389–40.
54 Boroviczény, Aladár, *A Király és Kormányzója*, Európa, Budapest 1993, 19–20. Until 1919, Garami was one of the most prominent leaders of the Hungarian Social Democrat Party. He was economics minister in the radical democratic revolutionary government of Mihály Károlyi.
55 Gyula Károlyi was a member of the Hungarian Upper House and the prefect (főispán), of the county of Arad where he had his estates. After being a lieutenant in the Hussars on the Russian front during the war, he returned to politics in 1919. He was of the same family as Mihály Károlyi, but of another branch.
56 Romsics, István, *Bethlen István*, Magyarságkutató Intézet, Budapest, 1991. 86–87.
57 Ibid., 82.

minister in mid-October 1918, although he was the last person in history to hold that prominent position. When he arrived in Vienna, the monarchy was already de facto non-existent and the new leaders of German Austria did not welcome him wholeheartedly. He resigned from his post on October 31.

Lajos Windischgraetz had been minister for procurement in the Hungarian government during the war. Vilmos (William) Vázsonyi was a barrister and a liberal democratic politician, founder of the Democratic Circle in 1894. He was Jewish and was known for having fought for the 1895 granting to the Jewish religion status equal to that of the traditional Christian confessions of Hungary. As a Hungarian M.P. he defended the programme of the Democratic Party and then became minister of justice in two governments between 1917 and 1918. He was always a faithful legitimist and continued to defend the rights of the Habsburg monarch after the war.

Besides the above mentioned three, there were a great number of legitimists residing in Switzerland, such as Baron Musulin, Austro-Hungarian minister in Bern, Count Albert Apponyi, Léon de Vaux, k.u.k. diplomat, Col. Hussarek, brother of the former Austrian prime minister, Count Leopold Berchtold, former minister of foreign affairs, Count Esterházy (most probably Ferenc Esterházy) and Ambassador Gyula Szilassy, who was living at the Bellevue Palace Hotel in Bern, but who possessed a house and property in Bex (canton Vaud), where he was born.[58]

Andrássy, Windischgraetz and Vázsonyi, were among those who had set up a press organ in Switzerland called *l'Agence centrale*. French sources claim that its active members were Andrássy, Windischgraetz, Félix Vályi (the founder and editor of the *Revue Politique Internationale* in Lausanne) and a certain Harry Schmidt of Geneva, who had a Swiss diplomatic passport. Schmidt collaborated with the *Intelligenz Blatt* of Bern and was operating as liaison agent between legitimists residing in Hungary and those in Switzerland.[59] Other sources say that the agency was directed by a certain Rodolph

---

58 Document of the Czech embassy received from the Swiss police. Hungarian State Archives (henceforth MNL), K64, 3 cs., 1921-1-177, Gen. Berzeviczky to Khuen-Hederváry of Political Department and Amb. Kánya, Budapest, April 17, 1921.
59 Archives diplomatiques du Ministère des Affaires étrangères (henceforth ADMAE), Z Europe, 1918–1929, Hongrie, Propagande 65/1. Bern, March 25, 1919.

Kremmer, head of United Press Association.⁶⁰ The Austrian historian Otto Forst de Battaglia claimed being the leader of the *Agence centrale*.⁶¹

The *Agence centrale* was created with the financial support of a rich Austrian industrialist and Swiss resident, Baron Andreas Veitsberger⁶² and was based in Lucerne; its purpose was to bring "anti-Bolshevik propaganda to the Swiss press by exaggerating Bolshevik danger in Austria and Hungary".⁶³ At least this was the way it was seen by H.M. Minister Sir Horace Rumbold in Bern. After Mihály Károlyi gave over power to the Communist dictatorship of Béla Kun, the danger was proven to be fact and consequently had not been exaggerated. But Rumbold did not stress the most important aims, which were to inform Western politicians of the true situation in the region of the destroyed monarchy, to keep in touch with the supporters of the emperor in the different Successor States and to realise Emperor Karl's plans by influencing the international press regarding the necessity of a Danubian Confederation.⁶⁴

There were also other legitimists in Switzerland more or less connected to the *Agence centrale*, such as Julius Bornemisza, who was Austro-Hungarian consul in Romania and became Hungarian consul in Bern, a journalist and politician, he was an active propagandist trying to influence the Bernese *Bund* newspaper by giving great sums of money, but without much success. Ödön Beniczky, an agrarian of the Smallholders Party, was chief of propaganda of the legitimists in Switzerland. He won over the prelates of Fribourg and the Benedictine monastery of Einsiedeln to the cause and was doing propaganda through them.

The agency's modus operandi was to set up a network of bureaus around Europe. This was realised with the help of a Danish export company that founded an economic telegraphic agency with offices in all the major cities

---

60   MNL, K64, 3 cs., 1921 -1 -177, Gen. Berzeviczky to Khun-Hederváry and Amb. Kánya, Budapest, April 17, 1921.
61   Forst de Battaglia, Otto, "Restauration der Habsburger", in *Europäische Geschrpäch: Hamburger Monatshefte für auswärtige Politik*, VIII, Heft 11, 1930, 5–7. This is confirmed by Heinz Rieder, *Kaiser Karl. Der Letzte Monarch Österreich-Ungarns 1887–1822*, Munich, Callwey Edition, 1981, 297; Fiziker, Róbert, *Habsburg kontra Hitler, Legitimisták az Anschluss ellen, az önálló Ausztriáért*, Budapest, Gondolat, 2010, 20, 178.
62   ADMAE, Z Europe 1918–1929, Hongrie Propagande 65/1. Bern, March 25, 1919.
63   National Archives (henceforth NA), Foreign Office (henceforth FO) 371 3529, 36671, Rumbold to Curzon, 1. March 1919.
64   Windischgraetz, Ludwig, *Ein Kaiser kämpft für die Freiheit*, Verlag Herold, Wien, 1957, 137–138.

of Europe that would distribute news on the economic situation in the countries of the Danubian region. The agency also served as a centre for keeping contact with Karlist circles in the various countries. In two months' time, the agency had sister offices in Prague, Belgrade, Budapest, London and Paris that were in touch with the main opposition newspapers and sending out propaganda for an economic union of Danubian States.[65]

The Paris office was especially successful and was gaining results. In summer 1919 a member of the Paris buro met with Aristide Briand, who told him that Clemenceau was wrong to have destroyed the Danubian Monarchy. Karl responded by sending his Bourbon-Parma brother-in-law, Sixte, to Paris. Later, in August 1919, Andrássy himself was sent to meet Briand and give him a memorandum on Karl's plan.

Apart from his secret diplomatic activity in the service of his monarch, Andrássy involved himself in publishing articles. As early as March 1919, he and many other legitimists believed there was little hope to save the monarchy in German Austria and as a result concentrated their activity on Hungary. Félix Vályi gave Andrássy the opportunity to write two articles on the future of Hungary in the *Revue* during his stay in Switzerland. These articles reveal his thoughts about Hungary and Central Europe, and both mention the necessity of creating a federalised Central Europe. He also underlines the danger of punishing Hungary, which would again push it into the arms of pangermanism. Andrássy wrote:

> Personne en Hongrie ne demande aux puissances occidentales de léser les intérêts réels, essentiels et non imaginaires de leurs alliés tchèques, roumains et yougoslaves. Il s'agit uniquement d'abandonner les visées territoriales impérialistes de ces jeunes nations dont l'intérêt vital n'est nullement incompatible avec le maintien d'une Hongrie viable.[66]

---

65 Ibid.
66 "No one in Hungary is demanding that the western powers compromise the real, essential, and non-imaginary interests of their Czech, Romanian, and Yugoslav allies. It is strictly a question of abandoning the imperialist territorial aims of these young nations, whose vital interest is in no way incompatible with the upholding of a viable Hungary." Andrássy, Gy., "La Hongrie et la Paix", *La revue politique internationale*, vol. XI, no. 36, 1919, 12–22.

And he proposes instead of separatism: "si au lieu de créer des irrédentismes nouveaux, on se contente d'une autonomie complète pour toutes les races du pays."[67]

In another article, he praises President Wilson who, "under the influence of the genius of his country",[68] had been able to solve the problem of self determination of nationalities by subordinating it to the general interest. The precondition for solving the nationalities problem is to maintain the integrity of Hungary to avoid the continual struggle of the Hungarians for their means of existence. Maintaining the thousand-year-old Hungarian state "with autonomy for the races within it, who are in the minority, would endanger the existence neither of the latter nor of Hungary's neighbours nor, lastly, the peace of the world. The only obstacle to this solution lies in the boundless ambition of the Czechs, the Roumanians [sic] and the Serbs [...]." Andrássy was still hoping the peace treaty would solve the border problem: "[...] we cannot believe that after the lessons of the present war it would in any way endanger the maintenance of peace if a curb were to be placed on the unjustified ambitions of such smaller states."[69]

These lines show that Andrássy was open to conceding broad autonomies to the minorities of pre-1918 Hungary in the frame of the Realm of Hungary that could have been the first step to a federal Kingdom of Hungary. He was a federalist, since he was open to an alliance with other states of the old monarchy once those had handed back the regions of Hungary they had conquered. However, in his political program presented in Hungary in 1920 he was to elude such an unpopular question. Indeed, the aim of post-revolutionary Hungary was to restore the country to its pre-1918 borders, and any reference to a "federal" solution was strongly unpopular in the counterrevolutionary atmosphere that prevailed then. Andrássy's conception, mentioned in the *Revue politique internationale*, was as far as the Hungarian political elite, left or right, could go. Not even the radical democrat Jászi or an Andrássy could conceive of a Hungary separated from its pre-1918

---

67 Ibid., 20.
68 Andrássy, "National Self-Determination", *La revue politique internationale*, vol. IX, no. 37–38, 1919, 185.
69 *Op. cit.*, 186.

regions. Concessions could go only so far as to accept a Hungarian state with autonomous regions within its borders. Hence, it would hardly be sufficient to convince the Allies.

The Legitimists back in Hungary

The first of the counter-revolutionary governments was based in Arad, which was occupied by the Romanian army. The government then moved to the town of Szeged, in May 1919, which remained Hungarian, and created the Szeged Government. Its objective was the return of order and of the pre-armistice regime. After the fall of the Commune brought about by the advance of the Romanian army and its occupation of Budapest, the former *homo regius* (a sort of viceroy) of King Karl, Archduke József, took over as head of state with the title of Governor of Hungary, giving the impression that the Habsburg monarchy was back in Hungary. Parallel to these events, Admiral Miklós Horthy, a member of the Szeged Government as Minister of Military Affairs and Commander of the National Army, created for himself the title Supreme Leader (fővezér) of the Army—dissociating himself from the Szeged Government— and entered the capital with his army.[70]

Since the Republic, followed by the 1919 Republic of Councils, was disastrous for Hungary, the conservatives had a good argument to revert to the pre-1918 regime, and the majority of the Hungarian population was supportive of this. However the form of government that Hungary would choose was still undecided, and no decision was taken by the national government to clarify this.

The only political group that would vote for a republic was the Socialist Party. As their influence was very feeble and the population at large was royalist, they had few supporters and thus little chances to achieve their goal.[71]

Who were the candidates for the throne other than the legitimate monarch and his descendants? For the free electors, there were not only Hun-

---

70   Ormos, Mária, *Hungary in the Age of the Two World Wars 1914–1945*, Atlantic Research and Publications, Inc., Highland Lakes, NJ, 2007, 60–61.
71   Service Historique de l'Armée de Terre (henceforth SHAT), 7N Hongrie, 2885, no. 465, 8–9. Mission Mil. français en Hongrie (no date 1919).

garian but also foreign candidates. Among the latter, those who had the best chances, according to French information, were an English prince, the Duke of Teck, who had some Hungarian roots[72] and was the brother of Queen Mary of Great Britain, and the Duke of Connaught[73] and Prince Cyril of Bulgaria, second son of King Ferdinand, whose names appeared as well.[74]

Among the Hungarian pretenders was Albert of Habsburg-Teschen, the son of Field Marshal Frigyes (Frederic) of Habsburg-Teschen. The family was resident in Hungary, and Albert's mother was Princess Crouy of Belgium. The Crouy family was traditionally considered as descendants of the royal Hungarian Arpadian dynasty, thus some anti-legitimists—such as Gömbös—were trying to use this as an argument to legitimise Albert's candidacy.

Yet Archduke József of the Hungarian Palatine branch of the Habsburg Dynasty remained the *favorit*.[75] He was very much a Hungarian, since his branch had been residing in Buda for many generations. He was popular, had democratic leanings and did not wish to bring back the old feudal system of the Hungarian magnates.[76]

On August 7, 1919, the archduke became head of state as Regent of Hungary and nominated the first post-communist government in Hungary after negotiations and acceptance of the Entente. This was a logical choice, since he was the *homo regius* nominated on October 27, 1918, by King Karl to defend his interests in Hungary. He was the one who had nominated Mihály Károlyi as prime minister on October 31, 1918.

Archduke József behaved quite unfaithfully to his monarch and cousin as he became a candidate to the throne. He did not refuse the flattering approaches of the supporters of his candidacy. Karl got wind of this and was quite furious. As Entente pressure was too important, the project of making József king was set aside; but Entente opposition was uneven. On one

---

72 The duke's, and his sister, Queen Mary's grandmother was a Hungarian, Countess Claudia Rhédey from Transylvania, which justified such a choice.
73 Prince Arthur, Duke of Connaught (1850–1942) was the third son of Queen Victoria. He was governor general of Canada (1911–1916), www.geocities.com/naciones_unidas_queenvictoria/arthur_biog
74 Andrássy, "National", 186.
75 The *Palatinus* was the hereditary viceroy or governor of Hungary. The first Habsburg who became hereditary *Palatinus* was Archduke József, brother of Emperor Francis I.
76 SHAT, 7N Hongrie, 2885, no. 465, 9, Mission Mil. française en Hongrie, (no date, 1919).

hand, József was very strongly attacked by Thomas Hohler, high commissioner of the British legation in Budapest. On the other, the Quai d'Orsay had a secret plan to put József on the throne as king of Hungary, which will be detailed below. On February 7, 1920, the Entente (Conférence des Ambassadeurs) sent a note to the government emphasising that no member of the Habsburg family could be head of state in Hungary. A new head of state had to be chosen.

In March 1920 Horthy was elected "Governor of Hungary" by the Hungarian Parliament under military control but with the approval of Britain. Logically, this appeared to entitle the country to be a monarchy again, and a ministerial decree announced that this was again the case. The names of public institutions were prefaced by the words "Royal Hungarian",[77] which undoubtedly reassured the legitimists, who thought that the return of the crowned king was imminent. But the internal situation was far from being so simple, and the decree reignited an already latent row. Parliament separated into two groups on the royal question. On one side was the coalition party, the United National Christian Party (KNEP), which was strongly legitimist, and on the other was the Smallholders Party, Kisgazda Párt (KGP), most of whose members were "free electors". Yet there were two sorts of legitimists: the Karlists, who wanted to precipitate the restoration, and the moderates who would wait for a better moment.

The battle between the legitimists and free electors was harsh. Andrássy, who became the leader of the legitimists, expressed the will to restore King Karl IV. When revealing his political program as a member of Parliament, Andrássy said that "the sovereignty of the crown of Saint Stephen comprises the sovereignty of the whole nation."[78] He decided to avoid the question of the existence of a legitimate king in order to evade any provocation of the free electors in the very unsubtle political arena. It was evident to him that the free electing law would be reactivated only if there was no heir to the throne. As the monarchy had not ceased to be and the Pragmatic Sanction

---

77 Admiral Miklós Horthy de Nagybánya was elected governor or regent on March 1, 1920. Benda, Kálmán, *Magyarország történeti kronológiája*, III, Akadémia Kiadó, Budapest, 1982, 872.
78 Andrássy, Gyula, *Miskolci programbeszéd*, Budapest, 1920, 10.

of 1713 was still the law, even if *Personalunion* was over, there was no reason for the election of a new king.[79] His opinion was that in order to avoid any conflict between the free electors and the legitimists, the "royal question" should not be an issue prior to signing the peace treaty. Once that danger was over and the king reinstalled, the monarch should respect the wishes of the Hungarian Nation and accept no other crown without consulting it. What was important for Andrássy was that the king represent Hungarian interests abroad and be concerned with its territorial problems.

Karl eventually accepted the condition that he would be the king only of an independent and national Hungary,[80] and by doing so, he responded positively to a new nation state of Hungary, which would rule out any possibility for him to become monarch in Austria—though, personally, he was still dreaming of a multinational confederation. This promise did not suffice to convince the free electors, who saw restoration in Hungary as a gateway to the crown of Austria. They also considered Karl to be a German prince and not a Hungarian one. For them the end of the Dual Monarchy and the letter of Eckartsau[81] meant that it was necessary to elect a national king. Despite Prime Minister Teleki's and Horthy's calls to table the royal problem, discussions continued. By then the legitimists were really dominant in the governing party.

On February 2, 1920, at the Paris Peace Conference, the Hungarian delegation was told that the Allies were hostile to the restoration of the Habsburgs—followed by the February 7 note, quoted above, from the Conference of Ambassadors. Instead of ending the debate between legitimists and free electors, it made it even worse. In fact, the Hungarian population was scandalised by the decision to limit the scope of its internal policy after the Treaty of Trianon (July 4) had confirmed that 71 percent of Hungary's territory was alienated, and it reinforced the legitimist camp.[82]

Even though the Commune in Hungary had ended and the return of the conservative government to Budapest was now a fact, Vienna still remained

---

79 Ibid.
80 Kardos, *A legitimizmus alternatívái*, 27–28, November 8, 1920, Karl to Horthy.
81 The so-called letter of abdication from the crown of Hungary signed in Eckartsau.
82 Iordache, Nicolae, *La Petite Entente et l'Europe*, IUHEI, Geneva, 1977, 30.

another centre for malcontent legitimists. There were Austrian, Czech, Yugoslavian and Polish legitimist officers in Vienna, and Hungarian officers of Horthy's army went to meet them in October 1919 with the purpose of buying ammunition, but without success. This ammunition was destined to reinforce Colonel Antal Lehár's—the brother of the Hungarian operetta composer—Hungarian army, based mainly in Sopron (in German, Oedenburg), this military corps was ruling western Hungary and was attracting many Hungarian but also malcontent legitimist officers from the Successor States, of which one third were Austrians. The west of Hungary had consequently become a centre for legitimist malcontents.[83] Antal Sigray was nominated by the Hungarian government and reconfirmed by Horthy to become high commissioner of western Hungary, and in this position he was plotting with Lehár to declare the autonomy of Hungary's Western Comitats and put them under the rule of King Karl IV.[84] Therefore, by the end of 1920, western Hungary had become the strongest bastion of the legitimists in the Danubian region. The monarchist movement of western Hungary and of Austria was directly financed by the Hungarian government.[85]

The question remains whether there were Hungarians who really wanted the restoration of the Austro-Hungarian Monarchy in its entirety or at least the restoration in both Austria and Hungary. An anonymous "confidential" Hungarian report mentions the possibility of a Danubian Confederation in a united Austro-Hungarian form. It also describes that it would be in Hungary's interests if the monarch were to be restored in Vienna first. For the report's author, the restoration in Austria and Hungary could only be an advantage to Hungary, unless, of course, the monarch was to use his power in Austria to the Hungary's disadvantage.

His arguments were that having Karl as a monarch in Vienna would be much better than having Karl Renner or an Ottokar Czernin (former minister of foreign affairs under the monarchy) as Austria's leader. Karl could counter the Slavonic bloc (Czechoslovakia, SHS Kingdom) much more effi-

---

[83] 7N Hongrie 2885, Rapport: Armée hongroise, October 29, 1919.
[84] NA, FO 371, 4862/C13700, Johnson (H.M. High Commissioner) to Curzon, December 8, 1920. Johnson was the new high commissioner, replacing Hohler.
[85] MNL, K64, cs. 1, 22/Res 1919, December 10, 1919.

ciently with a united Austria-Hungary, and not only would it have greater influence on Central European politics, but it would also solve the problem of western Hungary (Burgenland), which was awarded to Austria at Trianon.

The most interesting feature of this document, written by an Austro-Hungarian legitimist, is that the restoration in Austria would probably mean the disintegration of Czechoslovakia and of the SHS Kingdom. Answers to the questions posed by this document's author, along with his own interpretations, are presented in subsequent chapters. Suffice it to say here that the author did not realise that in September 1920 Austria could not restore the monarchy even if it were wanted by its people and government. The existence of this confidential document from the Hungarian Ministry of Foreign Affairs shows that there were supporters of a large Danubian Confederation[86] comprising Austria and Hungary together, and that this alternative was not ruled out in interwar Hungary.[87]

Emperor Karl's Postbellum Plan

Karl of Habsburg was born in 1887, only two years before the Mayerling tragedy and the death of the heir apparent, Archduke Rudolph. After the tragedy, it was Franz Joseph's younger brother Karl Ludwig who was to follow Rudolf on the throne, but when he died in 1896, his elder son Franz Ferdinand became heir apparent. Given that Franz Ferdinand had a morganatic marriage in 1900, his descendants could not become monarch. Hence it was his younger brother Otto, father of Karl, who was next in line after Franz Ferdinand. Otto died in 1906 and Karl became next in line after Franz Ferdinand.

Franz Joseph intensified the intellectual education and military formation of his pious grandnephew Karl and related to him with paternal feelings. Karl also had close relations with his uncle Franz Ferdinand. He learned many things from his uncle on politics and the nationalities issue. He was conscious that he would have to reform the dualist system, as his uncle was

---

86 As usual, the true nature of the state is not detailed, and therefore I cannot enquire whether it is more of a federation or confederation.
87 MNL, Oszkár de Charmant Manuscripts. Confidential, 844–49 ff.

planning to do, but not only as a trialist state, limited to three nations with the project of giving Czechs or Southern Slavs the same rights as Hungary. Karl did not agree with this project limited to Trialism and thought that he should reform the monarchy into a federation that would give all peoples of the monarchy equal chances.[88] But when Karl ascended his two thrones in the middle of the war (1916), he would decide not to affect the changes he had foreseen as necessary. He was asked by the influential Hungarian prime minister, Count István Tisza, to come to Budapest as soon as possible to be crowned as king of Hungary without reforming the monarchy. Eventually he decided that these reforms could wait until the end of the war, even though the different nationalist groups were becoming impatient for reforms. The Hungarian coronation bound his hands, and he could not change anything in Hungary. This situation brought him to make his declaration federalizing only the Austrian part of the Dual Monarchy in October 1918.[89]

After Emperor Karl's efforts to save the monarchy by federalizing it at the end of World War I, and the disintegration of Austria-Hungary that followed in November, there was little hope of recreating a large Central European federal or confederal entity. The most important person who relentlessly held to the idea that the salvage of the Habsburg Monarchy, as a con/federal state, was still possible was the monarch himself. Rumours persisted that the emperor had written down his own *post-bellum* plan, but it was not until 2004, when the relevant papers were finally published, was there written evidence of a confederation project conceived by the emperor, except for a few documents known and published in the 1980s in Vienna, most of which were only personal accounts, not notes authored by the emperor himself.[90]

It is in the archives of the Vatican's "foreign affairs" department, the Secretariat of State, that one can find the most important written sources setting out Emperor Karl's post-bellum plan to federate the Successor States of Austria-Hungary. There is much speculation about his knowledge of the prob-

---

88 Cordfunke, Erik, *Zita, La dernière impératrice 1892-1989*, Ed. Duculot, Paris, 24–25, 33.
89 Ibid., 48.
90 Eric Feigl, *Kaiser Karl, Persönliche Aufzeichnungen, Zeugnisse und Documente*, Amalthea, Vienna, 1984, 301–2. As historian of the cause for beatification of Karl of Habsburg, Elisabeth Kovács published the sources she used for the cause in 2004: Kovács, E., *Untergang oder Rettung der Monarchie*, t. II, Documenten, Böhlau Verlag, Wien, 2004.

lems of Central Europe, and posterity usually questions his understanding of the situation and the true relevance of his political steps. There is no doubt that Karl was a very young emperor— not specifically schooled to be a monarch—who inherited a large state entangled in what was then the largest war in history. War was followed by catastrophes: defeat, famine, revolutions and the disintegration of the multinational Empire-Kingdom.

The first questions to be addressed are whether his plan was relevant at this stage in 1919. It is also important to understand the role of the Vatican and the pope, to whom the letters on the Danubian Confederation were directed; and finally, one would like to understand why Karl counted especially on Britain and later on France to help him rebuild the Danubian area.

During the 1914–1918 war, the Holy See wanted to strengthen the Dual Monarchy. But as the war went on, the Vatican's Secretariat of State considered that Austria-Hungary could only survive if reorganised into a federation of nation states. The disruption of the Monarchy into small, independent nation states did not favour the Vatican in its aim to retain its disciplinary power over the clergy of the dissolved Monarchy and, if necessary, reform it. The policy of appointing nuncios to the new Successor States was initiated in 1920.[91] This did not mean that Pope Benedict XV himself would not have preferred to see Karl maintain a Catholic and federative monarchy in Central Europe. In fact, he held him in high regard, for Karl of Austria-Hungary was the only World War I belligerent to have listened to and tried to put into practice the papal appeal for peace in 1914.[92]

> Nous prions et conjurons ardemment ceux qui dirigent les destinées des peuples d'incliner désormais leurs cœurs à l'oubli de leurs différends en vue du salut de la société humaine. Qu'ils considèrent que assez de misères et de deuils accablent cette vie mortelle et qu'il y a assez de sang versé ; qu'ils résolvent donc à entrer dans les voies de la paix et à se tendre

---

[91] C.A. Macartney Papers, Bodleian Library Manuscript Department (henceforth Bodley MS), Report of the Foreign Office Research Dep., "The Vatican and the Successor States", February 18, 1944.
[92] Schönborn, Card. Christoph, "Carlo d'Austria: Imperatore e Re", in *L'Osservatore Romano, Supplemento*, no. 229, Domenica 3 Ottobre 2004, 14.

la main. Ils mériteront par là les bénédictions de Dieu pour eux et pour leurs nations et ils auront hautement mérité de la société [...]⁹³

Pope Benedict considered Karl his spiritual son,⁹⁴ which is why Karl decided to send a confidential letter describing his ideas on Central Europe to the most appropriate person, his spiritual father, the pope.⁹⁵

The First Letter to Benedict XV

Following the armistice, Emperor Karl signed two proclamations considered by some as letters of abdication: one for Austria in German (signed at Schönbrunn Castle in Vienna on November 11, 1918) and one shortly thereafter for Hungary in Hungarian (signed at Eckartsau Castle on November 13, 1918). These two letters of "abdication" are crucial for the understanding of Emperor Karl's first letter to Pope Benedict XV.

On February 28, 1919, Karl wrote a "strictly confidential" program of federalization of the now partitioned Empire-Kingdom to Pope Benedict XV, calling upon him for help with "une confiance toute filiale et de lui parler à coeur ouvert" (with filial confidence and open heart).⁹⁶

Karl started his letter to the pope by emphasising that there was no question of his abdication and that he was forced to sign a manifesto (referring to the Schönbrunn letter concerning Austria) that he did not consider a declaration of abdication.⁹⁷ The manifesto reads as follows:

---

93 "We beg and beseech ardently that those who direct the destinies of the peoples henceforth incline their hearts to forget their differences, with a view to the welfare of human society. That they might consider that enough misery and grief assails this mortal life and that enough blood has been spilled; that they therefore resolve to embark on the paths of peace and extend their hand to each other. They will in this manner merit the benedictions of God for themselves and for their nations and they will have highly merited from society ..."
"'Exhortation aux catholiques du monde entier'of September 8, 1914 of Pope Benedict XV", in Latour, Francis, *La papauté et les problèmes de la paix pendant la première guerre mondiale*, L'Harmattan, Paris, 1996, 306.
94 Ibid., 15.
95 The letters were published by Elisabeth Kovács following my research at the Vatican in Kovács, E., *Untergang...*, t. II, 2004.
96 Archivio della Sacra Congregazione per gli Affari ecclesiastici straordinari (Vatican State Secretariat Archives) (henceforth AE), Austria, 525, prot. 88.527.
97 "Je n'ai pas renoncé au trône et je suis décidé à ne jamais abdiquer. Dans l'état austro-allemand j'ai été forcé, par la révolution, de signer une proclamation moyennant laquelle je déclarais vouloir m'abstenir,

Seit Meiner Thronbesteigung war ich unablässig bemüht, Meine Völker aus den Schrecknissen des Krieges herauszuführen, an dessen Ausbruch Ich keinerlei Schuld trage.

Ich habe nicht gezögert, das verfassungsmässige Leben wieder herzustellen und habe den Völkern den Weg zu ihrer selbständigen staatlichen Entwicklung eröffnet.

Nach wie vor von unwandelbarer Liebe für alle Meine Völker erfüllt, will Ich ihrer freien Entfaltung Meine Person nicht als Hindernis entgegenstellen. Im voraus erkenne ich die Entscheidung an, die Deutschösterreich über seine künftige Staatsform trifft.

Das Volk hat durch seine Vertreter die Regierung übernommen. Ich verzichte auf jeden Anteil an den Staatsgeschäften.

Gleichzeitig enthebe Ich Meine österreichische Regierung ihres Amtes. Möge das Volk von Deutschösterreich in Eintracht und Versönlichkeit die Neuordnung schaffen und befestigen. Das Glück Meiner Völker war von Anbeginn das Ziel Meiner heissten Wünsche.

Nur der innere Friede kann die Wunden dieses Krieges heilen.[98]

---

en attendant, de tout acte gouvernemental, laissant à la nation le soin de décider de l'avenir. Je me considère comme nullement engagé par cette déclaration parce qu'elle m'a été extorquée à un moment où je ne disposais plus des moyens voulus pour étouffer la révolution. Mon armée se trouvait encore engagée au front, tandis qu'ici mes troupes m'avaient complètement abandonné, à tel point qu'il ne me restait, finalement, pour me protéger, que des élèves de deux écoles militaries." [I have not renounced the throne, and I am determined never to abdicate. In the Austro-German state I was forced by the revolution to sign a proclamation in return for which I would declare my willingness to abstain, while waiting, from every government act, leaving to the nation the charge of deciding its future. I consider myself as in no way obligated by that declaration because it was extorted from me at a moment when I no longer had the means at my disposal necessary to quell the revolution. My army was still engaged at the front, whereas here my troops had completely abandoned me, to the point where, in the end, all that remained to protect me were the students of the military schools.] AE, Austria, 525, prot. 88.527.

[98] "Since ascending the throne I have continually endeavoured to lead my Peoples out of the horrors of war, for the outbreak of which I bear no blame. I have not hesitated to reinstate a life that is constitutionally based and have opened for the Peoples a path to the independent development of their statehood./ Filled, as ever, with unalterable love for all my Peoples, I do not want my Person to be an obstacle to their free development./ I acknowledge in advance the decision that Germany-Austria will make regarding its future form of government./ The People have taken over the government via their representative./ I resign from all participation in the affairs of state./ I simultaneously dismiss my government of Austria./ May the people of German Austria create and fortify the new order in unity and a spirit of reconciliation./ The happiness of my Peoples has been the goal of my most fervent wishes from the beginning. Only internal peace can heal the wounds of this war." Kovács, E., *Untergang...*, doc. 123, 414–15.

The legal formulation of the letter does not straightforwardly imply abdication and carefully avoids the fateful word. It could be interpreted as a declaration implying only the suspension of his regal functions for an undefined period of time. However, owing to the state of affairs in Austria and to the ambiguousness of the manifesto, the archbishop of Vienna, Cardinal Piffl, considered it a declaration of abdication in his letter of December 30, 1918.[99] In other words, the Catholic Church considered the Schönbrunn letter to be referring to rump Austria as such.[100]

If we consider Karl's "Manifesto" written as King of Hungary, the problem is similar. He describes it to Benedict XV in these words: "Comme roi de Hongrie, également, sous la menace de voir ma maison à tout jamais détrônée, je me suis trouvé dans la nécessité de donner une déclaration semblable à l'autre."[101] In the case of Hungary the declaration was much shorter than the Schönbrunn one:

> Nem akarom, hogy személyem akadályul szolgájon [sic?] a Magyar nemzet szabad fejlődésének, mely iránt változatlan szeretettel vagyok áthatva. Ennél fogva minden részvételről az államügyek vitelében visszavonulok és már eleve elismerem azt a döntést, mely Magyarország jövendő államformáját megállapítja.[102]

If we consider Karl's concept that in a Danubian Confederation headed by him there could exist different forms of government,[103] then it is not surprising that Karl contested the interpretation of these letters as "declarations of abdication", since he implied in both declarations that nations will be able to choose their form of government.

---

99 AE, Austria, 525, prot. 86.573.
100 Letter from Valfré di Bonzo, nuncio in Vienna, to Sec. of State Gasparri, November 1918, AE, Austria, 529, prot. 84.396.
101 "Similarily as King of Hungary, under the menace of seeing my house dethroned for ever, I found myself in the necessity to give a similar declaration as the other." AE, Austria, 525, prot. 86.527.
102 "I do not want my person to be an obstacle to the free development of the Hungarian Nation, towards whom we still feel a great affection. I therefore resign from all participation in state affairs and I accept in advance the decision that Hungary will take regarding its form of government." Kovács, *op. cit.*, no. 125, Ekartsau, November 13, 1918, 419–20.
103 Feigl, *op. cit.*, Faszikel no. 38, Handgeschriebene Weisungen Seiner Majestät, Allgemeine Richtlinien, 301. We will return to this question in later pages.

Interpreting the Eckartsau letter as a letter of suspension is more obvious than doing so for the Schönbrunn letter, but, in short, both of them avoid the word "abdication".[104] The Schönbrunn declaration was definitely closer to an abdication, however.

It appears from British Foreign Office correspondence in 1921 that not only the author of "the Hungarian declaration" was contesting its value. Britain—as well as its allies—refused to consider this note as a letter of abdication and was pressing the Hungarian government to get a second and more convincing letter from King Karl.[105]

In his same letter to the pope, Karl warns of the dangers of an Anschluss to Germany:

> Quel sera, désormais, le sort de l'Autriche-Hongrie? Pour le moment, il est fort question de la réunion des provinces allemandes de l'Autriche à l'Allemagne, un projet qui agite très fort les esprits et qui a beaucoup d'adeptes dans les milieux radicaux et socialistes et qui, s'il se réalisait, signifierait la fin de l'Autriche en tant qu'état catholique. Il écarterait à tout jamais cette autre solution que je considère comme la seule possible et désirable et offrant des garanties de durée et de consolidation, et qui consisterait à faire renaître l'ancienne monarchie sous forme d'une fédération des états nationaux qui se sont organisés sur son ancien territoire. Cette seconde solution compte également de nombreux partisans, surtout parmi les éléments modérés et conservateurs, parmi les honnêtes gens, en général, mais la terreur qu'exercent les radicaux les paralyse et les empêche de se prononcer ouvertement dans ce sens.[106]

---

104 Ozer Carmi says: "D'après la loi magyare, pour qu'un acte d'abdication soit valable il doit être contresigné par le Président du Conseil, et l'abdication acceptée par les deux Chambres du Parlement." [According to Magyar law, in order for an act of abdication to be valid, it has to be countersigned by the President of the Council, and the abdication accepted by the two chambers of parliament.] Carmi, Ozer, *La Grande-Bretagne et la Petite Entente*, Droz, Genève, 1972. The nature of the letter—suspension of his functions as king—is confirmed by Gyula Wlassics, president of the Hungarian Parliament, in a document published by Prof. Kardos from ELTE University Budapest. Kardos, József, *A legitimizmus alternatívái Magyarországon (1918–1946)*, Korona Kiadó, Budapest, 1996, 9–10.

105 "I consider that it would be impossible for the Allied Governments to regard as an act of abdication, or even renunciation, a document which has been carefully worded in order to avoid giving any such impression." London, September 21, 1921, from Secretary of State S.P. Waterlow to H.M. High Commissioner in Budapest, Mr. Hohler, NA, FO 371/6105, 60–61 ff.

106 AE, Austria, 525, prot. 88.527. A few months later Karl would reiterate the danger of an Anschluss in more precise terms in a letter to President Poincaré: "[...] l'Entente devrait exiger pour

J'admets que cette union si elle doit se refaire, devra, à la suite des évènements, prendre une forme très changée et toute nouvelle. Mais je ne vois cette fédération que comme monarchie, avec un souverain légitime.
Tout président élu appartiendrait forcément, par ses origines, à un des états nationaux, ne pourrait être accueilli qu'avec méfiance par les autres nationalités et, par là, porterait en soi le germe de la discorde et de nouveaux désordres. Un inconvénient, un danger que ne présenterait pas la dynastie indigène, planant, pour ainsi dire, au dessus des différentes nationalités.[107]

He continues by explaining the structure of the new federal monarchy. First he explains that it would have common institutions (points as appeared in his letter):

---

l'Autriche allemande de nouvelles élections basées sur la délimitation territoriale telle qu'elle aura été fixée. Mais avant d'exiger ces nouvelles élections, l'Entente doit statuer d'une manière absolument claire, quelles seront les conditions de paix dans le cas d'une renonciation définitive à l'union avec l'Allemagne et quelles seraient les conditions dans le cas contraire. L'effet moral en serait d'une importance extrême sur la mentalité publique et exercerait une influence transcendante sur le résultat des élections." [The Entente should require new elections for German Austria based on the territorial delimitation as it will have been fixed. But prior to demanding these new elections, the Entente must give rulings in an absolutely clear manner regarding what will be the conditions for peace in the case of a definitive renunciation to the union with Germany, and what would be the conditions in the contrary case. The moral effect of this would be of extreme importance for the public mentality and would exert a transcendent influence on the result of the elections.] Kovács, E., *op. cit.*, doc. 166. 508–10, Dr Henri Seeholzer (in the name of Karl) to Poincaré, Prangins, June 10, 1919.

107 "What, henceforth, will be the fate of Austria-Hungary? For the moment, there is a significant push to reunify the German provinces of Austria and Germany, a project that is causing a great stir among minds and which has many followers in the radical and socialist milieus and which, should it be realised, would mean the end of Austria as a Catholic state. It would forever cast aside that other solution which I consider as the only possible and desirable one and as offering guarantees of long duration and consolidation, and which would consist in bringing about the rebirth of the ancient monarchy in the form of a federation of the national states that have organised themselves on its ancient territory. This second solution likewise has numerous supporters, especially among the moderate and conservative constituents, among the decent people generally, but the terror being exercised by the radicals paralyses them and prevents them from openly declaring themselves in this sense./ I admit that this union, in the event that it must remake itself, will, in the wake of events, have to take on a very changed and completely new form. But I view this federation exclusively as a monarchy with a legitimate sovereign. / Every elected president would inevitably, by his origins, belong to one of the national states, he could be received by the other nationalities only with distrust, and would thus carry within himself the seeds of discord and fresh disturbances. An inconvenience, a danger which the indigenous dynasty would not present, hovering as it were above the different nationalities." AE, Austria, 525, prot. 88.527.

1. les rapports avec l'étranger (diplomatie)
2. l'armée
3. commerce, postes et chemins de fer, navigation, avec un parlement fédéral et les ministères respectifs.[108]

For the rest, each state would have complete autonomy, its own constitution and even its own governmental form, which meant that republics would also be accepted into the confederation. Emperor Karl considered this as natural, since there were republics, like Hamburg, that had been members of the Holy Roman Empire. His project does recall the structure of the Dual Monarchy with its three common ministries: Foreign Affairs, Finance and Defence.

He continues by arguing why the monarchy is necessary:

J'ai la conviction qu'une fédération danubienne de ce genre, et monarchique, sera seule capable d'empêcher que la vielle monarchie de mes ancêtres ne devienne à l'instar des Etats des Balkans, le théâtre de guerres sanglantes et de luttes interminables. Déjà les différentes petites républiques à peine constituées, font la guerre, plus ou moins ouverte à tout ce qui est catholique. Et considérant l'énergie des Allemands de l'Empire et connaissant, d'autre part, le caractère faible et débonnaire de mes Allemands d'Autriche, tout porte à craindre qu'une union politique de ces deux éléments ne pourrait se produire qu'au détriment du catholicisme.[109]

These words show not only that the monarch was well informed but also that he could foresee in which direction Germany was heading: the January Spartakist uprising in Berlin was to be followed by the April Commune in Munich; Bolshevik danger was therefore imminent in Bavaria. A union

---

108 1) Foreign relations (diplomacy); 2) Army; 3) Commerce, postal service, railway, navigation, with a federal Parliament and related ministries. Ibid.
109 "I have the conviction that a Danubian federation of this genre, and one based on monarchy, will alone be capable of preventing the old monarchy of my ancestors from following the example of the Balkan states and becoming the theater of bloody wars and interminable battles. Already the different small republics, having barely been constituted, are waging more or less open war on everything that is Catholic. And considering the energy of the Germans of the Empire and recognizing, on the other hand, the weak and easy-going character of my Germans in Austria, everything points toward the fear that a political union of these two elements could not but come about to the detriment of Catholicism." Ibid.

of Austria with such an unstable Germany could indeed endanger Catholicism. Even if the Commune was vanquished, one can still argue that Karl had fought a war as an ally of Germany and was confronted with a Prussian militarist mentality in regard to which he was apprehensive. In other words, no matter what sort of radicalism—right or left—Karl was dreading, he was quite aware of the consequences of such a union. Sooner or later, his 1919 fears would reveal themselves to be prescient: the 1938 Anschluss with a strongly anticlerical Nazi Germany represented a true danger to Catholicism.

The following paragraph shows a monarch who was less acquainted with realities contemplating the alliance of the cross and the sword as the solution to the region's problems:

> C'est, je ne le cache pas, ma propre cause que je plaide, en même temps que celle de notre religion. Mais l'autel et le trône, ces deux pouvoirs d'institution divine, ne sont-ils pas appelés à marcher de pair, étant seuls capables, par leur union, et rétablir l'ordre et, surtout, de le maintenir? Puissent, Saint-Père, nos efforts réunis arriver à endiguer le bolchevisme qui, dans chacune de ces petites républiques, approche à pas de géants. [...][110]

He then comes to the point: "Les gouvernements [of the Successor States] étant impuissants à y porter remède, nous n'espérons le salut que d'une intervention étrangère."[111] He recognises that without external help, Central Europe cannot be saved and asks for the Pope's intervention.

Knowing the papacy's, and his own situation, it is difficult to imagine that Benedict XV could have helped in re-establishing the monarchy in a confederal form or stopped the tide of Bolshevism on Danubian Europe. Was Karl asking

---

110 "It is, I do not deny it, my own cause which I am pleading, simultaneously with that of our religion. But the altar and the throne, these two powers of divine institution, are they not called to march side by side, being alone capable, by their union, of re-establishing order and, above all, of maintaining it?/ May, Holy Father, our reunited efforts succeed in holding back Bolshevism which, in every one of these small republics, is approaching with giant steps. As the governments are powerless to bring about a remedy for this, we can only hope that salvation will occur through foreign intervention." AE, Austria, 525, prot. 88.527. He was right in regard to Bavaria with the installation of the April Commune.
111 "As the governments [of the Successor States] are powerless to bring about a remedy for this, we can only hope that salvation will occur through foreign intervention." Ibid.

for the Vatican's intervention as a last resort? As Emperor of Austria, Apostolic King of Hungary and a profound Catholic, Karl had been relying on Vatican diplomacy and its advice all through the war. At this moment, he was counting on the Church's diplomacy to get foreign forces involved in stopping Bolshevism and then bringing back order with the help of the Church. His anxiousness to act against the imminent threat— which arrived in Hungary only a few weeks later, in March 1919, in the form of a Bolshevist regime— shows that he was, yet again, well informed regarding the situation in Central Europe. He had already mentioned this danger in February 1918, when he predicted a revolution in Austria and southern Germany within six months.[112]

As is known, foreign occupation (French and Romanian) did stop Bolshevism in Hungary, but it did not enable Karl to reoccupy his royal apostolic throne. At this point, the future variant of Habsburg Monarchy—limited to Hungary or to a confederation of independent states— was not yet decided, especially in France. Karl was still counting on an opportunity to negotiate the survival of the Empire-Kingdom.

Pope Benedict's response of March 26 was most polite but did not offer real support, only moral encouragements:

> Noi facciamo voti per il migliore avvenire di coteste popolazioni, da Noi tanto benamate per il sincero loro attaccamento a questa Sede Apostolica e cosi care ancora a Vostra Maestà. Quando si pensi a tutto ciò che Ella ha fatto per il bene dei popoli a Lei affidati della Provvidenza divina, non meraviglia il constatare come nell'animo Suo, pur dopo i gravi rivolgimenti politici, permangano le migliori disposizioni ed i piú cordiali sentimenti verso di essi.[113]

At the time as these exchanges of letters, the Vatican was observing the events in Central Europe. On March 16, 1919, the apostolic nuncio to Vien-

---

112 NA, FO 371, 3133, 175–76 ff. After declaring the Republic of Councils in Budapest, Béla Kun had planned to bring the Commune to Vienna, a plan which eventually failed.
113 "We vow for a better future for these people, whom We love for their sincere attachment to this Apostolic See and who are so dear to Your Majesty. When thinking of all You have done for the good of the people entrusted to You by divine providence, it is no wonder to observe how in Your heart, even after serious political upheavals, the finest disposition and the most cordial sentiments persist towards them." Response of the Pope: AE, Austria, 525, prot. 88.527.

na, Teodoro Valfré di Bonzo, wrote to Secretary of State Pietro Gasparri: "Non credo che si possa sperare in un ritorno monarchico, tale l'antipatia o l'indifferenza che regna per gli Hasburgo."[114]

But then he also added:

> Ho però saputo che l'Imperatore sempre fidente nella buona stella della sua famiglia non pensa affatto ad abdicare. Egli dice che se si considera la stato in cui si trovava l'Austria quando sono avvenute le elezioni, se si pensa che molte provincie che sono occupate e molti uomini che sono prigionieri non hanno potuto dare il loro voto, deve apparire chiaramente che le elezioni ultime non rappresentano la volontà di tutta l'Austria tedesca, che quindi egli ha tutte le ragioni per non considerarsi ancora legato dall'impegno preso nell'atto di ritirarsi dagli affari.[115]

However, the secretary of state did not take much notice of these remarks. He was already drawing up a letter to Karl Seitz, president of the Constitutional Assembly of the newborn Republic of Austria, that would recognise the new Austrian state in December 1919.[116] Karl was already considered a deposed monarch. It should not be forgotten that the Vatican's rush to recognise the new republic was clearly a way of ensuring its future influence in the Republic of Austria, which remained a strongly Catholic country. This step was typical of pre-Lateran policy to ensure that the pope—who was still a prisoner of the king of Italy— would have bilateral relations with this geographically reduced Successor State. However, this was not the only reason: Karl's wife, Empress Zita, considered Secretary of State Gasparri an enemy of historic Austria.[117]

---

114 "I do not think that one can hope for a return of the monarchy, such is the antipathy or the indifference that reigns towards the Habsburgs."
115 "It came to my knowledge, however, that the Emperor, evermore confident in the good star of his family, is not thinking of abdicating at all. He says that if one considers the state in which Austria found itself when the elections occurred, if one thinks that many occupied provinces and many imprisoned men could not cast their vote, it must be clear that the last elections do not represent the will of all German Austria, and therefore he has every reason not to consider himself still bound by the commitment made in the act of withdrawing from affairs." AE, Austria 525, prot. 89, 848.
116 The document relating to the recognition is in dossier: AE, Austria 525.
117 Feigl, *op. cit.*, Vienna, 1984, 347–48.

The Second Letter

In Karl's second letter, this time sent from exile in Wartegg (Switzerland),[118] he added two points that he omitted to mention in his first letter:

> Premièrement, en constituant l'état fédératif il serait de grande importance de le créer neutre. L'histoire a démontré clairement qu'un état composé de plusieurs nationalités reste fermement uni en temps de paix et même, pour cette raison, est une forte garantie pour le maintien de celle-ci [la paix]. Par contre en temps de guerre cet état est soumis à de violents tiraillements si l'une ou l'autre des nations qui en font partie se trouve dans un camp adverse.

He then underlined the necessity of common representation at the Peace Conference, as opposed to separate delegations:

> Deuxièmement, que l'Autriche-Hongrie soit représentée à la Conférence de la paix, non seulement par les délégués des différents Etats nationaux qui se sont formés sur son ancien territoire, et qui actuellement sont en lutte les uns contre les autres, mais aussi par une représentation commune: car tant d'intérêts communs, surtout en questions financières, ne peuvent être avantageusement traités que s'ils sont représentés en bloc vis-à-vis des anciens adversaires.[119]

It was certainly not the interest of the leaders of the Successor States to be represented commonly as members of Austria-Hungary. Czechoslovakia,

---

118 This letter was sent to Cardinal Gaetano Bisleti as intermediary. The Cardinal had married Karl and Zita at the Castle of Schwarzau (Austria) in 1911.

119 "First, in setting up the federative state, it would be of great importance to create it in a neutral fashion. History has clearly demonstrated that a state composed of several nationalities stays firmly united in times of peace and, for this reason, is even a strong guarantee for the maintenance of the same (of peace). On the other hand, in times of war this state is subject to violent frictions if the one or the other of the nations that make up a part of it finds itself on an opposing side./ Second, that Austria-Hungary be represented at the conference of peace, not merely by the delegates of the different national states that have formed upon its ancient territory and which are presently fighting one against the other, but also by a common representation: for so many common interests, particularly in financial matters, cannot not be handled to advantage unless they are represented collectively vis-à-vis ancient adversaries."

which did not exist before 1918 and had everything to gain from the Peace Conference, considered itself as independent from Austria-Hungary, which was responsible for the war. Serbia and Romania, which were on the victors' side and were gaining new territory and population, would both protest in the most vigorous way had the Entente obliged them to send leading members of the newly gained population to join a common representation of Austria-Hungary. What Karl still did not want to accept was the unwillingness of the Entente to recognise the existence of Austria-Hungary as a whole, given that it had chosen to destroy it.

> Les anciennes légations, bien qu'en état de liquidation, fonctionnent toujours puisque les petits états nationaux à l'exception des Tchécoslovaques ne sont pas encore reconnus et, espérons-le, ne le seront pas d'ici longtemps. Quand à Vienne, un diplomate désire avoir une information, il ne s'adresse pas à Mr Bauer, mais à l'ancien ministère des affaires étrangères. Un grand avantage de la représentation commune serait que le courage des hommes politiques, qui encore aujourd'hui déplorent la désagrégation de l'Empire, serait puissamment soutenu.
> La crainte seule, que la manifestation de leurs sentiments désavantagerait leur petit état vis-à-vis des autres, surtout si cet état était le premier à se prononcer, retient beaucoup d'hommes politiques et les empêche de faire connaître franchement leurs opinions.
> C'est le premier pas qui coûte: alors les peuples liés entre eux depuis des siècles écouteront avec empressement la voix de la réconciliation et comprendront que leur véritable intérêt est de redevenir unis.[120]

---

[120] "The ancient legations, although in a state of liquidation, continue to function since the small national states, with the exception of the Czecho-Slovaks, are not yet recognised and, let us hope, will not be recognised for a very long time. As for Vienna, if a diplomat desires to receive information, he does not address himself to Mr. Bauer, but to the old ministry of foreign affairs./A great advantage of common representation would be that the courage of men of politics, who deplore to this day the disintegration of the Empire, would benefit from powerful support./ The fear alone, that the expression of their sentiments would cause their small state to be at a disadvantage with regard to others, particularly if this state was the first to express itself, holds many men of politics back and prevents them from making their opinions known openly./ It is the first step that counts: thus the peoples connected among themselves for centuries will listen attentively to the voice of reconciliation and will understand that their true interest lies in becoming united again." Letter to Cardinal Bisleti — playing the role of intermediary— April 17, 1919: AE, Austria 525, prot. 90. 154.

It is true that the common Ministry of Foreign Affairs still existed in 1919, though undergoing liquidation.[121] There is an interesting example to illustrate this: Switzerland refused to recognise any other ministry of foreign affairs than the old joint one until October 31, 1920, thus recognizing the Austro-Hungarian envoy in Bern until that date. Most of the other envoys had left and liquidated their representations towards the end of 1919, but this was still not the case in April of that year, when this letter was written, and Karl was right to underline this fact in order to influence the course of things to his, and the Empire-Kingdom's, advantage.

There may be doubts about the accuracy of the reports he received or the advice of the advisors surrounding him in Switzerland. However, it is difficult to know the number of politicians of the Successor States who had remained secret legitimists. In Hungary, many would show their colours soon.[122] Ivo Banac[123] and especially Jasna Adler[124] have established that there was important Croatian republican and pro-Habsburg resistance alike against Serb domination after the creation of the new Slovene Croatian Serb (SHS) Kingdom. It was not easy, though, for nations now considered as minorities to resist when the Entente powers had already decided their fate.

There was, however, a problem when Karl mentioned the "little nation states" that were not recognised, except for Czechoslovakia. In fact there were no little nation states other than Hungary and Austria, which became nation states de facto after losing their territories with minorities. The other parts of the monarchy were annexed to already-existing states that qualified themselves as nation states, such as Croatia to the Serb Kingdom and the even more ethnically mixed Transylvania to Romania.

Emperor Karl's letters to the pope can give the impression that he did not totally grasp that during the war deals were struck with Italy, Romania

---

121 Matsch, E., *Der Auswärtige Dienst von Oesterreich (-Ungarn), 1720–1920*, Vienna, 1986, 170–73.
122 In August 1919, the country was taken over by a "governor", Archduke Josef von Habsburg, Karl's *homo regius*. Hungary was again reuniting with continuity after the hundred days of the Republic of Councils.
123 *The National Question in Yugoslavia*, Cornell University Press, Ithaca, London, 1988.
124 The Croatian historian, a former lecturer of the University of Geneva, has made a remarkable thesis on the forced union of Croatia with Serbia. She has worked mainly with Croatian and Austrian archival sources. Adler, Jasna, *L'Union Forcée, La Croatie et la création de l'Etat yougoslave (1918)*, Ed. Georg, Geneva, 1997, 328, 340–41, 350–51.

and especially the Czech politicians in exile.[125] The Czechs had managed to guarantee their position on the side of the victors and present themselves and the Slovaks as victims of Austro-Hungarian authoritarianism. There was, therefore, not much hope that the Entente countries would respond to such a plea. However, Karl considered that he had to convey to the person he trusted the most, Benedict XV, his concerns about his people.[126]

The Emperor's Personal Notes on the Danubian Union

As a supplement to the Danubian Confederation project that was sent to the pope, it is important to show some of the emperor's private notes on the subject in which he describes the form of the confederation: "Our principal aim is a Danubian Confederation [...] an economic alliance of all the so called 'Successor States' under their legitimate sovereign."[127]

The content of this draft is as follows:

- the elimination of customs borders, *Zollgrenzen,* between the member states;
- at the federal level, the emperor would be supported by a chancellor and an economics minister responsible to the federal Parliament;
- there would be a common defence, but each country would have its own foreign ministry and its own army as a contingent of the federal army;
- republics could also be member states;
- small or large, the member states would have equal rights;
- owing to its economic nature, the federation could not have an active or aggressive foreign military policy and should have a form of neutrality;

---

125 Let us not forget the Czech legions that were present in the French and Italian armies in exchange for the Entente's support to their cause. They were also present in Siberia supporting "white" Russian troops fighting the Bolsheviks.
126 It did take a year for the press to get hold of the Vatican's implication in a restoration. See NA, FO 371 4650 Austria, 169–71ff., July 27, 1920, *Agramer Tagesblatt: Plan for a Danubian Confederation.*
127 Feigl, *op. cit.,* Faszikel No. 38 Handgeschriebene Weisungen Seiner Majestät, Allgemeine Richtlinien, 301.

- conflicts between states would be dealt with by a Court of Justice with members of the states;
- the emperor would not have the authority to get involved in conflicts between member states;
- the emperor would nominate the chancellor and the economics minister;
- the emperor would be the supreme commander of the federal military forces and represents the federation abroad;
- in Austria, the monarchy would be based on the English example;
- there would be respect of the autonomy of the *Länder*;
- no militarism, possibly a Swiss militia system.[128]

These notes are much more elaborate than those he sent to the pope. Though not dated, they were probably written after the Vatican letters.

Since the plan outlined is a sketch, it lacks many essential aspects related to the functioning of a federal system, such as: how common decisions are taken, how the member states are represented or how the federal Parliament expresses itself. And we do not know if the member states delegate or submit themselves to the con/federal organs or centre. At first glance, the plan seems to have the criteria of a confederation, since all members can have their own foreign ministries, but at the same time, the confederation would have a common army and a common economics minister, which are already aspects of a federation. There is even a contradiction: each country could have its Ministry of Foreign Affairs, but the emperor would represent the state abroad. Does this mean that the emperor would represent only the states that do not decide to have their own Foreign Ministry or would represent them all? He might have been conceiving an idea of a subsidiary system of ministries. But he does not mention, as in his first letter to Benedict XV, a common "diplomacy". For all these reasons, it is difficult to decide whether this embryonic plan, called a "Danubian Confederation", is truly a confederation. The editor of the document points out that the content of this plan was duplicated almost in its entirety by André Tardieu, the later prime minister of France in the early 1930s, when he prepared his project, known as the

---

128 Ibid., 301–2.

"Tardieu Plan", for a new Danubian Confederation.[129] Whether it was copied remains a hypothesis, but there are certainly similarities.[130] Naturally, Tardieu conceived it without Habsburg involvement.

Karl's proposal specified that the numerous questions relating to this federation had to be dealt with by specialists: a monetary and customs union, freedom of circulation, railway conventions, shipping channels, post, telegraph and telephone. Finally, economic interests would be represented externally.

Karl did not forget to defend the territorial interests of Austria and Hungary in his proposals, written just after the St. Germain and Neuilly (he means Trianon, which was discussed by the Allies and Hungary in Neuilly) peace treaties

> Pour en arriver à cette fédération il faudrait concéder à l'Autriche et à la Hongrie une révision des traités de St-Germain et de Neuilly, révision faite dans ce sens que ces petits états ne seraient pas contraints d'emporter toutes les charges — sous la condition toutefois qu'ils tendraient la main à leurs anciens compagnons.[131]

Ever since the nineteenth century, the idea of a Danubian Confederation was a recurrent idea in the minds of revolutionary politicians and was later adopted by the Habsburgs themselves. The survival, and later salvation, of the Empire-Kingdom depended on its realisation. In 1919, the idea of a Danubian Confederation was late in being proposed. It had been late already in October 1918, but this did not mean that diplomatic efforts were not to be ventured to save the idea.

---

129 Ibid., 301.
130 The "Tardieu Plan" for a Danubian Confederation was mainly a Central European trade union, involving the Little Entente states with Austria and Hungary, which could have been developed further but which failed following the Stresa Conference in 1932. It was to break the isolation of Austria and Hungary by the Little Entente and limit the influence of Germany in the region. Ferencuhova, Bohumila, "La Tchécoslovaquie et le Plan Tardieu", *Revue d'Europe Centrale*, Strasbourg, Centre d'Etudes Germaniques, no. 2, 1997, 1–14.
131 "In order to achieve this federation, it would be necessary to concede to Austria and to Hungary a revision of the treaties of St-Germain and of Neuilly, a revision made in the sense that these small states would not be forced to bear all the burdens – provided, however, that they would extend their hand to their long-standing companions." Prangins, December 1919, Letter to His Holiness, Kovács, E. *op. cit.*, no. 180, 543–45.

CHAPTER II

Karl Tries Britain and France

The Danubian Confederation and Britain

The People of Influence at the Foreign Office

The emperor enjoyed a good reputation in the British Foreign Office. Permanent Under-Secretary Lord Hardinge remarked that the young emperor was most anxious to make peace with the Entente: "His first act, on his accession, was to break Count János Forgách,[132] head of the political section of the Common Foreign Ministry, as having been the author of Austria's ultimatum to Serbia, which the young Emperor described as a criminal document."[133] And then Lord Hardinge praised his positive intentions: "It was well known that the young Emperor Karl was sincerely desirous of peace and that he hated the war and deprecated the original cause of it."[134]

His reputation came from Karl's sincere efforts to negotiate a separate peace with the Entente during the war. On the one hand, there were negotiations initiated by the emperor through his brothers-in-law, Sixte and Xavier de Bourbon-Parma—who were both officers of the Belgian army—with Clemenceau. On the other, the English negotiations are much less well known but have been covered by Hungarian historians.[135]

It is not the purpose of this book to go into details concerning these 1916 negotiations; however, it is useful to show that their failure was considered in Brit-

---

132 Among the warmongers there were other Hungarians like Forgách: Foreign Minister Count Leopold Berchtold and Count Alexander Hoyos, Berchtold's chef de cabinet, also considered a Hungarian (born in Fiume) but with an English mother. They all favoured a more aggressive foreign policy for Austria-Hungary. Tunstall, Graydon A. Jr, "Austria-Hungary", in Richard F. Hamilton & Holger H. Herwig (eds.), *The Origins of World War I*, Cambridge University Press, Cambridge, 2003, 125.
133 Hardinge, Lord, *Old Diplomacy*, John Murray, London, 1947, 209.
134 Ibid., 220.
135 Arday, Lajos, *Térkép csata után: Magyarország a Brit külpolitikában 1918–19* (Hungary in British foreign policy), Magvető, Budapest, 1990.

Chapter II

ain as having been the responsibility of Austria-Hungary, which did not want to make concessions until the last months of the war. Sir Horace Rumbold, one of the British mediators during the secret negotiations, said in April 1918:

> If there is to be any justice in the world the Central European Empires ought to be completely smashed [...] we find it difficult to decide which is the stronger feeling in my mind, the hatred of Germany or the contempt of Austria. They are a pretty pair and [I] still believe that they will receive proper chastisement.[136]

In short, the Foreign Office claimed that it had made an effort to save the Austrian Empire. By April 1918, Britain was no longer interested in saving it, but there were still some British officials who wanted to do so, in some form, until October 1918 and even beyond.[137]

The negative effect on the Foreign Office, from Austria-Hungary's perspective, was the influence of the so-called New Europe Group. From 1915, this group, led by Henry Wickham Steed, editor of the Times from 1919, and R. W. Seton-Watson, an influential historian and political activist specialised in Central Europe, elaborated a policy that would redraw the map of Central Europe by accepting that all nations of the Habsburg Monarchy had the right to independence.[138]

---

136 Rumbold to de Bunsen, April 15, 1918, Rumbold Papers, Bodleian Library, Oxford. Bátonyi, G., *Britain and Central Europe 1918–1933*, Oxford, 1999, 11.

137 Such is the case of Captain Leo Amery, a half-Hungarian intelligence officer in the Balkans and influential member of the War Cabinet Secretariat and the later First Lord of the Admiralty, 1922–4, and member of the Paneuropean Union of Count Coudenhove-Kalergi. He defended the idea of saving the Habsburg Monarchy as a Danubian Confederation. Amery's views were sent to the war department and the PID by Robert Cecil, who sympathised with the former's ideas. FO 371/3136, 177223/W3, Minutes of Capt. Amery, London, October 24, 1918.

138 R.J.W Evans offers a severe criticism of Seton-Watson and Wickham Steed in regard to "their attitudes to empire" by saying: "Certainly they were no apologist for the expansionist, flag waving imperialism of the Tories: [...] Seton-Watson was a patriotic Scot, who for some time concealed his roving commission under the nom de plume of "Scotus Viator"[...]. But equally most do not, any more than their Victorian ancestors, seem to have registered an inconsistency between support for the British Empire and condemnation of despotic, decadent multinational authority elsewhere. Wickham Steed was only exaggerating from widespread premise when he explained the complications of Austria-Hungary by reference to the behaviour of tribes on the Indian frontier." Evans, R.J.W, "Great Britain and East-Central Europe, 1908–48: A Study in Perceptions", *The First Masaryk Lecture*, Kings College, London, 2001, 12–13.

In March 1918, Lord Hardinge created the Political Intelligence Department of the Foreign Office. He was assisted in reorganising the ministry by Sir Eyre Crowe,[139] an expert on Germany who succeeded Hardinge as permanent under-secretary for foreign affairs in 1920.[140] Though Seton-Watson was not a member of this department—he worked in the War Office's Enemy Propaganda Department—he had a great deal of influence and was the *maître à penser* of quite a few of its members, such as Lewis Namier[141] who was the specialist on Central European questions.

Another important Foreign Office figure was Francis Oppenheimer.[142] Though not a member of the Political Intelligence Department (PID), Oppenheimer was a financial and economic expert at the Foreign Office and was asked to help evaluate the situation in Austria. He was favouring the idea of a Danubian Confederation and was hostile to the annexation of Austria by Germany. He was prejudiced against the Germans but found "the Austrians a lovable race".[143]

Having German roots,[144] Crowe was suspected of being favourable in his approach to Germany after the end of the war;[145] just as Oppenheimer was concerning Austria. All these people, especially Seton-Watson and Namier, were influential on Central European questions and had their say in the future of region.[146] In these conditions, obtaining British support for a Danubian Confederation, in which the role of Budapest would be central, was diffi-

---

139 He would become head of the political section of the British delegation to the Peace Conference from June 1919.
140 Bátonyi, *op. cit.*, 12.
141 Namier was the disinherited son of a Jewish landowner from Galicia, a province of Austria. His true name was Ludwik Bernsztejn Niemirowski. He was interested in and strongly prejudiced about Central Europe. Evans, R.J.W, *op. cit*, 11–12. Namier opposed Amery's idea of creating a Danubian Confederation. FO 371/3136, 177223/W3, London, November 7, 1918, Namier's notes to Amery's Memorandum.
142 Goldstein, E., *Winning the Peace*, Clarendon Press, Oxford, 1991, 80.
143 Bodleian Library, Oxford, Manuscript Dep. (henceforth Bod. MS) Oppenheimer papers Box 6/2 Memorandum by Sir Francis Oppenheimer for the P.M. Paris, June 3, 1919.
144 Eyre Crowe, the son of the British Consul General, was not only partly educated in Germany (Düsseldorf and Berlin) but also had a German mother and wife. Goldstein, *op. cit.*, 80.
145 Hardinge said about him, "He was so palpably German... Further, I mistrust the soundness of his judgements." Though Crowe claimed, as early as 1907, that Germany wanted to dominate Europe and the world, he became more nuanced towards it after the war. Ibid., 80. (E.g.: He favoured Germany over Poland and Lithuania when reorganising the map of Europe. Ibid., 127.)
146 Namier opposed Leo Amery's idea of creating a Danubian Confederation. FO 371/3136, 177223/W3, Namier's notes to Amery's Memorandum, London, November 7, 1918.

cult. Not to say that a Habsburg restoration would be countered outright by the PID team,[147] which explains why Britain had shown only little interest, after World War I, in a Danubian Confederation in general. The Habsburgs were considered by many in the Foreign Office as the staunch ally of Germany during the war and, therefore, as unacceptable candidates as a head of state in Central European countries, as was Kaiser Wilhelm for Germany.

Very soon after the war, pro-Habsburg emissaries were sent to Bern to influence future decisions of the Entente in favour of a Danubian Confederation and to influence Britain against supporting the German Anschluss of Austria by underlining its danger. Professor Lammasch, the last prime minister of the Austrian Empire, was sent to Switzerland as a delegate of the new Austrian Republic to attend a conference of the League of Nations. He tried to propose a loose confederation of neutral republics including Lower and Upper Austria, Salzburg, Tyrol, Voralberg, the German portion of Styria and Carinthia—in other words, the *Länder* of the new Austrian Republic—and the German portions of Hungary (in Baranya county and Western Hungary).[148] Another Austrian sent an important study on the Danubian Confederation and a *Zollunion* to Sir Francis Oppenheimer.[149] But the interest shown was lukewarm.

The British Foreign Office was continuously bombarded, through its embassies or directly, with similar letters, studies and essays on the Danubian Confederation, and it could not ignore, without assessing them, these sometimes lengthy papers.

The Aide-Mémoire to the Pope

After writing both letters of "abdication", Karl left for Switzerland after the Federal Council (government) there allowed him entrance. Karl and Zita and their children left Austria on March 24, 1919, escorted by a British officer, Lieutenant Colonel Edward Strutt, who had been sent by King George V of Britain.

---

147 Namier was one of those strongly opposing a Habsburg restoration and he thought that the Anschluss of Austria to Germany was the soundest solution; an idea with which Hardinge fully agreed. Goldstein, *op. cit.*, 129. Czechoslovakia was strongly supported by him. Ibid., 138.
148 NA, FO 371, 3529, 507–509 ff. Sir Rumbold's dispatch, March 19, 1919.
149 Bod. MS, Oppenheimer 6/2, Dr Karl Schlesinger's letter and study to Oppenheimer Zurich, July 30, 1919.

Their first destination was Castle Wartegg at Lake Constance (Bodensee) before eventually arriving on May 20, 1919, at their residence in a large villa belonging to the Napoléon family in Prangins at Lake Geneva (Lake Léman). They continued their correspondence with Vatican from there.

In an *Aide-Mémoire* to the Holy Father, sent on December 2, 1919, from Bern with an introductory letter by Luigi Maglione, the special papal envoy to Switzerland, Karl wrote that England seemed interested in the federal project that he had previously sent to the pope, and he asked the pope to intervene on his behalf:

> Grâce aux nombreux courants qui se manifestent dans toute l'ancienne monarchie, il pourrait se faire, que les Anglais, mal informés, ne renoncent à la réalisation de leurs excellentes intentions. Je prie donc sa Sainteté de vouloir bien, si Elle le juge possible, de faire suggérer aux Anglais, de la manière qui Lui paraîtra convenable, de tenir compte des communications que j'aurais à faire, peut-être des avis que j'aurais à donner. Ce n'est, Dieu sait, pas de la présomption de ma part, mais par la force des choses je me trouve placé en dehors des partis et au-dessus des aspirations nationales de mes sujets, ce qui,—tous mes peuples m'étant également chers,— me semble être une garantie suffisante de mon impartialité.[150]

That Karl was still counting on English support is not surprising. It is due; first, to the fact that British diplomacy made efforts to save Austria-Hungary nearly up to April 1918; disinterest came later.[151] Second, Britain had saved Karl and his family by sending a Catholic officer to escort them to safe haven in Switzerland. In his December letter, Karl's hopes were still concentrat-

---

150 "Thanks to the many trends that are finding expression across the entire former monarchy, it could be that the English, poorly informed, will not give up on their excellent intentions. I therefore beg Your Holiness to consider, should He deem it possible, suggesting to the English, in whatever manner will seem appropriate to Him, that they take into account the communications I would have to make, perhaps the opinions I would have to give. God knows this is not due to presumption on my part, but rather I find myself placed by the force of circumstance beyond the parties and above the national aspirations of my subjects, which – given that all my peoples are equally dear to me – strikes me as a sufficient guarantee of my impartiality." AE, Austria 526, no. of protocol does not appear, only letter no. 3151.
151 See Valiani, Leo, *The End of Austria-Hungary: The definitive account of the collapse of a great Empire*, Secker and Warburg, London, 1973, 264–66.

ed on getting Protestant England to help and to do so through the Vatican, which proved unsuccessful. However, he had no alternative other than to turn to England, because the other Entente country that was strongly Catholic, and where the pope might have had better chances of being convincing, was still controlled by the anti-Habsburg Clemenceau government.[152]

There is no evidence that, the Vatican sent a response to Karl's *Aide-Mémoire*, nor was there a letter on the subject sent to the Foreign Office. The ecclesiastical prefect notes the following: "per il secondo punto [intervention of England] non credo che la SS [Sancta Sede]essere in grado di intervenire."[153]

There are, indeed, no signs of a letter from Secretary of State Gasparri to the British foreign minister, Lord Curzon, on this matter. The Vatican must have already been discouraged by Curzon's previous response concerning Habsburg affairs. On May 29, 1919, Cardinal Gasparri asked Curzon to help the Habsburgs regain some property in Bohemia, on the grounds that the king of England had "generously taken under his protection the emperor and his family" by leading them to safe haven in Switzerland and might want to finish his work of "charity and justice if he would take under his protection the private possessions of the emperor and his august family."[154] The answer that Curzon wrote to H.M. minister to the Holy See, Count John de Salis, was reproving:

> Government cannot make representations to the Czechoslovak Government with regard to ex-Emperor's estates in Bohemia.
> That there is no foundation for statement in Vatican communication that the King of England had taken persons of ex-Emperor and his family under his protection.

In other words, these measures were taken for humanitarian reasons only, and, Curzon finished, "You should explain to the Vatican in whatever way you think will best be accepted [...]."[155]

---

152 Yet, this did not restrain him from trying even France and asking his Swiss lawyer to act as intermediary. Feigl, *op. cit.*, 298–300.
153 "Regarding the second point [intervention of England], I do not believe that the Holy See is able to intervene." AE, Austria 526, 68 f.
154 NA, FO 380 (British Legation to the Holy See)/ 22, 418 f.
155 NA, FO 380/ 22, 435 f.

But then the question remains why Gasparri's—and subsequently, Karl's—entreaty for English intervention and assistance might seem clumsy and somewhat naïve. However, if one looks at the journal of Lieutenant Colonel Strutt—the officer entrusted with the mission of protecting and escorting the emperor out of Austria—one might form a different picture: "I was handed the following message from [General] Tom Bridges [Chief of the British Military mission to the Army of the Orient], Constantinople: 'You will proceed at once to Eckartsau and give the Emperor and Empress moral support of British government'," and, Strutt continues, "we disagreed as to the interpretation of 'moral support'."[156]

As Gordon Brook-Shepherd, the English author who had access to the private archives of Emperor Karl, says of Strutt: "This newcomer was to develop for the Emperor of Austria and his family an almost passionate devotion [...] with a fervour second only to his loyalty to his own King." This behaviour caused indignation in London.[157] As a result, it is understandable that the Vatican— as well as Karl, the main person concerned— had the impression that England's intentions were really favourable.

But these were not isolated cases. High ranking British officers with Habsburg sympathies were far from uncommon: Admiral Ernest Troubridge (president of the Inter-allied Danube River Commission) is mentioned as having such feelings, and Lieutenant Colonel Thomas Montgomery-Cuninghame (the British military representative in Vienna) as being in favour of a Habsburg restoration and a Danubian Confederation.[158] Major General William Thwaites, director of military intelligence at the War Office, underlined the need to foster a Danubian Confederation.[159]

Another personality who might have sympathised with such ideas was Count John de Salis, H.M. minister to the Holy See. He was a Catholic, an

---

156 Brook-Shepherd, Gordon, *The Last Habsburg*, London, 1968, 229–30.
157 Ibid., 228. He was even advising the emperor and even served him in diplomatic missions. When Curzon discovered this, he was outraged, but the War Office spared him greater problems by limiting itself to an army consul reprimand. NA, FO 371 6102, C6930/180/21.
158 Bátonyi, G., *op. cit.*, 20–22. Lojkó, Miklós (ed.), *British Policy on Hungary 1918–19, A Documentary Sourcebook*, SSEES, London, 1995, no. 173, 287–88.
159 Zsuppan, F.T, "The Hungarian Red Army as Seen through British Eyes", in Pastor (ed.), *Revolutions and Interventions in Hungary and Its Neighbour States, 1918–19*, War and Society in Central Eastern Europe 20, New York, 1988, 92. Bátonyi, *op. cit.*, 24.

English gentleman, a descendant of an old, originally Protestant Swiss family from the canton of Graubünden. There are references in the Foreign Office archives indicating that his superiors were speculating about appointing a Protestant as his successor.[160] This shows that certain members of the Foreign Office were still suspicious of their Catholic diplomats, especially when they were sent to the Vatican.

The Vatican's role as the link between Karl and Britain remained relevant for many reasons: Karl was sent a Catholic officer to bring him to safe haven; H.M. minister to the Holy See was a Catholic of Swiss German origin, like the Habsburgs themselves; many of the key officers of the War Office were sympathetic to the Habsburgs. Karl, as well as the *Secretariato di Stato*, could consider Britain as the best choice between the two Entente states to approach in relation to the future of Central Europe. Moreover, Karl could use the Vatican for this purpose, knowing that with John de Salis he might even have a sympathetic intermediary.

The lack of an answer did not discourage either Karl or his emissaries and counsellors. Prince Ladislas Lubomirski—an emissary of the emperor and "a person with close relations to the French Embassy"[161]— sent a letter to Lord Acton, H.M. ambassador in Bern, explaining that Karl was very much against Germany and wished for a strong entente with the Western powers that would guarantee a prosperous future for the nations of Central Europe. The letter also specified the necessity of uniting the Danubian nations in a manner that would not compromise the absolute independence of the Successor States.[162]

---

160 The document has been destroyed but a reference card of the Foreign Office Archives sums the problem up in a few words. NA, FO 371 W22/94595/F9851.
161 NA, FO 371 3529/84515, Acton H.M. Minister in Bern to Curzon, Bern, June 2, 1919, letter from Prince Lubomirski on visit to Emperor Karl.
162 Ibid.

A French Visitor at the Foreign Office

The First and Second Visits of a French Marquis to the Foreign Office

Emperor Karl did not give up his efforts to convince the Foreign Office of the necessity of a Danubian Confederation. At this point a person who is never mentioned in biographical literature relating to Emperor Karl comes on the scene: the mysterious Marquis de Castellane.

Though there is no mention of his first name in the Foreign Office documents, the marquis was well known in Paris and even in London society as Boni (Boniface) de Castellane, a *député* (member of the French Parliament) of his own ancestral constituency, the commune of Castellane. He was a person known in the upper circles of society for his elegance, wit and brilliance and for his marriage to Miss Anna Gould, one of the richest heirs of the American industrial aristocracy. After his divorce in 1906, Castellane found himself broke and had to make a living by becoming an art dealer, but this did not mean that he did not continue to meet the great and powerful of the day. He was sometimes even sent on special missions by the government. Proof of this is that Poincaré himself, the then president of the French Republic, sent Castellane in 1914 on a mission to the Balkans to inquire about the people behind Archduke Franz Ferdinand's assassination.[163]

As he wrote in his memoirs, he had been introduced to the exiled Emperor Karl during a secretly organised meeting near Lake Geneva in Lausanne and then travelling together with Karl to Prangins the same day. This meeting was organised by his friend Dr Henri Seeholzer, who was the emperor's Swiss lawyer and who had published some of Castellane's political ideas.[164] The meeting was organised most probably in 1919 and not in August 1920, as presented by Castellane's biographer.[165] Castellane was very moved by the prospect of meeting Karl who hoped he could count on him to rebuild the

---

163 Fejtö, *op. cit.*, 382.
164 Castellane, Boni de, *L'art d'être pauvre*, Les éditions Du Crès et Cie, Paris, 1925, 240.
165 Mension Rigau, Éric, *Boni de Castellane*, Paris, Perrin, 2008, 223. This for the simple reason that the Foreign Office archives confirm that Castellane called on Lord Hardinge on December 22, 1919, after having met Karl in Lausanne—unless, of course, there would have been an unlikely second meeting that the marquis omitted to mention in his memoirs.

Europe he conceived of. The idea, shared by the French aristocracy in general, consisted of isolating Germany by reinforcing Austria.[166] Karl assured Castellane of his love of France and his desire to be understood by French politicians, and Karl asked the marquis if he could get in touch with the British Foreign Office. He considered Britain to be well disposed towards him since the officer Britain had sent to Vienna to escort him to Switzerland had saved him from great dangers.[167] This is the only clue the marquis gives in his memoirs regarding his Habsburg mission to England, and it does not mention what it was or would have consisted of. Castellane visited the Foreign Office several times on this matter and made a great effort to represent the political interests of Karl.

Castellane appeared at the Foreign Office on December 22, 1919, calling on Lord Hardinge—permanent under-secretary of state for foreign affairs—whom he knew previously in Paris. He explained to Lord Hardinge that Karl had clarified to him "how it would be impossible in the future for the small States into which Austria-Hungary had been broken up to stand alone, and that the only remedy to prevent Tyrol, Austria and Bohemia [...]" from operating a rapprochement "towards Prussia would be the formation of a Danube Confederation."[168]

The presence of this document and the lengthy ones that follow in Foreign Office archives strengthens the hypothesis that the Vatican did not pass on Emperor Karl's request for help from Britain. It is the probable reason why Karl felt it was necessary to get in touch with the Foreign Office, this time directly through a French envoy to Lord Curzon.

The most interesting feature of Castellane's comments to Lord Hardinge is that he mentioned the emperor's quite severe position on Hungary:

---

166 Castellane recalls: "Je vis de près se préparer les folies qui nous menèrent aux traités de Versailles, de Trianon, de Sèvres, de Saint-Germain. La conception générale des hommes d'Etats péchait par la base, et se trouvait contraire au développement logique de l'Histoire et à nos intérêts. On balkanisait l'Europe au lieu d'européaniser les Balkans; et l'on détruisait l'Autriche au profit de l'Allemagne, au lieu de diviser l'Allemagne au profit de l'Autriche... " (I saw from up close the follies that led us to the treaties of Versailles, of Trianon, of Sèvres, of Saint-Germain. The general conception of statesmen rested on false principles and ran contrary to the logical development of History and of our interests. Instead of Europeanizing the Balkans, Europe was Balkanised; and Austria was destroyed to the benefit of Germany, rather than dividing Germany to the benefit of Austria ...). Castellane, *op. cit.,* 226.
167 Ibid., 242–43.
168 NA, FO 371 3533, 3/168530/5445, Lord Hardinge's report, London December 22, 1919.

> The only danger that he [the emperor] could fear from such a Confederation would be that Hungary might in the end play the part which Prussia has played in the German Confederation. That Hungary would have a monarchy is indisputable, and he himself had received several invitations to become King of Hungary. In that event he would do his utmost to prevent Hungary playing in the future the role of Prussia.[169]

Through Castellane as his spokesperson the emperor showed some reservations regarding Hungary and also showed that he wanted to avoid that part of the monarchy becoming the leading state of the confederation. On the one hand, Hungary's aim was to recoup the regions occupied by enemy forces and recreate greater Hungary, on the other, Karl's was to create a confederation of nations out of pre-1918 Austria's, but also out of Hungary's, complicated ethnic landscape. This reaction was not at all surprising, since Archduke Franz Ferdinand had already planned to break Hungary up into smaller entities. One of the anomalies of this message is that the emperor would never have stated that he was invited to be king of Hungary when he still considered himself as such.

Castellane invited Hardinge to come and discuss this topic directly with the ex-emperor, but Hardinge declined the invitation arguing that:

> the question was not pressing, for such a Confederation could not possibly be created for some years, especially in view of the great bitterness which seems to prevail amongst the newly created States, who appear to vie with one another in trying to cut each other's throats. Until a better feeling prevailed amongst them the idea of a Confederation was out of question, [...].[170]

Hardinge's answer was straightforward: he had underlined that Britain would not support the emperor's idea for the time being.

---

169 NA, FO 371 3533, 3/168530/5445, Notes on Lord Hardinge's report of December 22, Vienna, January 13, 1920.
170 Ibid.

In spite of Hardinge's negative reply, Castellane's description of Karl's Danubian Confederation project was sent to British diplomatic missions in Vienna, Budapest, Bern, Paris, Prague, Washington, Belgrade and Rome, and it was passed on to the prime minister. This wide dissemination showed how seriously Hardinge took the fact that the Emperor-King was thinking of restoring the monarchy; and the fact that a Frenchman—with an impressive network in the French political world—was his emissary could only have worried Britain even more.[171] Hardinge's concern was to be proven right only by dint of the French emissary's insistence. Indeed, on February 13, 1920, Castellane sent a note from Karl to Lord Balfour, lord president of the Council, by the intermediary of Karl's Swiss lawyer, Henri Seeholzer, in which Karl explains that he is "the best and the only guarantee" against Austria's "too intimate relations with Germany". He recalled that his manifesto of October 1918 had aided the secession of the different nationalities from the Empire-Kingdom without the effusion of blood. He protested against those who considered the dynasty as an enslaver of minorities and made every effort to find a solution to the discords, even if he was limited by the Hungarian Constitution. He was ready to grant universal suffrage to Hungary in order to give fairer representation to the minorities of the Kingdom of Hungary, but the majority of the Hungarian Parliament opposed it.[172]

The Third Visit of the Marquis de Castellane to the FO

On July 30, 1920, the Foreign Office reported that the marquis again called on Lord Hardinge after having handed to Curzon five studies, titled "Inclosures", on the Central European situation, stressing the necessity to create a Danubian Confederation.[173] If one refers to the discussion with a member of

---

171 NA, FO 371 3533, 3/168530/5445, Lord Hardinge's report on meeting with Marquis de Castellane of December 22, 1919, London, January 13, 1920.
172 Mension Rigau, *op. cit.*, 225–26.
173 173 NA, FO 371 4714, 2590/2509/52, 4–5 ff., Mr Ronald Campbell's (private secretary to Curzon) interview with the Marquis de Castellane. In his biography of Castellane, Eric Mension-Rigau gives us more details on the marquis' stay in London: He met Curzon at a dinner and mentioned the papers and their contents, especially his idea to organise a meeting of Karl with an important English politician in the Swiss Jura or the Engadine. Lord Curzon answered: "We will consider this document." Mesion-Rigau, *op. cit.*, 226. It is interesting to note that, when visiting England in 1923, Cas-

the Foreign Office —a certain Mr Campbell, private secretary to Lord Curzon, Castellane's major argument was that a German–Italian–Russian alliance, and Central European malcontent nations such as Hungary, would endanger the existence of Britain and France within a year. He went as far as to say that France and Great Britain would be completely absorbed by the malcontent European states. He then added, as recalled by Campbell:

> The Marquis de Castellane took the opportunity to express at some length his apprehensions regarding the future of France and that of this country, both of which he endeavoured to convince me would be involved in war within a year against a combination of Italy, Germany, Russia and the aforesaid Danubian states, unless effect could be given to the ex-emperor's project, which the marquis seemed to regard, not only as a panacea for the present disturbed state of Europe, but even as the only bulwark against complete absorption of France and Great Britain in the near future by hostile elements of Europe enumerated above.[174]

In his "Inclosure II" he is much less pessimistic than in his oral statements to Campbell. Castellane mentions a German, Austrian, Russian and Italian alliance, but without mentioning the destruction of Britain as a consequence.[175] There are three ways to interpret this vague statement. First, that he was referring to an alliance of the unsatisfied nations (Germany, Italy and Russia), to which we can add the revisionist camp made of smaller nations (Austria, Hungary and Bulgaria), against the satisfied ones. Second, he may have been hinting at a counter-revolutionary alliance, since the White Russians of General Wrangel were receiving German as well as Hungarian support to prepare the counter revolution in Russia from, respectively, Ludendorff and Horthy. Third, he could have well been aiming at the Bolshevik danger from Russia eventually leagued up with the anti-Bolshevik malcon-

---

tellane was the guest of Lord Curzon at his country estate in Hackwood, and that he even accompanied him to the House of Lords. Castellane, *op cit.*, 263–68.
174 NA, FO 371 4714, 2590/2509/52, 4–5 ff., Mr Campbell's (private secretary to Curzon) interview with the Marquis de Castellane.
175 Ibid., 9 f.

tent nations of Germany and Hungary. Indeed, the British Foreign Office was much alarmed by this specific danger, as Hugh Seton-Watson writes about the concerns of his father, R.W. Seton-Watson:

> Seton-Watson shared the view, widespread at that time though subsequently shown to be unsound, that the Russian Bolsheviks were agents of Germany. He feared a resurgent unholy alliance of German and Hungarian militarism in co-ordination with Bolshevik revolution.[176]

If it is true that there was nothing strange in such fear after a war during which Germany had sent Lenin to destabilise Russia, it still remains that neither of these scenarios was to happen in the near future. However, the marquis and most probably Karl were dreading a right-wing alliance headed by Prussian officers, since the Bolshevik danger had ceased to be an imminent threat as a consequence of the overthrow of the Republic of Councils in Hungary by Romanian and French forces by the end of summer 1919. The officers of the French military mission in Budapest were, indeed, dreading tsarist and German plots. This is confirmed by French military intelligence sources.[177]

Castellane's logical fears announcing an imminent threat from the alliance of the unsatisfied nations were too far-fetched at the time. In 1919 such a menace from countries that were significantly reduced and soon to be exaggeratedly punished by the Peace Treaties could endanger neither France nor Britain. Hence it sounded strongly unconvincing to the Foreign Office.

The Foreign Office could not possibly have understood such a far-fetched and bizarre catastrophe scenario, especially when Castellane was said to be announcing it as occurring within a year. Was he only trying to intensify the effect of his papers or did he truly believe that the danger was that alarming? It probably did more harm to his credibility than if he had written a slightly less tragic scenario.

---

176 Seton-Watson, Hugh, "R. W. Seton-Watson and the Trianon Settlement", in Király, Béla K., Peter Pastor, Ivan Sanders, (eds.), *Essays on World War I: Total War and Peacemaking, A Case Study on Trianon*, Brooklyn College Press, distributed by Columbia University Press, New York, 1982, 8.
177 SHAT, 7N Hongrie 2885, Mission militaire française en Hongrie, télégrammes no. 2623 (July 1, 1919) and no. 797 (July 4).

In the first of the four "Inclosures" that can be found in the Castellane file of the FO (the fifth is missing), the marquis came forward with more astonishing remarks on Germany. On one hand, he speculated that Bismarck, in favouring the separation of Hungary from the Austrian Empire—thus creating the double state of Austria-Hungary—had the possibility of its destruction in mind. This seems a bit far-fetched, as Bismarck is known to have considered Austria as an ally and as necessary for the balance of Europe. On the other hand, his remarks on what Germany had to gain from the Anschluss are much more interesting:

> By the fact of its territorial cessions in the East and the West Germany loses populations which were never devoted to her and enthusiastically greeted their new masters who were no others than their ancient ones [such as France in Alsace]; she would have got in exchange about seven millions of German Austrians who, with the Magyars and the Croatians, had been her best and surest allies; she could moreover reasonably expect a most intimate junction with Hungary and an alliance with Italy. In this way Western Europe would be separated from the East by a barrier hardly to be overwhelmed, and, moreover, Germany would see the road reopened which leads to Baghdad and the Ukraine. Better conditions for the possibility of a great revenge war can hardly be imagined.

Castellane here put his finger on a very sensitive point of British foreign policy. Britain was less interested in Central Europe than the Middle East which it was now controlling. An interpretation of the geopolitical situation that shows the possibility of Germany becoming a concurrent of Britain in the region would certainly attract more attention form the Foreign Office than the German question limited to Central Europe.

His concern regarding an Anschluss of Austria to Germany is the main topic of his paper which brings him to the following conclusions:

> The events have proved ever since a fact, that has certainly been foreseen in Paris, and that is, that so-called national states, being totally independent from one another and having broken every kind of link between each

other, are perfectly incapable of leading a life of their own. That is to say, that, without mentioning their complete autonomy which nobody thinks of contesting, they want an economic fusion which could deliver them from political antagonism that makes them blind to their real interests as well as to those of the rest of Europe.

The Danubian Confederation is the only solution to guarantee to Central Europe peace and economical prosperity. [...] But never will one be able to take that way as long as Hungary is in prey to perturbations of the movement of the so-called independence and Austria to those of the pangermanist propaganda.[178]

There is no doubt that he was trying to convince his readers that the isolation of the new born Successor States would make their survival quasi impossible. However, it is precisely in these months (July–August 1920) that the Little Entente was being set up secretly in Prague, first on a military basis before joining some economic aspects to it. Its creation united three countries against Hungary and the Habsburgs, and then against Austria and Italy, when the latter decided to create a triple alliance among Rome, Budapest and Vienna in 1927. So, in fact, no real economic federation could be born out of antagonisms which would lead to the formation of two distinctive camps. The lines below introduce the reader to the problem of Hungary and the role of Karl in Hungary:

To speak more concretely, the tendency to compel the king not to accept another crown without the consent of the Hungarian Parliament is destined to prevent the return of the crowned king whom the pangermanists know to be hostile to their plans and to the junction of Austria and Hungary based on their mutual consent: Hungary will be compelled to establish a political link with Germany, but she would not be allowed to come even to an economic arrangement with Austria.

In Castellane's view the failure of a re-union of Austria with Hungary in a confederation resulting in the former's isolation would contribute to

---

178 NA, FO 371 4714, 2590/2509/52, Enclosure I.

convincing, through Pangerman propaganda, those Austrians against Anschluss to eventually accept it as the least worst of solutions.[179]

In his letter of November 8, 1920, to Horthy—written at a later date than the Castellane papers—Karl had indeed promised Horthy to guarantee the independence of Hungary. Karl considered that the Pragmatic Sanction[180] and the dynasty's indivisible and inseparable rule over its Austrian hereditary lands and Hungary had ceased to exist, due to the end of the Austro-Hungary Compromise and the Personalunion of 1867. There is, yet, an important nuance in this letter that doesn't contradict Castellane's views but opens a possibility of enlargement:

> [...] si j'arrivais à reprendre le pouvoir souverain en Hongrie, je ne pourrais accepter ce pouvoir dans n'importe quel autre Etat, sans qu'une convention conclue entre la Hongrie et cet Etat reconnaisse l'indépendance absolue de la Hongrie et lui garantisse surtout la direction des affaires étrangères, sa représentation diplomatique à l'étranger et l'indépendance totale de l'armée hongroise.[181]

Moreover, Castellane thinks, in his first paper, that Hungarian independence can be used by Pangermanists to join Hungary to Germany as well, which can be again countered by the Danubian Confederation.[182]

Many accusations were made against Hungary, especially by Prague, that the Hungarian leadership, and especially the entourage of the newly elected regent, Miklós Horthy, was plotting with Prussian officers in Munich[183] to overcome the Peace treaties. Horthy's secret papers prove this to

---

179 Ibid.
180 Document ratified by the Hungarian Diet (1723) recognizing the female branch of Habsburg (Maria Theresia) to succeed to the throne of Hungary.
181 "If I succeeded in regaining sovereign power in Hungary, I could not accept this power in any other state unless an agreement reached between Hungary and this state recognises the absolute independence of Hungary and guarantees to it above all control over foreign affairs, its diplomatic representation abroad, and the total independence of the Hungarian army". In Werkmann, Karl Baron de, *Le calvaire de l'Empereur 1918–1922*, Paris, 1924, 135–37.
182 NA, FO 371 4714, 2590/2509/52, Enclosure I.
183 Especially with Ludendorff, which I have mentioned above. Szinai, Miklós, László Szűcs (eds.), *Horthy Miklós titkos iratai* (Horthy's secret papers), Kossuth, Budapest, 1962, 33–38.

have been so,[184] and the Marquis de Castellane was again well informed when he mentioned this to the Foreign Office.

Last, Castellane goes as far as to name one person, in fact the most instrumental one, among the pro-Germans of Hungary: Captain Gyula Gömbös of the joint k.u.k. general staff, a prominent anti-Habsburg of the postwar period. He also mentions the revisionist and militarist organisation MOVE (Magyar Országos Véderő Egyesület, Association for the Defence of Hungary)[185] of which Gömbös was the leader:

> The congenial policy between Berlin and Budapest appears particularly clear in an organisation which is presently very strong in Hungary: The "MOVE" which works under the direction of captain Goemboes [Gömbös]. This organisation has representative offices in Berlin and Vienna. The great danger lies in the fact that this organisation disposes to-day of perhaps greater power than the government itself; [sic] than in the complete ignorance in which numerous members of the Move are left as to the financial resources the abundance of which allow the suspicion that they are not from Hungarian origin only.[186]

Born into Hungarian petty nobility, with a Swabian mother, Gyula Gömbös was always an adept of the Pangerman cause and had great influence on Horthy. He was one of the *homines novi* born out of the Szeged Government and one of the twelve captains, as they were referred to, who influenced as well as served the regent.[187] MOVE was a counterrevolutionary organisation set up to defend Hungary from another Commune and defend Hungarian interests after the country was attacked from all sides in order to reduce it to its present Trianon treaty borders. It was truly under Gömbös's influence. In other words, Castellane paints a rather plausible picture of the Hungarian situation.

---

184 Letter of Ludendorff to Horthy, Munich, August 19, 1920, Szinai, Miklós, Szűcs, László (eds.), *Horthy Miklós titkos iratai*, Kossuth, Budapest, 1965, 33–39,
185 A military organisation for the defence of Hungary.
186 NA, FO 371 4714, 2590/2509/52, Enclosure I.
187 Bécsi, Zoltán, "Les officiers du Palais Royal (1920–1921)" in *Revue d'Europe centrale*, vol. III, no. 1, Strasbourg, 1995, 115–32; Gergely, Jenő, *Gömbös Gyula*, Vince Kiadó, Budapest, 2001, 77–104.

On the question of Austria, he warns of German propaganda but also writes that Germany did not currently have the means to annex Austria and had to deal with its own economic problems first.

> Yet Austria's union with Germany so far as it may be considered as the base of a still greater enterprise is for every German the first and most important aim of German policy; it is for him an irrefutable axiom. But this movement in favour of the union is not entertained to effectuate the junction to-day or to-morrow [sic]. For the present moment it only tries to prevent the economic cooperation of the states issued from the Austro-Hungarian monarchy so as to break any economic link between them.[188]

The analysis is very precise and again quite accurate, as the Anschluss of Austria was tried twice. When Germany felt strong enough to initiate the first Anschluss attempt in 1934, the Austrian government was already against it, unlike in 1919 when Otto Bauer was specifically hastening it.[189]

Castellane concludes by stating his solution to the problem: "The pangermanist propaganda in Austria, the movement in favour of independence in Hungary can only be efficaciously subdued in one way, and that is by drawing the outlines of a Danubian Confederation."[190]

In this paper, Castellane gives a stunning analysis of the consequences of an Anschluss and even mentions Germany's *Drang nach Osten*. His analysis appeared farfetched, as such ideas were not yet commonplace in France, but became so later.[191] The lack of understanding of the true threat that Ger-

---

[188] NA, FO 371 4714, 2590/2509/52, Enclosure I.
[189] Kerekes, Lajos, "Az Anschluss és a Dunai Konfederáció 'Alternatívája' Otto Bauer Külpolitikájában 1918–1919-ben", in *Történelmi Szemle*, 14 (3–4), 1971, 442–464. The second Anschluss attempt by Hitler was the successful one, even though, once again, the then chancellor of the Austrian Republic, Kurt von Schuschnigg, was opposing it. He was openly a legitimist and wanted the restoration of the Habsburgs and hoped that Archduke Otto would become emperor and remilitarise Austria to defend it against Hitler. In 1936, however, it was already too late to start the reconstruction of the Austrian Empire and the k. u. k. army.
[190] NA, FO 371 4714, 2590/2509/52, Enclosure I.
[191] Henri Soutou considers, when writing about Bainville's very similar previsions, that ideas of dissequilibrium of Europe caused by the Peace Treaties were not yet commonplace in 1919 and 1920. Sotou, Georges-Henri, "Préface" of Dickes, Christophe, ed., *Jacques Bainville, L'Europe d'entre deux guerres 1919–1936*, Godefroy de Bouillon, Paris, 1996, 4.

many represented resulted in peace treaties that partitioned Austria-Hungary and not Germany, leaving the latter a united state when it could have been portioned to its pre-1871 form of many independent monarchies and states in which local patriotism could have been enhanced by reinforcing their still existing identities and characters gained after the treaties of Westphalia (1648).

A certain number of Foreign Office specialists made remarks on the papers. The Castellane papers were directed by Curzon to Sir Eyre Crowe for "exam and eventual report".[192] The latter wrote that the scheme of an "Economic Federation" under the sovereignty of the ex-emperor "remains quite vague and nebulous—is described as easily realised as everyone in the former monarchy is in favour of it".[193] If it is true that Castellane does not explain the sort of federation it would be, the statement that it is easily realised does not portray what the marquis explains. In fact, he argues that it would be in the true interest of the Danubian populations.[194] It becomes even more obvious in the second paper, where he says that "effective alliances can only be carried out if they are advantageous to all interested parties".[195]

The Second and Third "Inclosures"

In the second "Inclosure", before explaining "how the British government is to set about to give effect to the scheme", Castellane warns of the consequences of not trying to solve the problem of Central Europe and expresses the danger of "balkanisation" and the alliance stated earlier of Russia, Germany, Austria and Italy, which would bar the route to British colonies in Asia.

His hints of how to realise this federation are, first, to let all states formed out of the Dual Monarchy know that they could expect economic help from England only if they would enter into a federation. To promise the defeated countries (Austria and Hungary) an amendment of their peace treaties

---

192 NA, FO 371 4714, 2590/2509/52, 3 f., Remarks by Crowe July 31, 1920. Crowe was head of the Western European section of the Political Intelligence Department of the Foreign Office, before becoming under-secretary of state for foreign affairs.
193 Ibid., 2 f.
194 Ibid., 4 f.
195 Ibid., 'Inclosure II'.

under the condition they comply with England's wishes. To advise victorious countries that investment of English capital on a large scale could only be taken into consideration for such economic unity. His next points are, second, to instruct diplomats to "work in that direction"; third, the nomination of a British High commissioner "under the pretence of protection of British interests"; fourth, to get English enterprises interested in the Federation; and finally, to influence public opinion with a special fund created for this purpose, since the population of these countries were being misled and things were advancing against their interest. After reading the points, a member of the FO remarked that by making this confederation, "England is to blackmail the states formed out of the former Austria-Hungary."[196]

Castellane finished his second "Inclosure" with the following words: "A serious opposition [to a Danubian Confederation] will be made only by the pangermanists because their ambition of ruling Europe and the whole world would be crushed by the creation of a Danubian Confederation."[197] The accuracy of this sentence can only be understood if we consider that what he predicted did eventually happen: Germany did enact its Pangermanist plan. But he does not weigh the fact that France's vengeance in Versailles will only have a stimulating effect on German people's drive for resurrection and domination. He is similarly unaware of the opposition of most of the Central European Successor States to the Danubian Confederation, which would be suggested by France in 1920.

Another member of the FO, Sir Alexander Cadogan, considered the papers as Austrian propaganda, the aim of which was exactly the contrary. In spite of this harsh beginning, Cadogan nuanced his remark by admitting, "We have done and continue to do what is possible to break down economic barriers between the new states formed out of the Austro-Hungarian Monarchy."[198] The only problem was that the will to support an economic federation was not sufficient. A military alliance or federation was even more

---

196 Ibid., 1 f.
197 Ibid., 11 f.
198 NA, FO 371 4714, 2590/2509/52; Sir Alexander Cadogan was a member of the Vienna Legation during the war and a member of the Central Office of the FO before he became head of the League of Nations section at the FO in 1923.

essential, and Cadogan was to continue, "[...] there are obvious dangers in the proposal for a Danubian Federation, of which the Italians are particularly apprehensive."[199] Castellane projected "the possibility of an alliance between Russia, Germany, Austria and Italy" that would pose a certain danger for Britain, but he did also send a whole paper, "Inclosure V", on the new Triplice. That paper quoted a letter that Italy's ambassador wrote to Otto Bauer, foreign minister of Austria: "'Italy must sooner or later break with England. To bring this about, Italy will make the union of Austria with Germany possible'." The Italian foreign ministry laid down two conditions, one of which was "that Austria must not maintain friendly relations of such an economic character with other succession states [sic], as these States depend on France and England."[200] This "Inclosure V" was entitled "Germany and Italy, The New Triple Alliance" and was commented upon as having been written "by some German personality".[201] Italy, being dissatisfied with what it got for joining the Entente in 1915, played a double game by supporting the vanquished states of the war. For the time being, Italy opposed a Slav-dominated alliance in the Danubian basin, but it also opposed—together with Great Britain—a Franco-Hungarian rapprochement.[202] London and Rome saw eye to eye on the matter, and the FO could neither share nor believe these French concerns, conveniently labelled as German propaganda by the FO staff.

In "Inclosure III" Castellane makes his biggest mistake by explaining how Karl should meet secretly with a senior British diplomat in the Jura Mountains or on a boat on Lake Geneva. As a result, the Foreign Office gave little credibility to the papers as a whole. They provoked the following remarks from a member of the FO: "This scheme is to be utterly fantastic and undeserving of serious consideration [...] Castellane, by no means devoid of intelligence, is far more at home as a leader of fashion and a collector of 'bibelots' than as an exponent of practical politics."[203]

---

199 Ibid.
200 Ibid., 16–17 ff.
201 FO staff remark signed E.P., July 31, 1920, Ibid., 1 f.
202 Ádám, Magda, *The Little Entente and Europe (1920–1929)*, Akadémia Kiadó, Budapest, 1993, 120–21. [First published in Hungarian: *A Kisantant és Európa*, Akadémia Kiadó, Budapest, 1989.]
203 Signed E.P., July 31, 1920, NA, FO 371 4714, 2590/2509/52, 1 f.

Sir Eyre Crowe added another remark: "It is indeed difficult to read these effusions with patience. They are not worth the time consumed in doing so."[204] Castellane did not argue his case strongly enough, but his remarks can certainly not be considered as effusions. They make much sense for a reader of today, because we know what happened during the interwar period. Castellane, however, lacks in-depth analysis and explanations of how these events could happen and why Entente politics could lead to this end if the Confederation was not created. Castellane had set up the worst case scenario after understanding the unbalanced nature of post-war Europe. The situation in Europe could have evolved in many different ways, but Castellane's negative scenario was, quite sadly, close to reality.

Remarks from senior British diplomats give a good picture of a certain lack of understanding of the Central and Eastern European situation in the Foreign Office, and they show a certain ignorance of the by then (August 1920) well-advanced and publicly-known diplomatic efforts of France to create a Danubian Confederation centred in Budapest.[205]

Indeed, by the time all these "Inclosures" were sent to the FO, its staff had received a press article presenting France's and the Vatican's role in the creation of a Danubian Federation. Sir Alexander Cadogan concluded that the article was "an echo of the movement" that Castellan was a representative of.[206] The Foreign Office was slowly realising the importance of Castellane's seemingly private initiative to convey his and the emperor's fears and plans. British diplomacy wasn't the only one to express apprehension regarding these plans. The Italians followed suit.[207] But how did the Castellane project become so "famous" as to be known by the Italians as well? Castellane may have been touting the project to other foreign ministries of Europe, but a more plausible answer is that it came to be known in the Italian Foreign Ministry through the British diplomats, since the report of Lord Hardinge on the meeting with Castellane had been sent to most of the British representations in Europe, among them Rome.

---

204 Ibid., 2 f.
205 To be described in Chapter III.
206 NA, FO 371, 4650/C2979, 168 f.
207 FO 371 Italy FO 371 C2690/2690/62, Sir Alexander Cadogan mentions Italian concerns regarding the Marquis de Castellane's project (no date).

Chapter II

To conclude, we should ask whether these thoughts are those of Castellane or of Karl. One cannot answer this question with certainty, but all in all it is evident that whoever put them together was a visionary considering Germany's threat in the future.

The description of Castellane's Danubian Confederation is important not only because it portrays many of Karl's ideas on the topic, but because it is the earliest description of such a plan written by a French politician to be found in both the Quai d'Orsay and the British Foreign Office archives. The concerns expressed by both London and Rome relating to the "Castellane Danubian Confederation" confirm the international anxiety provoked by this plan. It also portrays the view and fears of France concerning Germany and the malcontent nations.

Concomitant with this, British policy exhibited a certain lack of understanding towards a Habsburg Central Europe. The emperor was proposing a sort of commonwealth of states of the old Habsburg Dual Monarchy that Britain did not want to accept, even though Britain created a similar alliance after it lost some of its colonies, the aim of which was and still is to maintain a link with the countries born out of the British Empire.

A lack of perspicacity and strong resentment of the major ally of Germany in the war made many in the Foreign Office the enemy of any kind of federal form of Habsburg Monarchy, though not excluding a confederation or collaboration of Central European states in general.

Karl's letters to the pope, as well as the Marquis de Casellane's letters, show what were probably Karl's last efforts to save Central Europe as a Habsburg political entity. His conception of the region was that of a union of nations which should never be separated, as exemplified by the motto of the Austro-Hungarian Monarchy: *Indivisibiliter ac Inseparabiliter*. His efforts to re-establish unity and his concern for the future of his subjects were truly genuine. Karl might have been late in proposing a federal solution for Cisleithania, but he did not lose an opportunity to warn the Entente of the necessity of such a solution for the region. If we consider what became of Central Europe after his death, we can only admit that his concerns were to the point. The cutting up of the old Empire-Kingdom into many little states made them easy prey to the larger countries with imperialistic designs on this wealthy and strategic region. Pan-Slavism, in the form of Soviet Communism, and Pan-Germanism, in the form of German Nazism, were the two threats that destroyed Central Europe by enslaving it and kidnapping it from Western Europe.

To conclude on Britain's approach to the question of a Danubian Confederation, it becomes apparent that there were indeed two groups: on one hand, the New Europe group (inspired by Wickham Steed and Seeton-Watson) and the people of the Political Intelligence Department—the breeding ground of anti-Habsburg opinion[208]—were influencing the Foreign Office; and on the other, was the military officers group, which sympathised with the old Hungarian aristocracy and the Habsburgs. No matter how important the dissentions were in the Foreign Office on the question of the Habsburg Monarchy, it was clear that "there was a general consensus in London that a power vacuum should not be allowed to occur, and it was hoped that the most useful common links between the Successor States would not be broken and that some form of customs or economic union might be effected."[209]

The exiled emperor's *pro memorias* to the pope and the Castellane "Inclosures" cannot be considered and studied separately. They are both part of the greater picture that explains Karl's intentions and endeavours to win British support for his project. The problem is that both the channels he chose were the wrong ones. London considered neither Pope Benedict XV nor the Catholic French marquis as the right interlocutors.

Thanks to Mension-Rigau's biography, we know more about the Marquis de Castellane. He has confirmed that the marquis had an immense French and international network and had influence in many circles. Castellane was trying before and all through the war to argue for the necessity to save Austria-Hungary. In this aim he would visit Clemenceau and President Poincaré in July 1914, right at the beginning of the war, to try to stop France from declaring war on Austria-Hungary and would say that there was a plot to destabilise the Habsburg Monarchy that would have consequences for the whole of Europe. Other interesting information about the marquis is that he was con-

---

[208] Rothwell, V.H., *British War Aims and Peace Diplomacy, 1914–1918*, Oxford University Press, Oxford, 1971, 224.
[209] Goldstein, *op. cit.*, 131.

vinced of a Russian plot to kill Archduke Franz Ferdinand.[210] He was also active in helping the emissaries of Karl, such as Sixte de Bourbon-Parme, to meet the right people.[211] Thus it was not in 1919 that Castellane conceived the plan stemming from the idea that something had to be done to preserve Austria-Hungary or some form of it. He liked Central Europe, and he was even related to one of the most prominent families of that region through his aunt, Princess Radziwill, and he understood this part of Europe and its empire-kingdom.

Karl's Plan and France

Karl's Secret Contacts with France

Karl had many emissaries, during the war and after, who had the mission of getting in touch with the French. The most famous of these was his own brother-in-law, Sixte of Bourbon-Parme, who in 1917 was negotiating a secret separate peace treaty with Clemenceau; which failed, as Clemenceau had no intention of ending the war. This did not dissuade the emperor from finding ways of keeping in touch with French politicians and leaders, both before and after the war ended.

Baron Gyula Szilassy, an Austro-Hungarian diplomat, claimed that "it is a fact that France already in October 1918 tried everything 'secretly' to save the Austro-Hungarian Monarchy. I myself brought such a message in extremis from the French Gov. to H.M."[212] In other words, this would mean that

---

210 Mension-Rigau, Eric, *Boni de Castellane*, Paris, Perrin, 2008, 180–186. With his anti-Russian theory the conservative Castellane was echoing pacifist socialist leader Jean Jaurès, who accused the Russian ambassador Izvolsky of financing nationalist pro-war newspapers in Paris. Some authors say that the assassination of the French anti-war socialist leader Jean Jaurès had been supported by the Russian Ambassador in Paris, Izvolsky, in order to stop Jaurès' anti-war propaganda, which was influencing large segments of public opinion. François Fonvieille-Alquier, *Ils ont tué Jaurès*, Paris, Robert Laffont, Paris, 1968.
211 Mension-Rigau, *op.cit.*, 209.
212 The author's private archive: Gyula de Szilassy's notes commenting on Boroviczény's book: *Der König und sein Reichverweser* [1924]. This is confirmed by the activity of the French diplomat Dutasta, who was sent to Bern during the last weeks of the war by Clemenceau in order to make a last try to get Austria-Hungary out of the war. La Roche, Louis-Pierre, "L'affaire Dutasta: les dernières conversations diplomatiques pour sauver l'Empire des Habsbourg", in *Revue d'histoire diplomatique*, 1994/1.

Clemenceau's government continued to speculate on how to save the monarchy even after the unsuccessful dealings with Czernin. In fact, Czernin had made reference in a 1918 speech that Clemenceau wanted Alsace-Lorraine as separate peace terms. Clemenceau considered this as calumny and published the secret letters of Karl, in which the monarch suggested these border adjustments himself. It goes to the credit of Clemenceau that he still kept contact with Vienna diplomacy after the Czernin crisis, though he did not wish to end the war without France's total victory.

There were exchanges of letters as early as September 1918 between Austria and France via the French embassy in Bern which show that the emperor had informed the French government of Austria's intention to federalise the Austrian Empire and to discuss another peace project.[213] Whether there was willingness on the part of the French Government to maintain some form of Austrian Monarchy in October 1918 cannot be ruled out; the opinion that prevailed was that not much could be done to save it. François-Émile Haguenin, head of the press bureau and intelligence officer of the French embassy in Bern, wrote to the French foreign minister in September: "L'impuissance radicale de l'Empereur et de son gouvernement, la terreur que leur inspire l'Allemagne, l'attitude décisive prise par l'Entente envers l'Autriche, bien d'autres raisons encore empêchent de considérer le projet autrichien autrement que comme une manoeuvre anachronique [...]."[214]

Szilassy's remarks leave questions regarding whether certain French diplomats would have not envisaged saving the monarchy before the armistice was signed. After the war, however, the Quai d'Orsay had started making more efforts in that direction. But what did Karl do to convince France of his post-bellum plans? Parallel to his efforts to try Britain via the Vatican and Castellane, Karl took the initiative of contacting France again after the war. It is interesting to look at the letter his Swiss lawyer, Dr Seeholzer,[215] sent to

---

213 Kovács, *op. cit.*, no. 108, 386–388, Bern, September 18, 1918, Haguenin à Stephen Pichon, Min. des Aff. Étrangères.
214 "The drastic powerlessness of the Emperor and of his government, the terror that Germany inspires in them, the decisive attitude taken by the Entente towards Austria, and many other reasons besides, make it difficult to consider the Austrian project as anything other than an anachronistic manoeuvre [...]." Ibid., 386, footnote 2, Paix séparé, 104, 196–97 ff., Haguenin à Pichon, September 17, 1918.
215 Dr Seeholzer was a particularly useful agent for the emperor. He had access to most of the French ministries, knew President Poincaré, but also had contacts in the Vatican. During the war he kept

President Poincaré on June 19, 1919, carefully avoiding Clemenceau. In this letter, Seeholzer describes the emperor's ideas about some of his nations and makes some new points about Central Europe.

Karl reveals a new element, the danger posed by Italy's policy to cut Western powers from the East: all attempts at a union between Germany and German-Austria must be stopped, for Italy would use this opportunity to create a large block.[216] He continues with his advice regarding the Anschluss:

> [...] Il serait fort désirable que l'Entente notifie clairement au gouvernement de l'Autriche-Allemande qu'un régime qui se déclarerait nettement et sans pensée contre l'union, qui chercherait un rapprochement loyal avec les Etats nouvellement constitués et qui se ferait représenter par des délégués munis d'instructions conformes à ce programme, qu'un tel régime trouverait des vives sympathies au sein de la Conférence de Paris.[217]

Here Karl saw eye to eye with French foreign policy and he could back the French claim against the Anschluss. Karl did not want a Danubian Confederation at all costs. He stressed the necessity of first liquidating financial affairs in order to avoid the conflicts provoked by the dissolution of the Empire-Kingdom. It was only with said conditions that reconstruction and a Danubian confederation could be managed. He also suggested that the Successor States should be put under the presidency of a French or English delegate to help the different parties to an understanding.[218] This point does

---

contacts with the Thonon and Evian French Secret Service Office and was therefore considered a suspicious person by the Hungarians. Hungarian National Archives (henceforth MNL), K 64, 7 cs., 1922-48-96, Hungarian Embassy (signature illegible) to Count Bánffy, Ministry of Foreign Affairs, Bern, March 22, 1922.

216 With Germany and other malcontent countries.

217 "It would be greatly desirable for the Entente to inform the government of Austria-Germany in no uncertain terms that a government that would openly and without thought declare itself against the union, that would seek a loyal rapprochement with the newly formed states, and would have itself represented by delegates bearing instructions in conformity with this program, that such a regime would find strong sympathies within the Conference of Paris." Kovács, E., *op. cit.*, doc. 166, 508–10, Dr Seeholzer to Poincaré, Prangins, June 10 or 19, 1919.

218 "La totalité des Etats succédant à l'ancienne monarchie devrait être formellement engagée à s'entendre sous la Présidence d'un délégué français ou anglais quant à la liquidation systématique de l'ensemble de leurs affaires jusqu'ici communes et solidaires, et en particulier des questions financières, dans lesquelles règne encore un chaos absolu. La reconstruction irait de pair avec la liquidation." (The totality of the states succeeding the former monarchy should be formally engaged in

not seem strange when one reads a report written, surprisingly, by a communist officer of the 1919 Commune in Hungary: "The Entente alone is able to restore order in the country and within one week. The English are most respected and their arrival in the country would be greatly welcomed by the majority of the population, who would also be greatly pleased if Hungary should become an English dominion."[219]

In his letter, Karl indicated that he had a French contact person in mind for future discussions: "Enfin, l'Empereur est convaincu qu'il serait de grande utilité que l'Entente désigne un personnage compétent de nationalité française qui s'entretiendrait personnellement avec le souverain, dont les vues sont d'autant plus impartiales qu'il est placé au dessus des nationalités [...]."[220]

In another letter, the identity of the French liaison is confirmed. Indeed, Karl had an old channel to Paris in Bern, François-Emile Haguenin, and Karl suggested that this diplomat, through Seeholzer, should be the contact person. Karl had excellent contacts with him because already in September 1918 he had played the role of intermediary in Bern between Karl's emissaries and France.[221]

Apparently, the emperor did not get much of a response, because less than a month after Dr Seeholzer's letter, Karl approached the French Embassy in Bern stressing that he himself was the only possible link which could be utilised by the Allies for the purpose of influencing an economic union between portions of Austria-Hungary. However, there seemed to be traces of a change of behaviour by the French diplomats. It appeared that: "There is a strong current of opinion, though not unanimous, at French Embassy in favour of recommending appeal to French Government."[222]

---

reaching an agreement, under the directorship of a French or English delegate, in regard to the systematic liquidation of the entirety of their affairs hitherto both joint and several, and in particular regarding financial questions, in which absolute chaos continues to hold sway. The reconstruction would proceed in concert with the liquidation.) Ibid.

219 Lojkó, M. (ed.), *British Policy on Hungary 1918–1919, A Documentary Sourcebook*, SSEES, London, 1995, enclosure with no. 192, Major Lajtos' account on the situation in Budapest, dated: Vienna, July 9, 1919.

220 "Lastly, the Emperor is convinced that it would be extremely useful for the Entente to designate a competent person of French nationality who would have a personal discussion with the sovereign, whose views are all the more impartial as he is positioned above the nationalities [...]." Kovács, E., *op. cit.*, no. 166, 508–10

221 Ibid., no. 108, 386–88.

222 NA, FO 371 3529/98726, Lord Acton's decipher, Vienna, July 5, 1919.

Chapter II

Would he soon be able to harvest the fruits of his efforts? Karl was resolved to continue his quest to convince France of the necessity of the restoration. Using clerical channels again, he was able to send a "top secret" message stressing the need to restore the monarchy and recreate an alliance of the Successor States on economic terms in order to avoid the Anschluss. He presented a series of arguments to convince France of this: first, that German Austria cannot survive long in its current form; second, that the Habsburgs, as a Catholic dynasty, cannot have a Germanophile policy and has to be directed towards the Slavs; third, that France cannot show interest in this plan, especially because of Italy, but it can still hinder the Anschluss by at least contributing to its failure and letting the monarchists get organised in Austria and by informing Karl that there would be no opposition to this. Karl considered himself to be the solution to keeping Germany away from Central Europe:

> Je puis garantir à la France, que si l'Autriche allemande et la Hongrie—qui elle aussi penche vers l'Allemagne—reviennent sous mon sceptre, et que tous les états formés sur le sol de la monarchie se rallient dans les questions économiques, le rattachement à l'Allemagne aura à tout jamais vécu. En ce qui concerne la démocratie saine. [...] Le peuple ne veut rien savoir du rattachement à l'Allemagne, mais si c'est sous les formes démocratiques d'aujourd'hui qu'un référendum se faisait, je crains bien que le rattachement ne soit voté. Je crains bien qu'aujourd'hui, en France, on veuille croire à tout ceci. Si le rattachement se fait, la France a inutilement perdu des milliers de ses meilleurs fils, et le militarisme prussien recommencera tout de suite. A l'Autriche allemande se joindra la Hongrie, et un jour viendra où les Tchécoslovaques et les Yougoslaves pourront être en grand danger, d'autant plus qu'aujourd'hui déjà, l'Italie cherche l'amitié de l'Allemagne. De cette manière la 'Mittel-Europa' serait faite, et au lieu des Hohenzollern ce sera Noske qui serait à sa tête. C'est moi un ami de la France, qui vous l'assure. Le prince Rupprecht de Bavière a une chance, paraît-il, de rallier une grande partie de mes pays alpestres sous son sceptre. Pour empêcher cela, mes fidèles veulent me persuader de faire de la politique pangermaniste. Je ne le ferai jamais.[223]

---

[223] "I can guarantee to France that, if German Austria and Hungary—which also tilts toward Germa-

Through these words, Karl assured the French that he was strongly on their side and that he wanted to build his Central European policy on strong French support. This message is a key document for understanding policy that would unfold in 1920 and 1921.

Political changes in Paris with the departure of Clemenceau could serve Karl's interests.[224] A premonitory sign came from Aristide Briand, who had been prime minister and foreign minister from 1915 to 1917[225] and had dealt with the Emperor-King's envoys for a separate peace during the war.[226] In summer 1919, a meeting took place with one of Karl's envoys who asked for Briand's support to arm the Hungarian counterrevolutionary forces against the Commune to reoccupy Budapest, which eventually meant the restoration of the old order. Briand gave his total support to the project.[227]

A change of government did bring with it new conceptions of Central Europe in the Quai d'Orsay at the beginning of 1920. The secretary general of the French Foreign Ministry, Maurice Paléologue,[228] was inspired by the idea of Danubian Confederation. The capital of the new federation was to be Budapest, and Paléologue decided to discuss it directly and secretly

---

ny—return beneath my sceptre, and all the states formed on the soil of the monarchy join together in regard to economic matters, the union with Germany will have lived for ever. Concerning healthy democracy, [...] The people desire to know nothing of the union with Germany, but if a referendum were to take place under the democratic forms of today, I fear that the union would be voted in./ I am afraid that today, in France, people wish to believe all of this. If the union takes place, France will have lost thousands of her best sons in vain, and Prussian militarism will begin again right away. Hungary will join German Austria, and a day will come when the Czecho-Slovaks and the Yugoslavs could be in great danger, particularly given that Italy is already seeking friendship with Germany today. In this manner 'Middle Europe' will take shape, and in place of the Hohenzollerns it will be Noske who stands at its helm. It is I, a friend of France, who assures you of this. Prince Ruprecht of Bavaria has an opportunity, it appears, to gather a large portion of my Alpine countries beneath his sceptre. In order to hinder this, those who are loyal to me wish to persuade me to engage in Pan-German politics. This I will never do." Kovács, *op cit.*, II, no. 170, 523–25, Kaiser Karl to Msgr. Georges Prudent Bruley des Varannes, Prangins, July 3, 1919.

224 As early as summer 1919 and parallel to Karl's letters sent to Paris, emissaries of Karl were approaching Aristide Briand (who would become Président du Conseil in 1921), to ask him to hasten the end of the Commune in Budapest and support restoration in Hungary. Briand supported the project, and it was the French army that went to back Horthy's new National Army, the aim of which was to liberate Budapest from the Bolsheviks.

225 Bély, Lucien, Georges-Henri Soutou, et al (eds.), *Dictionnaire des Ministres des Affaires Etrangères 1589–2004*, Fayard, Paris, 2005, 469–78.

226 Brook-Shepherd, Gordon, *op. cit.*, 80, 99, 147, 256.

227 Windischgraetz, *Ein Kaiser kämpft*, 142–43, 158–59.

228 It is interesting to note that Paléologue was the son of a Romanian prince of phanariote descent, a member of the imperial family that once ruled the Greek Empire.

Chapter II

with Budapest (the Paléologue Plan is discussed in Chapter III). The second political change, which brought Briand, a man who seemed even more interested than Paléologue in Karl's project, into power (January 1921) is discussed in Chapter VI.

Regarding a Bavarian-Austrian–southern German confederation plan, Karl was against it, and even Sir George Clerk, the British commissioner in Prague, was quite sure of that.[229] Karl could be relieved that France had forbidden the Anschluss at Saint-Germain and that it had the same opinion of the Anschluss as did he himself.

At this point, Karl put on paper some of his other remarks and fears concerning the dangers of a still-relevant union of Austria with Germany:

> Le traité de St-Germain avec beaucoup de sagesse, s'est opposé à la réunion de l'Autriche avec l'Allemagne. Néanmoins nous constatons un mouvement unioniste dans les pays autrichiens de langue allemande, et ceci pour deux raisons, dont l'une est plausible et l'autre trompeuse. La première se base sur le fait que l'Autriche, telle que nous la voyons aujourd'hui, séparée de ses voisins, livrée à elle-même, est incapable de suffire à ses besoins. La seconde,—la raison trompeuse,—par laquelle on induit les peuples en erreur, tâche de démontrer que le salut repose uniquement dans l'union avec l'Allemagne. Si cette union se faisait, la Hongrie serait nécessairement forcée à se rattacher au bloc allemand et par conséquent, les populations,—la Tchécoslovaquie et la Yougoslavie, seraient pour ainsi dire serrées dans des tenailles. Il en résulterait cette Europe Centrale dont Naumann a évoqué l'image, ce bloc massif qui séparerait à jamais l'Europe occidentale des Balkans. Une création de ce genre rendrait illusoires pour l'Entente les fruits d'une victoire remportée au prix d'immenses sacrifices. Cette énorme agglomération sinon entièrement germanique, du moins sous l'hégémonie absolue de l'Allemagne, n'est compatible ni avec les intérêts de l'Angleterre, ni avec ceux de la France, et aucune de ces Puissances ne saurait en admettre la création.[230]

---

229 NA, FO 371, 4644/C10739, Lindley to Curzon, Prague, November 3, 1920.
230 "With a great deal of wisdom, the treaty of St-Germain was opposed to the reunion of Austria with Germany. Nevertheless, we observe a unionist movement in the German-speaking countries of

The document concludes that the Entente should pressure the Successor States to accept this Central European union by offering them economic support if they would accept.[231]

This memorandum was written after Hungary had been liberated from the communists and Austria's independence had been guaranteed. The new situation opened the prospect of Karl's return in both of his states. Having refused the Anschluss, the Treaty of St-Germain encouraged Karl to call on France for support when making further steps in the direction of restoration and a Danubian Confederation.

Bainville and Royalist Influence in the Quai d'Orsay

The concept of a Danubian Confederation was also supported by a member of Action française—a nationalist, Catholic and monarchist movement—in the person of one of its leading figures, the historian and journalist Jacques Bainville, a later member of the Académie française. Bainville's sympathy towards the Habsburgs and their monarchy already appeared in his pre-war writings. As a response to French liberals who were for the partition of the Dual Monarchy, he wrote that the dissolution of Austria-Hungary would create a constant diplomatic problem for France: "An Italian kingdom without counterweight and master of an entire sea, a German empire with nearly eighty million inhabitants, both facing a power of small and middle sized Czech, Magyar, Serb, Greek, and Romanian

---

Austria, and this for two reasons, of which one is plausible and the other deceptive. The first is based on the fact that Austria, as we see the nation today, separated from its neighbours, left to its own devices, is incapable of meeting its needs. The second—the deceptive reason—by which the peoples are being misled, attempts to demonstrate that salvation lies solely in the union with Germany. Were this union to occur, Hungary would be forced by necessity to join the German block, and consequently the Slav populations—Czechoslovakia and Yugoslavia—would be as though caught in the jaws of a pair of pliers. The result would be this Central Europe of which Naumann has evoked the image, this massive block which would forever separate Western Europe from the Balkans. A creation of this kind would render the fruits of a victory won at the price of immense sacrifices illusory for the Entente. This enormous conglomeration, if not entirely Germanic, then at least under the absolute hegemony of Germany, is compatible neither with the interests of England nor with those of France, and none of the Powers could allow its creation." Kovács, *op. cit.*, II, no.180, "Memorandum nach dem Konzept Seiner Majestät", Prangins, December 1919.

231 Ibid.

states". In other words, "the existence of Austria-Hungary is indispensable to France".[232]

After the war, Bainville was even more concerned by the unwillingness of the victor states to preserve the Austro-Hungarian monarchy as a strategic counterweight to Germany, and the victors' handling of the remnant state of Austria seemed to him an open invitation to German domination of the area. Furthermore, he reproached the Allies for

> [...] being so foolish as to dismember Germany in the east and still expect to enforce the settlement on the Rhine. The German state, left unified and strong at its core, had been provided with irresistible temptation to "fish in the troubled waters" of Poland, Czechoslovakia, and Austria, fledgling states with German-speaking populations whose independence could not easily be defended by Western power.[233]

For Bainville, there was no doubt that the treaty of Versailles would be put to the ultimate test in the mid-thirties due to the anarchical state of affairs in Central Europe. He announced that Germany, confronted with the superior powers of the Allies in the west, would begin to move against the Successor States of the Habsburg monarchy as soon as the Allied forces left the Rhineland.[234] He was right.

In 1920, Bainville published his famous *Les conséquences politiques de la paix*, in which he described the catastrophic effects of the peace treaties, which were the results of amateur politicians. He showed that the wrong states had been cut into pieces, while Germany had been left in its entirety. Here again he mentioned the importance of Austria-Hungary and even proposed to rebuild a new political entity in its place. But he announced that it would not happen without another crises and another conflict.[235] It is inter-

---

232 Bainville, J., *Journal*, I, November 28, 1912, see: Keylor, William R., *Jacques Bainville and the Renaissance of Royalist History in Twentieth-Century France*, Louisiana State University Press, Baton Rouge, London, 1979, 130.
233 Keylor, *op. cit.*, 137–39.
234 Ibid.
235 Bainville, Jacques, *Les conséquences politiques de la paix*, librairie Arthème Fayard, Paris, 1920, 209.

esting to note that Bainville mentioned points that Castellane had presented to the FO, such as the alliance of Germany with Russia, but Bainville had a far better pen and wrote it down much more convincingly. He also avoided assigning a date to an event he thought would happen in the future even if it is most probable.[236]

Bainville's severe positions towards Germany were the result of having thoroughly studied German history and having spent time in Bavaria. He first became a great admirer of Germany, its efficiency and flourishing economy and then saw the danger that a strong Germany represented for France. Let us not forget that Bainville said in 1920 that Germany would become "social-national", would occupy Czechoslovakia and partition Poland with Soviet Russia. Bainville made severe remarks against France's past foreign policy too. He blamed both Napoleon I and III for having created Germany and Clemenceau for having kept it together instead of partitioning it back into its pre-1871 situation of a plurality of states. Clemenceau's other sin was to put so much pressure on Germany as to consolidate its unity, nationalist feeling and spirit of revenge.

The same year he published the above-mentioned book, Bainville edited a document in his journal *La Revue universelle* titled "Le règne et les idées de Charles Ier empereur d'Autriche".[237] Although he leaves the author of the document in doubt, it is certain that the line of thought is very close to that of Karl, and it is proof that Bainville was not only an advocate of the Danubian Confederation and the restoration of King Karl but was also in contact with the group surrounding the Emperor-King.

In a short paragraph Bainville presents a Francophile emperor, friend of the Entente, who tried to separate himself from Germany during the war; he then reproduces the anonymous project itself. Its most interesting feature is the section about the Successor States and the remarks on Croatia and Czechoslovakia: "La Tchécoslovaquie, faible par le grand nombre de ces habitants non tchèques, et la Jougoslavie [sic] dont les populations slovènes et croates orientées vers l'ouest ne se sentent nullement à leur aise sous la

---

236 Montador, Jean, Jacques Bainville, Historien de l'Avenir, Ed. France Empire, Paris, 1984, 132.
237 Bainville, Jacques, "Le règne et les idées de Karl Ier Empereur d'Autriche", in *La Revue universelle*, vol. III, no. 14, October 15, 1920, 129–50.

domination serbe, devraient être vivement engagé par l'Entente à consentir à l'entrée dans une confédération à base économique."[238]

This document shows how the legitimists saw the ethnic problem that would endanger the stability of the new artificial "nation states" created out of the Habsburg Monarchy.

Bainville was one of the most visionary French intellectuals of his time, and his arguments concerning Central Europe and the whole of Europe in general were set up with considerable accuracy and with a brilliant historian's knowledge of the past and the logic of French geopolitics. Even if serving the ideology of French nationalists, Bainville is revealed to have been a supporter of an enemy monarchy (Austria-Hungary), the downfall of which France had contributed to in the name of serving its own interests, which Bainville considered as a grave mistake.

It is difficult to estimate the influence of Action française on the Quai d'Orsay in regard to the question of the Danubian Confederation. Yet it is obvious that the Quai d'Orsay was being encouraged by the French high commissioner in Budapest, Fouchet, to sponsor a journey to Budapest by Bainville "à titre de moyen de propagande" in order to develop Franco-Hungarian cultural and intellectual relations, for the author was much appreciated in Hungary because of his articles.[239] In general, Jacques Bainville's influence in the Quai d'Orsay is proven. His articles influenced public opinion, and through his friends he influenced French politics. He had influence on President Poincaré through the godfather of his son, Léon Bérard, who was the president's secretary,[240] and on Briand through his friend Emile Buré, Briand's private secretary.[241] Bainville wasn't the only royalist to influence

---

[238] "Czechoslovakia, weak in regard to the large number of its non-Czech inhabitants, and Yugoslavia, whose Slovene and Croation populations with their western orientation do not feel at all at ease under Serb domination, should be actively engaged by the Entente in consenting to entry in a confederation established on an economic basis." Kovács, E., *op. cit.*, no. 166, 508–10.

[239] As Fouchet says, Bainville could also profit from this visit to understand more about Central Europe. Fouchet wanted to use Bainville as an instrument of France's image-making in Hungary. AD-MAE Z Europe, Hongrie Propagande 65, Fouchet à Millerand, Budapest, July 31, 1920, 32 f.

[240] More than just being the secretary of Poincaré, Bérard was Minister of Education from 1921 to 1924. Keylor, William R., *Jacques Bainville and the Renaissance of Royalist History in Twentieth-Century France*, Louisiana State University Press, Baton Rouge, LA, 1979, 135, 163.

[241] Dikés, Charles, *Jacques Bainville. Les lois de la politique étrangère*, Paris, 2008, 120.

the government. The staff of Philippe Berthelot, Briand's chief of cabinet, was described by the left-wing press in 1915 as being full of royalists. And like Bainville in 1920, in 1915 the royalist Denys Cochin was sent on a mission to Greece by the earlier Briand government.[242] And last but not least, Bainville was a close friend of Maurice Paléologue. In 1935, only a few weeks before Bainville's death, Paléologue sponsored him to become the successor of President Poincaré as a member of the Académie française.[243]

Bainville's reflections obviously show their parentage in Castellane's thoughts, who knew him. Both Castellane and Bainville feared Wilson's ideas on the self determination of peoples, which went against the continuity of history and which were applied after the war.[244]

Both Bainville and Castellane were representatives of a certain conservative France, la *vielle France*, and they both admired the Austrian Empire. This goes back at least to the politics of Talleyrand, which imagined Austria as the bulwark of Europe, or even further back to Madame de Pompadour's influence on Louis XV to re-establish relations with Austria as an ally of France. Both men had this ancestral understanding of Europe's balance of power, the centre of which was based in Vienna. Without Austria as an empire, stability in Europe was lost.

---

242 Keylor, *op. cit.*, 100–101, 135; Dikés, *op. cit.*, 120.
243 http://www.academie-francaise.fr/les-immortels/jacques-bainville (12.02.2016).
244 Castellane met Wilson's military advisor Tasker Bliss who, like him, believed that the Habsburg Monarchy should be preserved. Mension-Rigau, *op. cit.*, 229.

CHAPTER III

The New Centre of Danubian Europe?

*"La puissance qui dominera la Hongrie possèdera la clef de voûte de l'Europe Centrale."*²⁴⁵

French Policy towards Hungary

The First Traces of a French Orientation in Hungary's Post-Bellum Diplomacy

French sympathy was growing in Hungary among certain politicians such as Count Pál Teleki and the then diplomat and later foreign minister (1938–1941) István Csáky. There were also pro-French diplomats such as Pál Hevesy and Baron Gyula Szilassy, both legitimists. Gyula Szilassy, Hungarian minister in Bern, explained that to get ready for the peace treaty, Hungary has to be prepared to lose territory and provide aspects of autonomy to its non-Hungarian citizenry:

> Nous pourrons nous estimer heureux si celles-ci se bornent à la cession de quelques comitats limitrophes d'une population roumaine ou slovaque compacte.
> On me dira que la France tient absolument à ses clients et voit dans une forte Tchécoslovaquie et une grande Roumanie les piliers de la puissance dans la vallée du Danube, tandis que l'Amérique et l'Angleterre verraient sans crainte une fédération hongroise de nationalités douées de droits égaux.²⁴⁶

---

245 "The power that will dominate Hungary will possess the key to Central Europe." ADMAE, Z Europe, Hongrie 60, 140–49 ff., Fouchet à MAE (Foreign Ministry), Budapest, December 11, 1920.

246 "We will be able to count ourselves fortunate if these limit themselves to the transfer of some limitrophe counties characterised by a compact Romanian or Slovak population./ It will be said to me

He was supporting a rapprochement with France, since for him France was to decide the fate of Hungary, and France had to be won over in order to be favourable to Hungary. To solve the territorial problem, Szilassy's solution for Hungary was a federation. He proposed an entente with Yugoslavia and an economic union later:

> Enfin il serait utile de terminer la "défense" en exposant les avantages que l'Entente et notamment la France retireraient d'un fédéralisme hongrois qui lui devrait la vie et qui formerait avec la Pologne et la Yougoslavie un rempart invincible contre le Germanisme et le Bolchevisme à la fois, alors qu'une Hongrie étouffée—toute notre histoire en fait foi—ne se résignera pas à ce sort. Dans ce cas la vallée du Danube deviendrait une seconde Macédoine qui finirait par graviter dans l'orbite de l'Allemagne, tandis qu'une Hongrie satisfaite et convertie assurerait la domination de la culture française de Constantinople à la frontière allemande.[247]

French propaganda in Hungary started quite early. In 1919 reports show an interest in Hungary and in making France more popular in the region.[248] France had a much more elaborate plan involving Hungary than did Britain or even the Successor States of Austria-Hungary. Szilassy in this report was one of the first Hungarian diplomats to announce the advantages of a rapprochement with France.

---

that France is absolutely attached to its clients and sees in a strong Czechoslovakia and a large Romania the pillars of power in the Danube valley, whereas America and England will view without fear a Hungarian federation of nationalities endowed with equal rights." MNL, K64, cs. 1, 996/Res. Szilassy à M. Károlyi, Bern, February 9, 1919. Szilassy continued to represent Hungary after the communist takeover. He was, however, asked to resign when Horthy came to power. He then retreated to his Bex estate in Canton Vaud. His house there still exists as a gift to the town council by the Szilassy foundation. His son left his library to the University of Lausanne library in Switzerland.

247 "Finally, it would be useful to end the 'defence' by exposing the advantages that the Entente and particularly France would gain from a Hungarian federalism that would owe its life to it, and which would, with Poland and Yugoslavia, form an invincible bulwark against Germanism and Bolshevism at once, whereas a stifled Hungary—our entire history bears witness to this—will not resign itself to this fate. In this case, the valley of the Danube will become a second Macedonia that will end up gravitating into the orbit of Germany, while a satisfied and converted Hungary would assure the domination of French culture from Constantinople to the German frontier." Ibid.

248 7N Hongrie 2885, 1919, Mission Mil. française en Hongrie, lettre no. 465, 8–10 ff., lettre no. 292 du Gén. Graziani au Ministre de Guerre, Budapest, November 2, 1919.

The French Plan for a Danubian Confederation

I had planned, initially, to cover Central European federalist projects and their reception at the Quai d'Orsay. However, there was one main project which was a French initiative. Whether it was a response to the many letters from Karl or a truly French idea is difficult to tell. It was certainly an idea which had been talked about in Paris, at least since Prince Czartoryski, and more than a half a century later it would become a political option for France.

One of the mysteries of French foreign policy for many decades was the French project of a Danubian Confederation centred in Budapest, rather than in any of the victor (Allied and associated) states, and the French Republic's alleged sympathy for the defeated Habsburgs.

Before embarking on a description of the French project, its interesting historiography deserves mention. For quite a long period the sole documents available were the Hungarian ones published before the war.[249] A book had been published on the Little Entente as early as 1923, in which the author mentioned the French policy towards Hungary,[250] yet a more serious study had to wait until Piotr Wandycz's *France and her Eastern Allies* in 1964.[251] He wrote:

> This policy, imperfectly known, constituted an interesting chapter in the annals of the Quay d'Orsay [...] did it proceed from a well-thought-out plan for a new French orientation in East Central Europe? Until all documents, especially those in the French archives, become available, it is difficult if not impossible to pass judgement on this phase of French diplomacy.[252]

---
249 Deák, Francis, Dezső Ujváry, (eds.), *Papers and Documents Relating to the Foreign Relations of Hungary* (henceforth *PFRH*), I: 1919–1920, Budapest, 1939. The embargo on French Foreign Ministry documents was lifted in the 1970s.
250 Mousset, Albert, *La Petite Entente*, Paris, 1923.
251 Wandycz, Piotr, *France and Her Eastern Allies 1919–1925*, Minneapolis, 1964.
252 Wandycz mentions Renouvin's and Duroselle's general manuals on international relations as the only French historians to have mentioned this plan. (Duroselle, J.B., *Histoire diplomatique de 1919 à nos jours*, Paris 1957, 36. Renouvin, P., *Histoire des Relations Internationales*, vol. IV, Paris 1953–58, 280–81. Duroselle, J.B. (ed.), La Politique étrangère et ses fondements, Paris, 1954, 24.) Ibid. 187. But Re-

Since then, a Hungarian scholar, Magda Ádám,[253] has thoroughly studied French Foreign Ministry documents—liberated from embargo since the 1970s—to give a precise picture of these negotiations and the answer to Wandycz's question, which we will also try to answer at this point.

After the presidential elections of January 1920, a new government was formed by the new president of the Republic, Paul Deschanel (February 18–September 21, 1920), with Alexandre Millerand (who would succeed Deschanel as president) as President du Conseil (prime minister) and foreign minister, and Maurice Paléologue, the former wartime ambassador to St. Petersburg, as secretary general of the Foreign Ministry. They replaced the Poincaré-Clemenceau duo. Both governments had the same concerns regarding Central Europe: the German and Soviet threats.

Until the change of government—the departure of Clemenceau—the policy towards Central Europe was quite anti-Hungarian. France wanted to achieve its aims by weakening the losers of the war via severe peace treaties and by building strong alliances with their central and south-eastern European allies: the policy of *vae victis*. Legends persist until today regarding Clemenceau's assumed "hatred" of Hungary.[254] It is, indeed, true that Clemenceau wanted to achieve peace as fast as possible. His contemporaries saw him as wanting a peace treaty as one way to continue war: *"une paix malpropre créerait un état de guerre perpétuelle où le militarisme des Alliés pourrait affirmer sa souveraineté sur le nouvel ordre européen"*.[255]

This does not mean that after Clemenceau's departure a new turn in foreign policy was impossible. Since the beginning of the peace process there were rows in French political circles regarding the way France would handle the Central European problem. However, it remains a matter of curiosity that the new direction taken by the Quai d'Orsay came before the signing of one of the most severe peace treaties (June 1920) ever imposed on a sov-

---

nouvin did write a more in depth article, as he was the only historian to have access to this Quai d'Orsay material before it was released: "Aux Origines de la Petite Entente", *Etudes européennes, Mélanges offerts à Victor L. Tapié*, Publication de la Sorbonne, Série 'Etudes', vol. 6, 1973, 489–500.
253 Ádám, *Little Entente*.
254 This is still commonplace in twenty-first-century Hungary.
255 "… *a dirty peace* would create a perpetual state of war where the militarism of the Allies could affirm its sovereignty over the new European order." Gobron, Gabriel, *La Hongrie mystérieuse*, Paris, 1933, 55.

ereign state, detaching 71 percent of Hungary's territory. But the severity of the peace treaty is less surprising if we consider that by the beginning of secret French–Hungarian negotiations in March 1920, Hungary's new shape was very near to its June 1920 contours, and its frontiers were pretty much decided by the earlier territorial gains on Hungary by its neighbours. Hungary was only delaying the signing of a peace *Diktat* it did not want to accept in the hope that some change to the harsh conditions and huge loss of territory would be implemented. Count Albert Apponyi, the head of the Hungarian delegation, went as far as to leave Paris in protest. France had to find another way of bringing Apponyi back to the negotiating table, and Paléologue's new approach to the Central European problem was part of the secret strategy.[256]

An anonymous paper published in January 1920 relating to the French interests in Central Europe reveals the true intentions of the French government regarding Hungary and its role in Central Europe. Titled "La question hongroise et l'intérêt français", it states that the equilibrium of Central Europe centres on Hungary: the map reveals it, and history is witness to it.[257] The author of this *étude* says that Germany supported dualist Hungary in order to fulfil its—not yet realised—aim to create a German *Mitteleuropa*.[258] Only new Hungary could realise the new Central Europe by its adhesion to a structure built on economic agreements and national independence. Its other members would be Prague, Belgrade and Vienna under an allied or at least a French protectorate. Then the paper moves on to describe what was to be changed in Hungary: the shift of property; the awkward suggestion of transforming Hungarian agriculture into a system of cooperatives as in Switzerland or Denmark; important infrastructure work on railways and rivers to enhance traffic; the organisation of trade between East and West. Hungary would become the banking centre of the region, since it already had the existing infrastructure. This report was probably the basis of Paléologue's own project.

---

256 Ádám, *Little Entente*, 55.
257 ADMAE, Z Europe, Hongrie 58, 4–9 ff. La question hongroise et l'intérêt français, author unknown, Paris, January 5, 1920. Same document in *Documents diplomatiques français sur l'histoire du basin des Carpathes* (henceforth *DFBC*), II, no.150, 330–33.
258 This is indeed confirmed by the Naumann plan for Central Europe.

These ideas show us why Hungary and its capital Budapest were of interest to the French, but the question might occur why Vienna, the capital of the old empire and geographically so close to Budapest, was not chosen to be the centre. The first problem was that a left-wing government was in power in Vienna. In Hungary a counter revolutionary conservative system had been re-established and its consolidation was underway, earlier supported by the French army. This was very important for foreign investment. Hungary was also a solid point from which to support Poland, which was at war with Soviet Russia. An exogenous element should not be overlooked. Britain had a strong toe hold in Vienna and had obtained control over shipping on the Danube. France was to counter this by using Budapest as the centre of its economic domination over the Danubian region and as a bridgehead into the Balkans.[259]

Budapest had other advantages similar to those of Vienna. It was the large capital of a former great power and had not only the infrastructure but also the economic and banking structures of a large state. This was evidently too large for Trianon Hungary but the ideal size for a Danube–Balkan Europe. France could easily move to Budapest and direct its new Central European influence from there.[260]

If the establishment of such a plan was decided, it was also because the Millerand administration had decided that France had to become the reactionary and anti-communist force of Europe. This meant that no diplomacy was attempted with Soviet Russia[261] and that it had to support Poland against Soviet Russia and the conservative forces in Hungary against a new Bolshevik revolutionary attempt orchestrated by Russia. But to realise this, it had to recognise that it had gone too far in the destruction of Central European unity; with the return of conservative powers in Hungary, a window of opportunity had opened to re-establish a solid entity in Central Europe starting from Hungary.

How many members would the Confederation have? The new government thought that an alliance only with the victor states was not sufficient. Their aim was to foster reconciliation with all the countries of the region, the

---

259 This is the result of Dr Bátonyi's research in the NA. Bátonyi, *op. cit.*, 120.
260 ADMAE, Z Europe. Hongrie, 58, 4–9 ff.
261 Husson, Edouard, Preface of Jacques Bainville, *Les conséquences politiques de la paix*, Gallimard, Paris, 2002, XLV–XLVI.

victorious and the defeated alike. A "balkanised" Central Europe politically and economically weakened, could not be strong enough against the German and Russian menace. Clearly, France's fears were not really different from those of Emperor Karl.

Into what political system would this union be placed: a monarchy or a republic? Millerand left the door open to a monarchy: "La France est prête à aider la Hongrie et à rétablir l'union avec les pays successeurs de l'ancien Empire. L'idéal serait que la Hongrie devienne une république mais la France ne l'empêchera pas s'il [sic] choisit la monarchie."[262] In general, as historian Magda Ádám has put it,

> the leaders of the Quai d'Orsay wished to unite the small Successor States, whether 'winners' or 'losers', either within a Danubian Confederation or with the help of a Habsburg restoration. For a while the two concepts existed simultaneously. At the beginning the first one was tried, and later, when it turned out that all Danubian states [including Hungary] were opposed to this French scheme, the second was pushed forward.[263]

It also seems that the Marquis de Castellane's positions were pretty much in accord with those of the new French Foreign Ministry.

How large would this confederation be? There were two concepts, a maximal and a minimal one. The first would have five members (Austria, Hungary, Czechoslovakia, Yugoslavia and Romania) and was dominated by anti-German trends, and the second considered only the union of Hungary, Romania and Poland and was dominated by anti-Soviet trends. And again the two conceptions of a Danubian Confederation and a Habsburg restoration existed in parallel,[264] but one would not exclude the other, since Paléologue and especially Fouchet preferred that Archduke József become king of Hungary rather than the crowned king, Karl IV.[265]

---

262 "France is prepared to assist Hungary in re-establishing the union with the successor states of the old Empire. The ideal would be that Hungary become a republic, but France will not stand in the way if it chooses monarchy." ADMAE, Z Europe, Hongrie 46, 120–24 ff.
263 Ádám, Little Entente, 48.
264 Ibid., 49. Wandycz, op. cit., 196.
265 ADMAE, Z Europe, Hongrie 60, 90–97 ff., Fouchet à Millerand, Budapest, November 6, 1920.

Chapter III

Was the Paléologue Plan launched after realising the severity of the treaty to be imposed on Hungary; or was the launch simply the reality of France's interests in Hungary as the centre point of the region? Obviously, the second factor prevailed. Suffice it to say that without a change of government, no such negotiation would have been possible.

France's general policy in the region is well summarised in an article in the German language newspaper of Zagreb, the *Agramer Tagesbalatt*:

> They did not care much about the disappearance of the Habsburg State, which they now regret on account of the unwillingness of the Successor States to unconditionally follow the French policy. It was less the fear that the addition of six million German Austrians would make Germany too strong than to take away Germany's influence in the Danubian States that gave rise to the idea of a Danubian Confederation.[266]

It would be superfluous after Ádám's in depth research on the so-called Paléologue Plan to present a second study of this plan. Yet, it is necessary to summarise the negotiations before one tries to understand the intricacies of French policy—diplomatic and military alike—and bring new elements to this complex period. Ádám's interpretation shows that the French Foreign Ministry's policy, triggered by the above mentioned pangermanist and Soviet threats, was first to promise economic, then political support to Hungary in exchange for French economic influence in Hungary. The secret negotiations with Hungary were started during March 1920. The nomination of a French high commissioner to Budapest was the first step of this policy.[267]

The Hungarian government offered to place their national railway and Danubian waterways under French authority and allow for a strong presence in Hungary of the Schneider-Creusot firm, which already owned many enterprises in the Successor States, such as the Skoda works in Czechoslovakia. It is obvious that the true interest of Hungary in this deal was motivated by the hope that France would help it gain back some of its lost territory; in

---

266 NA, FO 371 4650, C2979, FO translation of an extract from the *Agramer Tagesblatt*, July 27, 1920.
267 ADMAE, Z Europe, Hongrie 46, 120–24. Eventually, it was not the diplomat Doulcet but Fouchet who was chosen for the position of minister in Hungary.

other words, a partial revision of its borders. Hungary also had a second demand, which was to gain support to form a larger army, until then limited by the peace negotiations in Versailles to around 35,000 men.[268]

On one hand, territorial revision was very difficult to realise because of resistance by the Successor States to letting go of any land, even if inhabited in the majority by Hungarians; and the Entente had a great problem clearing the regions of the Czech and Yugoslav forces attributed to Hungary by the treaty. On the other hand, France could see taking an interest in the second point, since Poland was at war with Soviet Russia[269] and France was, at first, willing to support the creation of a regular and more important Hungarian army in order to support Poland as a buffer against Bolshevism. French backing for such an idea was growing when the Soviet army was operating successful counterattacks in Ukraine against Poland. In return for support to Poland, France made it clear that it would grant Hungary some of its wishes. In other words, it was the minimal project that was, for the time being, launched. However this was not an easy venture.[270]

If a confederation was to be built, negotiations would have to start with neighbouring countries. It was with Poland that Hungary had the strongest of common interests. Both nations had territorial claims on Czechoslovakia, and both could conceive of wiping Czechoslovakia off the map. Hungary wanted its "Upper Hungary", that is the new region of Slovakia, back and Poland wanted Teschen.[271] Count Csekonics, the Hungarian envoy in

---

268 *DFBC*, II, doc. 221, 500–505, Halmos (Hungarian government's envoy to Paris) à M. de Saint-Sauveur, director of Schneider-Creusot, Paris, April 14, 1920; doc. 247, 547–8, Fouchet à Millerand, Budapest, May 19, 1920; no. 260, 567, Fouchet à Millerand, Budapest, June 10, 1920; Ibid., no. 283, 594, Saint-Sauveur à Millerand, Paris, June 10, 1920.
269 Poland was France's most important ally against Germany and the Soviet Union, and it had to guarantee its survival. Wandycz, *op. cit.*, 196.
270 Ádám, *Little Entente*, 75–79; Carmi, Ozer, *op. cit,*, 28–29; *DFBC*, II, doc. 212, 493–94. Renouvin, P., "Aux origines", 491–93.
271 Polish Czieszyn was a coal-rich medieval duchy of Poland until the fourteenth century, then until 1918 it was part of the lands of the Crown of Bohemia. The district was comprised only 350 square miles with a population of 227,000 (1910 Austrian census), of whom 65 percent were Poles. It was divided in 1918 (November 5) by the local Czech and Polish national councils in anticipation of a final decision to be made at the Peace Conference. It cut the region in two, a Czech and a Polish zone, depriving Czechoslovakia of coal and cutting its sole rail access to Slovakia. Since France did not support the Czech claims over the Polish part, the Czechs occupied Polish Teschen on January 23, 1919, when Poland was in armed conflict with Ukrainians, Russians and Germans over boundaries. On February 1, the Council of Ten obliged the two countries to sign an agreement redividing the re-

Warsaw—and a legitimist—was urging his government to reoccupy Upper Hungary in order to cut, as soon as possible, the Czechoslovak–Russian corridor that endangered Poland and Hungary alike.[272] In a letter to Marshal József Piłsudski, Horthy expressed his concern about Romania being a factor that could ruin the plan of reoccupying Slovakia.[273] Horthy asked the general to oppose this by convincing the Romanians to remain neutral.[274] This was ever so urgent, since Csekonics thought that a secret agreement had been struck between Romania and Czechoslovakia to guarantee the former's intervention if the latter was attacked by Hungary.[275] In an earlier interview with Csekonics, Piłsudski told the Hungarian envoy that Poland would remain neutral in the case of a Hungarian–Czech conflict and that it would do its best to hold Romania back. Very soon, Romania showed interest in Paléologue's proposition for a Romanian–Hungarian alliance.[276]

Hungary also made overtures towards other Successor States. Given that it was impossible to deal with Czechoslovakia due to Edvard Beneš' suspiciousness towards Hungary, the Hungarian Foreign Ministry chose Yugoslavia. Acting on the information that Czechoslovakia was preparing a military agreement with Yugoslavia, a Hungarian emissary was sent to approach the Yugoslavs, but they refused to meet with him.[277]

Of course Paléologue saw his Danubian Confederation in a different way. He described it to Beneš as being necessary because Hungary was in the middle of the Danubian region and could not be ignored, as it was an explosive and dangerous force. The aim was to moderate this force and, if necessary direct it. He suggested to Beneš that he ask the Romanian forces of Bukovina to help defend the Sub-Carpathian region, for doing that

---

gion pending its final disposition to the Peace Conference. In April, the Councils (Councils of Four and of Five) referred to Poland and Czechoslovakia the question of Teschen, to be settled through negotiation, which led to the continuation of the fight over Teschen and its radicalization. It resulted, eventually, in the Conference of Ambassadors' decision to divide the region itself, leaving both countries frustrated. Mamatey, Victor S. (ed.), *A History of the Czechoslovak Republic 1918–1948*, Princeton University Press, Princeton, 1973, 33–36.

272 MNL, K 64, 1 cs., 74–78 ff,.Csekonics to Foreign Min. Kánya, Warsaw, March 1920.
273 Ibid. Hungary had renounced reoccupying Transylvania by force for the sake of Romanian support.
274 Ibid., 79–80 ff, Project of letter, March 2, 1920.
275 Ibid., 83–84 ff, Csekonics to Kánya. Warsaw, March 23, 1920.
276 *DFBD*, II, no. 196, 460, Paris, 23 March 1920, Paléologue-Ghika Conversations.
277 Ibid., no. 218, Fontenay à Milleraud, Belgrade, April 12, 1920.

would discourage Hungary from attacking Czechoslovakia.[278] For Paléologue the larger Confederation, including Czechoslovakia, still remained the better solution.

Hungary's plan for Polish–Hungarian union was actually elaborated earlier than Paléologue's proposal. In March 1920 a Polish–Hungarian alliance with Romania was in preparation in order to guarantee these two countries' neutrality when Hungary would reoccupy Slovakia. As a result Hungary was on the verge of creating a Little Entente of its own. France was therefore unwillingly supporting an alliance that was isolating Czechoslovakia. Hungary, naturally, avoided mentioning its scheme to reoccupy Slovakia, and it continued its negotiations with Paléologue in the hope that it could convince France to support it in its quest to recoup territory. The Polish–Hungarian project was never put into action because France eventually did not let Hungary enlarge its army. The question remains whether the Quai d'Orsay knew about the Hungarian–Polish plan to occupy Slovakia. This question is revisited in the chapter on Slovakia.

The Problem of the Lettre d'Envoi

It is timely to mention the French strategy to make Hungary sign the treaty of Trianon: the *lettre d'envoi* or transmittal letter, which left the door open to territorial revision. It mentioned the following:

> Fidèles à l'esprit dont elles se sont inspirées en traçant les frontières fixées par le Traité, les Puissances alliées et associées sont cependant préoccupées du cas où la frontière ainsi tracée ne correspondrait pas partout avec précision aux exigences ethniques ou économiques.
> [...] Peut-être une enquête menée sur place fera-t-elle apparaître la nécessité de déplacer, en certains endroits, la limité prévue par le Traité. Pareille enquête ne saurait être actuellement poursuivie sans retarder indéfiniment la conclusion d'une paix à laquelle l'Europe entière aspire. Mais,

---

278 ADMAE, Z Europe, Tchécoslovaquie 65, Paléologue on discussions with Beneš, Paris, July 29, 1920.

lorsque les Commissions de délimitation auront commencé leur travail, si elles estiment que les dispositions du Traité créent quelque part, comme ils est dit plus haut, une injustice qu'il est de l'intérêt général de faire disparaître, il leur sera loisible d'adresser un rapport à ce sujet au Conseil de la Société des Nations.

Dans ce cas, les puissances alliées et associées acceptant que le Conseil de la Société [des Nations] puisse, si une des parties en cause le lui demande, offrir ses bons offices pour rectifier à l'amiable le tracé primitif, dans les mêmes conditions, aux endroits où une modification aura été jugée désirable par la Commission de délimitation.[279]

If it is true that these paragraphs opened possibilities of territorial revision, they did not, however, give the Hungarians the chance to report to the League of Nations directly but rather to the Boundary Delimitation Commission in question.[280]

The Hungarians were trying to see in it the possibility of a future revision of the Trianon treaty. In fact, it was exactly Paléologue's purpose to make Hungary believe that a revision was possible. The negotiations took months, and Hungary sent many memoranda to Paris for acceptance. Paléologue was constantly renewing promises in order to urge Hungary first to sign the treaty and then, once that was done, to sign the economic agreement with

---

279 "True to the spirit that inspired them in tracing the borders fixed by the Treaty, the allied and associated Powers are nevertheless preoccupied by the case where the border thus traced would not correspond everywhere with precision regarding ethnic or economic exigencies./ [...] Perhaps an investigation conducted on site will cause the necessity to arise of displacing, in certain areas, the boundary provided for by the Treaty. Such an investigation could not presently be undertaken without delaying indefinitely the concluding of a peace to which all of Europe aspires. However, once the Demarcation Commissions have begun their work, if they judge that the stipulations of the Treaty create somewhere, as stated above, an injustice regarding which it is in the general interest to make it disappear, they will be at liberty to address a report on this subject to the Council of the Society of Nations./ In this case, the allied and associated Powers accept that the Council of the Society [of Nations] may, should one of the parties at issue demand it, offer its good offices to rectify the original tracing amicably, under the same conditions, at the locations where a modification would have been judged desirable by the Demarcation Commission." Lettre d'envoi des Puissances Alliées et Associées à M. Apponyi, président de la Délégation Hongroise signed by Millerand, May 6, 1920. Litván, György (ed.), *Documents Diplomatiques français sur l'histoire du bassin des Carpates, 1918–1932*, Akadémia Kiadó, Budapest, vol. 2, 1993, doc. 231, 520–23.

280 The Allied Boundary Delimitation Commissions were responsible for drawing the new frontiers between two countries. There were such commissions for each border: Austria–Hungary, Czechoslovakia–Hungary, SHS Kingdom–Hungary and Romania–Hungary.

France that would have meant a partial takeover of the Hungarian economy. Lazare de Montille, Paléologue's *chef de cabinet*, went as far as to say that Hungary could tear the treaty to pieces once it felt strong enough to do so and that, when that time came, Hungary could count on France's support.[281] This shows how keenly France wanted to get Hungary into its sphere of influence and use it for its own *Osteuropa Politik*.[282]

From the French point of view, and from that of the French officials involved in the peace treaty, the *lettre d'envoi* was not a very clear document, being somewhat ambiguous. A French author strongly supportive of the Hungarian cause claims that a certain General Meunier, the head of one of the Boundary Delimitation Commissions, said the existence of the *lettre d'envoi* showed that the Millerand government thought the peace was "*mauvais*", simply bad, since the letter was trying to get the Hungarians to accept a peace which was unacceptable. The general was not an isolated case, other French politicians also interpreted the *lettre* in the same vein.[283]

The French MP, friend of Hungary and later *résistant* Charles Tisseyre (1880–1945), shows that there were also those who tried to explain why the letter was not to give any illusions to the Hungarians. French MP Charles Guernier wrote in his report proposing the ratification of the treaty:

> The tendentious interpretation put on M. Millerand's letter handed to the Hungarian Delegation together with the Treaty, the chimerical hopes hung upon it, oblige us to make some complementary precisions. […] The high motives of equity which dedicated M. Millerand's letter of envoy must not be travestied by an interpretation which would lead to nothing less than the annihilation of the Treaty itself. It must not be forgotten that the fixing of the Hungarian frontiers was the object of the most minute care on the part of each of the Allies, and every point having been discussed a perfect solidarity was established at all points. Some one case,

---

[281] PFRH, I, doc. 368, 371–72, Count Csáky, special representative in Paris, to Count Teleki, Hungarian Min. of Foreign Affairs Paris, June 19, 1920.
[282] At this stage I have enough evidence to contradict Albert Mousset's statement that this policy was an "ephemeral misunderstanding". Mousset, *op. cit.*, 18–20.
[283] Gobron, *op. cit.*, 147.

considered in an isolated position, might perhaps call forth a rightful censure but is certainly compensated by an advantage in some other point, so that in rectifying the one from motives of equity one would be led to commit what would in reality be a much greater injustice.[284]

This report shows evidence that Hungary was not to dream of any changes. It is a fact that the peace treaty was full of injustices towards Hungary, but France would not change that. It is easy to conclude that Hungary, so desperately in search of an ally that could help revise the treaty, would not bow to the wishes of France without an important territorial concession. The possibility of a revision of Trianon was the condition in exchange for which Hungary would accept the Paléologue Plan. Without revision, Hungary would look for support elsewhere.

But what were Millerand's true intentions? After the peace treaty, Paléologue—not in office as secretary general any more—sent a note to Millerand written by an unnamed, obviously Hungarophile, French industrialist criticizing the *lettre d'envoi* as not being respected by the Quai d'Orsay. It stated in this note that members of the Conference of Ambassadors and of the Quai d'Orsay had told the writer that the transmittal letter could not change the stipulations of the treaty. But in the opinion of the industrialist: "La lettre d'envoi, en conséquence de laquelle la Hongrie a signé le traité, devrait être considérée comme nulle et non avenue puisque le but unique et le sens de ce document, partie intégrante du traité, était de modifier les duretés et les injustices de ce traité par la façon dont il devrait être exécuté."[285]

Millerand's answer to Paléologue showed quite a bit of irritation:

Vous n'aviez évidemment pas lu avant de me la remettre la note que vous m'aviez laissé hier soir; car vous n'auriez pas manqué de faire remarquer à son auteur que les 'divers personnages compétents de la Conférence

---

284 Tisseyre, C., *An Error in Diplomacy, Dismembered Hungary*, Mercure, Paris, 1924, 63–64.
285 "The cover letter as a result of which Hungary signed the treaty should be considered null and void, since the sole aim and the intent of this document, an integral part of the treaty, was to modify the severities and the injustices of this treaty in the manner in which it was to be carried out." Archives Nationales de France (henceforth ANF), Fonds Millerand, Dossier Paléologue, Lettre d'un industriel français.

des Ambassadeurs et du Quai d'Orsay' qui lui ont dit que la lettre d'envoi du Traité de Trianon ne peut modifier nullement les stipulations du Traité, n'ont fait que confirmer l'interprétation que vous-même comme moi n'avons cessé de donner, pendant notre passage au Quai d'Orsay, et qui est d'ailleurs la seule correcte et admissible.[286]

Paléologue answered with an embarrassed letter:

L'occasion m'est ainsi offerte de vous assurer que, si je vous parle avec une entière franchise et une complète liberté, je m'exprime toujours au dehors avec beaucoup de réserve sur les questions où l'on peut croire que je m'inspire plus ou moins de vos opinions c'est la condition tacite et nécessaire de la confiance que vous me témoignez et dont je vous suis si reconnaissant; c'est peut-être aussi le seul moyen que j'aie de vous aider un peu dans votre lourde tâche.[287]

There is no trace of a letter sent with the French industrialist's note, but his response gives us some indication of his position. Paléologue seemed to believe that there had been a revocation of the *lettre d'envoi* and that France had not been faithful to its commitments toward Hungary.

The inconsistency of the *lettre d'envoi* is one of the key elements of the lack of success of the French attempt to create a Danubian Confederation. After the elections, in September 1920, Paléologue was replaced by Philippe Berthelot. Paléologue had to play the role of scapegoat for the failed plan and had to resign.

At this point, when the Paléologue Plan was declared a cul-de-sac by the new secretary general of the Quai d'Orsay, one can say that Castellane's

---

[286] "Obviously you had not read the note you'd left me last night prior to sending it to me; for you would not have failed to remark to its author that the 'various competent personages of the Conference of the Ambassadors and of the Quai d'Orsay,' who told him that the cover letter of the Treaty of Trianon can in no way modify the stipulations of the Treaty, only confirmed the interpretation that you yourself, like me, never ceased to give during our travel to the Quai d'Orsay, and which is, moreover, the sole correct and admissible one." ANF, Fonds Millerand, Millerand to Paléologue, May 6, 1921.

[287] "The occasion is thus afforded me to assure you that, if I speak to you with complete frankness and total liberty, I always express myself on the outside with a great deal of reserve regarding the questions where one can think that I am more or less inspired by your opinions – it is the tacit and necessary condition of the trust that you express in me and for which I am so grateful to you; it is perhaps also the sole means I have to help you a bit in your weighty task." Ibid., Paléologue to Millerand May 6, 1921.

papers sent to the Foreign Office at the beginning of 1920—indifferent to whether or not Paléologue had knowledge of the marquis' attempt—reveal the extent of their importance and portray Paléologue's quasi obsession to deter Germany by creating a Danubian Confederation centred in Budapest instead of Vienna.

The Geopolitical value of the Paléologue Plan

What was the Danubian Confederation's true security program apart from the usual argument of avoiding the Anschluss? The destabilization of the balance of power provoked by the disappearance of the Habsburg Monarchy would be replaced by a confederation of all the lands and Successor States of Austria-Hungary (Hungary, Austria, Czechoslovakia, SHS Kingdom, Poland and enlarged Romania)—except for the South Tyrol, the Trentino, Trieste and Gorizia, given to Italy. Under this umbrella the following would be united: practically the whole ethnic population of the two leading nations (Austrian Germans and Hungarians); the new state made out of a part of Austria-Hungary (Czechoslovakia); two states that pre-existed the end of the war (Poland and Romania), which received a large part of Austria-Hungary; and eventually a pre-existing Kingdom of Serbia, which became a kingdom of three nations, though later only accepted the notion of one nation, the Yugoslav nation. By uniting them in the same confederation — all the Successor States, in their entirety, in a confederation—Paléologue would consolidate the key strength of this new ensemble under French control, which would go from sea to sea, from the Baltic to the Adriatic, and would therefore become even more efficient than Austria-Hungary, which only touched the Adriatic. Thus the Confederation would become a *cordon sanitaire* against Soviet Russia and would even replace France's old ally, Tsarist Russia, to the east.

The confederation would not only be a bulwark against Russia but also against Germany. It would naturally avoid the Anschluss but would also prevent Germany from occupying the Sudetenland.[288] Eventually it would pre-

---

288 There were, indeed, visionary persons in France who understood the true meaning of the faulty Versailles system. We have seen Castellane and Bainville, and of course Paléologue and Millerand. There was also a Hungarian Francophile industrialist and diplomat, Károly Halmos, who under-

vent Germany and Russia from partitioning Poland again. Thus the Paléologue Plan was a program that would have established a new balance of power that could have countered the threats that Germany and Soviet Russia potentially represented.

French–English Rivalry and the Creation of the Little Entente

The Hungarian historian György Ránki claimed that both France and Britain were competing for hegemony in the Danubian basin.[289] Britain got control of the Danube and was speculating on how Vienna could become the centre of its interests in the region; to which France responded with its plan of a Danubian Confederation. But a much more nuanced interpretation can show that Britain, under the influence of the PID, was not all that interested in Central Europe in 1918–19—except for the Danube, which connected Central Europe with the Black Sea, linking it to the Middle East—and was initially ready to leave Austria to Germany.[290] It is evident that after the French Confederation Plan was launched, Britain could not ignore it and got more involved in the region. It started supporting Beneš's plan of a Little Entente in the expectation that it would accept malcontent countries when they decided to give up their territorial claims.[291] If we admit that Britain did accentuate its involvement in the region, then it is undeniable that there was a power struggle between Britain and France. But the nature of their approaches was different: France was advancing economic solutions in order to solve political ones with a Danubian Confederation; whereas Britain was preoccupied by the economic consequences of a partitioned Central Eu-

---

stood the devastating effect of the new order as early as March 1920. He doubted, earlier than Bainville, that Czechoslovakia would always be strong enough to stop their three million Germans from joining the rest of their people across the border. In this case, Germany would get through peace what it could not get through war and Hungary could only bow to Germany's will. *DFBC*, II, no. 189, Paris, March 18, 1920, Halmos à Paléologue. This would match with some of the arguments of Bainville in his *Les Conséquences politiques de la paix*, published in autumn 1920.

289 Ránki, György, *Economy and Foreign Policy: The Struggle of the Great Powers for Hegemony in the Danubian Valley*, Boulder, New York, 1983, 440.
290 "The PID whole-heartedly supported Otto Bauer's pan-German argument", Bátonyi, *op. cit.*, 23.
291 Ibid., 43, 178–79.

rope.²⁹² Yet it would be premature to conclude that France was for a Danubian Confederation and Britain for a Little Entente, since the role of France appeared to be much more ambiguous, as we will see.

The Military versus Diplomacy?

There is a widespread view, even in the academic milieu, that the Little Entente was the child of France. There can be no doubt that it was not, and that it was a reaction to the Paléologue Plan and to the danger of a Habsburg restoration in Hungary.

The French government's intention concerning Hungary, and its opposition to the Little Entente were made clear in a telegram from Prime Minister Millerand to most of the French legations of Europe on August 24, 1920:

> Je vous ai communiqué un télégramme de M. Daeschner en date du 22 août relatif à la négociation d'une alliance entre la Tchéco-Slovaquie, la Yugo-Slavie, la Roumanie et éventuellement la Pologne et la Grèce en vue du maintien de la paix dans les Balkans. L'idée qui préside à la constitution de ce groupement est de prendre des garanties contre la Hongrie, la convention serbo-tchèque contenant même des dispositions en vue d'une coopération éventuelle contre les Magyars.
>
> Une telle politique présente le grave inconvénient d'isoler le gouvernement magyar, qui sera inévitablement tenté de se rejeter du côté de l'Allemagne pour y trouver un appui. Notre souci constant est au contraire, en vue de prévenir les conflits, de rechercher les éléments de rapprochement et d'entente entre les divers Etats de l'Europe centrale. C'est surtout pour être à même de travailler plus efficacement à la réalisation de ce dessein, que j'ai encouragé un rapprochement économique entre entreprises françaises et entreprises hongroises. Le développement de l'influence française à Budapesth [sic] paraissait propre à servir la cause de la paix, en

---

292 The difference in the English and French approaches to the problem is well portrayed by the works of two highly influential scholars, one English and one French: Keynes who wrote his famous *The Economic Consequences of Peace* (1920) and Bainville who wrote, as an answer to Keynes, *The Political Consequences of Peace* (1920).

donnant à tous nos Alliés de l'Europe centrale certaines garanties contre le renouveau de la politique de conquête en Hongrie.

Dans ces conditions l'adhésion de la Pologne (Varsovie), de la Grèce (Athènes) à la combinaison projetée risquerait d'aggraver la division de l'Europe centrale en deux camps et d'augmenter ainsi les chances de conflit. Nous n'avons donc aucun intérêt à ce que le gouvernement auprès duquel vous êtes accrédité entre dans un groupement orienté de la sorte.

Je vous prie d'examiner sous quelle forme, particulièrement discrète, il vous paraîtrait possible de signaler au gouvernement polonais (Varsovie) et grec (Athènes) les inconvénients d'une politique qui risque de solidariser les intérêts hongrois avec les intérêts allemands et de rendre plus difficile dans l'Europe centrale l'établissement de relations normales entre les Etats issus de la désagrégation de l'Empire habsbourgeois.[293]

The French press, as well, expressed its negative reaction to the Little Entente, which echoed the government's perception. Bainville expresses his concern in *L'Action française* (September 4, 1920) explaining that it would serve "neither France, nor Europe". The only approval came from the right-

---

[293] "I have communicated to you a telegram from M. Daeschner with the date of 22 August relative to the negotiation of an alliance between Czechoslovakia, Yugoslavia, Romania, and ultimately Poland and Greece, with the aim of upholding peace in the Balkans. The idea prevailing in the constitution of this group is to have guarantees against Hungary, with the Serbo-Czech convention even containing stipulations with a view to eventual cooperation against the Magyars./ Such a policy presents the grave disadvantage of isolating the Magyar government, which will inevitably tend to throw itself over to the side of Germany in order to find support there. Our constant worry to the contrary is, with the intent of preventing the conflicts, to research the elements of rapprochement and entente among the diverse States of Central Europe. It is especially in the name of working more effectively toward the realisation of this goal that I have encouraged an economic rapprochement among the French companies and Hungarian companies. The development of French influence in Budapest seemed well suited to serving the cause of peace, in granting to all our Allies of Central Europe certain guarantees against the renewal of the politics of conquest in Hungary./ Under these conditions the adherence of Poland (Warsaw), of Greece (Athens) to the projected combination would risk aggravating the division of central Europe into two camps and thereby increase the possibilities for conflict. Therefore we have no interest in seeing the government to whom you are accredited enter into a group thus oriented./ I ask that you investigate under what form, particularly discreet, it would seem possible for you to signal to the government of Poland (Warsaw) and that of Greece (Athens) the disadvantages of a policy that risks the solidarization of the Hungarian interests with the German interests and thus renders the establishment of normal relations between the states in Central Europe derived from the disintegration of the Habsburg Empire more difficult." ADMAE, Z Europe, Hongrie 47, 71–72 ff. Telegram from Prime Minister Millerand to most of the French legations of Europe, August 24, 1920.

wing *Echo de Paris*, which said that France can't be alarmed by a system that aims to stabilise an order that it had contributed to create.[294]

Millerand's letter shows that he was afraid of the same symptom that he dreaded with Austria: Hungary as well would fall into the arms of Germany. He was also concerned that other countries would join the Little Entente and make it even larger by growing both towards the north and south; though this alliance looked much more like a *cordon sanitaire* that could isolate Russia from Germany from the Baltic to the Adriatic. Except that Hungary would be a revisionist peninsula in the middle of it.

As is usual with historical research, some elements have emerged that prove that France's policy was not that consistent. This inconsistency appears in the French army's approach to Hungary during the same period. But first, its worth noting that there were officers that were in line with the Quai d'Orsay. General Graziani, the French chief of the Inter-allied Military Mission in Budapest, sympathised with Hungary's fate. He had a discussion with the Hungarian prime minister, who said that, like Britain and Italy, France should also show some signs of its willingness to favour Hungary. The prime minister added: "Wouldn't it be possible to bring certain rectifications to the borders of the project of treaty?"[295] Graziani answered that they could make a few positive remarks in the press, but France could not upset its friends in Romania, the SHS Kingdom and Czechoslovakia. This answer shows that General Graziani was in accordance with Millerand's approach that no border rectification could be envisioned.

Other French military representatives reported that the Germanophile magnates, among them Andrássy, were plotting to restore King Karl,[296] who was Germanophile himself: "L'Empereur Charles personnifie le règne réactionnaire, l'omnipotence des magnats, l'ostentation germanophile et la reconstitution de l'Empire austro-hongrois."[297] In these reports, there seems to be a confusion between two groups: on the one hand, the supporters of a union of Austria and Bavaria under Prince Ruprecht Wittelsbach, in which

---

294 Renouvin, P., *Aux origines*, 489.
295 *DFBC*, II, no. 212. Graziani à Lefèvre, Budapest, April 10, 1920.
296 SHAT 7N Hongrie 2885. Rapport Mensuel, August 1, 1920.
297 "Emperor Charles personifies reactionary rule, the omnipotence of the magnates, Germanophile ostentation, and the reconstitution of the Austro-Hungarian Empire." SHAT 7N Hongrie 2885. Rapport Mensuel, December 1, 1920.

Hungary would have kept its independence but could have joined Austria–Bavaria in a federation;[298] on the other hand, Karl and his legitimist followers who were openly anti-German and refused to be part of such a Bavarian alliance. In fact, the Ruprecht party was in competition with the Karlist party to get Austria. There certainly were Germanophile Hungarian aristocrats, but to claim that Andrássy was one of them ignores his personality.[299]

The question arises whether French military representatives were at all informed of their country's foreign policy or they simply decided to ignore it. The French confederation plan of Millerand had leaked in the press, and no one could ignore it; still, the army was probably not informed of the Quai d'Orsay's legitimist alternative. To sum up, the French officers were much more anti-Habsburgs than the politicians, since they had fought against the Germans in the trenches and despised anyone who spoke German.

There is another reason for this anti-Austrian approach. Many French officers were strongly biased in favour of the Czechs, not only because of the strong French presence in Prague—the creators of the Czechoslovak army—but also because during the war there was a Czech military legion, wearing French uniforms, integrated into the French army. The French officers were dealing with comrades in arms whom they had fought with during the war. Two high ranking French officers sent to Prague were under the spell of the Czechs: General Maurice Pellé and General Eugène Mittelhauser. Pellé was head of the French Military Mission to Prague and chief of general staff of the Czechoslovak army until December 1920; Mittelhauser was first commander of the Western Army Group in Slovakia, and then became both head of the French Military Mission and chief of general staff of the Czecoslovak army, following Pellé, until 1926. Both officers were instrumental in forming and leading the new Czechoslovak army. As a Czechoslovak commanding officer, Mittelhauser had been fighting the Red Hungarian troops of the Commune, who were attempting to reconquer Upper Hungary, then Slovakia.[300]

---

298 SHAT 7N Hongrie 2885. Rapport Mensuel, August 1, 1920.
299 On the character of Andrássy see Kardos, József, *Legitimizmus, Legitimista poltikusok Magyarországon a két világháború között*, Korona, Budapest, 1998, 9–23.
300 Janco, Anton, "La France et la création de l'armée tchécoslovaque", in *Le rôle de la France dans la création de l'Etat Tchécoslovaque (1918)*, Presses de l'Institut d'études politiques de Toulouse, Toulouse, 1993, 64.

Chapter III

The role of French officers in Czechoslovakia, as the de facto creators of the Czech army, was unclear. They held high military ranks as Frenchmen and key positions in the Czechoslovak army. As chief of staff, Mittelhauser was the representative of Czechoslovakia to sign the first military agreement between Czechoslovakia and the SHS Kingdom—represented by Colonel Danilo Kalafatović—on July 31, 1921, which was the first step towards the Little Entente.[301] However, an earlier agreement was signed at Konopiště (the former castle of Archduke Franz-Fredinand) between the general staffs of the same states under the supervision of Pellé, then chief of general staff of the Czechoslovak army (November 2, 1919).[302] Another Czechoslovak–Yugoslav agreement of "alliance" was signed on August 14, 1920, eventually followed by the aforementioned military agreement in July 1921. In other words, a French officer, Pellé, was behind a document that aimed at countering French foreign policy in Central Europe in 1920. In some ways, the clever Czechs had outsmarted the French by pulling them into their Central European plan. Except that the French officers were not unwilling to embarrass the Quai d'Orsay. By the time it was Mittelhauser's turn to sign the military agreement with Yugoslavia in summer 1921, the Briand Government was much less hesitant to back the agreement with the pro-Little Entente Philippe Berthelot, then in command of the Quai d'Orsay as its Secretary General. Obviously both pro-Czech generals had shown disapproval towards any French military agreement with Hungary.

The high-ranking officers fell into two camps with regard to a military agreement with Hungary. Generals Mittelhauser and Pellé, and Minister of Defence Eugène Lefèvre-Pontalis rejected *à priori* the whole idea. The second group, whose key members were Marshal Foch and General Gamelin, suggested extreme cautiousness.[303]

---

301 SHAT Fonds Foch 1K 129; Ferencuhova, Bohumila, "La vision slovaque des relations entre la France et la Petite Entente (1918–1925)", in *Nations, Cultures et sociétés d'Europe centreale au XIX et XX siècles, Mélanges offerts au Professeur Bernard Michel*, Publicatons de la Sorbonne, Paris; Kalhous, R., *Budováni armády*, Melantrich, Prague, 1936.
302 Ferencuhova, *op. cit.*
303 ADMAE, Z Europe, Hongrie 47, 88–90 ff. Cable de Pellé à Foch, July 27, 1920. Cable of Gen. Gamelin, July 31, 1920; *PFRH*. I., doc. 587, 578–79.

We can already draw a certain number of conclusions concerning French politics in Hungary. First, until the arrival of Berthelot to replace Paléologue as secretary general of the Quai d'Orsay, France's policy tended to be pro-Hungarian, and as soon as news of a possible Czechoslovak, Yugoslav and Romanian alliance reached the ears of Millerand, he showed preoccupation and alarm about such an eventuality. Second, it seems that the majority of French military officers sent to Central Europe never really sympathised with Hungary's fate and were even going the opposite way to French foreign policy. Thus it is safe to say that France's policy was ambiguous towards Hungary and even towards Central Europe in general. First the Foreign Ministry supported Hungary and the idea of a Danubian Confederation, and then it backed off due to new politics and as a consequence of the creation of the Little Entente—an alliance its own military had contributed toward creating—which it decided to use, once it was there, for its own purpose.

After supporting plans for an alliance between Prague and the SHS Kingdom (in the prospect of seeing it become a larger group of countries or even a Danubian Union, integrating most of the Central European countries and avoiding isolating some of them), Britain had to admit that it was outsmarted first by Beneš and then again by France, which took the new creation under its wing. Neither of the two states really wanted a Little Entente, but both contributed in a way to its creation, and in the case of France to its reinforcement and then survival.[304] Therefore, Britain was to take the side of Hungary for a short while before Hungary was to fall, together with Austria, into the arms of Mussolini as the leader of the malcontent states in 1927.

Why did the Quai d'Orsay's support for Hungary end? As the Foreign Office would say, France did not have the means to help Hungary, since France was in a very difficult economic and financial situation.[305] Though this remark might not have been totally irrelevant, France was not only to invest in but also to profit from Hungary's and the region's growth, since French industry, through Schneider-Creusot, had taken over many enterprises in other Successor States. But the fact that the French army had a different policy

---

304 Ádám, *Little Entente*, 218–19; Bátonyi, *op. cit.*, 177–78.
305 ADMAE, Z Europe, Hongrie 58, 154–62 ff.; Fouchet à Millerand May 12, 1920.

was a strong enough reason to see the French project of a Danubian Confederation fail. The departure of Paléologue from the Quai d'Orsay was equally important.

British Tactics against French Policy

After the war and before the signing of the Trianon Peace Treaty, Anglo–French rivalry was appearing in Central Europe. Hungary was becoming the pivotal state of this rivalry, which is no surprise, since Hungary was one of the two states of the Dual Monarchy.

Once the new Hungarian counter revolutionary government had moved back to Budapest in 1919, Britain started showing much interest in Hungary, and the British envoys considered Horthy as their man. Horthy was considered to be close to what they would define as an English gentleman, and Britain had confidence in and counted on him to keep order in Hungary after the revolution.[306] Prime Minister Bethlen was also an Anglophile—highly esteemed by the British[307]—and his task was to consolidate the regime and put Hungary back on its pre-war liberal-conservative path.

The Foreign Office consistently opposed French policy towards Hungary and Central Europe, which seemed irrational to them. They truly had little understanding for this project: after destroying the Habsburg Monarchy and supporting the creation of Czechoslovakia, France suddenly decided to support the claims of Hungary, putting it at the centre of its Central European policy and to some extent flirting with the idea of restoring the Habsburgs. Britain soon realised that it could play a role in countering France's pro-Hungarian and then pro-Danubian Union policy. But this did not mean that the diplomats sent to the different capitals of Successor States were completely objective. Some of them became champions of the interests of the states they were sent to. H.M. commissioner in Budapest, Thomas Hohler, found his niche and became a champion of Hungary's territorial claims.[308]

---

306 *DBFP*, vi, 402, Campbell to Leeper, Budapest, November 23, 1919.
307 Romsics, *Bethlen*, 99.
308 *DBFP*, series I, vol. 13, no. 78.

Nevertheless, as discussed earlier, the small group of the PID kept a close vigil and prevented the Treaty of Trianon from being altered.

Britain was not the only country to follow France's intrigues with anxiety. Italy was equally concerned by France's approach toward recreating the Habsburg Monarchy, or even something similar without the Habsburgs that could endanger the Italian World War I acquisitions.[309] The Italians also showed concern about the French initiatives towards a Danubian Confederation as described by Castellane.[310]

In Czechoslovakia, Beneš was afraid of such an alliance and worked to convince Britain that after creating the tripartite military alliance, he would broaden it by integrating Poland and Austria, as he claimed in his article published in 1922 in *Foreign Affairs*.[311] Since Poland had designs on the Teschen region in Czechoslovakia, Beneš told Take Ionescu—the Romanian foreign minister—that an alliance including Poland should have to be compatible with the common interests of both Czechoslovakia and Poland.[312]

Beneš was able to win the sympathy of George Clerk, H.M. minister to Prague, for this purpose.[313] The FO put Clerk's ideas into effect in order to counter French policy in the region by influencing Romania. So, Great Britain decided to employ a diplomacy that made the smaller French project of union a failure (Hungary, Romania and Poland).[314] Inspired by the French, Romania was preparing itself to sign a military treaty with Poland. In the interest of pushing forward this agreement, Maréchal Joseph Joffre visited Bucharest (August 1920) to convince the Romanians to take part in the war against Soviet Russia,[315] while Hungary was ready to support Poland in the same war. In October 1920 Prime Minister Lloyd George and Cur-

---

309 FO 371 C5059/2455/3, Conversation between M. Bridgeman and the Marquis della Toretta, Italian minister to Vienna, Vienna, August 21, 1920.
310 NA, FO 371 C2690/2690/62, Sir Alexander Cadogan mentions Italian concerns regarding the Marquis de Castellane's project (no date), see Carmi, *op. cit.*, 25.
311 "The Little Entente", *Foreign Affairs*, I, (1922–1923), 72.
312 Carmi, *op. cit.*, 28
313 Clerk was impressed by Beneš's idea to create a Central European block. *British Documents on Foreign Affairs* (henceforth *BDFA*), I, Clerk to Curzon, Prague, October 17, 1920, no.145; Clerk to Curzon, Prague, November 26, 1920, no.168. Ádám, *Little Entente*, 94.
314 NA, FO 371, C7503/4025, Rattigan (H.M. Minister to Bucharest) to Curzon, Bucharest, September 20, 1920.
315 NA, FO 371, C4426/4025, Rattigan to Curzon, Bucharest, August 18, 1920.

zon influenced Romania to reach an agreement with Soviet Russia. Britain considered Piłsudski to be a dangerous and inexperienced character who would bring the Entente into conflicts it did not want. Frank Rattigan, H.M. minister to Bucharest, saw great danger in putting the fate of the Little Entente into the hands of such an adventurer. He also advised better diplomacy towards Russia, which would bring about the recognition of the union of Bessarabia with Romania. In short, after direct talks between Beneš and Ionescu, and after British pressure was exerted, the direction of Romania's alliance changed (Czechoslovakia and SHS Kingdom) and became more oriented against Hungary than against Russia, as stated by Ionescu,[316] which meant that Britain knew the true purpose of the Little Entente.

We know that one month earlier H.M. high commissioner to Budapest had claimed that the French were "doing their best to promote better understanding between Hungary and Roumania [sic] and are against the idea of the 'Petite Entente'." But the French minister to Bucharest, Émile Daeschner, was of a different opinion. He thought that the members of the Quai d'Orsay were "acting short-sightedly" and "apparently desire to make Hungary the base of their Central European policy." In his opinion, however, it was doomed to be a failure.[317] In other words, not all the French diplomats voiced the same approbation for the Danubian project.

Neither the little nor the bigger French project of a Central European Union was supported by Britain; indeed, it was outright opposed to it. Britain not only hindered Quai d'Orsay policy but chose to intervene—more than providing simple encouragement—in order to support the creation of the Little Entente.

Consequently the FO had a role in contributing to the creation of the Little Entente in its strategy to counter the Quai d'Orsay, while in Czechoslovakia an embryonic military Little Entente was supported by the French army. But eventually, neither France nor Britain was the creator of the Little Entente. Beneš created it, and he was able to manipulate France and Britain in the interest of the newly established Republic of Czechoslovakia.

---

316 Carmi, op. cit., 28–29.
317 DBFP, series I, vol. xii, no. 221, Rattigan to Curzon, Bucharest, Sept. 17, 1920.

A comparison of the situations in the ministries of France and Britain reveals two very different pictures: most of the high-ranking English officers were quite aware of the fact that a strong and federalised Central Europe was necessary. As discussed above, there were officers who were supportive of a Danubian Union and even some who sympathised with the Habsburgs. In contrast, the Foreign Office was mostly against a Habsburg restoration and strongly opposed a French-sponsored Danubian Confederation centred in Budapest. This stand was to be fostered by the Millerand government's policy to use the Confederation plan for French domination in the Danubian region. What comes to light are the ambiguities of the British foreign and defence policies, which lacked a creative stabilizing plan in Central Europe. We can conclude that different ideas were clashing, and internal communication was not good enough to have the same policy in the War Office and the Foreign Office.

One could say, with slight irony, that the Danubian Confederation would have been a success if an "ideal" Entente policy had been created by combining the French Ministry of Foreign Affairs with the British War Office. This combination would have probably contributed to the realisation of the Danubian Confederation, since these two ministries would have been in "entente" with each other.

As noted above, there seems little doubt as to the role of religion when one compares the politics of these two countries. On one hand, in Protestant Britain there was little Habsburg sympathy in either of the two ministries (Foreign and War). There was, however, a certain regret among quite a few officers and even some diplomats regarding the destruction of such a grand empire, but only a few openly supported restoration.[318] On the other hand, in France the Catholic and noble milieu did have an influence on the support that Paléologue, an aristocrat himself, or later Briand[319] gave to restoration and recreation of a Danubian entity.

---

318 Carmi, *op. cit.*, 52–54.
319 I will come back to Briand's support for Karl in my chapter on the year 1921. Marquis de Castellane's visits to the Foreign Office can be interpreted as an attempt to sound out the opinion of Britain before the Paléologue Plan and Briand's much more discreet approaches.

France's somewhat adventurous projects in Hungary certainly had a destabilizing effect on the region, but at least France left a door open to an alternative to the Versailles-Little Entente system it was strongly contributing to setting up. Yet, it had missed the opportunity of proposing to work in concert with Britain to find a solution for the region.

Britain had a more logical approach and a policy involving less intrigue. Its approach was to wait until the Central European countries actually consolidated before they would propose an economic cooperation or union. Yet Britain, being an island, did not show understanding of France's fear of the potential danger that Germany, its direct neighbour, could represent in the future. The Foreign Office's problem was that the Central European question was left in the biased hands of a very small group, and moreover H.M. government had little time to waste on a region where it had few interests.

The Treaty of Trianon and British–French "Més-Entente"

The Treaty of Trianon as Ethnical Chaos

What followed the *letter d'envoi* attached to the Peace Treaty was the signing of the Treaty on June 4, 1920, in the Gallerie des Cotelles of the Grand Trianon palace in Versailles and the ratification of the document. The choice of this location does not seem innocent; it even had a gruesome element. Trianon was the favourite place of Queen Marie-Antoinette, the daughter of the highly esteemed queen of Hungary, Maria-Theresa. The French Revolution had cut off Marie-Antoinette's head, and her mother's kingdom was cut into pieces at her favourite place of residence.[320] It was, in a way, like chopping off her head again and making a statement to both the Hungarians and Austrians alike that for the second time the French Revolution had triumphed over the Habsburgs.

---

320 The location might have been even worse had it been signed in the Little Trianon palace, which were her favourite apartments.

Hungary was reduced from 282,870 km² (with Croatia, 329,000) to 93,000 km². Its population was reduced from 18.26 million to 7.6 million: 4000 km² were seceded to Austria along with 292,000 inhabitants, among which were 26,000 Hungarians; 63,000 km² were attached to Czechoslovakia, with 3.5 million inhabitants comprising approximately 700,000 to 1 million Hungarians. To Romania was given 102,000 km² with a population of 5.5 million among, which were 1.6–1.7 million Hungarians. Finally to Yugoslavia, 21,000 km² with a population of 1.6 million, of which 467,000 were Hungarians. In total 2.8 to 3.2 million Magyars found themselves in all the countries surrounding Hungary.[321]

The Slovaks, representing 2 million souls, and the Sudeten Germans, about 3.123 million, were now in centralized Czechoslovakia, with the Czechs dominating with 6,831,120. But the Hungarians, when added to the Germans, both non-Slav nationalities, already represented 4 million. Had the Slovaks joined this number, the Czechs would have been outnumbered by adding the 745,000 Ruthenians and 76,000 Poles now also living in Czechoslovakia. If considered one nation, the Czechoslovaks represented 8,798,000 of a total of 13,374,364 inhabitants in 1921. [322]

Croatians now incorporated into the SHS Kingdom represented about 3,700,000 in a country of 12 million inhabitants. Among these 12 million were 1 million Slovenes separated earlier from Austria, 5 million Serbs and the 470,000 Hungarians and other smaller nationalities.

Eventually totalling a population of 18 million, Romania had gained 5,265,000 inhabitants, among them 1.7 million Hungarians and 750,000 Germans. These nationalities, including 1 million Jews and representing only 28.8 percent of the entire population of Romania, had little effect on the unitary nation state of Romania.[323]

---

[321] The numbers differs in different Hungarian publications. It was difficult to calculate the exact number as certain citizens had double or more identities and spoke one or more languages: Glatz, Ferenc, "A kisebbség kérdés tegnap és ma", *Historia Plusz*, Historia Alapitvány, Budapest, 1993, 11; Romsics, Ignác, *The Dismantling of Historic Hungary: The Peace Traty of Trianon*, 1920, Social Sciences Monographs, Boulder, CO, 2002, 169–70.

[322] Glatz, "A kisebbség", 11; Galántai, József, *Trianon és a kisebbségvédelem*, Maecenas, Budapest, 1989, 24–32; Glatz Ferenc, *Minorities in East-Central Europe*, Europa Institute Budapest, Budapest, 1993, 39.

[323] Glatz, *Minorities*, 53, 48; Galántai, József, *A Trianoni Béke Kötés 1920*, Gondolat, Budapest, 1990, 90.

Chapter III

French-British "Més-entente" at the Peace Conference

Having seen the consequences of the treaty, it is timely to get an understanding of its reasons and the key moments of the peace talks. The French people had suffered greatly in the war as the front with Germany was mainly in France. They considered Austria-Hungary, as Germany's co-belligerents, to be likewise responsible for their four years of suffering. Since Austria-Hungary was not able to separate from Germany and was eventually even submitted militarily to Berlin towards the end of the war, the bitterness of many Frenchmen was almost as strong against Austria-Hungary as against Germany. Despite that, some in France had a soft spot for Austria—even Clemenceau, who had many friends in Vienna—but towards Hungary there was much less sympathy. This resentment was built up during the war and even earlier by historians such as Ernest Denis and Louis Eisemann in France and Seeton-Watson and Wickham Steed in Britain, who considered Hungary to be crushing its nationalities and unwilling to give them autonomy. Austria had made an effort before the war by giving regions such as Polish-inhabited Galicia a certain amount of autonomy. As we have seen, Karl had tried, and even more radically, to federalise the monarchy in October 1918, but Hungary simply refused to apply the points of the Manifesto to Transleithania.

Among other reasons for wanting to punish Hungary was that the Entente considered that it had had an important role in starting the war with key civil servants like the Hungarian Count Forgách. Then there was Béla Kun's Commune, which represented the threat of Communism in Europe and which fought against the Allies after the armistice in order to spread communism and regain territory for Hungary.

The Hungarian Delegation was presented with a draft peace treaty on January 15 at the Hôtel de Madrid in Neuilly. It matched the articles in the Versailles and Saint-Germain treaties in 290 of 364 cases.[324] Apart from the frontiers that were already established earlier, the draft forbade Hungary to reunite with Austria; demanded protection of rights for non-Hungarian minorities, including education in their mother tongue; limited its army to

---

324 Galántai, *op. cit.*

35,000 men; limited the number of new officers by imposing regulations on new officers and proscribing general conscription; forbade the manufacture or purchase of military vehicles such as tanks, naval vessels or aircraft; confiscated Hungary's Danube fleet; and eventually imposed reparations, to be determined by the Reparations Commission, that were to be paid over a period of 30 years from 1921.[325]

Once the draft peace treaty was presented and studied by the Hungarian delegation, the leader of the delegation, the legitimist Count Albert Apponyi, extensively questioned the terms because, as he claimed, they would amount to national suicide. For Apponyi, a proud Magyar aristocrat, it was almost impossible to conceive of the carving up of a thousand-year-old nation and state with a grand and ancient history by other proud and old nations. He responded that Hungary could not accept the borders without revision as doing so violated the principle of nationality defended by both the Conference and, passionately, by President Wilson, who had left Paris after the Versailles treaty. Yet the Conference rejected all arguments for maintaining Hungary's territorial integrity, even though Hungary would have accepted plebiscites in all disputed territories. The financial and economic clauses could not be met because of the impact of occupation by the Successor States and the effects of the Allied economic blockade. Philippe Berthelot representing the French head of government, Millerand, was open to no other alternative. For their part, the British and Italian prime ministers, Lloyd George and Francesco Nitti, were more open to Apponyi's arguments.[326]

The Hungarians started mobilizing contacts in London and in the British Parliament, which aired the Hungarian question in both Houses. The probable outcome was that Lord Curzon argued, at the Council of Heads of Delegation meeting on February 25, that the Hungarian answer to the draft treaty could not be ignored; it should be discussed by the three Allied leaders and more detailed matters should be referred to the Council of Ambassadors meeting in Paris.[327]

---

[325] Ibid, 90–92; Cartledge, Brian, *Mihály Károlyi and István Bethlen*, Haus Publishing Ltd, London, 2009, 96–97.
[326] Cartledge, *op. cit.*, 95.
[327] Ibid., 99–100; Romsics, *The Dismantling*, 133.

Chapter III

The debate on Hungary heated up at a meeting of the Council of Heads of Delegation at 10 Downing Street on March 3, 1920. Berthelot described the Hungarians as not having been the original settlers of the region, and as having "always proved themselves to be a most treacherous people" whose "statistics were notoriously untrustworthy".[328] Lloyd George responded: "Did M. Berthelot really believe that it would lead to peace in Central Europe if it were discovered afterwards that the claims of Hungary were sound, and that a whole community of Magyars had been handed over like cattle to Czechoslovakia and to Transylvania [sic, Romania], simply because the conference had refused to examine the Hungarian case?"[329]

These British arguments were supported by Nitti at both Council meetings, but Berthelot was against any amendment of either territorial or financial provisions of the treaty. The French blocked any re-negotiation of the peace treaty.[330] The only step that could be taken was to send the issue to the Council of Ambassadors and Foreign Ministers. Unfortunately for Hungary, this Council had received a memorandum by Allen Leeper of the Foreign Office, who was a great supporter of Romanian and Yugoslav territorial claims.[331]

Since the victors in the war had promised most of Hungary to the new Successor States and Romania during the war, only small changes could be envisaged, and Lloyd George himself was conscious of the fact that Apponyi should have concentrated on the details of the new frontiers instead of attacking the whole treaty.[332]

While the sessions with the Hungarian Delegation were ongoing in Paris, the Danubian (Paléologue) Plan negotiations with Hungary were to be started in March. Millerand understood that some sort of gesture had to be made towards Hungary. The French government had behaved most harshly toward the Hungarian delegation, whose members were under quasi house arrest in the Hôtel de Madrid in Neuilly; yet in the second phase, after March, the Quai d'Orsay team (headed by the Romanian boyar's son

---

328 *DBFP*,1919–1939, 1st Series, Vol. VII, no. 46, 384.
329 Romsics, *The Dismantling*, 134; *DBFP*,1919–1939, 1st Series, Vol. VII, no. 46, 386.
330 Cartledge, *op. cit.*, 101.
331 Romsics, *The Dismantling*, 135; *DBFP*,1919–1939, 1st Series, Vol. VII, no. 54, 440–449
332 Cartledge, *op. cit.*, 97–98

Maurice Paléologue) treated Hungary almost as Central Europe's most favoured state. While in March Berthelot was still referring to Hungarians as swindlers, in August Millerand was asking his diplomats to bar the route to the Little Entente in order to protect his Budapest-centred plan. This letter is ample evidence that the Paléologue Plan's aim was not just about getting the Hungarians to sign the treaty, it was really about a consolidating plan for the Central European region.[333]

At first glance, the French tactics were quite clever, alternating the carrot and the stick. After all, the French government got Hungary to sign a very harsh and penalizing peace that had already been postponed. But Hungary would have had to sign it anyhow, as it had no real choice to refuse it. Looking at the situation more closely, a more mitigated picture emerges. France failed to create a Danubian Confederation and to establish its economic and banking headquarters in Budapest. It also failed to hinder the creation of the Little Entente by its own war-time allies. In conclusion, it seems that France had neither the economic means nor the political will for a constructive and stable Central European policy.

Britain had a more direct and, one could say, more balanced approach to the Hungarian question during the peace negotiations. It did not promise things it could not deliver to Hungary. Both Lloyd George and Nitti did show more understanding towards Hungarian grievances and could foresee the dangers of a dissatisfied and revisionist Hungary that Italy would soon come to support.

The incredibly punitive measures imposed on Hungary—reparations, limitations on the military, the drastic reduction of territory—looked similar to those of the Versailles treaty itself. The two treaties were similar not only in geographical location but also in that they were similarly harsh on both Hungary and Germany. Regarding Germany, the Allies insisted more on reparations and the occupation of the Rhineland, to serve as a *cordon sanitaire*, and less on reducing its territory that was inhabited mostly by Germans. Significantly, the Trianon conditions were even harsher than the

---

333 We will come back to this interesting letter in our next section. ADMAE, Z Europe, Hongrie 47, 71–72 ff. Telegram from Prime Minister Millerand to most of the French legations of Europe, August 24, 1920.

Chapter III

Saint-Germain conditions, since Trianon awarded a part of western Hungary, now called Burgenland, to Austria—which was not less responsible for the war than Hungary—on the basis of ethnicity. Yet Trianon did not regard the regions on the borders with Romania, Czechoslovakia or the SHS Kingdom with Hungarian ethnic majorities as deserving the same equitable treatment. Thus Austria's territory became much larger than the original medieval Archduchy of Austria. Now Burgenland, Styria, Voralberg, Tyrol (without Süd Tyrol), Carinthia and Salzburg became part of Austria because they were German speaking. There was talk of granting Voralberg to Switzerland, but that did not happen because the latter refused. In two cases self-determination was not applied in regard to Austria: Süd Tyrol, the large German-speaking region that Austria lost to Italy and the Sudetenland, which became Czechoslovak. In this case, too, self-determination was not applied. Concerning Hungary, Apponyi would say to the Supreme Council that not even Germany, Austria or Bulgaria was to go through territorial changes of such magnitude.[334] Following Germany, it was Hungary's turn to consider the peace it was offered as a *"Diktat"*.

After Trianon, Italy was the first to support Hungary's revisionist claims. Which was not surprising, as Italy was also dissatisfied and built up its own irredentist claims. In the 1930s Britain was to follow the path of reconciliation with Germany because the Versailles treaty had failed to appease that vanquished state. The hard peace that France imposed on Hungary as well was going to bring the latter on a forced itinerary of revision, and given its location on the map, it could hardly resist the temptation of aligning itself with an equally revisionist Germany that had become Hungary's western neighbour in 1938.

Almost immediately after the armistice, the Croats and Slovaks would also start their resistance to assimilation into the new successor "nation" states. The Wilsonian dream of self-determination proved to be just a bluff, because it was applied in practically none of the Successor States. Ethnic Hungarians had no real chance to a fair plebiscite on the choice of their future homeland, with the exception of the town of Sopron/Oedenburg, which chose to remain in Hungary.

---

334 Cartledge, *op cit.*, 96.

The End of the Monarchy and the Peace Treaty

The peace conditions that came from above and were imposed on Austria-Hungary by Wilson in January 1918 were belatedly accepted by Karl, who encouraged the different nationalities to create their own national councils in October. The conditions marked the last act in the destruction of Austria-Hungary, a phenomenon triggered by an external factor: the Fourteen Points. The internal factor was that no solution was applied earlier to the nationality problem in Austria-Hungary. But there was another aspect linked to the external one: the different national councils hastily declared independence from the Monarchy so as to withdraw themselves of any war responsibility linked to Austria-Hungary's participation on the wrong side, that is, being the losers. Thus, the atmosphere of general disintegration could no longer be stopped. For those nationalities not already allied to the Entente during the war, separation from Austria-Hungary was crucial in order to negotiate an advantageous peace. At least they thought so, and this thinking was also followed by the Károlyi government when it declared Hungary's independence.

Assigning war responsibility for the Duplice and its allies in the peace treaties was essential for the Allies. Any questioning of this responsibility could make the whole edifice of Versailles crumble. The aim of the revisionist movement was, therefore, to prove that the responsibility was shared. Tsarist Russia, the first state to mobilise its army at the German border in 1914, having disappeared, it was no longer possible to compile an accusation against this Panslavist empire—the supporter of its little brother Serbia—and try to prove its responsibility for the war. Such an accusation would eventually have led to the assignment of shared responsibility by both the Allies and the Duplice, meaning that the Allies would have to allow revision.

Despite the fact that there was no possibility, for the time being, of reconsidering war responsibility, the revisionist movement did advance over time and its international leadership was embraced wholeheartedly by Germany, enabled by Britain's appeasement policy.

The problem of the Paris treaties lay in their lack of impartiality and equitable treatment between winners and losers. This was not the case in 1815, when France's territorial integrity was spared, unlike that of Austria-Hungary in 1919–1920. The big difference between 1815 and 1918 is that France was not partitioned. Henry Kissinger wrote that in 1815 there was "a conciliatory peace [...]; a balance of powers; and a feeling of shared legitimacy."[335] This impression of shared legitimacy was lacking in Paris, which was neither equitable nor did it give the impression of legitimacy for all parties. These considerations are among the key reasons for the failure of the Versailles system.

---

335 Kissinger, Henry, *Diplomatie*, Paris, Fayard, 1996, 271.

CHAPTER IV

The Croatians' Struggle for Autonomy

The Zagreb National Council and the Army

Southern Slavs, Yugoslavs…

It is important to use the right words, in its meaning of the day and not of today, to describe notions relating to the Slavonic peoples and the region between Hungary and the Adriatic Sea, as each of the terms appeared in a specific historical context.

In general, the terms South or Southern Slavs or Yugoslavs will be used here to describe the population called (until not so long ago, when Yugoslavia still existed) Yugoslavs. Originally, Yugoslavs (as they described themselves) were only the Southern Slavs of the Habsburg territories—Croatians, Slovenes, Bosnians and Serbs and not including the Serbs of the Kingdom of Serbia. The adjective "Yugoslav" is best delineated by the Yugoslav Committee of London,[336] which represented the Southern Slavs living in the Dual Monarchy during World War I. The Serbs of the Habsburg Monarchy—including Bosnia-Herzegovina— were called *Prečani* by the Serbs of the Kingdom of Serbia.

---

[336] The Yugoslav Committee's leaders were Ante Trumbić, Franco Supilo, Ivan Meštrović. They acted as the representatives of Habsburg Southern Slavs. Supilo pleaded for a union with Serbia with a federation of peoples with equal rights, or a federation of all Slavs living in the former Dual Monarchy. The other members were for union with Serbia. Supilo left in 1916 but the Serbs undermined the international recognition of the Committee in order to keep its hands free for Greater-Serbian ambitions. In the negotiations with Serbia, the Yugoslav Committee defended the view of post-war Yugoslavia as a federation of peoples. The form of the new state was negotiated in Corfu and resulted in the Declaration of Corfu signed on July 20, 1917. The new state would be a kingdom, and the questions of the future state organisation and the majority required in the constituent assembly would be settled later. At the end of the war both parties would differ on the interpretation of the agreement. Stallaerts Robert, Jeannine Laurens, *Historical Dictionary of the Republic of Croatia*, Scarecrow Press, Inc., Lanham, MD, London, 1995, 234–35.

The SHS (Slovene, Croat and Serb) State—also called SHS State (H for *Hrvat*)—was the first state proclaimed in Zagreb on October 19, 1918, which united Serbs, Croatians and Slovenes of the Habsburg Monarchy without Serbia.[337] The SHS Kingdom appeared once the union of the SHS State and the Kingdom of Serbia was signed. The term "Yugoslavia" was already being used in French diplomatic correspondence before its official adoption in 1929, when King Alexander Karađorđević centralized the administration, introduced a dictatorship and changed the name to "Yugoslavia" or "Kingdom of Yugoslavia".

Serbs of Croatia were already known as "Serbo-Croats" during the Austro-Hungarian Monarchy, but the term could also apply to a Croatian who accepted the union with Serbia, and in that case also to a member of the Serbo-Croat movement.

Slovenian-Croat-Serb National Council of Zagreb

Croatia-Slavonia held a special place among the countries of the House of Habsburg. It formed an integral part of the Crown of St. Stephen, but it was autonomous. Considering the agreements of 1868, Croatia had its own parliament, the *Sabor*, a Ban (a sort of governor representing Budapest), a local government and a minister of Croatia in the Council of Ministers in Budapest. Thus Croatia had constitutionally-recognised autonomy, a unique case in Transleithania. A French observer commented on the nature of this status: "Elle [La Croatie] n'est pas satisfaite de cette position, car elle aspire à l'indépendance complète, mais cette autonomie représente une valeur, petite, il est vrai, mais une valeur quand même."[338]

When Emperor Karl made his federalizing manifesto on October 16, 1918, in response to Wilson's Fourteen Points, the Slovene–Croat–Serb National Council (a de facto national assembly)—comprising the Southern Slavs or Yugoslavs of the Austro-Hungarian Monarchy—took a series of de-

---

337 Ibid., 234–35.
338 "It [Croatia] is not satisfied with this position, for it aspires to complete independence, but this autonomy represents a value, small, it's true, but a value nonetheless." ADMAE, Z Europe, Yougoslavie 40. f. 17. Politique en Croatie, September 12, 1918.

cisions in five points. Among the points were the demand of uniting the Slovene, Croatian and Serb-inhabited territories in an independent state and the rejection of the imperial manifesto of federalization, which implied the refusal of "any future proposal directed towards a solution resolving partly our national exigencies."[339] Another point of the declaration demanded that their own delegates represent their interests at the peace conference. Wilson, for his part, considered the Fourteen Points to be outdated and that it was their decision and not his to determine whether Austria-Hungary could satisfy their rights and destiny.[340]

But there were still Croatian politicians who wanted to find a legal solution with Vienna and Budapest. On October 21, a delegation of the originally republican but now more and more pro-Habsburg Croatian Party of Pure Rights (Čista Stranka Prava) led by its president, Aleksandar Horvat, travelled to Bad Ischl, the imperial summer residence[341] to ask the monarch to grant Croatia the same status as Austria and Hungary, in other words to recognise Croatia as a third state (trialism). Karl told the delegation that he was ready to accept the new state, but he needed the Hungarian Parliament's green light to relieve him of his coronation oath regarding the integrity of the Hungarian Crown. While the legitimist delegation was in Austria, Wilson's message was published in the Croatian papers, and demonstrations were held to celebrate the independence of Croatia. In the general confusion, a big demonstration was organised for October 22, with 50,000 people arriving to celebrate the Yugoslav State of the Monarchy. The Kronrat (Crown Council including Hungarian Prime Minister Sándor Wekerle), disconnected from realties on the ground, had decided that same day to refuse the unity of Czechoslovaks. Concerning the Yugoslav question, Karl decided that the two governments had to take measures to let the Southern

---

339 *Jugoszláviai 1918–1941, Dokumentumok*, Szeged, 1989, no.27. Even though after its radical decision not to accept any new form of contract with Habsburgs, one has to underline that the National Council kept good relations with the court aristocracy: Ban Mihailović became joint commissioner of Foreign Affairs and Count Rulmer became president of the Agricultural Committee of the Council. ADMAE, Z Europe, Yougoslavie 24, 2–6 ff., Résumé d'impression du Ct Carbonnier, Att. Mil. en Serbie, Belgrade, November 29, 1918.
340 Adler, *op. cit.*, 245.
341 Kazimirović, Vasa, *NDH u svetlu nemačkih dokumenata i dnevnika Gleza fon Horstenau 1941–1944*, Nova knjiga, Beograd 1987, 56–57.

Slavs unify within the Monarchy, even though Wekerle opposed this idea and wanted the union to happen only "within the Crown of Saint Stephen".[342]

Back in Zagreb, the National Council, suddenly not knowing whether their freedom came from Wilson or Karl, went to see the Croatian ban, Mihailović, and asked him what the reaction would be if the Council were to declare its legal attachments with Hungary as null. Not knowing what to answer, the ban consulted the Hungarian prime minister, who said that it would be for the Peace Conference to decide. Then the ban turned to Karl, who said that he would not oppose it, but it was the Sabor that had to decide.[343]

As there was no clear response from Vienna or Budapest and Croatian interests needed to be defended, the legitimist Party of Pure Rights decided to join the new National Council of Zagreb, though it was not accepted by the coalition ruling the Council and by Croatian Serb politician Svetozar Pribičević—vice president of the SHS National Council and later an independence fighter.[344] Nevertheless, the Party of Pure Rights would reappear later at the SHS Kingdom's Constitutional Assembly elections.

In Budapest, positions were slowly changing. The new National Assembly of Hungary recognised the autonomy of all nationalities of Hungary on the basis of the right to self-determination within Hungary. It also recognised the Polish, Ukrainian, Czechoslovak, Austrian-German and Yugoslav states and wished to enter in political and economic alliance with them. The Yugoslav State was at last confirmed as a federated state of the Monarchy![345]

Eventually it was the Croatian Sabor, recognised by all belligerent governments and with respect for the right of self-governance, that made the decision to create a sovereign state of Slovenes, Croats and Serbs on October 29, 1918:

> [...] all relations first between the Croatian-Slavonian and Dalmatian Kingdom and second between the Hungarian Kingdom and the Austrian Empire will cease to be. [...] the Croatian-Hungarian Compromise [1868 compromise] will be wiped out and annulled. [...] Dalmatia, Cro-

---

342 Adler, *op. cit.*, 232–233, 247; Benda, *op. cit.*, 840.
343 Adler, *op. cit.*, 247.
344 Ibid., 255–56.
345 Ibid., 250.

atia, Slavonia (comprising Rijeka) is declared completely independent from Hungary and Austria.[346]

This new state was created out of the territory of Croatia-Slavonia, Dalmatia and Carniola, but no decision was taken to separate from the Habsburg dynasty. On the same day, the Serbo-Croat Coalition majority had the Sabor transfer its political authority to the National Council of Zagreb, and with this political power, the National Council also received the military power.

The story continued then in Geneva. The *procès verbal* of the Geneva Conference (November 6–9)—a gathering of the Croat and Slovene representatives and the Serb Government—shows that "the Serb Kingdom and the National Council of Zagreb sets up a ministry to organise the united SHS State."[347] With this, a period opened that would last until June 28, 1921, the day of Vidovdan,[348] when the Constitution was published.

Referring to the Zagreb National Council's declaration of October 19, 1918, the SHS Kingdom was declared in Belgrade on November 18 with the following words:

> The Slovene, Croat and Serb who revolted on the territory of the Austro-Hungarian Monarchy and created a temporary independent nation state—inspired by the theory of national unity and supported by the great democratic concept, that all peoples have the right to decide of their fate—have showed their willingness already in the National Council declaration of October 19 to unite in a unitary Nation state with Serbia and Crna Gora [Montenegro], which state will comprise all the territories where Southern Slav ethnic groups live.[349]

The problem was that there was no mention of the form of union with the Kingdom of Serbia in the October 19 declaration. Was there going to

---

[346] Declaration of the Serb–Croat–Slovene State, *Jugoszláviai 1918–1941, Dokumentumok*, no. 28.
[347] The *process-verbal* of the Geneva Conference, *op. cit.*, no. 29.
[348] June 28 is the day of the assassination of Archduke Franz Ferdinand in 1914 and the day of the battle of Kosovo Polje in 1389.
[349] Declaration of the Creation of the SHS Kingdom, *op. cit.*, no. 33.

be some form of autonomy for the joining entities? There was, however, a hint as to the nature of this union with the words "unite in a unitary Nation state", obviously an assimilative nation state that would force all nationalities into one Serbian-led Yugoslav nation. On November 23, 1918, Serb occupation ended the independent SHS State. On December 1, union with the Kingdom of Serbia was achieved under pressure and without any plebiscite. In reaction to this, the next weeks and months would see the development of resistance and revolts, both political and military alike.

This sequence of events shows clearly that the Croatians had no intention initially of joining the Kingdom of Serbia in a new state. What they wished for was an independant Yugoslav state. There was also an intention of remaining in some form within the Monarchy, and it was the activity of the Croatian Serbians that brought the new Yugoslav state under Svetozar Pribičević to unite with Serbia-Montenegro.

France's Policy and its Unreliable Diplomat in Belgrade

Just before the armistice, France was against the creation of a greater Serbia. Neither Stephane Pichon nor Philippe Berthelot—then deputy director of diplomatic and commercial affairs—would officially support the union of Serbia with the Yugoslavs of Austria-Hungary before an agreement was struck between them; this was due to the Treaty of London with Italy. Clemenceau even promised Vittorio Emanuele Orlando (who represented Italy at the Paris Peace Conference) on November 5, 1918, not to recognise any Yugoslav State before the application of the clauses of the armistice. Clemenceau, had a completely different picture of central-south-eastern Europe and on November 15 he went as far as to say to Ante Trumbić, the Croat leader who became the first foreign minister of the SHS Kingdom, that the Yugoslavs of the Dual Monarchy should consider whether they wanted to be associated with Austria in a Danubian Confederation. His intention was, naturally, to avoid Austria's Anschluss to Germany.[350]

---

350 Pavlovic, Vojislav, *Une conception traditionaliste de la politique orientale de la France, Le vicomte Joseph de Fontenay, envoyé plénipotentaire auprès du Roi Pierre 1er Karageorgevitch (1917–21)*, http://istorija.tripod.com/fontenay.htm, (7.24.2018), 3.

Such was not the policy of Joseph de Fontenay, the French envoy to Belgrade since 1917, who was in complete symbiosis with Nicola Pašić—prime minister of Serbia and of the SHS Kingdom (from December 1, 1918)—in his aim to build a strong greater Serbia that could counter "German" (German and Austrian alike) influence in the Balkans and would avoid submitting Serbia, like during the Obrenović dynasty, to the Habsburgs. Fontenay considered the Serbs as the liberators of the Southern Slavs from Habsburg domination. He was also against a confederation[351] of Yugoslav states, which he felt would only bring instability, as they would be under the influence of neighbouring states such as Italy, which was positioning itself as Austria's successor in the Balkans.[352] As we will see, Fontenay's remarks hastened the development of anti-Croatian sentiments in Belgrade. His intrigue-laden diplomacy was to bring many other worries to the Quai d'Orsay.

Military Resistance

One of the main forces of Croatian resistance was to be found among Austro-Hungarian officers of Croatian origin, and one of the main figures in this group was General Stephan Freiherr (Baron) Sarkotić von Lovcen. The general proved to be quite authoritarian during the war, when he became governor or *Landeschef* of Bosnia-Herzegovina after the assassination of Franz Ferdinand. He sympathised with the ideas of Josip Frank, the founder of the *Hrvatska Čista Stranka Prava* (Croatian Party of Pure Rights). The Frankists advocated the Trialist solution of Archduke Franz Ferdinand, which consisted of the unification in an autonomous union of Croatia-Slavonia (part of the Kingdom of Hungary), Dalmatia and Slovenia (which were in Austria), and Bosnia-Herzegovina (which was a condominium of both Austria and Hungary). The greatest enemies of the Frankists were the Serbs, and Sarkotić took ruthless measures against Serbs who were plotting for a pan-Serbian Kingdom.[353]

---

351 There is no mention whether he was thinking of a Confederation or more of a federation that the republican Croats such as Radić were asking for.
352 ADMAE, Z Europe, Autriche 51, Fontenay à Pichon, Paris, Octobre 24, 1918.
353 Banac, Ivo, *The National Question in Yugoslavia: Origins, History, Politics*, Cornell University Press, Ithaca, NY, 1984, 89–95, 397.

Chapter IV

Sarkotić remained in Sarajevo after the desertion of his troops. The only faithful soldiers who remained with him in Sarajevo were a battalion of the Galician Guard, made up of Ukrainians. The National Council of Zagreb demanded his immediate resignation on October 30, 1918, but he refused and remained in Sarajevo.[354] Sarkotić did eventually resign as Landeschef of Bosnia-Herzegovina on November 1 in front of a delegation of the National Assembly of Bosnia-Herzegovina, to whom he declared: "Now you have the power." Nonetheless, they continued to await his decisions until November 3, 1918.[355] This indicates that the Bosnian Muslims were not as comfortable with the changes that they were undergoing and with the switch of sovereignty from Vienna–Budapest to Belgrade. Sarkotić would leave on November 5, when his Galician Guard dissolved, and Serb troops were approaching Sarajevo. He said goodbye to his staff and headed to Zagreb, where he was arrested.[356] There, he was held for ten days at the Hotel Palace, where he tried to commit suicide three times before he was finally released and asked to leave Croatia as soon as possible. From there he went to Vienna and then to Graz.[357] Before his resignation, Sarkotić was hoping to create a separate Croatian or Yugoslav army with himself at its head, and this solution was, in his view, the only way to hold the Serbs back.

Another k. u. k. officer shared Sarkotić's concern. Colonel Slavko Kvaternik was the National Assembly of Zagreb's chief of General Staff and official advisor of the old Austro-Hungarian Supreme Head Quarters.[358] He was opposed to the Serbs and was close to Ivo Frank, son of Josip Frank, Kvaternik's brother-in-law. Kvaternik thought that in the new government "the actual officers will not stay in their positions, especially if they are Croatians." His words were soon to be confirmed.[359]

---

354 Spence, Richard B., "General Stephan Sarkotić von Lovcen and Croatian Nationalism", *Canadian Review of Studies in Nationalism*, XVII, 1–2, 1990, 150.
355 Adler, J., *L'Union Forcée: La Croatie et la Création de l'Etat Yougoslave (1918)*, Geneva, 1997, 282–83.
356 The departure of Sarkotić is presented very differently by Adler than by Spencer. The latter says that Sarkotić tried to hold on to his position and had to deal with a lot of mass demonstrations. Ibid.
357 Ibid., 300.
358 Kvaternik was Josip Frank's son in law and was later one of the founders, with Ante Pavelić, of the pro-nazi Ustaša Mouvement, though married to an ethnic Jew (Olga Frank's father converted to Catholicism from Judaism).
359 Adler, *op.cit.*, 327.

Kvaternik was sent by the Yugoslav Council of Zagreb to visit the Belgrade office of General Paul Henrys (commander of the French eastern army) in order to present his project to set up an army. They already had 15,000 men and could raise 50,000, with abundant weapons. They only lacked uniforms. Coinciding with the visit, the National Council of Zagreb voted for the dissolution of the old Yugoslav army and the reconstruction of it with Serb officers. The reaction of the French minister of war, Pichon, to any of these solutions was negative, and he favoured only one solution, that of subordinating the Croatians to the Serbs.[360]

Following the armistice (November 3), on November 5 Clemenceau ordered General Franchet d'Espèrey to occupy Bosnia-Herzegovina and the area north of the rivers Danube and Sava (in the direction of Voivodina and Croatia) in order to support the political and military interests of Serbia. This green light was in direct contradiction to the thoughts Clemenceau expressed later on (November 11) supporting an Austrian-Yugoslav federation.[361] In fact, Clemenceau considered that he had to defend the political interests of Serbia exclusively in Bosnia-Herzegovina and north of the rivers Sava and Danube, but he did not mention Croatia. However, he did say that Franchet should "occupy regions that are strategically important for peacekeeping and continuation of military operations" and all this in conformity with article 4 of the Armistice of November 4.[362] To the north of the Sava was the inland part of Croatia, and since Italy wanted the Adriatic coastline, such Serbian occupation was not in contradiction to Italy's interests. The Serbs did not have to be asked twice to move into Croatia.

Following the breakup of Austria-Hungary, local national committees were created in towns and communes all across Croatia as representatives of the Zagreb National Assembly's power. The only problem was that these committees were self-proclaimed, and Zagreb had absolutely no control

---

360 ADMAE, Z Europe, Yougoslavie 54, 65 ff. Paris, December 4, 1918, Prés. du Conseil à Ministre des Affaires étrangères (onwards MAE); ADMAE, Z Europe, Yougoslavie 54, 67ff., 1918, Pichon à Fontenay, Paris, December 12; ADMAE, Z Europe, Yougoslavie 54, 68–69 ff, Pichon à Prés. du Conseil, Paris, December 4, 1918.
361 Adler, *op. cit.*, 291–92.
362 Clemenceau à Franchet d'Espèrey, Paris, November 6, 1918, *Les Armées françaises dans la Grande Guerre*, Paris 1934, 8 vols., vol. 3, Annexes I, document no. 1751, 508, 509.

over them. The committees created by Serbs sent emissaries to the Serbian army inviting it to occupy their villages and towns. As a result, on November 5 Zagreb received sixteen calls from Croatian localities asking for help against Serbian invasion.[363]

Not even a month after the green light from Paris, the Serbs, led by Kvaternik, started cleansing the Croatian forces of all Croatian officers and integrating those who remained into the Serb army. In reaction, there were revolts on many military bases. In Kostajnica, a meeting of the local national committee had to be interrupted because of a conflict between two groups, one shouting "long live the Republic" and "down with King Peter" and the other hailing the King of Serbia. In Osijek, there was a danger of confrontation between the Serb army and the SHS one. In Bjelovar, 600 legitimist soldiers shouted as they fled: "Listen to the voice of the knight, listen to our lord, King Karl."[364]

The capital, Zagreb, was soon to be the scene of violence. On December 5, a pacific and popular cortege went through the streets headed by 200 soldiers of two Croatian regiments of the old Habsburg army carrying Croatian flags. The participants shouted, "Long live the Croatian Republic", "Long live Radić" and "Down with King Peter". This degenerated into an armed confrontation with troops loyal to the SHS Council and resulted in fourteen deaths and more than twenty casualties. The Serb troops disarmed the protestors and occupied the city.[365] A large number of soldiers were arrested, and a Serb colonel was charged with the task of reorganising the Yugoslav army by demobilizing those of the old Austrian regiments who remained.[366]

On December 10, 1918, Milan Pribičević, head of the Serbian military mission in Zagreb, communicated to all governments that were successors of Austria-Hungary (Zagreb, Sarajevo, Ljubljana and Split) that the old k.u.k. army will be dissolved, and the new army will be made of the Serbian army and its volunteers.[367]

---

363 Adler, *op. cit.*, 292-93.
364 Ibid., 328.
365 Ibid.
366 ADMAE, Z Europe, Autriche 59, Bureau des Nationalités à Pichon, Berne, November 11, 1918.
367 Adler, *op. cit*, 330.

Historian Jasna Adler claims that with the military occupation, the nucleus of resistance was finished.[368] But it should not be forgotten that there were other uprisings of Croatian troops later in 1919, such as those in Našice, Zagreb, Bjelovar, Maribor (Slovenia) and Varaždin, which were described by a Croatian agent of France:

> Des évènements caractéristiques se déroulaient dans la vieille garnison du célèbre régiment de Warasdin Nr 16 à Bjelovar. Le commandement de cette garnison fut confié à un capitaine, qui était déjà en retraite pour son agitation serbophile. Les postes les plus élevés furent occupés par les officiers Serbo-croates, pendant le vieux régime, accusée de trahison. Les garnisons réunies en parade, refusent de prêter le serment. Un détachement Serbe avec un commandant Serbe prit le commandement. Les officiers reçurent l'ordre d'occuper leurs nouveaux postes en Serbie et Bosnie. Refus d'exécution et jusqu'à ce jour ces officiers attendent les évènements.[369]

Two regiments in Maribor—Marburg (Slovenia)—and Varaždin had revolted at the same time as Italian troops were moving across their demarcation line while claiming that they wanted to occupy Ljubljana.[370]

Slovenian soldiers who refused to serve the king of Serbs were imprisoned. Other Slovenes wanted to liberate them, but the Serbs opened fire on them. Many soldiers were killed, but the Slovenes were victorious, liberated the prisoners and fled into the mountains of Bachar [Bakar] with materiel and cannons. As analysed in a report of a Croatian agent close to the

---

368 Ibid.
369 "Characteristic events were taking place in the old garrison of the celebrated regiment of Warasdin No. 16 in Bjelovar. The command of this garrison was entrusted to a captain who was already retired for his Serbophile agitation. The most elevated posts were occupied by the Serbo-Croatian officers, during the old regime, accused of treason. The garrisons united in parade refuse to take the oath. A Serb detachment with a Serb commander took over command. The officers received the order to occupy their new posts in Serbia and Bosnia. Refusal to carry out orders and to this day these officers are awaiting events." ADMAE, Z Europe, Yougoslavie 40, f. 76 f., d'un agent à l'essai, May 16, 1919.
370 ADMAE, Z Europe, Yougoslavie 40. 100 f., Fontenay à MAE, Belgrade, April 30, 1919; op. cit., f. 83, 27 Juillet 1919, Fontenay à Pichon.

Croatian autonomist Peasant Party: "This revolt, fruit of a great political deception, will have grave consequences."[371]

It seems that some French observers, in this case military men, had realised that the situation in Croatia and Slovenia was much to the disadvantage of the Yugolsavs of Austria-Hungary:

> Les causes directes des mutineries de Maribor [Slovenia] et de Warasdin [Croatia], semblent être les suivants: Les Serbes considèrent les Officiers [sic] et soldats Yougo-Slaves comme des ennemis vaincus. Les soldes ne sont pas unifiées et de nombreux avantages sont faits aux militaires Serbes. L'équipement, l'habillement, la nourriture des soldats Yougo-Slaves sont déplorables.
>
> Les Serbes ont eu la prétention de constituer les divisions Yougo-Slaves sur le même modèle que les divisions Serbes. De ce fait ils se heurtent tous les jours à des difficultés, qu'ils cherchent à résoudre de la façon la plus brutale. Je citerai par exemple, le cas des sous-officiers supérieures ; de l'ancienne Autriche, qui étaient pourvus d'un grade assez important, et redeviennent des caporaux de la nouvelle Armée, le grade correspondant aux leurs n'existent pas dans l'Armée Serbe.
>
> Les Officiers:—La question des Officiers est beaucoup plus grave encore. La grande majorité des Officiers Yougo-Slaves [sic], servant dans la division de la Drave, (j'ignore ce qui se passe en Croatie) n'a pas encore été reconnue par le gouvernement Serbe,— La situation de ces gens d'une instruction et d'une éducation moyenne très convenable, qui servent naturellement dans l'armée S.H.S. qui se sont battus dernièrement pour la cause commune contre L'Autriche allemande ; et qui peuvent d'un moment à l'autre être renvoyés chez eux, comme des domestiques, sans pension, est extrêmement précaire.
>
> Un certain nombre d'entre eux provient des régions occupées par les Italiens. Sans fortune, ayant tout perdu pendant la guerre, quelques uns se sont échappés de Trieste, etc… pour venir servir ici. Quelle sera leur attitude quand on refusera de les accepter dans cette Armée.

---

371 ADMAE, Z Europe, Yougoslavie 40, 90 f., Compte rendu (exposé d'un personnage du parti Radic), August 5, 1919.

De vieux Colonels illettrés et à la retraite sont appelés ici pour prendre la place des techniciens Slovènes et anciens Chefs de service, qui deviennent de ce fait des employés subalternes.
Les officiers ont eu une attitude parfaitement loyale dans les derniers incidents en sera-t-il de même plus tard, quand le 2 août dit-on, ils auront communications de la décision de Belgrade à leur sujet?
Certains d'entre eux m'ont prédit, que des événements semblables a ceux de Maribor, se produiraient à Ljubljana dès le retour des troupes Slovènes, qui se trouvent actuellement en Croatie [...][372]

This example in Slovenia was characteristic of the situation in Croatia as well and confirms the Croatian claim that they were newly led by people with little education.[373] This was also a cultural problem, a confrontation between

---

372 "The direct causes of the mutinies of Maribor [Slovenia] and of Warasdin [Croatia] seem to be the following: the Serbs consider the Yugoslav officers and soldiers as vanquished enemies. The wages are not unified and numerous advantages are granted to the Serbian soldiers. The equipment, the clothing, the food of the Yugoslav soldiers are deplorable./ The Serbs had the pretention of forming the Yugoslav divisions based on the same model as the Serb divisions. Hence, they daily come up against difficulties which they seek to resolve in the most brutal fashion. I would cite, for example, the case of superior non-commissioned officers of the former Austria, who held a rather important rank and become lance corporals in the new Army, [as] the rank corresponding to theirs does not exist in the Serbian Army./ The officers: The matter of the officers is far more serious. The great majority of the Yugoslav officers serving in the Drave division (I'm unaware of what transpires in Croatia) has not yet been recognised by the Serb government. The situation of these people of average training and education that is quite appropriate, who naturally serve in the army of the State of Slovenes, Croats and Serbs, who last fought for the common cause against German Austria, and who can be sent home from one moment to the next like domestic servants, without a pension, is extremely precarious./ A certain number of them hail from the regions occupied by the Italians. Without means, having lost everything during the war, some of them escaped from Trieste, etc. [...] in order to come and serve here. What will their attitude be when faced with the refusal to accept them in this Army./ Some old illiterate Colonels in retirement are called here to take the place of the Slovene technicians and old department heads who, as a result, become subaltern employees./ The officers had a perfectly loyal attitude during the final incidents, will this remain the case later on when on 2 August, it is said, they will receive communication of Belgrade's decision concerning them?/ Certain ones among them predicted to me that events similar to those of Maribor would come about in Ljubljana upon the return of the Slovene troops, who are presently located in Croatia [...]" ADMAE, Z Europe, Yougoslavie 40, 100 f., extrait du Cap. Lagarde de la Mis. française détachée à Ljubljana, Zagreb, August 15, 1919.
373 Later, in 1921, the French minister to Belgrade would say, "Les Croates étaient habitués à une administration catégoriquement meilleure que celle des Serbes [...] elle est abominablement primitive, simpliste, rustique; elle manque de souplesse et d'intelligence, d'activité. Et c'est certainement une des sources du mécontentement." (The Croats were accustomed to an administration that was categorically superior to that of the Serbs [...] it is abominably primitive, simplistic, rustic; it lacks suppleness and intelligence, activity. And it is certainly one of the causes of discontent.) ADMAE, Z Europe, Yougoslavie 48, 149 f., Clément-Simon à Briand, Belgrade, September 28, 1921.

Chapter IV

two worlds, between two different systems of values: the Vienna- (Western) orientated officers educated in Austria or Hungary—especially those from the General Staff Academy of Wiener Neustadt—practicing the Habsburg code of honour, which was tolerant and cosmopolitan, faced the nationalist and pan-Slav Orthodox zeal of the Serbs, inspired by Tsarist Russia.[374] The consequence was the departure of many highly educated k.u.k. officers, or their expulsion from the new Yugoslav army. Those who did not leave the country would join the subterranean anti-Serb resistance. But there was also a political resistance that would sooner or later lead to separatism.

The Graz Croatian Committee and the Others

The Graz Committee

In 1918, two parties were opposing union with the Serb Kingdom: the pro-Habsburg Pure Party of Rights and the Croatian Peoples Peasant Party of Stepan Radić.

The Pure Party of Rights (Čista Stranka Prava) or the Frank Party, was certainly the most important legitimist but also nationalist grouping. Its founder, Josip Frank (1844–1911), was a Jewish convert to Catholicism. The party was dissolved in 1918 with the end of the monarchy, as its members represented hereditary Croatian loyalty to the House of Habsburg. The Frankists issued an anti-unification manifesto on December 2, 1918, in which they stated that Croatia and its representatives had not been consulted on unification with Serbia and its dynasty. Shortly thereafter, having triggered the anger of the Serbs, their newspaper, *Hrvatska*, was banned, they were excluded from the interim Parliament of Belgrade (March 1, 1919), and their leaders, Josip Pazman and Valdimir Prebeg, were arrested on the orders of Svetozar Pribičević. After renaming themselves *Hrvatska Čista Stranka Prava*, the Croatian Party of Rights, they reappeared on the political scene and won just 10,880 votes in the 1920 parliamentary elections, as they

---

374 Zorach, op. cit., 173.

had appealed to a small stratum of society, but still a significant sector of the Croatian intelligentsia and petite bourgeoisie.[375]

The son of Josip Frank, Ivo or Ivica, was a barrister and politician who went into exile in Austria—with reason, since even the much less radical Radić was arrested with the two leaders of the Croatian Party of Rights in March 1919. Vienna became the meeting point of former Austro-Hungarian malcontent nationalities, among them a great number of Croatian malcontents, some of whom contacted the Hungarian ABC (Hungarian National Committee of Vienna, or Anti-Bolshevik Committee) in order to get organised for the post-Bolshevik period after the interval of the so-called Red Carnival in Hungary.[376] In May, the Croatian malcontents in exile, among them Ivo Frank, founded the Croatian Committee of Graz, which would then move to Vienna.

The Austrian police identified a number of Frank's acolytes, including a certain Vladimir Sachs, a Jew who, like Frank, lived in Vienna since August 1919, and some military officers such as k. u. k. Major General Wilhelm Stipetić and General Sarkotić, one of their leaders, as well as Lieutenant Colonel Stjepan (Stevo) Duić,[377] member of general staff and former commander of the Orient-Corps and Captain Niko Petričević, born in Temesvár (Timoşoara in Romanian) but of Croatian nationality.[378] Former Croatian police officers were also involved, such as Dr Emmanuel Gagliardi, practicing as a barrister, who moved from Vienna to Graz in February 1919, and Benno von Klobularic. The latter became a Hungarian police officer in Pozsony (today Bratislava) before the territorial dissolution of Hungary, thanks to the help of the legitimist Szmrecsányi, leader of the Peoples Party in Hungary and later a member of the ABC in Vienna. Klobularic was already considered an extreme Magyarone by the Croatians.

The role Duić played was crucial. He was the member of the Croatian Committee closest to Karl and was also the contact person between the monarch and the Committee. A brilliant general staff officer and friend of

---

375 Banac, op.cit., 260–63.
376 Boroviczény, Aladár, *A Király és Kormányzója*, Európa, Budapest 1993, 26–27.
377 Österreichisches Staatsarchiv (henceforth ÖStA), Neues Politisches Archiv (henceforth NPA) Karton (henceforth K) 425: Frank, f. 643; Confirmed by Hungarian Foreign Ministry report of Budapest, 21. November 1919: MNL, K 64, 2 cs., 1919–41. I.-21 res.
378 ÖStA, NPA, K. 425: Frank, 643 f.; K 762, 686 f.

the officer Milan Pribičević (brother of Svetozar [379]), he was nominated in January 1919 to assist the chief of staff of the First Serb Army in Novi Sad (Újvidék), a former Hungarian town in Serb-occupied Vojvodina. But very soon (in February) he handed in his resignation, and after visiting family that resided in Brünn, he joined the city of Graz, where he became a founding member of the *Hrvatski Komite* in May 1919.[380]

The Vienna police concluded that the members of the Croatian Committee did not agree with the new SHS Kingdom and were preparing a plan to unite autonomous Croatia with Hungary and German Austria in an economic federation.[381]

Klobularic played the role of contact person between the Hungarian Peoples Party and the Frank Party, and according to the police, the aim of the cooperation between these two parties was to reestablish the monarchical system in Hungary and Croatia.[382]

But Ivo Frank had a problem with this collaboration:

Nach einer vertraulichen Mitteilung scheint es, dass Dr Ivo Frank seinen ungarischen Bundesgenossen misstrauisch gegenübersteht, da er besorgt ist, dass diese insgeheim den Plan verfolgen, die aus dem Verbande des S.H.S. Staates etwa losgelösten Länder unter magyarische Vorherrschaft zu bringen.[383]

Because of this mistrust, Frank turned to Italy and sent Sachs to see if there was support in Rome for his plan. As the months passed, the Italian connection seemed stronger.[384]

---

379 Svetozar was a Croat politician of Serb nationality and was the first interior minister of the new SHS Kingdom.
380 ÖStA, NPA, B/1514/4, Manuscript: Duić, Mario, *Stevo Duić (1877–1934), Ein leben als Mitteleuropa zerbrach*; Banac, *op. cit.*, 168.
381 ÖStA, NPA, K. 425: Frank I., Dossier: Umtriebe der Frankpartei gegen den Bestand des jugoslavischen Staates 1919.
382 ÖStA, NPA, K. 425: Frank, 634–37 ff.: Polizeidirektion in Wien, November 20, 1919.
383 "According to a confidential source, it appears that Dr Ivo Frank is suspicious of his Hungarian allies, for he is concerned that they are secretly pursuing a plan to bring those lands that have been somewhat detached from the S.H.S. States under Hungarian dominance." Ibid.
384 ÖStA, NPA, K. 425: Frank, 644 f., Vertretung in Belgrad an das öst. Staatsamt für Aeuss., Belgrade, January 19, 1920.

It was, in fact, Karl's Hungarian advisor and member of the ABC, Aladár Boroviczény,[385] who introduced the plenipotentiary official of the Croatian malcontents[386] —who had not yet set up the Croatian Committee—to the Italian ambassador to Vienna, Prince Livio Giuseppe Borghese. In a second phase, the chief of the Italian military representation had advised the Croatians in August 1919 to meet the Italian irredentist Gabriele D'Annunzio, who was about enter Fiume with his legionaries. D'Annunzio would be able to help them against Serbia without compromising the Italian government, since it had to be in agreement with the French government at the Paris peace treaties. The Italians, however, were anxious to avoid a Habsburg restoration through *Personalunion* in any of the Successor States, and they insisted that Croatia should stick to the republican form and should be an ally of Hungary only in order to fight the Serbs.[387] As the news spread that Ivo Frank was a legitimist, the Italians' behaviour towards him became contradictory. Some praised him, such as Foreign Minister Sforza, who would promise Frank financial support; whereas Prime Minister Francesco Nitti wanted to have him arrested and expelled, since he was an adventurer playing a double game and working for the restoration of the Habsburgs.[388]

In August 1919, the Croatian Committee of Vienna decided to emerge into daylight and reveal its program to the Entente by transmitting a memorandum to the allied missions present in Vienna. The memorandum stated that it wished:

1. Une confédération comprenant des Républiques: Tchéco-Slovaque, Autrichienne, Hongroise, Yougo-Slave (sans la Serbie).
2. Chaque République aurait son autonomie. La fédération serait une fédération économique afin que toutes les Républiques puissent jouir des débouchés sur la mer que possèderait la Yougo-Slavie.[389]

---

[385] He was a k.u.k. diplomat and married countess Agnes von Schönborn, who was a *dame d'honneur* of Empress-Queen Zita.
[386] His name is not stated.
[387] In September 1919, Col. Duić told the Hungarians that Italy was not only supporting Croat aspirations but would also not oppose the union with Hungary. MNL, K 64, 2 cs., 1919–41.I.-1 res. 4–17 ff., report, Budapest (henceforth Budapest), September 29, 1919.
[388] Ledeen, *op. cit.*, 182.
[389] "1. A confederation comprising Republics: Czechoslovakia, Austria, Hungary, Yugoslavia (without

Austrians became more and more convinced that the Croatian Committee was not a group of republicans but, in fact, of Habsburg monarchists. It was becoming evident that Hungary was financing the group and that Italy was also supporting it. Frank was in fact travelling with Italian papers to Rome through Switzerland, as reported by the Austrian police.[390]

Ghilardi and the "HoR"

Leon de Ghilardi,[391] a Southern Slav politician and revolutionary of Albanian origin, set up the secret HoR (*hrvacki republikanski odbor*, Croatian republican committee) in the territory of the SHS State. In a secret memorandum that he presented to the Hungarian Foreign Ministry he stated: "Die Länder Kroatien, Slawonien und Dalmatien, dann Bosna und Herzegowina bilden einen freien, föderativen, souveränen Staat, der sich in Vollkommener [sic] Parität und Gleichheit an den 'Ungarischen Staat', als Staat zum Staate anschliesst."[392]

In the document, Ghilardi claimed to have organised a wide network of battalions all around the country, which were set up in the following way: Zagreb 22 companies; "Stubicadolna (Stubica) 10; Sv. Ivan Zel. 14; Dugoselo 11; Plemicki Velika Gorica 12; Sambor 14; Taska 9; Karlovac 12; Pisarovina 10; Urginmost 8; Glina 10; Petrinja 8; Sisak 10; Dvor 12; Kostajnica 1." All in all 15 battalions with 175 companies.[393]

Ghilardi was received at the Hungarian Foreign Ministry by Iván Práznovszky—the foreign minister's counsellor and soon envoy to Paris—and asked the Hungarian government to "get in touch with the anti-Serb organisations of the Southern Slav state and support them politically". He specified that their "main effort was against Serb hegemony and the Karađorđević

Serbia)/ 2. Each Republic would have its autonomy. The federation would be an economic federation so that all the Republics could enjoy access to the sea which Yugoslavia would possess." ADMAE, Z Europe, Yougoslavie 40. f., Bulletin de renseignements, author unknown Zagreb, August 16, 1919.

390 ÖStA, NPA, K. 425: Frank, Wien, December 14, 1919, Staatsamt für Äusseres für Hollinger in Belgrad.
391 Ghilardi was up to now an unknown actor not even mentioned in Ivo Banac's remarkable book on nationalism.
392 "The states of Croatia, Slovenia and Dalmatia, followed by Bosnia and Herzegovina constitute a free, federative, sovereign state that is joining the Hungarian State in complete parity and equality, as one state to another." MNL, K 64, 2 cs., 1919-41.I.-2 res., Streng reservat!
393 Ibid.

dynasty". The fact that "they are a republican organisation, does not mean that they are antimonarchists, it is only an instrument to their aim to overthrow the Karađorđević dynasty". He explained that they are friends of the Hungarians and that they want to form a Hungarian–Italian–Polish–Bulgarian and eventually Romanian alliance.[394]

Though Práznovszky thought that the project had minimal chances to be realised, he considered the program as useful to Hungary, due to its destructive effect on the SHS Kingdom and its benefit of bringing the Croatians and other sympathizing ethnic groups back into the Hungarian sphere of interest and opening Hungary's access to the sea again. He commented that even if, in the future, his country had a different stand towards Serbia's Balkan policy, it could not avoid the HoR's plan for the destruction of Serb hegemony, hence it was better to follow and support the project.[395]

Ghilardi wanted to create anti-Serb Hungarian organisations in Serb-occupied Hungary—Vojvodina and the Banat. He asked for 300,000 Crowns per month and a few thousand weapons from the Hungarian government for his project in general.[396] Práznovszky directed him to the *MOVE* and its leader Gyula Gömbös—with whom Ghilardi had some contact through a Hungarian officer named Major Imre Kleindin—who would take over the direction of the programme with the acknowledgement of the Hungarian government and Foreign Ministry. Práznovszky would conclude: "It seems more and more clear that I cannot continue to go with two corrupt states like the Southern Slav [SHS Kingdom] and the Czechoslovak, because they would only be a burden."[397]

During a second meeting at the ministry, Ghilardi claimed that the revolutionaries would be ready in a few months and would start their operation against Serb enslavement. He asked the Hungarian minister of defence to give him a number of officers to help organise the Hungarian population in occupied southern Hungary. This time the Foreign Ministry official was

---

394 MNL, K 64, 2 cs., 1919-41.I.-1 res., Praznovszky's report, Budapest, September 18, 1919, Praznovszky.
395 Ibid.
396 MNL, K 64, 2 cs., 1919-41.I.-1 res., 4–6 ff., Praznovszky's report, Budapest, September 18, 1919; confirmation in *op. cit.*, 14–17 ff., Praznovszky's report, Budapest, September 29, 1919.
397 *Op. cit*, Praznovszky's report, Budapest, Sepember 18, 1919.

Chapter IV

more careful and stated that Ghilardi's movement would wage its revolution against Serbia independently of Hungary if the latter did not wish to participate. In his view, the Hungarians would have to set up a civilian organisation for this purpose in order to avoid problems if the mission backfired. But there was an obstacle to cooperation: Gömbös refused to cooperate with Ghilardi because he considered him an "ambitious and unreliable person".[398]

The ministry had to find another officer and asked a certain Colonel Seyfert to set up "the Southern Slav action" backed by Hungary. But again, Gömbös refused categorically to work with Ghilardi, because he had known him a long time and he was absolutely unreliable. Both Práznovszky and Seyfert suggested Major Kleindin instead, who, though he considered himself not fit for the mission, would still agree to be the contact person and would find the right calibre officer for the mission.[399]

Major Kleindin served in Austria-Hungarian Yugoslavia for fifteen years and thought a Hungarian–Croatian rapprochement was feasible, and he would support it with all his might. He knew Sarkotić, Count Salis,[400] Colonel Lexa, the former military attaché in Sofia, Duić, Kvaternik and others. He would get in touch with the 1,500 Croatian officers in exile in Vienna, for they were well informed about the situation in Croatia. If they thought the moment was ripe, he would help using all the means at his disposal. Seyfert had set forth two conditions for his collaboration: the independence of Croatia and its union with Bosnia. Iván Práznovszky noted that this was a different action than the one now supported by the Foreign Ministry, and he would favour Ghilardi's plan first.[401] Duić also thought that their—the officers'—action should not be mixed with Ghilardi's action and that Ghilardi should not take part in the organisation process because he was not well thought of in Croatia. However, he could be useful in Albania, Bosnia and Dalmatia, and Hungary should perhaps give him a subvention for that.[402]

---

398 MNL, K 64, 2 cs., 1919-41.I.-1 res,. 7–9 ff., report (author unknown), Budapest, September 25, 1919.
399 Ibid.
400 Count Salis, a member of the Croat Committee, was a part of the same, many branched, Graubündenden family as the British minister to the Holy See. MNL, K 64, 2 cs., 1919-41.I.-21 res., Report, Budapest, November 21, 1919.
401 MNL, K 64, 2 cs., 1919-41.I.-1 res. , report, Budapest, September 27, 1919.
402 MNL, K 64, 2 cs., 1919-41.I.-1 res. 14–17 ff., report, Budapest, September 29, 1919.

The Former k. u. k. Officers

In Budapest the newly-installed Horthy regime supported the group and the organisation of the Croatian Legion, a volunteer force. They recruited Croatian POWs from Russia who were going home through Hungary.

The headquarters were first in Kőszeg (Vas County) and then Zalaegerszeg (Zala County) near the Croatian–Slovenian border. There were many contradictory estimations of the size of this force, and one source states that it was composed of six batteries, each with four cannons of Italian origin; and it was claimed that they had six battalions in Zalaegerszeg, each with 800–900 men.[403]

In September 1919, Duić was in Budapest to meet with Horthy and deal with the matter of the forces stationed in Croatia. He met with an official of the Foreign Ministry to whom he said that the situation in Croatia was rapidly approaching a crisis and that action by a union of independent Croatia with Hungary would start on October 15 and would finish in December. The grounds for military action were the Radić[404] and Frank constituencies, and each of the 22 constituencies that would provide a battalion. There were already 34 fully armed battalions assembled in commando forces whose centres were Zagreb, Sisek, Karlovac and Warasdin. Though Duić did not make mention of it, all four commandos seem to correspond with the HoR's companies, thanks to which we can conclude that Duić's Croatian Committee and the HoR forces were considered as one, or at least they were strongly connected.

In other regions, the Croatians would have 12 battalions which would be supported by Hungarian forces composed of the POWs given by Horthy and forces from Fiume composed of POWs held in Italy. The Hungarian forces would be composed of four regiments of Croatian soldiers who were

---

403 Banac, *op. cit.*, 264; Archiv Hrvatske, Rukopisna ostavstina Dr Milana Sufflaya, Box 2: Optuznica, 69. A British "Confidential Print" mentions a place called Blatno Jezero, which is the Croat name for Lake Balaton. Consul Maclean calls it "Balatok" in Hungarian and had probably no idea of where it was, and that it was a lake. Zalaegerszeg is northwest of Lake Balaton and confirms that the camp was most likely to the west of the lake. NA, FO 371 4669, C11466/307/19, Consul Maclean to Sir A. Young, Zagreb, November 6, 1920.

404 As I will show, Stepan Radić was leader of the autonomist Peasant Party in Croatia.

Chapter IV

fighting in Béla Kun's red army. The chief of the army could be either General Anton Lipostyak (Antal Liposcak in Hungarian) or General Mihalović.[405] Another member[406] of the Croatian Committee stated that there were five to six battalions organised by Lieutenant Colonel Kvaternik and these squadrons were waiting in Austria between Marburg, Pettau and Cilli.

Duić then mentioned the international implications of the action. He stated that Italy was not only supporting Croatian aspirations but would also not oppose the union with Hungary.[407]

Having approached the French, Duić said that Pichon was against the Croatian project. Yet he claimed that there was a French group around André Tardieu, then still a French MP, that was supportive of their aspirations. This fact seems very unlikely, since the latter wanted to make a corridor between Yugoslavia and Czechoslovakia to cut Hungary from Austria, which the Italians eventually opposed at the peace conference.[408] It is, however, possible that as with Hungary, the Quai d'Orsay had an unofficial secret plan regarding Croatia, but there are no traces of it.

Duić's plan was to be managed without bloodshed, and arms were to be used only as the last resort. Yet, it was difficult to imagine a relatively pacific takeover if Ghilardi was to be involved.

After Duić's visit, a new Croatian officer appeared in Budapest. First Lieutenant Crnković worked for the SHS Vlada (government) until October 1919, when he joined the Hungarian Ministry of Finance and was referent for Croatian affairs at the Hungarian Supreme Command. He wanted to join the Vienna Croatian Committee, and as the son of a vice-ban of Croatia he was considered the ideal contact person to connect the Committee and the Hungarian government. He, like all the other officers, believed in a *Per-*

---

405 Was Gen. Mihalović a relative of Antun Mihalović the last Hungarian ban of Croatia? I could not find a connection. MNL, K 64, 2 cs., 1919-41.I.-1 res. 14–17 ff., Budapest, September 29, 1919, report on Croatian situation and Yugoslav action; Balla, Tibor, *A Nagy Háború osztrák–magyar tábornokai: Tábornagyok, vezérezredesek, gyalogsági és lovassági tábornokok, táborszernagyok*, A Hadtörténeti Intézet és Múzeum Könyvtár, Budapest, 2010, 213–14.
406 Lieutenant Crnković was sent to join the Croat Committee of Vienna by the Hungarian Supreme Command, MNL, K 64, 2 cs., 1919-41.I.-21 res., report, Budapest, November 21, 1919.
407 MNL, K 64, 2 cs., 1919-41.I.-1 res. 14–17 ff., report, Budapest, September 29, 1919.
408 ADMAE, Z Europe, Autriche 53, Barrère (Min. à Rome) à Pichon. Tardieu was one of Clemenceau's chief advisors during the negotiation of the post-war peace treaties, Rome, February 14, 1919.

sonalunion with Hungary. Crnković said that the Committee and the parties supporting them were made up of Catholic monarchists and especially *kaisertreu* officers and clergy. Their aim was to restore the monarchy with an orientation towards Vienna, but if their plan did not work, than they could see an association with Hungary.[409]

The Hungarian diplomat who interviewed him, Villani,[410] concluded that the Vienna Croatian Committee was the central organ of Ghilardi's HoR, which considered Sarkotić and Frank as its heads.[411] As noted above, Duić's remarks on the battalions can only strengthen this fact.

In December, it was Klobularic's turn to visit Budapest. He went to the Foreign Ministry to negotiate the transfer of the Graz–Vienna Committee to Budapest, and, as he revealed, the Committee was financed by Italy. Frank and Duić were in Rome to get their 52,000 POWs—an exaggerated number—armed and put them at the disposal of the Committee. He also stated that Croatia would give Fiume to Italy in exchange; with one condition, that the harbour remained international. The plan concerning Croatia was to set up a Szeged-type government in Susak (an island just adjacent to Fiume) from where the operations would be controlled. When this army started to take action, the SHS State would be attacked on four sides: from Styria, from Fiume by the POWs, from the river Drave by Hungarians and from the valley of Stumnica by Bulgarians. For that reason, Klobularic would be negotiating with the land-marshal of Styria and was awaiting a delegation from Bulgaria.

This time, the Foreign Ministry was more reserved and feared that Hungary would be compromised by such a plan. Villani even questioned the presence of this Committee in Hungary.[412]

From these Hungarian reports it seemed that the Croatians were highly organised and that what they still needed was more munitions. It was also obvious that there was an important concentration of separatists around the

---

409 MNL, K 64, 2 cs., 1919-41.I.-21 res., report, Budapest, November 21, 1919.
410 The writer of the report would have been one of two brothers, both Hungarian diplomats of Italian origin, Barons Frigyes or Lajos Villani di Castello-Pillonico.
411 MNL, K 64, 2 cs., 1919-41.I.-21 res. report, Budapest, November 21, 1919.
412 MNL, K 64 1919, 41 I-21 res., The transfer of the Croat Committee to Budapest, Budapest, December 2, 1919.

concept of a confederation and that the role of the Habsburg monarch was most crucial for the majority of the Committee members who reported to the Hungarian Foreign Ministry. They were interested in a union, *Personalunion*, under the Holy Crown of Saint Stephen with a *Zollverein* and strong economic links, but apart from that, complete independence.[413] They obviously wished to see King Károly as the guarantor of respect for their independence in this union. Thus, the figure linking Hungary and Croatia was the legitimate monarch.

Later, on July 5, 1920, a treaty was signed in Venice between the representatives of the Command of Fiume (Giovanni Giuriati[414] and Giovanni Host-Venturi[415]) and the Croatian separatists, represented by Frank and Sachs. Another treaty bore the signatures of Jovan Plamenatz, president of the Council of Ministers and foreign minister for the King of Montenegro, and two Albanians, which confirms that there was an international Balkan alliance against the Kingdom of Serbia.[416] These treaties mentioned guarantees, on the part of Fiume, of supplies of arms and money for the separatists. The Croatians were promised 9,000 guns, 6 million bullets and 7 million lire (Italian currency). The treaty mentioned that the insurrection would start on August 1 in Montenegro and August 24 in Croatia and Albania. In return for these supplies and funds, the signatories promised to do all they could to destroy the SHS Kingdom. Italy's interest in these treaties stipulated that not only would Fiume remain Italian but also the cities of Zadar (Zara, I), Šibenik (Sebenico, I), Split (Spalato, I), Trogir (Traú, I) and Ragusa were to become "perpetually independent" and to constitute a loose federation or maritime league. The rest of Dalmatia was to vote on whether it was to be independent or belong to Croatia.[417]

---

413 Boroviczény, *op. cit.*, 27.
414 Irredentist leader and fascist politician, president of the free state of Fiume (1922–1923).
415 Irredentist leader and fascist politician. Founder of the Fiumese Legion that occupied Fiume with D'Annunzio.
416 "Mouvement offensive générale [sic] pour occuper tout le territoire serbe." These were the words of Giuriati to describe the offensive. Ledeen, *op. cit.*, 182–83.
417 The *Comandante* (D'Annunzio) was named as the "legitimate representative of victorious Italy" in the treaty. Ibid.

Gagliardi and Frank thought that Yugoslavia would be attacked by émigré armies of Croatians, Montenegrins and Macedonians, Bavarians, Albanians, Bulgars, Hungarians and the Styrian peasant legions (under Dr Willibald Brodmann's Untersteierische Bauernkommando)[418] and finally Italy.[419] However, it seems far fetched to consider that the occupation of the whole of Serbia was truly planned by Frank and even more so that this was possible.

By the end of 1920, the Serbs were waiting for an imminent confrontation and had concentrated their forces near the river Drave.[420]

The Hungarian sources are a rich complement to the French Quai d'Orsay sources and show only too clearly that the French were not clear-headed about the different ramifications of the separatist organisations. The Austrian police interrogations are even more limited, since the Graz–Vienna Committee members who were interrogated never spoke freely to the Austrians, whereas they did to the Hungarians, because they knew that Hungary was on their side and, even more, would probably support them.

The Peasants Party's Resistance

Radić, "the Rising Star"

The HPSS (*Hrvatska pučka seljačka stranka*, or Croatian People's Peasant Party) was founded in 1904. Its leader was Stjepan Radić, a republican who was often, though falsely, called a socialist by the French. He was born into a peasant family and educated in Paris at the *Ecole des Sciences Politiques* and was a brilliant politician with a many publications. A French diplomat wrote that he could have had "a profitable influence on the rural classes [...] to whom he was devoted body and soul". But the French considered him to have an unstable character. The diplomat even went so far as to claim:

---

418 The Bauernkommando was created in the locality of Straden, Styria, to defend the Austrian border against Yugoslavia. Hinteregger, Robert, "Abwehrmassnahmen an der untersteierischen Grenzen 1918/19", *Zeitschrift des Historischen Vereins für Steiermark*, 66, 1975.
419 Banac, *op. cit.*, 268.
420 NA, FO 371 4669, C11466/307/19, Zagreb, 6. Nov. 1920. Consul Maclean to Sir A. Young.

[...] si, par la suite d'un défaut mental il ne se laissait pas aller quelquefois à certains écarts de conceptions confinant à la spéculation pure qui le rendait étranger à ses auditoires ou qui les excitait à la révolte, suivant que l'orateur est incompris ou compris, et qui mettent les pouvoirs publics dans la nécessité de sévir contre lui.[421]

Radić was a pacifist and was called the "Croat Gandhi" because he wanted to attain Croatia's freedom through pacifist means. He was considered a demagogue, even though he nearly whispered when he gave a speech. In the words of Ivo Banac, Radić was one of the most able of Croatian politicians, "a romantic, and yet a pragmatist" who "illuminated the skies like the luminous flash of a meteor."[422]

Within months of the creation of the Yugoslav state, the Peasant Party publicly proclaimed its intention to seek Croatian national self-determination and to internationalise the Croatian question. As the Yugoslav monarchical system of government trampled on the rights of the Croatian peasantry in the name of *narodno jedinstvo*—Croatian–Serb national unity—Radić voiced his demand for a Croatian republic, national sovereignty, and a Croatian constituent assembly. Although he made reference to a federal Yugoslav republic, he insisted, much as he did in October–November 1918, that the Croatian people first had to possess the right to determine their future in a Croatian constituent assembly before such a federation could even be considered.[423]

The Peasant Party of Radić wasn't the only group that wanted autonomy or independence. The Chamber of Commerce of Zagreb voted an *ordre du jour* in which it specified that with respect to commerce, industry and supplies it regretted the annulment of Croatian autonomy and its members

---

[421] "[...] if, as a result of a mental defect, it was not possible at times to go to certain lengths of conceptions bordering on pure speculation that made him foreign to his audience or that incited them to revolt, depending on whether the orator was misunderstood or understood, and which place the public powers in the position of having to act against him." ADMAE, Z Europe, Yougoslavie 32, f. 71, Consul de France à Président du Conseil, Zagreb, August 12, 1920.
[422] Banac, *op. cit.*, 226.
[423] Biondich, Mark, *Stjepan Radic, the Croatian Peasant Party, and the Politics of Mass Mobilization, 1904–1928*, University of Toronto Press, Toronto, 2000, 163–64.

considered that the bad economic situation was related to this. The former bans (under Hungarian rule) of Croatia (Ivan Škrlec, Teodor Pejačević, Pavao Rauch) were seconding this agitation, and Radić's *Obzor* newspaper in Zagreb was continually urging independence and fighting against the united Serb–Croat–Sloven state.[424] Nor should one forget the Frankists, who were fighting equally for independence but were mostly in exile.

The Federalist

But if Radić was an independentist, was he also a federalist—and of what sort? Was he imagining a Croatia federated with the Kingdom of Serbia or with another country? And was he a republican or a disguised monarchist?

Fontenay, the French minister in Belgrade, was influenced by the Serbs and seemed to be persuaded that Radić was a legitimist and not a republican. Belgrade wanted to establish this as fact by giving many of Radić's *kaisertreu* telegrams, sent to Vienna during the war, to Fontenay.[425]

In fact, Peasant Party links to the Habsburg monarch in exile can be identified at a very early stage after the war. Windischgraetz claimed that, accompanied by Duić, Vladko Maček—the party's second-most important politician and a member of its main committee—was one of the first visitors to King Károly in Prangins.[426] But what was Maček's true approach to the problem just before, during and after the war?

Vladko Maček would have claimed that Radić secretly wanted the monarchy to lose the war in order to provoke its internal reorganisation. Radić's public speeches in the Sabor and statements in the press gave a totally different impression, such as the one that the Serbs had sent to Fontenay. In a speech given at the Zagreb Sabor in 1917, he claimed that the Habsburgs would be able to reunite the peoples of the Danube once the dynasty was

---

[424] ADMAE, Z Europe, Yougoslavie 40, 32–33 ff., Fontenay à MAE, "Agitation séparatiste en Croatie", Belgrade, February 21, 1919.
[425] ADMAE, Z Europe, Yougoslavie 40. f. 40 Etat-major 2ème Bureau au Ministère de la Guerre (henceforth MG), Zagreb, April 6, 1919.
[426] Windischgraetz, *Ein Kaiser kämpft*, 138.

liberated from the Hohenzollerns and the Hungarians.[427] To a certain extent, it would have been difficult to do otherwise than to support the Emperor-King, for all parties had to express loyalty to the Habsburg dynasty or risk the consequences. But in spite of his Russophilism and apprehension regarding Germany's growing might, his commitment to the reorganisation of the monarchy and fear of Serb expansion were stronger and led him to support the war effort. If it is true that the Great War would gradually challenge many of his loyalties, but in the early years of the war he could not envisage a solution to the Croatian Question outside the borders of the monarchy. In August 1914, he went as far as to declare that Serbia, Russia and France had provoked the war and that the monarchy could not lose, for its peoples were united behind the war cause.[428] A week earlier he had written that Franz Ferdinand had intended to reorganise Austria-Hungary and unify the Croatian lands in the course of autumn 1914.[429]

Radić believed that after the war two things could happen: either the status quo would be preserved and the Kingdom of Croatia "will be free and united within the monarchy" alongside "united resurrected Serbia and strong Bulgaria" or, if the monarchy were to collapse,

> the Slovenes, Croatians, Serbs and Bulgarians would have to find a solution, in which case the South Slavs would have to recognise their respective state traditions: the Croatians were the only historic political nation in the monarchy's South Slav region and the Serbs and Bulgarians were political nations on their respective state territories.[430]

At this point, he still believed that after the war the Croatian lands would be united, and all existing ties would be severed between Croatia and Hungary—but not from Austria. After Karl's accession, Radić had great expectations and hoped the new monarch would negotiate a separate peace with the

---

[427] ADMAE, Z Europe, Yougoslavie 40. f. 46, Extrait du discours de Radić au Parlement Croate, March 1917.
[428] Biondich, *op. cit.*, 122–3: *Dom*, August 27, 1914.
[429] Ibid., 282: *Dom*, July 8, 1914.
[430] Ibid., 126.

Entente and reorganise the monarchy into a federal state. Karl tried both, but he was unsuccessful with both. Even if Radić claimed that Serbs "are our brothers not only by language and spirit but also in any social respect", that did not logically entail unification with Serbia "because we have our thousand-year-old state and we want to remain in the monarchy".[431] Radić's true aim was Croatian unification within the Habsburg—Cisleithanian—Monarchy. When 1918 came and the Habsburg Monarchy disintegrated, Radić moved to the idea of independence, but not at any price.

In early 1919, Radić and the party thus effectively committed themselves to Croatian independence. The party's petition to Paris was supposed to demonstrate and, in the absence of elections at that time, legitimise the Croatian desire for an independent republic. By the end of March 1919, over 115,000 signatures had been collected. At the end of April 1919, Radić indicated to his wife that on the basis of this petition he hoped to be invited to Paris to present his case. Radić wrote to Maček:

> [...] all of our constitutional and elementary human rights have been trampled, it was only natural that I now demand from the Entente, from Europe, from Wilson, for cultural humanity, for our Croatian republic without any regard to the Serbs and Slovenes. [...] All our work and all of our endeavouring should be directed so that we Croatians establish a neutral peasant republic.[432]

From the French point of view, Fontenay wrote that the separatist movement was apparently under the direction of Radić but was, in fact, the work of the Frankists, who were relying on the Agrarian Party and claimed that the pro-Habsburgs had taken the republican name tag and would get rid of it and express their legitimism as soon as the separation was accomplished.[433] It is clear that both were involved in the separatist movement and their aim was to find foreign support in order to guarantee their independence.

---

431 Ibid.
432 Ibid., 164–65.
433 ADMAE, Z Europe, Yougoslavie 40. f. 32, Fontenay à Pichon, Belgrade, February 21, 1919.

Between 1919 and 1920 there was certainly no indication that republicanism would be abandoned anytime soon. Radić continued in 1919 and early 1920 to believe that a "Danubian federation" of some kind was still possible, though it appears that he saw such a federation as being largely an economic association. On May 28, 1919, Radić wrote that Austria would be revived, "except we fear that the whole of 'Yugoslavia', therefore Serbia too will enter into it". It is evident that he wanted Serbia to be excluded from such an association, and as the French reported:

> Le parti Radić-Frank, qui donne la note à l'opposition, inscrirait à son programme la formation d'une confédération du Danube, comprenant avec l'Autriche allemande et la Hongrie, des états slaves autonomes des Balkans y compris la Bulgarie [...] étant libre de choisir la forme de gouvernementale qui paraît le mieux leur convenir. Ce choix devrait faire l'objet d'un referendum populaire.[434]

In a series of letters written to his wife between August 6 and 8, 1919, Radić argued that Yugoslav federalism might have worked in the autumn of 1918, but that it was now too late for such a federation. Radić had, in fact, moved back to a reformulation of his broader vision of the East Central European Union that he advocated in summer–fall 1918, in the hope that a "Danubian federation" encompassing Austria, Hungary and Croatia would be formed. However, by December 1919, Radić had made slight progress toward accepting a federation with Serbia, and he wrote, "The main thing for us (*and the people*) is a republic = self-determination, and federalism = Norway towards Sweden and the opportune moment Norway from Sweden (1907)."[435] Nevertheless, in December 1919 Radić was still not fully committed to the idea of Yugoslav (con)federalism,[436] to which he would move in

---

434 "The Radić-Frank party, which sets the tone for the opposition, would write into its program the formation of a Danube confederation, comprising German Austria and Hungary, autonomous Slav states from the Balkans including Bulgaria [...] being free to choose the form of government that seemed to suit them best. This choice should become the object of a popular referendum." ADMAE, Z Europe, Yougoslavie 31, 101. Information "Secret", author unknown, Fiume, April 20, 1919.
435 Biondich, op. cit., 167–68.
436 Ibid.

the future. In other words, Radić was still strongly dedicated to his idea of independence and a Danubian confederation.

There is no doubt that Radić remained nostalgic for the Habsburg Monarchy even after the war and the destruction of the Dual Monarchy. His conception of an independent republic was possible as part of a confederal Habsburg Monarchy and was a way of saying no to the Karađorđević Monarchy. Radić knew that without an alliance with a bigger nation or nations, Croatia's survival as an independent state was impossible.

Contact with Italy and the Croatian Committee

On March 8, 1919, the Peasant Party adopted a nine-point resolution in which it refused categorically to recognise the Karađorđević dynasty or the work of the PNP (*Privremeno narodno predstavništvo*, Temporary National Representation)[437] as having any legitimacy in Croatia. It declared, among other things, its intention to send a petition to President Woodrow Wilson as a protest against Serb disrespect for the concept of self-determination of nations and demanded a neutral Croatian republic. Radić passed on the resolution to the French mission in Zagreb, which would have been what prompted the new SHS authorities to arrest him and other members of the party on March 25. Belgrade claimed to Fontenay that Radić was arrested because he had contacts with the Italians, with whom he was plotting against the SHS State (Kingdom). He was, indeed, awaited by Italian agents in Italy from where he was to lead the separatist movement;[438] at least that is what the Serbs wanted Fontenay to believe. Radić was in fact asking for Sidney Sonnino's (Italian minister of foreign affairs) support to let him go to Paris to defend Croatia's case at the Peace Conference.[439]

Three leading members of the Agrarian Party had been arrested and indicted on three counts: they asked for Italian support against Serbia; they would give Fiume to Italy in exchange for the latter's military support; and,

---

[437] First parliamentary body of the SHS Kingdom.
[438] ADMAE, Z Europe, Yougoslavie 40, 37 ff., Fontenay à Pichon, Belgrade, April 6, 1919.
[439] Documenti diplomatici italiani (henceforth DDI), 1918–1922, Serie 6, vol. II, Rome, February 25, 1919, Badoglio to Sonnino in Paris, no.502, 343–45.

finally, one of the party members wanted to convince a French journalist of his idea to bring French hegemony to Croatia.[440]

Whatever the reasons, true or invented, all opponents of the united SHS State were to be arrested: Radić and Maček[441] of the Peasant Party, Josip Pazman, Dr Vladimir Prebeg of the Party of Right.[442] By this action the Serbs wanted to crush the separatist movement definitively. But the Serbs had miscalculated by arresting Radić and his companions, since the separatist movement and the support from Italy— although less visible since the arrest of Radić—were still growing and were only stimulated by his arrest. Actions, such as the spreading of anti-unionist pamphlets, are good examples of the growing separatist propaganda and activity.[443]

As reports on how the Italians were implicated in the plans to destroy the SHS Kingdom were flowing into the French representations, Fontenay was persuaded that Italians were behind the Croatian plotters[444] but could not believe that it was a general movement: "d'aucuns [en Italie] poursuivent systématiquement la division de la Yougoslavie, dans l'espoir chimérique de jouer dans les Balkans l'ancien rôle de l'Autriche-Hongrie."[445] As a Croatian agent working for the French confirmed in his report on Italian influence in Croatia:

> Que la France se persuade bien: jamais nous ne nous soumettrons au régime serbe. Nous sommes joints aux Serbes pour établir un pays Yougo-Slave Karadjordjevic, une confédération de La Croatie, Bosnie, Herzégovine, Slovénie avec la Serbie tout en conservant et garantissant l'indépendance et la souveraineté de La Croatie, et surtout de la République. Nous n'avons pas secoué les Habsbourg pour reconnaître les Karad-

---

440 ADMAE, Z Europe, Yougoslavie 40. f. 80 d'un agent à l'essai (suite du rapport no.148, July 13, 1919).
441 Radić was held without trial in police custody for 339 days, even though he was a member of the Croat Sabor and had diplomatic immunity. Vladko Maček (1879–1964) was held for nine months.
442 Banac, *op. cit.*, 262.
443 ADMAE, Z Europe, Yougoslavie 40, 71–73 ff., Rapport du Gen. Guillot du April 21 au May 2, 1919, Paris, May 5, 1919.
444 Fontenay insists on Radic's links to Italy with a Serb document showing that anti-Serb pamphlets were prepared to be sent to Yugoslavia. ADMAE, Z Europe, Yougoslavie 40, 67 f., Fontenay à Pichon, Belgrade, April 27, 1919.
445 "… none [in Italy] systematically pursue the division of Yugoslavia, in the chimerical hope of playing in the Balkans the former role of Austria-Hungary". ADMAE, Z Europe, Yougoslavie 40, 32–33 ff., Fontenay à Pichon, "Agitation séparatiste en Croatie", Belgrade, February 21, 1919.

jordjevic. Nous sommes 2,600,000 Croates dont 25% seulement sont Serbo-Croates. [Serbo-Croats=Serbians of Croatia][446]

The agent continued, in this same menacing vein: "Les Italiens nous aideront pour gagner notre liberté, plus que nous en demandons aujourd'hui, et une autre fédération se ferait: ce serait La Croatie, la Slovénie, la Hongrie, la Roumanie et la Bulgarie."[447] These lines confirmed the secret reports, sent to the Quai d'Orsay, on the plan for a large Balkan and Danubian Confederation, and the internationalisation of the anti-Serb camp with Italy's participation.

Italian participation in the aim to destroy the SHS Kingdom was known in London as well, and an official of the Foreign Office confirmed that:

> I think it not at all impossible that efforts will be made in Hungary—probably in agreement with Italian circles—to detach Croatia from the Jugo-Slav [sic] state. In spite, however, of the known friction between the Serbs and Croatians I doubt whether the latter could easily be attracted to Hungary; The Croatians, though republican when confronted with a Serb dynasty, were on the whole personally very much attached to the Habsburg family.[448]

Italian intentions in Croatia were quite obvious, but their importance was still to be evaluated.

The Peasant Revolution of September 1920

The Peasant Revolution, known as the "Peasant revolt against Draft-Animal Registration",[449] was the only important insurrection that shook the SHS

---

446 "France must be persuaded: we will never submit to Serbian rule. We have joined forces with the Serbs to establish a Karađorđević Yugoslav state, a confederation of Croatia, Bosnia, Herzegovina, and Slovenia with Serbia, preserving and guaranteeing all the while the independence and sovereignty of Croatia, and especially of the Republic. We did not shake off the Habsburgs in order to recognise the *Karađorđević dynasty*. We are 2,600,000 Croatians of whom only 25% are Serbo-Croats." ADMAE, Z Europe, Yougoslavie 40, f. 78, Menées italiennes en Croatie « d'un agent à l'essai », May 16, 1919.
447 "The Italians will help us gain our liberty, more than we demand today, and a different federation will take shape: it will be Croatia, Slovenia, Hungary, Romania, and Bulgaria." Ibid., 75–79 ff.
448 NA, FO 371 4384, PID, 686 f., AWG Randall Remarks, December 8, 1919.
449 Banac, *op. cit.*, 248.

State in the period studied (1919–1920) and had general support throughout Croatia.

Until now scholars considered the revolt only as an insurrection triggered by farmers' anger at administrative decrees introduced by Belgrade. The most important of these ordered that the taxes in place since 1917 be augmented with a surtax of 100%, railway tariffs experience a 1,000% augmentation, and the value of domestic animals (especially horses) be reassessed, which was considered the gravest of offences against the farmers.[450] The problem was, however, much more complex.

A French intelligence report explained that the peasant revolutionary movement was based in the region of Osijek, and "its aim was the proclamation of an independent republic including Bosnia-Herzegovina".[451] The report claimed that the revolt was the result of intervention by the now-Budapest-based Committee, Frankist and Radić party militants, agents from Italy, Hungary, Bolsheviks from Russia, communists from the SHS Kingdom,[452] and malcontents in general. Newspaper propaganda attacked the Belgrade government intensely, insulted the Entente, and even affirmed that they could be saved by a Slavonic bloc headed by Russia and Bolsheviks.[453] Radić, who was then in prison and was a proponent of non-violence, once noted that he "was committed to a peaceful resolution of the country's political crisis," but "had to use all of his influence 'to prevent a revolution that others wanted to initiate believing it to be possible and successful'". It was apparent from the existing unrest that not all of his party members shared his view.[454]

In addition the peasant element, which was excited by propaganda and by the very events it had to experience, the Peasant Revolution also resisted

---

450 ADMAE, Z Europe, Yougoslavie 40, 149–50 ff., Consul de France à MAE, Zagreb, September 7, 1920. ADMAE, Z Europe, Yougoslavie 32, 116 ff., Consul de France à MAE, Zagreb, September 18, 1920, "Le marquage des chevaux au fer rouge lors du recensement en vue d'une réquisition éventuelle", ADMAE, Z Europe, Yougoslavie 40, 150–52 ff., Col. Deltel Att. Mil. à MG, Belgrade, October 14, 1920.
451 ADMAE, Z Europe, Yougoslavie 40. 86 f., Informateur "von", Bern, August 2, 1919.
452 Biondich confirms that "the Peasant Party's local leaders were involved in the revolt". Ibid., 167.
453 ADMAE, Z Europe, Yougoslavie 40, 150–151 ff., Col. Deltel Att. Mil. to MG, Belgrade, Oct. 14, 1920.
454 Biondich, op. cit., 167.

open recruitment to send Croatians to the Albanian front, some of whom deserted and remained in Albania to then join the separatist movement in Italy or Hungary.[455]

There were also military revolts, such as those that started in the regions of Sisak, Bjelovar, Zagorie, Krizevci, Zagreb and Warasdin (Varaždin)[456]— regions that were confirmed by the Croatian Committee members as having HoR companies. In these revolts, officers shot at civilians, with a large death toll. The Croatian head of the police in Zagreb, Zimperman, was suspected of having been informed ahead of time and of being part of the plot, since he was slow to mobilise his forces. Many Croatian recruits defected from the army: 184 of 200 deserted from the 5th infantry regiment. Some of them did so even before the beginning of the Peasant Revolution.[457]

These reports prove that it was a much broader uprising than simply a peasant revolt. It is, however, strange that the so-menacing Italian and Hungarian Croatian troops did not appear at the borders. Even if the operations were not a success, it showed that the Croatian population was receptive to the politicians opposing Serb domination, and it was probably all that the seemingly heavily armed and organised Hungarian–Italian–Croatian plot managed to provoke in 1919 and 1920.

Fontenay's Perception of Radić

According to Fontenay (April 1919), Radić's ideas were not shared by the majority of Croats, but only by Germanophile elements:

> [...] Raditch ne représente, en somme, qu'un groupe de paysans dont il a surpris la naïvité en leur promettant tout [...] désireux de rompre l'unité de

---

455 ADMAE, Z Europe, Yougoslavie 32, 116 ff., Consul de France to MAE. Zagreb, September 18, 1920; ADMAE, Z Europe, Yougoslavie 40, 150–151 ff., Col. Deltel, Att. Mil. à MG, Belgrade, Oct. 14, 1920. Albania was in conflct with Italy, Serbia and Greece which occupied the country since 1918. Albanians fought for independence and were able to recognise the independence of the Albanian state in March 1920, thanks to support from the USA.
456 ADMAE, Z Europe, Yougoslavie 32, 116 f., Consul de France à MAE, Zagreb, September 18, 1920; Ibid., 114–15 ff., Consul de France à Pichon, Zagreb, September 17, 1920.
457 Ibid., 114–15 ff., Consul de France à MAE, Zagreb, September 17, 1920.

l'Etat Serbe Croate Slovène afin de renforcer le Germanisme et d'affaiblir la ceinture destinée à contenir ces velléités de poussée vers l'Adriatique."[458]

Fontenay claimed that if Croatia really wanted to protest, it could do so in Parliament. But he seemed to ignore the fact that Radić was arrested for doing precisely that, among other things. Fontenay's ignorance of the number of people Radić represented and of France's true policy towards the Croatian republicans becomes even clearer when he writes: "On ne saurait d'ailleurs, dans aucun pays, tenir compte des idées personnelles que peut avoir chaque citoyen et en ce qui concerne La Croatie la très grande majorité ne partage pas les vues de M. Raditch". Fontenay not only ignored the growing influence of the Agrarian Party on the farmer population but also stereotyped them as a group of ignorant people. The end of his statement is the cherry on the top of the cake: "Pourrait-on songer à soutenir les agitations irlandaises contre l'unité de la Grande-Bretagne."[459] By going as far as to compare Croatia with Ireland he proves that he would not support self-determination for any nation, new or old, and would back Belgrade's policy totally; which is not to say that Fontenay revealed a strongly colonial perception of the problem. Croatia was to be considered only as spoils that would be snatched from Hungary to be attached to Serbia.

Fontenay's interpretation was in accord with the Serb way of viewing the problem of Croatian opposition: "Nous ne nous laisserons pas intimider par les Croates [...] formant un bloc d'opposition contre nous comme il était auparavant contre les Magyars."[460] As a result, they chose to position themselves in the same dominant, *Herrenvolk*, position towards the Croatians as the Hungarians did earlier; except that the Magyars had always accepted the Croatians as a "historical nation".

---

458 "In sum, Radić represents nothing more than a group of peasants whose naivety he surprised by promising them everything [...] desirous of breaking the unity of the Serb Croat Slovene state in order to reinforce Germanism and to weaken the bond destined to contain these vague desires of a push toward the Adriatic." ADMAE, Z Europe, Yougoslavie 40, 61 f., Fontenay à Pichon, Belgrade, April 11, 1919.
459 "Moreover, in no country would it be possible to account for personal ideas that each citizen can have, and in regard to Croatia the grand majority does not share the views of Mr. Radić [...] Could one dream of supporting the Irish agitations against the unity of Great Britain." Ibid.
460 "We will not let ourselves be intimidated by the Croatians [...] forming a block of opposition against us as it was previously against the Magyars." ADMAE, Z Europe, Yougoslavie 40, 80 f., d'un agent à l'essai (suite du rapport no. 148, July 13, 1919).

Radić's Climb to the 1920 Elections

Fontenay as well as Belgrade had misinterpreted the importance of the peasant movement. If there was no excitement when Radić was arrested in March 1919,[461] his popularity grew parallel to the growing numbers of malcontents until the day of the elections of November 28, 1920. But a few weeks before that date, Radić negotiated a coalition with the Croatian Union Party, which was joined by Count Teodor Pejačević, who was ban during the Habsburg Monarchy. In other words, the representative of the *ancien régime* had joined hands with the republican Radić.[462] As the Croatian Clerical party—which was viewed as being secretly in favour of Habsburg restoration—had joined the Union Party a bit earlier, there was now a second party that was secretly pro-Habsburg; the Frank party having been openly considered as such.[463]

On November 28, the Peasant Party won the rural districts, some of which gave Radić 90 percent of the votes. The town proletarians and bourgeoisie gave Radić's party only 6.77 percent, however this did not hinder it from becoming the largest party in Croatia, holding the largest bloc of Croatian ballots, and Yugoslavia's third largest party with 230,590 votes and 50 deputies in Belgrade.[464] The Croatian Union won 5.23 percent and the Frankists only 2.48 percent of all votes in Croatia-Slavonia.[465] As a result, among the MPs from Croatia-Slavonia, there were 50 Agrarians in coalition with the Frankists and the Croatian Union and the Clericals, with 6 seats, facing the 28 Democrats and Radicals. Since the 59 Croatian Communists had been excluded because of the anti-communist laws of the SHS Kingdom, Radić had exactly two-thirds of the recognised votes.[466] Those who elected communist parliamentarians would most probably have voted for Radić, if they had known that their vote would not be considered, and consequently the Agrarians would have represented an even greater danger to

---

461 ADMAE, Z Europe, Yougoslavie 24, 2–6 ff., Résumé d'impression du Ct Carbonnier, Att. Mil. en Serbie, Belgrade, November 29, 1918.
462 NA, FO 371/4669, 120 f., Consul Maclean to Young, Zagreb, Nov. 6, 1920.
463 NA, FO 371/4669, 121–22 ff., Consul Jones to Young, Sarajevo, November 10, 1920.
464 Banac, *op. cit.*, 227.
465 Ibid, 392.
466 ADMAE, Z Europe, Yougoslavie 48, 149 f., Clément-Simon à Briand, Belgrade, September 28, 1921.

Belgrade. In a bit more than a year, the concept of a Croatian Peasant Republic had become the dominant idea in Croatia.

Radić, in coalition with Frankists and the Croatian Union, not only had the majority in Croatia, but could have deadlocked Parliament in Belgrade if it had managed to attract the Yugoslav Muslims of Bosnia and Macedonia.[467]

The supporters of Frank and Radić were counting on their victory to bring about the separation of Croatia from Serbia. Two scenarios were imagined in the pro-Habsburg milieu: in a first phase, the separatist majority would either create a separate parliament in Zagreb and leave the Belgrade Parliament, or it would provoke a revolution against Serb centralisation. In a second phase, there would either be the creation of a little Croatia-Slovenia or the attachment of Croatia to Hungary and Slovenia to Italy.[468]

Interactions or Separate Ways

We know that Radić asked for Italian support, and it is evident that he had no way of avoiding doing so, since France refused to support Croatia's claims. We have seen that Ghilardi (HoR) and Ivo Frank (Graz–Vienna Committee) were preparing plans for great uprisings and military action in coordination with Italy in order to liberate Croatia and destroy the SHS Kingdom in coordination with other groups from Albania and Bulgaria.[469] It is also known that Italians, such as D'Annunzio, were prepared to provoke disorder in Yugoslavia. High ranking military officers, such as Deputy Chief of Staff Pietro Badoglio and Admiral Enrico Millo, governor of Dalmatia, and some elements within the government such as Foreign Minister Carlo Sforza were supportive of plans that would destabilise the SHS Kingdom.[470]

But what was Radić's true link to the Italians and to the Croatian Committee? If it is proven that Radić had contacts with Italian military and

---

467 NA, FO 371/4669, 122–23 ff., Notes on conversation with M. Jelavic, November 12, 1920.
468 ADMAE, Z Europe, Yougoslavie 40, 209–10 ff. Copy of compte *rendu* of Comte de Bombelles an Austrian aristocrat of French origin, Min. de France à Briand, Belgrade, June 15, 1921.
469 As my research does not cover these regions, I will not treat the latter aspects.
470 Ledeen, *op. cit.*, 180–81.

diplomats,[471] it is less clear whether he had contacts with D'Annunzio's Fiume Command directly. As argued by historians Banac and Biondich, the Graz–Vienna Committee would often pretend to be agents of Radić in order to elicit foreign support.[472] There are, however, many clues that tend to offer proof that Radić, or at least his followers or entourage, was dealing not only with D'Annunzio's Command but also with the Croatian Committee.

First, Giovanni Giuriati, a follower of D'Annunzio, claimed that he "had gone to Zara with two Croatian separatists" (followers of Radić) and had "arranged for a pro-separatist journal to be published in Zara".[473] Second, it is confirmed that not only Frankists but Radić himself favoured accepting Italian support to help save Croatia from Serbia.[474] Third, French intelligence reported that Radić was part of the Graz Committee.[475] There is no source to support the latter assertion, but there is little doubt that Radić was in contact with the Committee even if he was not officially a member of it.

French as well as Hungarian sources have often considered some members of the Frank Party to be members of the Peasant Party. They claimed that Prebeg and Pazman joined the Agrarians when the Frank Party was dissolved.[476] In fact, the Frank Party continued to exist under the new name "Croatian Party of Right", as mentioned earlier, and the two members were arrested in March 1919 not as members of Radić's party but as leaders of the Croatian Party of Right. This clearly shows the existence of a certain confusion in Paris and Budapest relating to the different malcontent parties.

Radić had cooperated briefly with the Frankist leadership and the Vienna Committee in 1918 and in 1921–22,[477] which means that Radić, though a

---

471 DDI, 1918–1922, Serie 6, vol. II, no. 502, 343–45, Badoglio to Sonnino in Paris, Rome, February 25, 1919. He was to be helped by the Italians to get to the Paris peace conferences.
472 Biondich, op. cit., 159.
473 Ledeen, op. cit., 181.
474 ADMAE, Z Europe, Yougoslavie 40. 54 f., Radić à Sonnino, Paris, April 7, 1919; ADMAE, Z Europe, Yougoslavie 40. 61 f., Fontenay à Pichon, Belgrade, April 11, 1919.
475 This document even implicated Radić in a Frankist plot to kill the king of Serbia see: ADMAE, Z Europe, Yugoslavia 40. 102–3 f., p.o. Le Ban, le Conseiller banal Dr Gojković à Renseignement, Zagreb, May 21, 1919.
476 As claimed by the son of Ban Crnković, the Croat Committee depended on Radić's party, which was joined by the Frank party MPs when it was dissolved, among which was the notary Prebeg. Budapest, November 21, 1919, MNL, K 64, 2 cs., 1919–1941. I.-21 res., report.
477 Biondich, op. cit., 159.

pacifist and a man who disliked the Hungarians, would try all possible channels in order to save Croatia from Yugoslav occupation.

Since the Peasant Party was the strongest party (without even considering the Frankists) in a system where there was universal suffrage, it is safe to say that the will of the Croatian people was for independence and that the leading members of parties that represented this were secretly or openly pro-Habsburg. Whether for reasons relating to tradition (like the Frankists) or because it was in the interest of Croatia (such as the leaders of the Peasant Party), by the end of 1920 the leading coalition (alliance of Frankist and Peasant Parties) was pro-Habsburg legitimist. The Serbs, with the help of France, were in the process of chasing the Croatians back into the arms of the Habsburgs. Yet it still remained to bring King Karl back to Budapest or Vienna, which would enable him to pursue his role as protector of the Croatians and Slovenes.

CHAPTER V

Slovaks: The Unwilling Czechoslovaks

The Fast-Paced Road to Resistance

The Hungarian Plans for Slovakia

Hungary's new prime minister, Count Mihály Károlyi—freshly appointed by the king's *homo regius*, Archduke József, on October 31, 1918—having declared the independence of Hungary from Austria on November 16, now had to face the dissolution of Hungary. It is not broadly known that Károlyi had issued a programme, as the new president of the Hungarian National Council, which claimed that the integrity of the Kingdom of Hungary could be saved by granting self-determination to the different nationalities. In doing so, Károlyi had followed Karl's October 16 declaration that would, this time, apply to Hungary.[478]

Meanwhile, Beneš sent the following remarks to Prague from Paris following the setting up of the provisional Czechoslovak government in Washington in October 1918:

> It is therefore extremely important that nothing happens in Bohemia that could [...] undermine the authority of either the government or its individual members [...]. It is not desirable "that another government be set up in Bohemia", or that anyone else should negotiate, "on behalf of the nation" with Vienna or Budapest on the federalization of the Habsburg state.[479]

After the Belgrade armistice of November 13, the Hungarian government sent troops to re-establish its authority over Upper Hungary (Slova-

---

[478] Benda, K., *op. cit.*, 840, 842; Macartney, C. A., *Hungary and her Successors*, Oxford University Press, London, 1937, 103.
[479] Zeman, Zbynek, Antonin Klimek, *The Life of Edvard Beneš 1884–1948*, Clarendon Press, Oxford, 1997, 32.

kia) and disperse the Slovak National Council of Turčiansky Svätý Martin, (Turócszentmárton in Hungarian and often referred to as the Council of Saint-Martin in Anglo-Saxon literature),[480] which was, eventually, dissolved by the Czecho-Slovak government on January 8, 1919. The Hungarians pushed the Czechoslovak forces in western Slovakia towards Moravia but could not drive all of them out of Upper Hungary.[481]

As the Hungarians seemed to have the advantage,[482] the new Czechoslovak commissioner to Budapest, Milan Hodža—a Slovak and former deputy of the Hungarian Parliament[483]—started unauthorised negotiations on November 26 with Oszkár Jászi, the Hungarian minister for nationalities, on Slovak autonomy within Hungary until there was a decision by the Peace Conference. Jászi's plan was to transform greater Hungary into a Switzerland-type federation of cantons in which territory would be distributed to the nationalities in a representative way. His so-called Slovak Imperium would be composed of the districts having a Slovak majority. The Slovaks would have a parliament, broad administrative autonomy and independent cultural affairs, and the official language would be Slovak.[484] They were the same terms that were put down in the Pittsburgh Agreement.[485] The discussions with Hodža resulted in the following design: a far-reaching autonomy in which power would be in the hands of the Slovak National Council, which would head the administration and would guarantee order through a National Guard subordinate to it. The autonomous territory would have a

---

[480] *DFBC*, doc. 55, 111–12, MAE (Pichon) aux Ambassadeurs de France à Londres, Berne, Bruxelles, Rome et Washington Paris, November 29, 1918.
[481] Mamatey, *op. cit.*, 31
[482] The Hungarian government claimed that as they did not have the military power they would negotiate. Szarka, *op. cit.*, 155.
[483] Milan Hodža (Slovak agrarian politician) was a former member of the Hungarian Parliament elected in 1905. He attended the St. Martin meeting in May 1918, organised by the Slovak National Party. He encouraged the creation of the SNC and was one of the signatories of the Martin Declaration. He created the National Republican Farmers Party in Slovakia (September 1919), which formed a coalition with the Slovak National Party that became the Slovak National Farmer's Party to fight during the elections of 1920. Kirschbaum, *Historical*, 73–74.
[484] Szarka, László, *A Szlovákok Története*, Bereményi Kiadó, Budapest, 1993, 155–56; Jászi, *Magyar*, 65. Jászi wrote that he could have struck an agreement not only with the Germans and the Rusyns but with the Slovaks as well.
[485] See following pages.

National Assembly and common affairs would be discussed by delegations from both the Hungarian and the Slovak Parliaments.[486]

But why did Hodža start such a negotiation when Czechoslovakia had been admitted to the Peace talks as one of the victors during the war and when Beneš had given instructions not to negotiate on federalisation? Lieutenant-Colonel Fernand Vix, head of the Allied Military Mission in Budapest (November 1918–March 1919), had told Hodža that the presence of the Czech army in Slovakia violated the Belgrade military convention between the Allied forces and the Hungarian government. Hodža answered that, if that was so, then the "Czechoslovak"[487] troops would retire from Hungarian territory.[488] Thus, Hodža had to conclude that he could not count on the Entente to keep Slovakia under Czechoslovak control and had to be compromising towards Hungary.

Prague could not dispute Slovakia being awarded to Hungary due to its feeble military forces, and it turned to diplomacy for help.[489] As General Franchet d'Espérey had failed to include Slovakia in the Belgrade armistice provision, Beneš protested in Paris to Pichon and Marshal Foch to allow Prague, as a recognised Allied government, to occupy Slovakia with its military forces.[490]

As there was no administrative boundary between Hungary and Upper Hungary, and since Slovakia, as such, had not existed in the past, Beneš decided to use the natural borders of the Danube and Ipoly rivers as the demarcation line between Czechoslovak and Hungarian forces, thus putting the fertile plain north to the Danube, mainly inhabited by Magyars, under Czechoslovak control. The French government accepted, and Pichon informed the Hungarian government—in a late night letter of November 29, 1918—that it had to evacuate Slovakia, but he did not mention where the demarcation line was located.[491] To add to the confusion, earlier on the same

---

486 *A Trianon Forrásai I, Dokumentumkötet*, Magyar Nemzeti Történelmi Társaság, Kaposvár, 1994, 158–59.
487 At that stage they were more Czech, if not exclusively, then Slovak.
488 *DFBC*, no. 57, 113–14 ff., Vix à Gén. Henrys, Commandant de l'Armée française d'Orient Budapest, November 29, 1918.
489 Mamatey, *op. cit.*, 31, 56.
490 Ibid., 32.
491 *DFBC*, no. 55, 111–12. Pichon à MAE, aux Amb. Londres Berne, Bruxelles, Rome et Washigton Budapest, November 29, 1918, 23:50h.

day Vix had sent a letter to General Henrys, commander of the *Armée d'Orient* (mentioned above), in which he said that the Hungarian government had complained many times of the invasion of "Northern Hungary" by Czechoslovak forces and suggested the departure of the Czecho-"Slovak" forces and that "ce résultat serait particulièrement apprécié à Buda-Pesth. Mon autorité se trouverait renforcée si ce résultat était obtenu."[492] In this same letter Vix wrote that Pichon stated that Hungary had to "retirer ses troupes du territoire tchéco-slovaque".[493] This proves that the French military had no idea of what the limits of Upper Hungary were and shows the arbitrariness of these limits.

As news came of French instruction to evacuate Upper Hungary, Hodža took a second, unauthorised, "liberty" of negotiating, this time regarding the demarcation line that had been lacking in the French instruction. An agreement was struck on December 6 with the Hungarian minister of defence, Béla Bartha, which would slide the demarcation line northward, to the disadvantage of Czechoslovakia, leaving the mountainous, poor and exclusively Slovak inhabited districts to Czechoslovakia, while maintaining the principal towns Kassa and Pressburg (to be called Bratislava, SK)—inhabited in the majority by Magyars—in Hungarian hands. The new demarcation line also left eastern Slovakia under Hungarian control, where Viktor Dvorčák, a Magyarone and leader of the Eastern Slovak National Council, founded an "East Slovak Republic" on the same day, "claiming that the Slovaks were a distinct nationality". This was the first attempt to create an independent Slovak state after the war; it fell on December 30, 1918, when Czechoslovak troops arrived at Košice (Kassa, H).[494] More to the east, Subcarpathian Hungary was attached to Czechoslovakia in April 1919 by the will of the Ruthenians, who were the majority population in this region.[495]

---

[492] "[...] this result would be particularly appreciated in Budapest. My authority would find itself reinforced if this result was obtained." Ibid., no. 57, 113–14, Vix à Gén. Henrys, Commandant de l'Armée française d'Orient, Budapest, November 29, 1918.

[493] "[...] withdraw its troops from Czechoslovak territory." Ibid., 55, 111–12.

[494] Mamatey, *op. cit.*, 32. Toma and Kovač claim that it was called the Slovak Peoples' Republic and declared on December 11, 1918, at Košice (Kassa). Toma, Peter, A., Dusan Kovač, *Slovakia, from Samos to Dzurinda*, Hoover Inst. Press, Stanford, CA, 2001, 69–70; Jászi, Oszkár, *Magyar Kálvária, Magyar Föltámadás*, Bécsi Mayar Kiadó, Vienna, 1920, 65. Heimann, M., *Czechoslovakia*, Yale University Press, New Haven, London, 2009, 44.

[495] A group of Ruthenes (a Carpatho-Ukranian ethnic group) of the Subcarpathian region of pre-1918 Hungary had set up a republic in Jasina (Körösmező, H), the Hutsul Republic (Eastern Subcar-

Naturally, Beneš accepted neither the new demarcation line nor the federalisation plan of Slovakia, and Hodža was definitely disavowed. Meanwhile, Jászi was trying to postpone a *fait accompli* in order to secure a plebiscite that would end in Hungary keeping Slovakia. Beneš did not waste time; he protested and had his original suggestion reinforced by the French government on January 20, 1919.[496]

It is appropriate to ask whether Hodža was truly convinced of the virtues of Slovak autonomy or accepted the idea only to induce Hungary to evacuate Slovakia. Jászi truly believed that Hodža had been won over to his idea, though the latter emphasised that this arrangement would be valid only until the Peace Conference.[497] Hodža claimed that he had accepted in order to induce Hungary to evacuate.[498] Indeed, what advantage would there be in federalising if centralisation was Prague's programme. If Beneš had not stopped the process, Hodža could have achieved the creation of Jászi's "Slovak Imperium", which would have been a *fait accompli* by the time of the Peace Conference. This situation would have certainly advantaged the Slovaks' autonomist claims towards Prague. Whether Hodža's openness to the project could indicate that, as a Slovak, he leaned towards the idea of auton-

---

pathia) near the old boarder of the Kingdom of Hungary in January 1919. It had a small cabinet and parliament but fell when the Romanian troops occupied the region in May 1919. Jasina was re-occupied by Hungarian Red forces in July 1919 before officially being granted to Czechoslovakia by the Trianon Treaty. Prior to these events, (July 1918) Gregory Žatkovyč, a Hungarian-born Rusyn (another word for Ruthene, though also considered as a different group of Carptho-Ukrainians), was brought up in Pennsylvania and was the leader of the Ruthenes of America (The American National Council of Hungarian-Ruthenes *Amerikans'ka Narodna Rada Uhro-Rusinov*). He approached President Wilson, who told him the only way the Ruthenes could get autonomy was to join Czechoslovakia. He made a deal with Masaryk and signed a "Declaration of Common Aims" (October 26, 1918) in Pennsylvania, with him granting autonomy to Rusyn's once Czechoslovakia was created. Žatkovyč was appointed governor of the autonomous Ruthenian territory from April 1920 to April 1921. Control of Cezchoslovakia over the Subcarpathian region was assured until the Trianon Peace Treaty. However, apart from the East Slovak Republic, there were two Ruthenian groups with different agendas: the Hungarian Ruthene National Council founded in Lubló (November 8, 1918) and that met again in Eperjes/Prešov under its leader Antonij Beskyd, which wanted to separate from Hungary; and the second group, set up in Ungvár (Uzhgorod), which wanted to remain in Hungary. Eventually it was the pro-Czechoslovak group led by Beskyd—who was invited to join the Czechoslovak peace delegation—which prevailed. Heimann, *op.cit.*, 37, 44–46, 61.
496 Macartney, op. cit., 103; Mamatey, *op. cit.*, 32.
497 Szarka, *op. cit.*, 155; Jászi wrote that he could have struck an agreement not only with the German and the Rusyn minorities but with the Slovaks as well had Hodža not received a *désaveu* from Prague. Jászi, *Magyar*, 65.
498 Mamatey, *op. cit.*, 32.

omy for Slovakia seems doubtful. Known to have been a convinced Czechoslovak, it is more likely that he needed to buy time.

Considering Hungary, the organisation of autonomies was not a surprise, since Oszkár Jászi had been preparing a plan during World War I to cut the old Realm of Saint Stephen into national autonomies. Some French sources claim that the autonomy of East Slovakia was proclaimed by Jászi, the committee of which was set up by Dvorčák.[499] Jászi, indeed, knew about the "East Slovaks", but he also knew that there was not a lot of support behind them, which meant that it was not worth supporting them and similar groups. As he said, "The main problem was not to save old Hungary but to realise a more logical and moral international order."[500] Jászi was against representing the policy of some members of the Károlyi government who, under the guise of accepting the conditions set by the Entente, would organise leagues for the integrity of Hungary back home and send secret agitators to occupied territories.

Jászi defended himself by explaining that three to four separate propaganda organs were working without his knowledge.[501] The most important of these was the *Területvédő Liga,* the League for the Defence of Territorial Integrity (henceforth TL). Though a civilian society, it had many military officer members who were organising propaganda and gathering intelligence information with government money, helping but sometimes countering its policy.[502]

---

499 As described by an anonymous French intelligence report, the Committee was made up of 20 members, two of whom were Slovak "creatures of Budapest". It further claimed that when the autonomy was proclaimed, these two members were excluded, and it was proclaimed only by Germans and local Hungarians of Košice. Dvorčák was proclaimed as its president, but the Slovaks forced Dvorčák to resignation. Then the Hungarians spread the rumor that the Czechoslovak envoy to Budapest, Hodža, had accepted this presidency. ADMAE, Z Europe, Tchécoslovaquie 34, 3 f., Prague, December 26, 1918, (without signature). Thanks to Polish and Hungarian propaganda, French Intelligence thought that a new Slovak Republic was to be created in federation with Poland. Ibid, 4 f., Capitaine Gaillard, Service de Renseignements d'Annemasse (in Savoy, on the border with Geneva), December 29, 1918, signed. In the next documents the intelligence officer writes that "the information on the impending creation of a Slovak Republic cannot be considered as serious." Ibid. document no. 70, 7 f.
500 Jászi, *Magyar,* 64.
501 Ibid., 67.
502 Tilkovszky Loránt, 'Területi integritás és területi autonómia', *Századok,* no. 3, Budapest, 2000, 555–96, see 556. Feketené Cselényi Zsuzsanna, "Magyarország Területi Épségének Védelmi Ligája megalakulásának körülményei és tevékenysége", *Egri Ho Shi Minh Tanárképző Főiskola Közleményei,* XVII. Eger, 1984, 113–26.

Jászi's project of federalisation would still have been possible during the war if the Hungarian governments had then anticipated their 1918 plight, but once the war was over it could have been feasible only if Hodža had been able and willing to bring it through with Prague.

From Pittsburgh to Saint-Martin

The main reasons that made the Slovaks turn against Prague also form the background for demonstrating in this chapter the very rapid change of sentiment between Slovaks and Czechs following the war and for the creation of Czechoslovakia.

A few months before the end of World War I, on May 30, 1918, the Pittsburgh Pact was signed by Slovak and Czech-American organisations and Masaryk, representing the Czecho-Slovak National Council.[503] The pact—drafted by Masaryk—clearly specified that "a political programme aiming at the union of the Czechs and Slovaks in an independent state comprising the Czech lands and Slovakia", but it is also stated that "Slovakia shall have its own administration, its own Diet, and its own courts." It would have its own "official language in the schools, in government offices, and public life generally."[504]

On October 28, 1918, the Czech National Committee in Prague declared the creation of the Czechoslovak Republic. Unaware of this declaration, a Slovak National Council was established at Turčiansky Svätý Martin (Saint-Martin) two days later (October 30, 1918),[505] the members of which made the "Martin Declaration". That declaration rejected the right of the Hungarian government to speak on behalf of the Slovaks, gave the Slovak Council this right and proposed a union in a common state with the Czechs. The Slovak leaders called themselves a Czecho-Slovak nation, which was not the

---

503 Czecho-Slovak National Council, recognised by the French government as the Czecho-slovak government on June 29, 1918, followed by Britain on August 9 and the USA on September 3. Mamatey, *op. cit.*, 85.
504 School of East European and Slavonic Studies (henceforth SEESS), Seton-Watson Papers (henceforth SEW) 10/2/1, Hlinka's Memo to Peace Conference; Kirschbaum, Stanislav J., *Historical Dictionary of Slovakia*, Scarecrow Press, Lanham and London, 1999, 126.
505 Felak, James Ramon, *"At the Price of the Republic" Hlinka's Slovak People's Party 1929–1938*, University of Pittsburgh Press, Pittsburgh and London, 1994, 22–23.

main goal of the Slovak nationalists but the recognition of the Slovaks as a distinct nation and autonomy for Slovakia. The word "Czechoslovakia" would come back to haunt them.[506]

An important point is that the Slovak leaders had become aware—only in summer 1919—of the fact that the Pittsburgh Pact defended their right to autonomy.[507] One of these leaders, the most prominent by far, was Andrej Hlinka who was to become the greatest figure in the fight for autonomy and independence. As in Croatia, the leader of the national movement was an educated and charismatic man, a Catholic as well, indeed, a priest. Reverend Hlinka had been the founder of the Slovak Peoples Party in 1913 under Hungarian rule and had a heroic political past. He was praised by Seton-Watson as a Slovak martyr[508] for having been arrested, condemned and imprisoned by the Hungarians for his anti-Magyar activity in 1907. After the war, in October 1918, he was the co-founder of the Slovak National Council, deputy of the Czechoslovak National Assembly and a signatory of the Declaration of the Slovak Nation. In November 1918, he founded the Slovak Clerical Council, which was composed of politically active clergy. Its aim was to defend the rights of the Catholic population and it recreated the Slovak Peoples Party—members of which were nicknamed the L'udaks—on December 19, 1918.[509]

But things went badly from the first for Hlinka's Slovak national movement, and he would not gain the confidence of Prague in order to influence politics in the direction he thought best for the Slovaks. It was Vavro Šrobár—the most important Hlasist[510] spokesman before the war and the only Slovak to sign the proclamation of the Czechoslovak state on October 28, 1918—who was chosen as he man in whom Prague placed its con-

---

506 Felak, *op. cit.*, 16.
507 SEW, 10/2/1, Hlinka's Memo to Peace Conference; Kirschbaum, *Historical*, 126.
508 SEW, 10/2/1, *Scotus Viator* by Andrej Hlinka, and *Hlinka and Scotus, Further Views.*
509 Mamatey, op. cit., 85; Kirschbaum, *Historical*, 71.
510 Originally proposed by a group of students influenced by the ideas of Tomas G. Masaryk in the periodical *Hlas,* "The Voice". They were partisans of a union of Slovaks with the Czechs. Kirschbaum, *Historical,* 70. Šrobár was a lawyer, deputy to the Czechoslovak National Assembly from 1918–23 and leader of the Slovak wing of the Czechoslovak Social Democratic Workers' Party. He was minister for Slovakia from 1919–20, a strong supporter of Czechoslovakism and an opponent of Slovak autonomy. As a physician "with a secular and liberal outlook" he totally opposed Hlinka's parochial clerical mentality as resembling that of Slovak peasants. Felak, *op. cit,* 25; Kirschbaum, *Historical,* 49.

fidence in establishing the Czecho-Slovak Revolutionary Assembly (Skalica government).[511] It was created in Prague on November 13, 1918, as a provisional national assembly, by the Prague National Committee with undivided authority and with power to draft and adopt a permanent constitution. The Assembly had 40 Slovak members, selected by Šrobár, among them Andrej Hlinka, the leader of the Slovak Peoples Party and his advisor František Jehlička.[512] Other Slovaks such as Ivan Dérer[513] and Milan Hodža had also travelled to Prague, but the Slovak delegation did not represent a cross section of the Slovak people.

Hlinka's Fight for Slovakia

It was unlikely that the Hlasist-dominated Slovak Club[514] would recommend and the National Assembly approve Slovak autonomy,[515] and the Slovak Peoples Party made that known to Prague. It also made it secretly known to the Hungarians of the ABC who had fled to Vienna during the Republic of Councils.[516]

Hlinka and František Jehlička, representing the frustrated and malcontent Slovaks, decided to defend their claims in Paris at the Peace Conference and left for France via Poland on August 27, 1919. As the representatives of the Allied powers were drifting apart on the question of the minorities, they might have had a fair chance of influencing the decisions to their favour.[517]

---

511 It became the Constituent National Assembly after the April 1920 elections. Kirschbaum, *Historical*, 38.
512 Rev. Franz Jehlička (1879–1939) a priest, professor of theology at the University of Budapest and member of the Hungarian Parliament in 1906–7, he was an advisor to Hlinka. He was deputy to the Czecho-Slovak Revolutionary Assembly in 1919. He helped recreate the Peoples party and accompanied Hlinka to the Paris Peace conference in 1919. He sought to influence Slovak politics from Budapest and Warsaw, where he created the Slovak National Council. (Mamatey, *op. cit.*, 84; Kirschbaum, *Historical*, 83).
513 Lawyer, journalist, signatory of the St. Martin Declaration (1918), and regional chairman in Slovakia of the Czechoslovak Social Democratic Workers' Party. Dérer was minister for Administration of Slovakia in 1920. http://www.historiecssd.cz/d/derer-ivan/ (21.4.2018).
514 Politicians who were appointed to represent Slovakia in the Czechoslovak Revolutionary Assembly organised into a Slovak Club. The deputies were also representatives of the major parties in Slovakia. Kirschbaum, *Historical*, 146.
515 Mamatey, *op. cit.*, 85.
516 Boroviczény, *op. cit.*, 30.
517 Mamtey, op. cit., 85.

Chapter V

They submitted a "Mémoire des Slovaques à la Conférence de Paix", which began as follows: "Nous ne sommes ni Tchèques ni Tchécoslovaques, nous sommes Slovaques tout simplement. La Slovaquie aux Slovaques. C'est au nom de la paix durable que nous réclamons l'autonomie de la Slovaquie."[518]

Referring to the Pittsburgh agreement, which recognised the autonomy of Slovakia, Hlinka stated that those who had taken political power did not want to hear about it anymore. "Not only do they want to create a Czechoslovak state but also a Czecho-Slovak Nation, which is an ethnographical monstrosity". For Hlinka the Slovaks had fallen from a Magyar hegemony to a Czech one. As there was no mention of a Slovak nation in the approval in Versailles of a Czechoslovak Republic (September 14, 1919), Hlinka was hoping that by his presence in Paris he could pressure Masaryk and Beneš to recognise Slovak autonomy and insert it into the Peace Treaty.[519]

When the Slovak Club got news that Hlinka was in Paris, they proposed to deprive him and Jehlička of their parliamentary immunity and to try them for treason. Of the two, it was Hlinka who went back to Czechoslovakia, and he was imprisoned for the second time in his political career, but this time by the Czechoslovaks in Moravia. Jehlička went to Budapest and acted as a paid Hungarian agent from then on. The Czechs and pro-unity Slovaks had managed to create their future enemies.[520]

As Hlinka had only demanded autonomy and not independence (the constitution had not been drafted yet), and he had not violated any law, he was not tried for treason. He was soon released and could return to Slovakia. In order to avoid having him campaign in the parliamentary elections, he was kept in Prague; this did not hinder him from being elected to the Assembly.[521]

By the end of 1919 the Czechs were losing ground in Slovakia as anti-Czech feeling was growing stronger among Slovaks. If the Hungarian propaganda and the newly-formed Slovak-Hungarian League were an important

---

[518] "We are neither Czechs nor Czechoslovaks, we are simply Slovaks. Slovakia to the Slovaks. It is in the name of lasting peace that we reclaim the autonomy of Slovakia." SWE, 10/2/1, Confidential: Hlinka's Memorandum to the Peace Conference.
[519] Ibid.
[520] Kirschbaum, Stanislav J., *A History of Slovakia: The Struggle for Survival*, Macmillan Press, London, 1995, 164–65.
[521] Ibid.

factor in the evolution of the anti-Czech feeling in the whole of Slovakia,[522] then the Magyarophile feelings in the economically important part of Slovakia[523] (the south) had to do more with the fact that the majority of the population of towns such as Pressburg (newly Bratislava) and Kassa (now officially Košice) had Hungarian as their mother tongue.[524]

After the elections in April 1920, Hlinka got a bitter surprise when he realised that his party had gotten only 12 seats in Parliament (17.6 percent) and that the Social Democratic Party polled 38 percent with 23 seats, and the Agrarians, the Slovak branch of the Czechoslovak Agrarian Party, got 18 percent in Slovakia and 12 seats.[525] In other words, they came in only third for a party that claimed to speak in the name of the Slovak people, and neither of the two other parties defended autonomy. The socialist ideas of the short-lived Soviet Republic had had an influence on the population and Hlinka was to combat this until "Red Slovakia would turn into a white one". In the future he would introduce national and religious issues into the 1920 elections.[526]

In order to become the dominant political group in Slovakia, the Peoples' Party sought influence everywhere it could, in cultural organisations, economic institutions, Christian-social trade unions and the Association of Catholic Students.[527] It eventually succeeded.

It is timely to ask whether Hlinka was just a federalist or also a legitimist. Boroviczény says that Hlinka, Dvorčák and Jehlička visited the ABC Committee in Vienna and/or the Hungarian government once it was re-established in Budapest and that they would have visited Karl in his Swiss exile as well.[528] It is known from Prince Windischgraetz that Hlinka sent

---

522 *DBFP*, vol. VI, no. 283, 378–79, Gosling to Curzon, Prague, 16 November 1919; *op. cit.*, no. 134, 182–83, Prague, Gosling to Curzon, August 23, 1919; *op. cit.*, no. 36, 71–73, Gosling to Curzon, Prague, July 11, 1919.
523 *Op. cit.*, no.134, 182–83, August 23, 1919, Gosling to Curzon; *op. cit.*, no. 36, 71. Prague, July 11, 1919, Gosling to Curzon.
524 Glatz, Ferenc, *Minorities in East-Central Europe, Historical Analysis and a Policy Proposal*, Europa Institute, Budapest, 1993, 40–41.
525 Felak, *op. cit.*, 29; Jelinek, Yeshayahu, *The Parish Republic: Hlinka's Slovak People's Party 1939–1945*, Columbia University Press, New York, 1976, 8; Kirschbaum, S. (ed.), *Slovak Politics, Essays on Slovak History in honour of Joseph M. Kirschbaum*, Slovak Institute, Cleveland, Rome, 1983, 166.
526 Jelinek, *op. cit.*, 8.
527 It was to supply the future leadership of the Party.
528 Boroviczény, *op. cit.*, 30.

his secretary, Harodek, to assure the monarch of the Slovak people's faithfulness.[529] Another clue is that while Karl was declaring that restoration in Hungary could be done in less than a year, the Czechoslovak propaganda was spreading the news that the menace of restoration was imminent in Prague. The Prague newspapers were underlining that Hlinka and his friends were receiving favourably the news of a return of a pro-monarchic government in Hungary.[530] Hlinka was surrounded by other priests such as Father Dr Florian Tománek, his old companion[531] and an outspoken legitimist who published pro-Habsburg articles with Father Ferdiš (Ferdinand) Juriga. Editor of the Pressburg-based *Slovenske Ludové Noviny* (Slovak People's News), Tománek was arrested, denied a legal trial and imprisoned.[532] Jehlička, also, was looking forward to restoration.[533]

In addition to the lack of respect for their wish for autonomy, four main factors alienated the Slovaks from the Czechoslovak idea. Two of these were indigenous: the Catholic Church's position and the high percentage of Magyarones (pro-Hungarian Slovaks) among intellectuals; and two were exogenous: the dictatorial Czechoslovak measures taken by Šrobár, and the legionaries' behaviour.

The Role of the Church

In Cisleithania, the famous Czech historian František Palacký as well as Masaryk interpreted their nation's history as a struggle between Hussitism, "representing progressive national spirit" and "the Catholic Counter-Reformation, which stood for reaction and oppression", which was backed by the Habsburgs.[534]

---

529 Windischgraetz, *Ein Kaiser kämpft*, 145.
530 Boros, Ferenc, *Magyar csehszlovák kapcsolatok 1918–1921-ben*, Akadémia, Budapest, 1970, 98; Boros, Ferenc, *Hongrois et Slovaques*, Press Publica, Budapest, 2002, 44.
531 Mamatey, *op. cit.*, 139.
532 ADMAE, Z Europe Tchécoslovaquie 45, Memorandum of Prof Kmoško and Fr. Jehlička (October 30, 1919); SEW/10/2/1, Reply of Seton-Watson to Memorandum of Prof Kmoško and Fr. Jehlička (no date).
533 MNL K26, 1921-38-1920, Jehlička to Jenő Tvrdy, Magyrone lawyer and close friend of Hlinka, December 31, 1919.
534 Felak, *op. cit*, 22–23.

In Transleithania, the liberal 1895 legislation had secularised Hungary, and after the war the Slovak priests were hoping to re-establish the influence of the Catholic Church in the country in order to better its economic situation and satisfy personal ambitions. The new rulers, the Czechs and their Slovak supporters, made a big mistake by reinforcing secularisation, planning the separation of church and state, nationalising primary and secondary education and bringing in agrarian reforms that threatened Catholic Church estates. As a consequence, they had frustrated the clergy and had made it an enemy.[535]

Hlinka denounced the Czechs as anti-clerical and as favouring the Lutheran Slovaks when assigning political positions.[536] The factors that led the Slovak Catholics to create a political party were: that the new government threatened them with secularisation and anti-clericalism; the exclusion of Catholics from serving in the administration proportionally to their numbers; the desire on the part of Slovak priests for career advancement in a de-Magyarised church; and finally, Hlinka's rivalry with Šrobár. An extra factor was that the Slovak church was still dependant on Esztergom, in the hands of Hungarian Prince Primate Cardinal Csernoch (a priest of Slovak origin),[537] who asked Hlinka and the Slovak clergy to resist the Czechoslovak Republic. Hlinka, however, answered that the Czechoslovak Republic was an irreversible fact.[538] The Czechs, too, held some of the cards, since Hlinka wanted to become the first Slovak archbishop in Slovakia, and they could influence him by voicing that possibility when necessary.[539]

Until Hlinka established the SPP, there is no evidence that he would have shown any public opposition to Czechoslovakian unity or demanded autonomy.[540] Once created, the People's Party attracted many priests and

---

535 Jelinek, *op. cit.*, 6. The Slovaks, in general, were shocked by Czech anticlericalism. 371/4383, PID, 6, memorandum on Czechoslovakia, November 1919.
536 Felak, *op. cit*, 22–23.
537 The Hungarian Catholic Church's strong interest in Upper Hungary found response in the Slovak clergy's ambitions. Tilkovszky Loránt, "Területi integritás és területi autonómia", *Századok*, no. 3, Budapest, 2000, 563.
538 Felak, *op. cit*, 22–23.
539 NA, FO 371/5823/C22435, Slovakia, Summary for October 1921. Jehlička was trying to influence Hlinka, too, by stimulating his will to become the first archbishop. Mamatey, *op. cit.*, 85.
540 Felak, *op. cit.*, 26.

with them their flocks. The party leadership was composed of priests as well as university professors due to the lack of Slovak intellectuals in a strongly agrarian Slovakia.[541]

The Magyarones of Slovakia

During the days of the Austro-Hungarian Monarchy, a Slovak patriot was a person who took part in the struggle against Magyarisation, but as historian James Felak wrote, since Slovakia had become Czechoslovakia "many Magyarones were undergoing a difficult psychological transformation: World War I and the creation of the Republic had transformed many values. Hatred of Czechoslovakia was still evident; reality had to be acknowledged and means of adjustment found, so these people changed from Magyarones into ardent Slovak nationalists."[542]

The transformation of Magyarones into "Slovak nationalists" was the way to resist the Czechs.[543] As an autonomist and anti-Magyar, Hlinka was closer to the Slavic Czechs, yet he accepted many Magyarones into the leadership of his party. This was mainly for two evident reasons: first, the Magyarones—who had chosen the Hungarian identity and language—were much better educated than authentic Slovaks, since they had access to the best education in the Realm of Hungary, and, as a result, could pursue higher-level careers; second, most priests were part of a Magyarised segment of Slovak society due to the fact that they were members of the Hungarian Catholic clergy (even Father Hlinka). In other words, two groups made up the bulk of the leadership of the SPP: the clergy and the Magyarones, who were often one and the same.

The strong presence of Magyarones in the SPP made Prague believe that the autonomists were in fact pro-Magyar irredentists, which was partly

---

541 Jelinek, *op. cit.*, 7. The elite of Slovakia was composed of Hungarian *bene possesionati* nobles and of a rich German bourgeoisie (the so-called Zipser Sachsen population of the northern German cities of Upper Hungary and the German burgers of Pressburg and Kassa). Some of the Hungarian nobles of Slovakia were of Slav origin but considered themselves Magyars.
542 Felak, *op. cit.*, 7.
543 Ibid, referring to Materna, Jozef, *Minulosť a prítomnosť slovenských autonomistov*, Bratislava, 1923.

true.[544] Author Yeshayahu Jelinek, who specialises in the SPP, claims that the autonomists— including most of the Magyarones—were for a Slovak autonomy in the frame of the Czechoslovak Republic.[545] This could be a general impression, but there are no statistics to claim that this was true; however one can look at the fate of the Magyarones described in this book. Vojtech Tuka and Jozef Tiso became leaders of the first Slovak Republic under German Nazi control. Jehlička, Juriga and others were anti-Czech separatists. All these Slovaks were, or had developed into, Slovak patriots or later into radical nationalists. A lot of them wanted, at least for a moment during the period studied, to reattach autonomous Slovakia to Hungary and, consequently, remained, to a certain extent, Magyarones.

Hlinka accepted Magyarone Slovaks in the SPP and would accept anyone who showed Slovak patriotism and would defend autonomy for Slovakia. An original example was Vojtech Tuka (1880–1946), professor of law, Magyarone, Slovak autonomist and member of Hlinka's party.[546] Tuka, like Jehlička, was in the pay of Hungary, unbeknown to Hlinka. His aim was to drive a wedge between Slovaks and Czechs and attach the former to Hungary.[547] Like Tuka, Jozef Tiso, the later president of the first Slovak Republic (1939–1945), was a Magyarone as well, though a "silent" one.

Prague's Assimilation Programme

Šrobár was appointed minister with full powers for the administration of Slovakia; his powers were dictatorial, and he did not shy away from using them. His tasks were to suppress social unrest, fire the civil servants under Hungarian influence and establish a Czechoslovak administration. He did

---

544 Jelinek, *op. cit.*, 7.
545 Ibid. The author claims this without any reference.
546 Ibid., 9.
547 He was surreptitiously in contact with groups such as Austrian monarchists, Italian Fascists, Hungarian irredentists and German Nazis in order to destroy Czechoslovakia. Felak, *op. cit.*, 32. With a strong foothold in the party's press and decision-making organs and the ear of Hlinka, he was able to become one of the party's most influential figures and became editor-in-chief of the party's press organ, *Slovák*, in 1922. Jelinek, *op. cit.*, 9. In summer 1921 he presented Hlinka with a draft of the SPP's autonomy proposal and was the author of the first autonomy submission to the Czechoslovak National Assembly.

not believe in the wisdom and patriotism of the Slovak masses and thought that, distorted by Hungarian rule, they did not see where their interests lay. Thousands of Czech officials came to Slovakia with Šrobár in order to assist him. Though in general, they increased efficiency in this mainly agricultural and backward former region of Hungary, the Czechs often lacked tact and differed in manners, culture and outlook. The Slovaks resented paternalism.[548] The new authority would impose and collect taxes more regularly than before and would distribute state positions to the Czechs.[549]

Hlinka claimed that the *Slovenská Ľudová Strana* had 90 percent of the Slovak population behind it and that as the party of autonomy, it was persecuted by the Czechs. The soldiers, Sokols,[550] employees and gendarmes persecuted the party, and even the postal services did not always deliver the party's letters and newspapers but destroyed them or held them back. The party's right to meet was limited and their gatherings were forbidden or dispersed, as in Žilina (Zsolna, H) on August 17, 1919, when the Czech militia dispersed the crowd and wanted to kill the orators.[551]

While Hlinka was in prison, until April 1920, Juriga tried to persuade the Slovak Club to defend a vague "self-administration and legislature on the provincial level", but without success, and the new constitution of February 1920 would not even recognise two different languages but only one: Czechoslovak. Six Ľudaks voted for the constitution but underlined that it did not mean they would abandon their aim of autonomy.[552]

Czechoslovakism was the main doctrine of the constitution, and the reasons for a centralised regime were evident: first, single nation equals single government; second, the Germans and Hungarians could demand national autonomy if it was accorded; third, there was a necessary control over Slovakia in order to avoid it falling back to Hungary. The Hungarian minority

---

[548] At a certain point, Šrobár was obliged to reprimand the Czechs for their religious intolerance by saying that "they have to acknowledge the piety of the Slovaks and not to offend their religious feelings". Reference to Šrobár's exposé of August 4, 1919, SSEES, SEW, 10/2/1, Hlinka: *Mémoire à la Conférence de la Paix, Les Slovaques sous le joug Tchèque*.
[549] Felak, James Ramon, *op. cit*, 21; Macartney, C. A., *Hungary and Her Successors: The Treaty of Trianon and its Consequences 1919–1937*, London, 1937, 124–27.
[550] Originally Czech patriotic gymnastic associations, but later also cultural associations.
[551] Felak, *op. cit.*, 28
[552] Ibid.

represented 21.6 percent of Slovakia's population, that is 650,547 individuals (1921 census). The Hungarians were both economically and politically dominant,⁵⁵³ and Prague would have a hard time integrating them.

There was another element of Czech repression and assimilation that was a strong factor in alienating the Slovaks: the legionaries.

The Problem of the New Czechoslovak Army

In June 1919, the Hungarian Communist forces moved into Slovakia. A Soviet Republic was declared in Eastern Slovakia. This post-war conflict proved to be a painful baptism of fire for the gestating Czechoslovak army because it showed the new army's unreliability in respect to officers and troops alike: "Czech troops showed unwillingness to fight for Slovakia; they were unreliable under fire, and many officers were degraded to the ranks. Numbers of men were shot for cowardice and insubordination."⁵⁵⁴ It was in these terms that Cecil Gosling, the British chargé d'affaire to Prague, described the situation. The Hungarian forces had to retreat under Entente pressure. Nevertheless, it was thanks to the French officers that the whole of Slovakia had not been occupied by the Czechs.⁵⁵⁵ By the end of the year, the Slovak soldiers were disobeying their Czech officers and were singing patriotic Hungarian songs "to show their dislike of the Czechs".⁵⁵⁶ The Czechs were frightened, but the returning Czech legions were to solve the problem.

The Legionaries

Three groups of Czech legionaries were fighting in Italy, France and Russia on the Allied side during the war. These legions were integrated into the respective armies, with the respective uniforms. The largest legion was in Russia, numbering to 50,000 men. As the Czech legion remaining in Russia

---

553 Mamatey, *op. cit.*, 95–97.
554 *DBFP*, vol. VI, no. 36, 71–73. Gosling to Curzon Prague, July 11, 1919.
555 Ibid.
556 *Op. cit.*, no. 332, 452, Gosling to Curzon, Prague, December 1, 1919.

played a leading role in igniting the anti-Bolshevik resistance,[557] it was the task of the legionaries coming back from France and Italy to occupy Upper Hungary at the beginning of 1919. They were the backbone of the forces that fought the Hungarian Red Army in 1919.[558]

Once they returned to their newly-independent homeland, the legionaries from Russia represented some 88,683 individuals.[559] Then the problem of demobilisation began, and as it was impossible to unite them after their return, many associations of legionaries were founded, among which the *Družina československých legionářů* (Company of Czechoslovak Legionaries) was the most radically nationalist and showed no compromise towards Germans and Hungarians.[560]

Minister of Finance Alois Rašin declared that no pensions would be paid to the legionaries, they were to be compensated differently, and the Parliament's law of May 1919 (art. No. 282 and no. 462) gave them the right and priority to claim positions as civil servants or to become employed by state companies. Another law, regarding the distribution of real property, also gave priority to the legionaries, and land would be given to them even if they were not farmers.[561]

The legionaries were placed especially in regions inhabited by non-Slav minorities, such as in the Hungarian-inhabited Csallóköz (Grosse Schüttinsel, D), where they were rewarded with land belonging to minorities. These legionaries also had the right to claim civil servant positions subsidised by the state, and they were one of the factors spurring anti-Czech resentment among the populations of Slovakia. Prague used them because they were a reliable force which could be employed against the Hungarian Red Army, and also Prague thought that it would be better if some stayed in Slovakia to supervise that region. This implantation and assimilation programme displeased not only the Hungarians and the Germans but also the Slovaks.

---

557 G. Thurnig-Nittner, *Die Tschechoslowakische Legion in Russland*, Wiesbaden, 1970. Boroviczény, *op. cit.*, 30; Windischgraetz, *Ein Kaiser kämpft*, 146.
558 Simon, Attila, 'Legionárius telepitések a két háború között', *Századok*, no. 68, 2004, 1368.
559 Ibid., 1368–69.
560 Ibid. See: Šedivý, Ivan, "Druzina ceskoslovenskývh legionárského hnuti v Ceskoslovensk", *Sbornik k dejinám 19. a 20*, 1993, 94.
561 Ibid.

Antipathy toward the legionaries and Prague was perceptible not only among the nationalities but also among the officers of the new Czechoslovak army.

The other organisation representing the legionaries was the *Svaz*, numerically the more important among the two. Beneš was trying to amalgamate the *Svaz* with the *Družina* under his direction but without success. By the end of 1920 the *Svaz* was becoming radicalised and was tending towards the left. The general conclusions of the conference held in Prague at the end of November 1920 were that:

> [...] the Legionaries would resist every attempt at a monarchist restoration, not only in Czecho-Slovakia, but also in the neighbouring States: that they would oppose any effort of the Poles to recover territory in Teschen which had been assigned to Czecho-Slovakia, and, if the Poles advanced for such a purpose, would strive to win back those districts which had been torn from Czecho-Slovakia.
>
> A somewhat platonic expression of a desire to live in friendship with the German elements was included in the findings of the Conference, and a resolution was passed to the effect that reaction, supported by secret forces inimical to the State, was raising its head, and that the Conference, representing 27,000 Legionaries, looked to Dr Benes and would not allow the clean shield of their self-sacrificing activities in the revolution to be besmirched.
>
> The Legionaries expressed themselves as determined, if need be, to overcome by revolution all obstacles to social reform caused by reaction, and as was to be expected, they protested strongly against the intention of the minister of national defence to with draw the vote from soldiers actually serving with the colours. [...]

The conference ended with the formal submission of the following formal demands to the State:

1. Socialisation of all big industries and mines.
2. Expropriation of big landowners without compensation

3. Confiscation of the property of "Mortmain"—that is, entailed property of the Church and of the aristocracy.
4. Separation of Church from State and of the Schools from Church.
5. Socialist reforms in the schools.
6. Reforms of the State Defence Force.[562]

British Commissioner Clerk's opinion was that such radical left-inspired demands were unexpected coming from soldiers who had fought on the side of the "white" Russian forces. The legionaries' contribution toward alienating the Slovak Catholic Church and Catholics from Prague seems obvious. It could well have contributed to pushing the landowning aristocracy and bourgeoisie, not solely of the Slovak part but also of the Czech part of the republic, to support Emperor Karl's restoration.[563]

Tensions in the Army

Concerning the new army, the radical measure taken by Prague was to exclude most of the non-Slav officers, among them a great number of ethnic Germans, by "restricting the number of minority officers by both *de facto* and *de jure* discriminations".[564] Zealous Czechs would administer Czech language exams in such a way that it was impossible for Germans to pass them. Once the new military education was established in the early 1920s, not many Germans and Hungarians wanted to join the officer candidate schools dominated by Czech and French officers.[565] Then there was the problem of the k. u. k. officers. Prague could not exclude them from the army since they were well-educated soldiers, but the legionaries were granted seniority over them.[566] In the 1923 statistics of the Czechoslovak army, former k. u. k. officers still represented 34.02 percent (one-third of the officers) of the new Czechoslovak army, as compared to 29.93 percent of former legion-

---
562 NA, FO 371 4721, ff. 95–7, Clerk to Curzon, Prague, November 30, 1920.
563 Ibid.
564 Zorach, J., "The Nationalities problem in the Czechoslovak Army", *East Central Europe*, vol. 5, no. 2, 1978, 171.
565 Ibid.
566 Ibid.

aries.[567] "Nearly all of the officers and common soldiers of the pre-war and war generations had undergone military training in the Austro-Hungarian Army."[568] Some sources even say that one third of the army would have been ready to revolt against the legionaries,[569] and this matches the percentage of k. u. k. officers. The arrest in Prague on September 9, 1919, of twelve persons accused of fomenting a monarchist coup was an extra element to support this hypothesis, since among those arrested were a number of officials of the National Defence Ministry.[570]

The formation of a young officer corps would take years, so there was no choice but that Prague had to keep the k. u. k. officers. In January 1921 the British military attaché would report, referring to the words of a French intelligence officer: "The question of the junior leading was one that gave their [the French] mission anxiety. The only reliable officers were the former Austro-Hungarian officers, who were mistrusted by the rank and file because of their political leanings."[571]

The quasi absence of Slovak officers in the k. u. k. army reappeared in the new Czechoslovak one. The Slovak recruits were a problem and were considered as "fodder". They complained that they were treated in a patronising fashion. As a measure to integrate them, they were sent to complete their military service in the Czech lands and in mixed regiments.[572] Naturally the Slovak officers who were successful in their military career felt bitter about the Czech domination. Czech officers argued that the Slovaks lacked adequate education to advance to the higher ranks. This claim was used to justify the status quo.[573]

In contrast to Yugoslavia, the new Czechoslovak state had enemies within, since it could not exclude the excellent k. u. k. staff, as Belgrade had done with the Croat officers. Among these officers could be found quite a few el-

---

567 *Manuel de statistique de la République Tchécoslovaque*, 2 vols., vol. II, Prague, 1925, 354.
568 Zorch, *op. cit.*, 170.
569 Windischgraetz, Lajos, *My adventures and Misadventures*, London, 1966, 124.
570 *British Documents on Foreign Affairs (BDAF)* Part II, series F, vol. 1, years 1919–1922, doc. 16, 27–28, Gosling to Curzon, Prague, September 13, 1919. They were released on September 25, 1919. BDFA, *op. cit.*, doc. 17, 28, Gosling to Curzon.
571 BDFA, *op. cit.*, doc. 148. 192–93.
572 Zorach, *op. cit.*, 177.
573 Ibid., 177–78.

ements critical of the new state. All these malcontents were a potential danger for the unity of Czechoslovakia. Hence, in the new Czechoslovak Republic, there were three main centrifugal groups: the minorities, former k. u. k. officers of the new Czech army, and the Catholic autonomists of the party of Hlinka.

From a Hungarian perspective—as described from Budapest by French High Commissioner Fouchet—the explanation for the Slovaks' change of alliance can be summed up in three points: a centralisation policy had replaced the granting of autonomy; the anti-religious (especially anti-Catholic) politics of Prague, and given that ideas and usages had been respected earlier by the Hungarians—which the French commissioner to Budapest recognised would advantage Hungary in the eyes of the majority of Slovaks; the spoliation of property in Slovakia. For all these reasons, Slovakia would be in favour of joining Hungary, except for the northwest of the country.[574] To these reasons can be added the dictatorial measures of Šrobár and the behaviour of the legionaries. Though these conclusions were seen through a Hungarian lens, they did make sense and represented existing reasons why Slovaks would want to leave Czechoslovakia,

The Slovak Exiles

The New Slovak–Hungarian Plan for Autonomy

After the departure of Jászi into exile as a consequence of the Commune, and the re-establishment of a conservative regime in Budapest, Hungarian propaganda continued its actions in Slovakia. Though a document mentions that "the Hungarians started financing the Slovaks during Béla Kun and the Ministry of Minorities continued this propaganda action called the 'Slovak Action' by financing the Slovak separatists", Jászi has revealed that this propaganda pre-existed the Commune.[575]

---

574 ADMAE, Z Europe Tchécoslovaquie 34, 152–56 ff., Fouchet à Millerand, Budapest, May 7, 1920.
575 K64, 1 cs., 9–33 ff., report (without signature).

Magyar propaganda and activity towards nationalities expressed itself in two different forms: on the one hand, the TL's (League for the Defence of Territorial Integrity) uncompromising policy to keep the Kingdom of Saint Stephen's territorial integrity without any form of autonomy or federalisation; and on the other, the more willing to compromise Ministry of National Minorities, headed by Jakab Bleyer, a Swabian Hungarian, which was newly established after the re-instalment of the conservative regime in Budapest. We will limit the scope of this study to the Ministry of Minorities' plans, since the TL was against granting autonomy.

The Ministry of Minorities was subdivided into different departments (German, Ruthene and Slovak), each of which was headed by a member of the respective minority, which allowed a certain level of participation by the minorities.[576] This sub-chapter looks at the projects born out of the policy and negotiations of the Department for Slovak Affairs (Tót Főosztály).

As mentioned earlier, the Republic of Councils had started re-conquering Upper Hungary in order to spread communism, though many Hungarian who joined the Commune considered it, first of all, as a national duty.[577] The same national and territorial motivations—embraced by most of the Magyars—stimulated the military and politicians who joined the counter- revolutionary army and government. It resulted in the persistence of occupation projects, usually jointly with Slovak separatists, one of which was an incursion into Slovakia at the level of Pozsony (Bratislava)-Losonc. Horthy (as commander-in-chief of the Hungarian army) had also prepared an occupation plan, the so called "pacification of Slovakia" operation. Naturally, these projects were strongly encouraged by the TL. In December 1919, all such operations were set aside by Prime Minister Huszár and Bleyer, because neither the military nor the political levels of preparation of Horthy's plan were acceptable. Huszár and Bleyer were not quite sure whether there was another solution. Since a military action could end in a fiasco and as the Slovaks could only be content if granted autonomy, they both thought that a construction based on national autonomies would have a greater ef-

---

576 K64, 1 cs., 2-1920-7-28 (508/vi), 416–19 ff., 1920 report, anonym.
577 Many officers who were former members of the k. u. k. atill rmy, joined the Hungarian Red Army and considered this reoccupation more as a national duty than an internationalist cause.

fect at the Peace Conference than an adventurous military action.[578] The postponement of all military actions was also due to the eminently explosive situation in Slovakia and the fact that the Slovaks would, they thought, separate from Bohemia by themselves.[579]

The atmosphere in Slovakia was explosive not only because of Prague's refusal to grant autonomy but also because of its refusal to hold a much-demanded plebiscite. This refusal confirmed Prague's anxiousness concerning the Slovak population's allegiance. It became clear to the Hungarians that the Slovaks would favour a reattachment to Hungary.[580] The response was, indeed, promising, because the representatives of the Germans, Romanians, Slovaks, Ruthenes and Croats of the Mura and Wends (Slav ethnic group among Hungarians in Zala and Vas counties of Hungary) sent their decision to the Hungarian prime minister requesting recognition of their rights, their renaissance in a Christian and democratic Hungary, and their belief in the concept of the Hungarian Apostolic Kingdom. And, last but not least, they assured Minister of Minorities Dr Jakab Bleyer of their total confidence and support. Suffice it to say that the issue of autonomies, in the frame of the reduced Kingdom of Saint Stephen, was advancing.[581]

A secret meeting took place at the primate of Hungary's residence in Buda with members of the government and all the nationality representatives, including Jehlička —now head of the Slovak section of the Hungarian Ministry for Minorities and founder of the Magyarophile Slovak Peoples Party (Magyarbarát Tót Néppártot) in Hungary— and Professor Michal Kmoško of the University of Budapest, a prominent Slovakian figure of Hungary.[582] The negotiations remained secret and were not made public because they were afraid of the TL's reaction. The following agreement was set up:

---

578 Tilkovszky, Loránt, "Területi integritás és területi autonómia", *Századok*, no. 3, Budapest, 2000, 566.
579 Bleyer was systematically against any such action. K 26, 1921-38-13, Budapest, July 22, 1920, "Declarations of Zoltán Szviezsényi [head of the Slovak section of the Min. of Minorities] on the meetings of the Ligue for Territorial Integrity", by A. Gálocsy; Tilkovszky, *op. cit.*, 568–69.
580 Ibid.
581 MNL, K27, 124 (1919–1920), Prime Minister Huszár's declaration to the Council of Ministers of January 3, 1920. Proceedings of the Council of Ministers.
582 Janek, István, František Jehlička: szlovák hazafi vagy Budapest ügynöke? ÚJ SZÓ ONLINE January 17, 2016. https://ujszo.com/panorama/frantisek-jehlicka-szlovak-hazafi-vagy-budapest-ugynoke (3.01.2019); Tilkovszky, *op. cit.*, 567

1. The Slovaks of Upper Hungary would be accepted as a distinct nation.
2. They would receive territorial autonomy.
3. Questions of education, administration, religion, charity would be the exclusive resort of the autonomy.
4. The Slovaks would have to install a governor in whose sphere of influence would be all administrative and judicial questions.
5. The Slovak parliamentarians would also be MP's of the Hungarian Parliament.
6. The Slovaks would have a Slovak minister in the Hungarian government.
7. A Slovak bishop would be elected.
8. And all non-Slovak speaking bishops would have to retire.
9. The nomination of bishops would be made by the Slovak bishops who would propose a list of candidates to the pope and the Apostolic King for election.
10. The creation of Slovak regiments in Upper Hungary.
11. Creation of a Slovak gendarmerie.
12. Slovak post and telegraphic services.
13. The state would support the educational system and Slovak autonomy with means similar to other regions of Hungary.
14. The rights of German and Hungarian minorities had to be defended.
15. Courses in Hungarian language and literature had to be given in the region to enable Slovaks to work anywhere in Hungary.
16. The Hungarians could send inspectors to control whether Slovak autonomy violated the given limits. However, the inspectors would only have consultative rights.
17. When conflict of opinion occurred. an objective and mixed tribunal would be set up;
18. Slovak autonomy would be mentioned in the Royal Oath and elevated to law.[583]

---

[583] Tilkovszky, *op. cit.*, 567.

Though Hungary was not transformed into a federation, the Slovaks would be granted an autonomy guaranteeing their self-rule. Yet these points did not guarantee a Slovak Parliament and local ministries.

All the points that Jehlička wanted were integrated into the proposal for autonomy.[584] The document showed in a clear way that Slovaks would be part of the Realm of Hungary with a crowned king. During the following days the proposal was accepted by the government (on January 9, 1920), and it was ready to be presented in Paris by the Hungarian Peace Delegation.[585] In spite of the results, Hlinka expressed his dissatisfaction to Jehlička, since Hlinka demanded an autonomous legislative body and refused that an official Hungarian be sent to oversee the Slovak governor.[586]

The Hungarian Peace Delegation left for Paris on January 5 under the leadership of Count Albert Apponyi. The choice of Apponyi was rather clumsy, given that he was, as Hungary's minister of education, the father of the infamous 1907 law on the Magyarisation of education known as the *Lex Apponyi*. He is less known for having fought for an autonomy proposal for minorities after the war.[587] Viktor Dvorčák, who took part in the elaboration of the autonomy proposal, became the Slovak member of the Delegation as the "expert on Slovak affairs". The day the Peace Delegation left for Paris, the Hungarian prime minister, Károly Huszár, could note that all the Slovak fractions considered that their future was in Hungary rather than in Czechoslovakia. The prospects looked good.[588]

On January 12, 1920, Apponyi submitted the Slovak autonomy proposal to the Peace Conference,[589] and on January 14, he explained that the framework within which the peoples of Hungary would like to live could not be

---

584 On the day when the Hungarian delegation arrived in Paris for the Peace negotiations, Jehlička became president of the new Association of Magyarophile Minorities (January 7, 1920). Tilkovszky, *op. cit.*, 568.

585 MNL K27, Proceedings of the Council of Ministers, box 124, December 1919. Jehlička explains that he was accompanied by Father Štefan Mnoheľ (another signatory of the St. Martin Declaration) to negotiate with Bleyer. Jehlička, *Father Hlinka's Struggle for Slovak Freedom*, Slovak Council, London, 1938, 33.

586 Tilkovszky, *op. cit.*, 575.

587 Jehlička wrote to a close friend of Hlinka that Apponyi's autonomy plan was ready and once it was accepted by the Council of Ministers, Apponyi would bring it to Paris. MNL K26, 1921-38-1920, Jehlička to Jenö Tvrdy, December 31, 1919.

588 MNL, K26, 1921-38-13, "Szviezsényi Zoltán nyilatkozatai".

589 *A Magyar Békétárgyalàsok, Jelentés*, vol. II, Magyar Kir. Külügyminisztérium, Budapest, 1920, note, 2.

decided by external persons but "[...] only by the People and its components: its nationalities and diverse social classes. I ask therefore the Supreme Council, to give the Hungarian people and the nationalities living on Hungarian soil the possibility to choose their future lives and the frame of their future relations after consultation and mutual agreement."[590]

The negative response was delivered by Millerand in his infamous transmittal letter, which said that Hungary was late with such proposals. If Millerand was correct in saying that the Hungarian government was late, it was, however, fallacious to claim that there was no need for a plebiscite on the basis that the nationalities had expressed their will in autumn 1918,[591] especially if one considers all that had happened in Slovakia and Croatia since the end of the war.

Šrobár wrote a very honest note to the Slovaks of America explaining the reasons why a plebiscite, an autonomy and a special national assembly could not be accepted in Slovakia:

"En vertu de l'accord de Pittsburg la Slovaquie aurait du obtenir une assemblée nationale, examinons ce fait d'une maniere objective. La population du Slovensko compte environ 3 millions d'âmes, dont 1,600,000 slovaques, 250,000 juifs, 500,000 russes, 155,000 allemands et plus d'un demi million de hongrois. Si l'assemblée nationale slovaque avait 300 membres, il y siegeraient 22 juifs, 50 russes, 15 allemands, 53 hongrois, donc 140 non-slovaques et 160 slovaques. Mais si ces slovaques seraient en pluspart des "slovaques octobristes". Ils auraient qu'une majorité de 20 voix, majorité, qui ne suffirait pas d'assurer le pouvoir au government pour 24 heures. Remarquons que les hongrois avaient une classe intellectuelle tres forte, et l'ont encore toujours. N'oulions pas que le Slovensko a été débordé par des magyars et des "magyarons". Nous supposons qu'aucun slovaque ne votera pour un magyar ou un magyaron! Est-ce possible a présent? La nation slovaque s'est elle éveillé durant ces 8 mois et ne votera-t-elle que pour des slovaques? Notre peuple connaît-il ceux, qui sont slovaques et ceux, qui ont renié notre cause? Bien au

---

590 *A Magyar Békétárgyalàsok, Jelentés*, vol. I, 16.
591 *A Magyar Békétárgyalàsok, Jelentés*, vol. II, 487–488, Millerand's *Lettre d'envoi*, Paris, May 6, 1920.

contraire. Nous avons des comitats (Bars, Hont, Nógrád, Abaúj, Zemplén, Szepes, Sáros, etc.) ou nous ne pouvions un fidele slovaque, qui soit apte de mener son peuple ! Immaginez vous une assemblé nationale slovaque, ou jamais un député slovaque ne devrait manquer! Et immaginez-vous une opposition de 140 membres. Non pas une opposition de langue slovaque, mais une de langue étrangere; cette assemblée nationale serait-elle dans ce cas une assemblée nationale slovaque? Ce serait un tohubohu et une auberge, ou les convives sont continuellement en querelle.".[592]

This note shows the motivations of the Czechophile minister of Slovak affairs. Let us admit that he was right, and that Czechoslovakia couldn't have survived if Slovakia had been granted autonomy. In this case, all the minorities should have been given autonomy, and if not a territorial one, then a personal one as imagined by the Austro-Marxist chancellor of Austria, Karl Renner—a politician of Moravian descent who had applied it successfully in a region of Moravia before the war. No matter what the arguments were, the Czechs and Czechophile Slovaks had not respected the clauses of the Pittsburgh Agreement, and the Hungarians had proposed an autonomy—though not light heartedly—that was much more attractive to many Slovaks than the Czechoslovak status quo.

The reaction to the refusal of a plebiscite in Slovakia was immediate. At a meeting held at the University of Budapest by the Federation of Philo-Hungarian National Minorities (Magyarbarát Nemzeti Kisebbségek Szövet-

---

[592] "Considering the Pittsburgh Agreement Slovakia should have been granted a parliament. Let us analyse the facts in an objective way. Slovensko's population is about three million: 1,600,000 Slovaks, 250,000 Jews, 500,000 Russians [Rusyns], 155,000 Germans and more than a half a million Magyars. [...] Even if most of the Slovaks were 'Octoberist Slovaks', they would only have a 20-voice majority which would not even be sufficient to hold the government in place for 24 hours. Let us underline that the Magyars had and still have a very strong class of intelligentsia. Let us not forget that Slovensko is full of Magyars and Magyarones. Let us consider that not one Slovak would vote for a Magyar or Magyarone! Is this possible today? Did the Slovak people awake during these eight months and will it only vote for Slovaks? Do the Slovaks know who the Slovaks are and who are denying our cause? On the contrary there are counties (Bars, Hont, Nógrád, Abaúj, Zemplén, Szepes, Sáros, etc... [H]) where we could not find one faithful Slovak that would be capable to lead his people. Let us imagine a Slovak parliament where not one Slovak deputy should ever be absent! And imagine an opposition of 140 members! Not a Slovak speaking opposition, but a foreign language speaking one. In these conditions would this parliament be a Slovak Parliament? It would be an inn where the guests would be constantly quarrelling." A Paix: 141 Hongrie, No XXIII, annexe 13. *A Magyar Békétárgyalàsok, Jelentés*, vol. II, 124, Note no. XXIII, Annex 13, Šrobár's Note.

sége) on January 23, 1920, Professor Michal Kmoško said that the Slovaks would not accept the peace treaty (Trianon) conditions, would fight for a plebiscite, and if the Peace Conference did not order a plebiscite, than there would be no peace in Slovakia.[593]

International Efforts seeking Support

The Slovak separatists did not limit their diplomacy to Hungary but were also building their international network. Besides their negotiations with and natural leaning towards Hungary, they were now in relations with Poland, which was also an enemy of the Czechs (Poland had a conflict with Czechoslovakia on Teschen), and they were still trying to influence the Entente. Even after Jehlička and Hlinka's unsuccessful journey to Paris, Jehlička continued to disseminate memoranda to the Entente nations.

For example, in October 1919, Jehlička and Kmoško[594] gave a memorandum to Sir George Clerk in Budapest on the Slovak Question.[595] Both personalities were now living and teaching in Hungary, and Seton-Watson accused them both of not truly representing the Slovak Nation.[596] But Seton-Watson overlooked, or simply did not know, that Hlinka was also actively involved in getting Hungarian support with the help of Jehlička.[597]

Jehlička and Kmoško continued their efforts in other directions, and in February 1920 they visited the German embassy in Vienna and explained that a separation of Slovakia with annexation to Hungary was being prepared and asked Germany to help. Jehlička and Kmoško explained that

---

593 Tilkovszky, *op. cit.*, 571–72.
594 Kmoško fled Budapest during the Commune and went to Slovakia. He returned to Budapest afterwards to become a university professor.
595 ADMAE, Z Europe, Tchécoslovaquie 45, 55 f. Stephen Osusky à M. Laroche, Paris, December 20, 1919; Ibid., Memorandum on Slovak Question by Francis Jehlička, deputy to Prague and Michal Kmoško, Professor of University (October 30, 1919).
596 Seton-Watson, the "Scotus Viator" can be equally considered as biased when presenting historically inexact facts as arguments: "In the course of the middle ages the Czech Kings were the rulers not only of the Czechs but also of the Slovaks and Magyars. On several occasions Slovakia was administrated by representatives of the Czech Kings and continuity of its political life was interrupted only during the domination of the last Hapsburgs." SSEES, SEW, 10/2/1. Reply to the Memorandum of Prof. Kmoško and Jehlička (not dated).
597 A. Boroviczény, *Op.cit.*, 29–30; A. Lehár, 'Egy katonatiszt naplója 1919–1921', in *Historia Plusz*, no. 11, Budapest, 1993, 42–43.

Horthy's Hungarian forces would cross the border and join the armed Slovak inhabitants. Poland would attack from the north, which would be necessary because Hungary would be attacked by Yugoslavia. The Germans assured the two Slovaks that they would not intervene in the politics of their neighbour states: "[...] dass sich Deutschland bei dem kommenden Konflict neutral verhält und inbesondere nichts gegen die Polen unternimmt, die voraussichtlich das Vorgehen der Slovakei unterstützen werden."[598]

Magyar Propaganda and Slovak Interests

To support the Slovak separatist movement the Ministry of Minorities had sent at least 7 to 8 million Crowns to Károly Bulissa, a Magyarone barrister from Prešov (Eperjes, H), who was heading the Slovak Central Office (*Tót Központi Iroda*), which was under the influence of the TL.[599] But the ministry soon recognised that he was an adventurer and a swindler. Minorities Minister Jakab Bleyer discovered that Bulissa had set up a large administration but was only a *Strohmann* (front man) and wasn't under political control, not to mention that he couldn't even speak Slovak. Besides Dvorčák and Jehlička, the Hungarians were keeping Bulissa as the "man behind the scenes". Bleyer advised the foreign minister to set up an inquiry on Bulissa, dissolve his group eventually and support Slovak leaders who had the support of the population.[600] The ministry had decided to eliminate the elements that Jehlička and Kmoško considered as not defending Slovak interests. But the removal of Bulissa and his accompilces was not making progress.

Hlinka's group (under František/Ferenc Unger, Hlinka's secretary) soon made their anger known to the Hungarians and threatened to start "action" without Hungary if they did not stop their unacceptable behaviour. The Hungarians' badly organised, and thus counterproductive, propaganda

---

598 "[...] that Germany will stay neutral in the coming conflict and in particular will undertake nothing against the Poles, who will likely support Solvakia's course of action." German Document no.10, Attaché Holzhauser to Wilhelmstr., Berlin, February 25, 1920, in Kirschbaum S. (ed.) *Slovak Politics*, 112–16.
599 K 64, 1 cs. ff. 9–34, Somssich J. Foreign Minister (henceforth FM) to staff, Budapest, January 26, 1920; op. cit., 35–45 ff., Bleyer J. Min. of Minorities to FM, Budapest, April 2, 1920. Tilkovszky, *op.cit.*, 564.
600 K64, 1 cs., 34–42 ff., Bleyer, Budapest, April 2, 1920.

made them lose a lot of time, and Bulissa's group remained active while little had been done to dissolve it.[601]

And what about the structure of the Hungarian "action", Hlinka's group was referring to? The action was to be centralised in two centres: one in Budapest, dealing with propaganda and military intelligence, and another in Pressburg that would work on internal organisation. The financial support would come through Vienna. The internal organisation would be done by the Slovak Revolutionary Committee recognised by Hungary and in diplomatic contact through a Hungarian chargé d'affaires. Outside of Slovakia, this committee would have a centre on neutral soil in Vienna with a smaller council of ministers. The members remaining in Slovakia would remain secret until the liberation. The new government would be representative of all of Slovakia's parties.[602] The liberation of Slovakia was to be accomplished by the Slovak national movement without the military support of Hungary, because the Hungarian nationalist detachments frightened the Slovaks, so order would have to be kept by local forces.

Another group, which was composed of the Slovak political parties close to the pro-Magyar Peoples Party (an association located in Budapest under Dvorčák's leadership) and the Kassa National Council, wanted to know if the Hungarians were ready to: act to liberate Slovakia; give over the organisation of the liberation to the Slovaks and support their action; recognise the pro-Hungarian Slovak National Council of Kassa as an active part of the action; and be ready to stop financing all other groups.

The Kassa National Council was waiting for moderate action that would augment pro-Hungarian sympathies in Slovakia.[603] One can see that the Hlinka group and the Kassa National Council each had a very similar approach to Hungarian support.

Meanwhile in Budapest, the Területvédő Liga was becoming so strong that not only the Slovak representatives in Budapest but also the Ministry of Minorities had to defend themselves and radicalise their position. As

---

601 K64, 1 cs., 256 ff. Report Budapest, June 20, 1920.
602 K64, 1 cs., 256 ff. Report, Budapest, June 20, 1920; K64, 1 cs., 1920-7-28 (505/vi), 416 f., A tót főosztály évi müködése.
603 K64 1 cs. 254–60 ff., Secret Report, Budapest, June 20, 1920.

Jehlička had left for Poland and was not under the influence of Hungarian pressure groups anymore, he could get Polish support for his negotiations with the Hungarians and the Slovaks who remained in Budapest. The minority representatives who stayed in Hungary were under pressure from the Területvédő Liga. They had to reject their plans for autonomy and claimed, in order to defend themselves, that it was Jehlička's fault that the autonomy project had been set up. Kmoško and Dvorčák were trying to convince Jehlička to come back from Poland.[604] The Területvédő Liga did not even spare the Hungarians who defended the cause of autonomy, and Apponyi as well as Andrássy got their share of criticism.[605]

The Krakow and Warsaw Committees

The other place of exile for the Slovak separatists was Poland. Jehlička created a Slovak National Council in May 1920 in Warsaw.[606] In Krakow, a Polish-Slovak Committee had been set up by professors at Krakow University, which became known as the Krakow Committee.[607] But in August 1919, the Hungarian ambassador in Warsaw was already writing to Bethlen (head of the ABC in Vienna) that those who wanted war with the Czechs wished to set up a Magyar-Slovak legion in Galicia and military circles in Krakow were very interested in such a project. Hungary proposed to pay all the expenses and would nominate a general staff officer of Hungarian origin from Upper Hungary as the head of the legion.[608]

In July 1920, Jehlička sent a letter to his archbishop explaining the Polish approach to the question of Slovakia and clearly criticising the Hungarian moves.[609] Jehlička thought that without Polish support the liberation of

---

604 Tilkovszky, *op. cit.*, 579.
605 Ibid., 577.
606 Kirschbaum, *Historical*, 83.
607 K64 1 cs., 292 ff., June 10, 1920.
608 K64 1 cs. 1919-41.I—4 res. Csekonics to Bethen (chief of ABC in Vienna),Warsaw, August 16, 1919.
609 Bobula, another Magyarone, said to Jehlička that the revolutionary committee after having expelled the Czechs would elect a parliament and would beat the Hlinka party. This parliament in which the Slovaks would be a minority would negotiate with the Hungarian Parliament on the concessions to be given to the Slovaks. K64 1 cs. 290-91 ff. Zakopane, July 2, 1920, Jehlička Ferenc to Card. Csernoch.

Slovakia from Czech rule was impossible. As described by him, there were two camps with regard to this question in Poland. One group was the officers, who were categorically against Slovakia's annexation to Hungary and preferred to see it become independent, but as a Polish protectorate. But according to Jehlička, another group, mainly politicians whose names were not disclosed, was ready to support the Hungarians against the Czechs but only if the Hungarians guaranteed the broadest autonomy to the Slovaks in advance. The Poles considered Dvorčák and Bulissa to be Magyarones and false Slovaks, and thought they were doing the project much harm.[610] The situation was even worse for Dvorčák, because he was accused of making up the story of his meeting with Prime Minister Ignacy Paderewski in order to lend importance to his person.[611] Jehlička advised the Hungarians not to support Dvorčák and Bulissa, lest Hungary lose the support of the Slovaks. These negative elements, among which Kmoško is also mentioned, wanted Slovakia's status quo ante in Hungary,[612] whereas František Unger, Hlinka's secretary, Jehlička and Hlinka wanted autonomy. Unger informed Jehlička that Hlinka did not see that there was any importance to which country Slovakia would be attached. The important point was that after the expulsion of the Czechs, the Slovak Parliament could decide the fate of Slovakia. Jehlička's position was "Slovakia's broadest autonomy in Hungary and the federation of Hungary with Poland".[613]

Poland was opposing Slovakia's return to Hungarian allegiance because it wanted Slovakia for itself. But now that Poland had military problems, it would accept a fait accompli if Hungary were to annex Slovakia, and it left Jehlička with a free hand in getting Hungary's support.[614]

A memorandum to the Polish foreign minister, Stanisław Patek, made no secret of such an alternative and proves that the Polish government was considering joint Polish–Hungarian military action:

---

610 K64 1cs. 1918–1920-7-4057, 66–67 ff. Jehlička to Card. Csernoch, Warsaw, June 12, 1920.
611 K64 1 cs., 1919-41-I-4 res., Csekonics to Bethlen in Vienna, Warsaw, August 19, 1919.
612 K64, cs. 1, Letter to Card. Csernoch, Warsaw, June 12, 1920; Unger refers to Hlinka's wish of discrediting Dvorčák. Ibid., 63–68 ff., Procès verbal.
613 It is difficult to evaluate whether Jehlička truly thought of a federation between Hungary and Poland or it was not more of a confederation. K64 1cs. 1918-1920-7-4057, 66–67 ff. Jehlička to Card. Csernoch. Warsaw, June 12, 1920.
614 K64, cs 1, 298–300 ff., Esztergom, Csernoch to Teleki, copy of Jehlička's letter to His Eminency, August 5, 1920.

[...] the interests of Poland as well as Hungary require a common border and cutting the corridor through which the Czechs wanted to link up with Russia and which for the time being remains a blind alley separating Poland form Hungary. Severing this alley can take place in one of three ways:
1. Hungary's recovery of Slovakia.
2. The establishment of an independent Slovakia.
3. The unification of Slovakia with Poland in some legal state form.[615]

Meanwhile, the League of Nations pressured Beneš to arrive at an agreement with the Slovaks, and Beneš had approached Hlinka to arrange a solution. Unger said that Hlinka should not give in to Beneš and make exaggerated demands that Beneš could not accept. The competition was therefore open between Czechs and Hungarians to seduce the Slovaks.[616]

A few months later (November 1920) the move toward rapprochement between Romania and Poland was intensifying. Budapest feared that Prime Minister Take Ionescu, who was known to be a great supporter of the Little Entente and was visiting Warsaw on November 1–2, would endanger the Polish–Hungarian plans. After the visit, Marshal Piłsudski, using a non-diplomatic channel, informed Budapest that Warsaw was still interested in cooperating and having a common border with Hungary.[617]

With regard to military preparations, officers from Hungary, who could be used to liberate Slovakia, were being transferred to Poland, as Hungary was under the severe military regulations imposed by the Entente, such as limiting its army to 35,000 men. In Poland, there were five regiments comprised of prisoners returning from Russia. About 3,000 supernumerary officers and NCOs were being transferred to Poland,[618] and a military coup was in preparation at the Polish border with Czechoslovakia.[619] This military coup was probably the incursion to destroy the Bohumin–Košice (Kas-

---

615 As edited by Janusz Cisek in "The Beginnings of Joseph Beck's Diplomatic Career: The Origins of his Diplomatic Mission to Admiral Horthy in October 1920", in *East European Quarterly*, XXVII, no. 1, March 1993, 131.
616 K 64, cs. 1, 1920–7, *op. cit.*, 63–68 ff.
617 Cisek, *op. cit.*, 135.
618 7N 2885. Prague, December 29, 1920, Rapport politique, Tchécoslovaquie (no signature), "Renseignements parvenu d'un membre de la police tchèque", which are claimed to be verified.
619 ADMAE, Z Europe, Tchécoslovaquie 45, 97–100 ff.

sa) strategic railway line described by General Mittelhauser and was to be performed by the Magyar–Slovak Legion, principally concentrated in Zakopane. It was divided into one to three small regiments of some 200–800 men each and was going through daily, though brief, training.[620]

France's Approach to the Problem

These negotiations between Hungary, Poland and the Slovak separatists had repercussions: the Czechoslovak government suspected a double attack, from Poland on Teschen and from Hungary on Slovakia,[621] and France was informed of the fact that certain Polish military circles were sympathising with the separatist and pro-Magyar Slovaks. There were two approaches to the problem, one from the Ministry of War and one from the Quai d'Orsay.

General Mittelhauser informed the Ministry of War of the existence of an irredentist organisation, part of Hungarian propaganda that was supported by certain Polish military authorities.[622] This is confirmed by Jehlička.[623] This organisation was the Magyar–Slovak Legion concentrated in Zakopane that is described above.[624] As some of this intelligence came from Prague, it shows that the Czechoslovaks knew and were quite concerned about the existence of Polish–Hungarian–Slovak military collaboration, which, as Mittelhauser underlined, put the French army in a very delicate position, as it still commanded certain Czechoslovak regiments and because both Czechoslovakia and Poland were France's allies. Mittelhauser tried to underplay the importance of such an anti-Czech organisation, and General Niessel, the chief of French military mission in Warsaw, confirmed that these movements were unimportant.[625]

---

620 7N 3105, EMA, 2ᵉ Bureau, without date; Ibid, no. 290/2 EM, Gen. Mittelhauser, Chef de la Mis. Mil. français à MG, Prague, January 13, 1921.
621 7N 3094, no. 301, Couget à Leygues, Président du Conseil, Prague, December 14, 1920.
622 7N 3105, Etat-Major de l'Armée (EMA onwards), 2ᵉ Bureau, without date; Ibid, no. 290/2 EM, Gen. Mittelhauser, Chef de la Mis. Mil. français à MG, Prague, January 13, 1921.
623 K64 1cs. 1918-1920-7-4057, 66–67 ff. Jehlička to Card. Csernoch, Warsaw, June 12, 1920. It seems, therefore, that French military intelligence was well informed.
624 7N 3105, EMA, 2ᵉ Bureau, without date; Ibid., no. 290/2 EM, Gen. Mittelhauser, Chef de la Mis. Mil. français à MG, Prague, January 13, 1921; Ibid., no. 440, EMA, 2ᵉ Bureau à Gén. Niessel, Chef de la Mis. Mil. français à Varsovie, Paris, February 11, 1921.
625 7N 3105, EMA, 2ᵉ Bureau, without date; Ibid, no. 290/2 EM, Gen. Mittelhauser, Chef de la Mis. Mil.

Chapter V

A month earlier, the approach the French minister took toward Prague was to minimise even further the importance of these preparations, calling them "rumours". Especially since Masaryk had received assurance from the Poles that "toutes les mesures seraient prises pour prévenir des tentatives contre la Slovaquie".[626] However, parallel to these military and diplomatic dispatches the Quai d'Orsay received a study describing a union between Hungary and Poland that would incorporate Slovakia. The Quai was therefore well informed of a Magyar–Polish plan, serious or not, to occupy Slovakia. The unsigned study in question, most probably written by a Pole, claimed that:

> La Pologne depuis plus de 1000 ans est en relations cordiales avec la Hongrie. Toutes deux royalistes et catholiques ont la même horreur du bolchevisme et l'ont prouvé. La Hongrie désire cette alliance—La Pologne ne veut l'accepter qu'avec la sanction de la France.[627]

It explained that the Czechs had been working against both French policy in the region and the existence of Poland during the Polish–Russian conflict:

> Nous ne pouvons oublier les horreurs que nous ont fait toujours et partout les Tchèques sans compter les dernières, lorsque manquant à tous leur engagements, au moment ou l'Europe, la chrétienté, la civilisation était en danger, et nous à l'agonie, ils ont retenu à deux reprises les munitions qui devaient nous sauver et que la France nous envoyait!?[628]

---

français à MG, Prague, January 13, 1921; Ibid., no. 440, EMA, 2ᵉ Bureau à Gén. Niessel, Chef de la Mis. Mil. français à Varsovie, Paris, February 21, 1921.

626 "[…] all measures would be taken to warn of attempts against Slovakia." 7N 3094, Couget à Leygues, Président du Conseil Prague, December 14, 1920, no. 301.

627 "For more than 1000 years Poland has enjoyed cordial relations with Hungary. Both royalists and Catholics share the same horror of Bolshevism and have demonstrated this. Hungary desires this alliance – Poland does not want to accept it without the sanction of France." ADMAE, Z Europe, Hongrie, no. 48, ff. 123–31. Thèse de l'Alliance Polono-Hongroise.

628 "We cannot forget the horrors that the Czechs have done to us always and everywhere without counting these last, when failing in all their engagements, at the moment when Europe, Christianity, civilization itself were in danger, and ourselves in agony, they twice withheld the munitions that should have saved us and which France sent to us!?" Ibid., 128.

The study concluded with the argument that the alliance with Hungary would enable the French to aid Poland from the Adriatic and that it would, consequently, be in France's interest to permit it.[629]

The diplomatic dispatches lead us to the question whether, in January 1921, the Quai d'Orsay had resolved itself to accept the Little Entente or was still flirting with the idea of realising the Polish–Hungarian–Romanian union.

As there is no trace of the Quai d'Orsay's intentions to inform Prague of the existence of a Hungarian–Polish plan for the destruction of Czechoslovakia, and given that the French War and Foreign Ministries were both diminishing the importance of such speculations, it can be deduced that not only did the Quai d'Orsay feel uneasy—due to its sympathy for both countries—but it was also still frustrated that Czechoslovakia was working against its past federalist efforts.

Though the establishment of a "cordon sanitaire" between Germany and Soviet Russia was the aim of France, and though the Polish–Hungarian plan corresponded perfectly to the Quai's fears, the Foreign Ministry could not allow itself to see two of its allies fight a war against each other. Hence its policy was to restore calm in the region and bring these two countries into an alliance.

Some Conclusions

What was the situation at the end of 1920 concerning the Slovak émigrés and dissident groups? Past literature on Slovakia (Mamatey, Kirschbaum, Macartney and others) has presented Jehlička, Dvorčák, Kmoško and others as Magyarones working for the Hungarians and as not truly defending the interests of the Slovak people.

Hungary's intriguing policy towards the Slovaks—under Területvédő Liga pressure—made Jehlička cautious and critical toward his friends who remained in Budapest (Dvorčák, Kmoško) and shows that, even though a

---

[629] Ibid., 123. Yet, it was difficult to imagine how to bring French aid from the Adriatic if the SHS Kingdom had been an ally of Czechoslovakia since August 1921, unless Croatia were separated from Serbia or that it went through Italy and Austria.

Chapter V

Magyarone, Jehlička was first of all a Slovak defending, like Hlinka (whom he represented), the interests of the Slovak people. It is, however, obvious that Jehlička initially preferred Hungary to Poland, but since he had moved to Poland and been nominated a university professor in Warsaw[630] he had become more and more critical of Hungary's counterproductive and intrigue-filled policy regarding the Slovaks. After Dvorčák, Bulissa and Kmoško were discredited, it became patent that the group led by Jehlička and representing Hlinka was the only legitimate one that could deal with the Hungarians or the Poles in order to separate Slovakia from Prague. But revelations in the Hungarian archives also prove that neither Dvorčák nor Kmoško was a traitor to the Slovak cause, since both took part in elaborating, in concert with the Hungarian government, the autonomy proposal accepted by the latter and submitted to the Peace Conference. It was only after the refusal of the Entente that the Hungarian government, under pressure from the Területvédő Liga, hardened its policy towards the minorities. To sum up, these revelations give us a new picture of these persons and show that they were all, like Hlinka, fighting for the same cause: Slovak autonomy, even if limited to more of an autonomy than a federation with Hungary. The other new aspect is the willingness of the Hungarian government to offer a certain degree of autonomy to the nationalities. The main supporters of this plan were two legitimists: Apponyi and Andrássy.

Some Slovak historians claim that the political concept of Czechoslovakism was based on the state-founding and newly created Czechoslovak nation, which was necessary in order to gain a majority in a country with 3 million Germans, 600,000 Hungarians and smaller minorities such as Rusyns, Ukrainians, Jews, Romanians and Poles.[631] In other words, the problem of Austria-Hungary vis-à-vis its many nationalities had been transferred to Czechoslovakia. But, had Czechoslovakia not taken a large fragment of the Hungarian-inhabited zone of the region they considered to be Slovakia and the largely Ruthene- and Hungarian-inhabited Subcarpathia,[632] it would

---

630 K 64, 1 cs., 299 f.
631 Kovac, Dusan, *Szlovákia Története*, Kalligram, Pozsony-Bratislava, 2001, 180.
632 The greatest concentration of the Hungarian minority was in the plains region, near the Danube and Ipoly rivers, and in Subcarpathia (especially in the towns of Beregszász, Munkács and Ungvár).

have had fewer minority problems to cope with. Not only did the Czechoslovak government not accept the fact of its multinationality, it also got greedy in its border-defining process when it occupied regions with a large majority of Hungarians.

It is fair to conclude that by the end of 1920 the Hungarians and Slovaks had been unsuccessful in realising their project of "confederation", either by military or diplomatic means.

CHAPTER VI

Habsburg or Little Entente?

August 1920–November 1921 and What Followed

The First and Second Return Attempts of Karl IV

Had it not been for the two 1921 attempts to restore King Karl, this study could have ended with the Peace Treaty of Trianon and the unsuccessful French attempts to create a Danubian Confederation. These attempts re-kindled some hopes for the Hungarians as well as for the nationalities and legitimist leaders that wanted separation from the SHS Kingdom and Czechoslovakia.

The attempts were among the most important events of the interwar period, not only for Hungary but also for the whole of Central Europe because they precipitated the creation of the Little Entente due to the Romania's adherence to the existing Czechoslovak–Yugoslav alliance. Their importance is also shown by the quantity of documents issued on the subject in Entente countries as well as in Hungary and Austria. A detailed description of the return attempts of the crowned King of Hungary is beyond the scope of this study and would not bring any important information on federative or centripetal movements in and around Hungary. It is important, however, to understand the support for restoration from France and what the reactions were to it in Croatia and Slovakia.

The Nature of France's Support in 1920

France's alleged support for restoration plans can be divided into two periods, a pre-Briand period (1920 to 1921) and a period starting with Briand's arrival at the Quai d'Orsay (January 1921). In mid-1920, Karl's contacts with France intensified through his Swiss lawyer, Henri Seeholzer.

Chapter VI

Emmanuel Peretti della Rocca, director of political affairs at the Quai d'Orsay, informed Karl in the summer of 1920, that the French government was not at all hostile to restoration in Hungary, "ni même tout à fait en Autriche; qu'il avait qu'à attendre son heure et le moment pourrait venir où on le prierait même de remonter d'urgence sur le trône."[633] Swiss diplomatic documents explain these French intentions by the fact that in summer 1920, Poland was on the verge of crumbling under the pressure of Russian forces, while Czechoslovakia was announcing that it was Poland's friend but not Russia's enemy, which meant that no one knew whether the Czechoslovaks would join the Russians if they were to find themselves face to face with them. In other words: "Hungary could be called to re-appropriate its secular role as the boulevard of Europe."[634] These words meant that with an unreliable Czechoslovakia and a menaced Poland, Hungary had a chance to become the military stronghold and the stable point of the "cordon sanitaire" that was being set up by France.

On one hand, both Henri Allizé, the French envoy to Bern after being posted in Vienna (March 1920), as well as Emmanuel Peretti della Rocca, expressed that France was not opposed to a restoration in Hungary and Austria. On the other hand, Jules Laroche, the deputy of the secretary general of the Quai (the pro-Little Entente Berthelot) told Seeholzer that he would inquire about these allegations. As a result, in October 1920, the French foreign minister, Leygues, made it known to Allizé that the assertions that a restoration would be in the interest of France are "de tous points inexactes".[635] It shows that before the arrival of Briand to the Quai d'Orsay, the Quai was already separated into two groups: a group of diplomats not opposed to the restoration of Karl and a group against this project.

---

633 "[...] nor even actually in Austria; that he had only to wait for his time and the moment could come when one would even beg him to ascend the throne again out of urgency."
634 *Documents diplomatiques suisses 1848–1945*, no. 8, doc. 66, 196–97, La Division des Affaires étrangères du Département politique aux Légations de Suisse, Bern, April 12, 1922. This was confirmed by Henri Allizé, French Ambassador in Bern, in a less enthusiastic way: "M. de Peretti lui [Seeholzer] avait dit qu'on ne verrait pas en France d'un mauvais oeil la restoration de l'Empereur Charles." (M. de Peretti himself [Seeholzer] had said that the restoration of Emperor Karl would not be viewed negatively in France.) ADMAE, Z Europe, Autriche 41, 256, Paris, October 11, 1920, Visite de M. Seeholzer.
635 "Inexact on all points." ADMAE, Z Europe, Autriche 41, ff. 261–2. Paris, October 14, 1920, Leygues à Allizé.

Briand and Karl

In January 1921 political changes brought Briand back to the prime ministerial chair together with the position of minister of foreign affairs. Certain sources, mainly gathered by Magda Ádám at the Quai d'Orsay archives, tend to show that Briand's return to government changed France's approach to the question of Karl's return to the Hungarian throne, but no source written by Briand himself has confirmed this. Since there are no minutes of the French Council of Ministers to show whether or not Briand took a stand on the question, we have to rely on international sources gathered from archives and personal memoirs and accounts to answer this question. But let us start by asking how far back the claimed special relationship between Briand and the Emperor-King went.

Karl's contacts with Briand started during the war, when the Emperor-King was trying to set up a secret peace settlement with France. The emperor's two emissaries, who were in fact the empress' brothers Sixte and Xavier of Bourbon-Parma, were both Belgian officers and thus could move freely in Paris and France. They were good friends of General Lyautey (an officer with royalist leanings) and acquaintances of Jules Cambon, the secretary general of the Quai d'Orsay, through whom they met with President Poincaré and Prime Minister Briand to negotiate a secret separate peace agreement with France.[636] Briand was accused by his political rival, the warmongering Clemenceau, of also carrying out secret peace talks with the Reich through a German diplomat, Baron Lancken (the Lancken Affair). However Briand, eventually, never met Lancken and was not prime minister anymore when this meeting was scheduled to happen (September 1917) under the control of President Poincaré. After the change of government (March 20, 1917) and its shift into more bellicose hands—Alexandre Ribot (March 20–12 September, 1917) and then Clemenceau (November 16, 1917–January 18, 1920)—than those of "the leftist" Briand, the negotiations would conclude unsuccessfully.[637]

---

636 Suarez, Georges, *Briand*, vol. 5–6, Plon, Paris, 1938, 52, 136–37.
637 Brook-Shepherd, *The Last Habsburg*, 144.

Chapter VI

The oldest biography of Briand, a multivolume work by J. Suarez, describes Briand's post bellum sympathy for the Habsburgs quite clearly:

> Briand était partisan d'une restauration des Habsbourg et ne s'en cachait pas. Il pensait qu'une dynastie qui avait conservé dans certaines régions du vieil empire d'aussi vigoureuses racines pouvait être, le moment venu, contre l'expansion allemande, un rempart plus efficace que les gouvernements précaires et mutilés par les traités. Contre le bloc germanique, ébranlé par les secousses de la guerre, mais qui ne tarderait pas à ressouder, les peuples et les races étalés comme une mosaïque entre l'Adriatique et la Mer Noire seraient bientôt incapables de se défendre, si un centre d'attraction puissant à la fois par la tradition et par le prestige ne les retenait pas et ne coordonait pas leurs éléments disparates. Mais c'eût été la fin d'un système dont Berthelot réclamait la paternité et dont Benes tirait, pour son pays, une suprématie injustifiée.[638]

There is no reason to doubt Suarez's statement, since many in the Quai d'Orsay supported a Danubian Confederation. Nonetheless, one additional step had to be taken in order to see if this sympathy towards Karl would bring concrete support.

The first time Briand's[639] post-war support for Karl is recorded is when Prince Lajos Windischgraetz claimed that in summer 1920, he met Briand for dinner in a private room of a restaurant near the Madelaine, where he transcribed Briand's remarks as follows:

> Si Charles de Habsbourg de sa propre initiative, sans toutefois provoquer, l'intervention armée des états nouvellement formés, pouvait réussir à

---

638 "Briand was a supporter of a Habsburg restoration and did not hide it. He thought that a dynasty that had preserved, in certain regions of the old empire, such vigorous roots, could be, when the moment came, a more effective bulwark against German expansion than the precarious governments mutilated by the treaties. Against the Germanic block, rattled by the shocks of the war, but which would not delay in reuniting, the peoples and the races spread out like a mosaic between the Adriatic and the Black Sea would soon be incapable of defending themselves if a centre of attraction that possessed power at once due to tradition and to prestige did not hold them check and did not coordinate their disparate elements. But this would have been the end of a system of which Berthelot claimed the paternity and from which Benes, for his country, would draw an unjustified supremacy." Suarez, *op. cit*, 238.

639 Briand was not yet prime minister.

s'établir et à se maintenir à Budapest, l'union de la Hongrie avec l'Autriche aurait la chance d'empêcher l'Anschluss de cette dernière à l'Allemagne. Dans ce cas le maintien de l'autorité impériale en Europe centrale pourrait devenir possible et même désirable. Comme de raison la France ne pourrait en aucun cas prêter officiellement main forte à une telle action expressément monarchiste; pourtant une fois établie dans la vallée du Danube l'attraction traditionnelle de la couronne des Habsbourgs aurait un effet efficace vis-à-vis des nouveaux états dont la composition est bien loin d'être assurés.[640]

It is interesting to note how these contacts were seen from Prangins. In the 1960s, the former empress, Zita, gave British journalist Gordon Brook-Shepherd a never-before published account of these relations and explained that Briand had made seven promises, a "seven-point verbal pact", most probably because the correspondence between Karl and Clemenceau had been revealed to the press by Czernin. This time no written form of the "pact" could be delivered for fear of seeing another indiscretion revealed to the press that would compromise France in the eyes of its allies. The points were:

1. immediate recognition of the emperor as soon as he had taken over as king of Hungary;
2. immediate setting-up of economic links;
3. immediate granting of French state credits;
4. French military aid should the emperor need it against foreign attacks;

---

640 "If Charles of Habsburg on his own initiative, yet without provoking the armed intervention of the newly formed states, could succeed in establishing and maintaining himself in Budapest, the union of Hungary with Austria would have the possibility to prevent the Anschluss of this last with Germany. In this case, the upholding of imperial authority in central Europe could become possible and even desirable. As one would expect, France could under no circumstances officially lend a hand to such an action, which was overtly monarchist; however, once established in the valley of the Danube, the traditional attraction of the crown of the Habsburgs would have a palpable effect vis-à-vis the new states, the composition of which was far from being assured." Windischgraetz claims that these were the exact words of Briand, which he noted word for word. Windischgraetz, *op. cit.*, 158–59. These descriptions are recalled by Windischgraetz in a similar way in most of his books on his life published in different languages. *Vom Roten zum Schwarzen Prinzen, Mein Kampf gegen das k.u.k.System*, Berlin, Wien, Verlag Ullstein, 1920.

5. a pledge, on the other hand, that no French troops would be forced on the emperor if he did not require them;
6. an undertaking to "look again" at the large territories of Hungary allotted to its neighbours and to "readjust the position to a certain extent";
7. a promise, as regards those same neighbouring states, to keep them in check and cut off all French credits on which they so heavily depended should they give any trouble.[641]

This pact looked quite similar to the Paléologue Plan and was not at all surprising if one considers the topics of the 1920 negotiations between France and Hungary. In other words, the reader has little reason to doubt former Empress Zita's account. Even the point expressing the possibility of borders readjustment was a plausible argument, as it had been raised, though eventually denied, by Millerand in his infamous *lettre d' envoi*.

The last direct encouragement was given to Sixte and to Strutt, the now British reserve officer who had led Karl and Zita to Switzerland, in February 1921.[642] Zita revealed that Strutt, himself, met Briand in the presence of Paléologue and Maréchal Hubert Lyautey and had discussed the exact position taken by the French prime minister, who "asked the emperor once again to take over the Hungarian throne as soon as possible and promised his support, naturally with the same condition as before, namely that the emperor would succeed in seizing power."[643] There is no reason to question these words, since they were secret and never to be published. There was, however, room for misinterpretation.

The Run-Up to Karl's First Visit

There could well be a connection between restoration of the Habsburgs and the irredentist claims of Hungary, as Karl IV had not signed the Treaty of

---

641 Brook-Shepherd, *The Last Habsburg*, 247.
642 On Strutt's report that he kept secret until after the failed visit of Karl in Budapest in NA, FO 371/6103, C6930/180/21, Col. Strutt to Cadogan, March 31, 1921.
643 Letter of September 29, 1930, from Count Degenfeld, secretary to Empress Zita to Baron Wiesner, legitimist leader in Austria, in Brook-Shepherd, Gordon, *The Last Empress, The Life and Time of Zita of Austria-Hungary, 1892–1989*, Harper-Collins, London, 1991, 160.

Trianon and many Hungarians and separatists of the Successor States considered him still to be the king of the old realm of Hungary and its peoples. His rights and those of his heirs covered the pre-1914 territory of Hungary that was now occupied by Romania, Czechoslovakia, the SHS Kingdom and Austria. The supporters of Karl believed that a Habsburg restoration would repudiate ipso facto the treaties of Trianon and Saint-Germain.[644] The argument was, therefore, very strong against placing at the head of the country a nationally-elected king who could not guarantee the legitimate territorial rights on the whole of the Realm of Saint Stephen.

At the Imperial and Royal Court in exile at Prangins, Karl was continually concerned to avoid any additional conflicts after the bloody world war. He was constantly waiting for the right moment to step into action and go back to Hungary, where the monarchy had been reinstalled. But in January 1920, Karl still considered his return as potentially dangerous, which is to say, he had been informed of the Slovak separatist efforts to return to Hungary. Thus he would postpone return.[645]

The then-existing literature—expanded by more recently published literature—on the question shows the following sequence of events. Karl had received the un-official support of the French head of government, Aristide Briand, and the royalist circles in the French Foreign Ministry, as well as guarantees that if he could convince Horthy, and create a fait accompli, France would recognise him as king of Hungary again. Karl was confident that Horthy, his governor in abstentia, would give the throne back to him, since Horthy had promised that he could return after the signing of the Trianon Peace Treaty. Horthy argued that the presence of Karl in Bu-

---

[644] Carmi, *op. cit.*, 35; Wlassics, G., "Az Eckartsaui nyilatkozat, a királykérdés" (1921), in Kardos, *A Legitimizmus*, 10–13.

[645] "Ich verweise nur darauf, dass die Wiederherstellung der Monarchie in Ungarn jetzt zum Anschlusse der Slowakei an Ungran und damit zu einem blutigen Konflikt zwischen Prag und Budapest und die westungarische Frage zu schweren Differenzen zwischen Österreich und Ungarn führen müssen. Mit anderen Worten: Der König von Ungarn müsste gegen sich selbst als Kaiser von Österreich, König von Böhmen etc. Kämpfen." (I only point out that the restoration of the monarchy in Hungary now must lead to the Anschluss of Solvakia to Hungary and therewith to a bloody conflict between Prague and Budapest and the west hungarian question must lead to strong differences between Austria and Hungary. In other words: the King of Hungary would have to fight against himself as Kaiser of Austria, King of Bohemia, etc.) Kovács, E., *op. cit.*, no. 189, 558–60, Karl an Fürst Lubomirski.

dapest before the signing would worsen the clauses that were against Hungary's interests. So, after Trianon, Karl thought that the moment was ripe. On March 27, 1921, he made a surprise visit to Budapest.[646] Horthy and his followers were completely dumbfounded by the arrival of the unforeseen guest, and because of the Entente pressures on Hungary that forbade the Hungarians to install their legitimate monarch, they refused to reinstate him on the throne. Even worse, Czechoslovakia and the SHS Kingdom considered the king's return as a *casus belli* and hence threatened Hungary's remaining territory. However, Horthy told the king that if he could bring a letter confirming Briand's willingness to accept a *fait accompli*, he might be willing to reconsider. Karl told him that this was Briand's secret plan and that the latter could not confirm this in writing as it was not France's official policy. Briand would only accept a *fait accompli*. As the king left, Horthy made the indiscreet choice to ask the French attaché about Briand's support instead of asking Hungary's representative in Paris, Praznovszky, to sound out Briand discreetly but directly.[647] The case against Horthy is worsened by the fact that, the next day, instead of asking Fouchet to confirm French support for Karl, he asked Fouchet to help him convince the king of the necessity of his departure from Hungary.[648] By that time, the Little Entente (Czechoslovakia and the SHS Kingdom) had gotten news of the king's presence in Hungary and started to protest. Beneš wanted to send an ultimatum to Hungary, which was avoided thanks to British intervention.[649] In short, external factors led by Beneš and eventually Fouchet's denial of Briand's support were added to the internal resistance expressed by Horthy and his circle.

From the perspective of the Hungarian representation in Paris, we get a different picture. Recently published documents have revealed that the Hungarian envoy, Iván Praznovszky, did make inquiries in Paris, but he could only meet Prime Minister Briand officially when he presented his ac-

---

646 To call this a return attempt would be a mistake; since the monarchy had been re-established, I prefer to call it the king's first visit to Hungary.
647 Ádám, *Little Entente*, 116.
648 Ormos, Mária, "Trón az ingoványon. Károly császár kísérletei egy birodalom megmentésére", *Rubicon*, no. 10, 2004, 15–16; Ormos, Mária, *"Soha amíg élek!"*, Pannónia könyvek, Pécs, 1990, 65.
649 Beneš did eventually send his ultimatum when the king had already left, Ormos, *Soha*, 77.

creditation letter as chargé d'affaires (October 11, 1921). He then left Paris the same day for a three-month holiday, during which time Karl's second return to Hungary occurred.[650] Earlier, when he was secretary of the Hungarian peace delegation, that is, the delegation of an enemy state vanquished by the Entente, Praznovszky had always been denied a meeting with Berthelot. If Berthelot was not ready to receive him in March/April 1921—even for a courtesy visit[651]—then it was even less conceivable for Praznovszky to be able to visit Briand, who also held the position of minister of foreign affairs. On the other hand, Prince Sixte—a Belgian allied officer—did have personal talks with Berthelot. Sixte was not representing the interests of Hungary but of his brother-in-law, who had more extensive plans than just regaining the crown of Hungary. It has to be underlined that after the departure of Paléologue from the Quai d'Orsay the opportunities for Hungarian emissaries and diplomats to meet with senior members of the Quai d'Orsay had been significantly reduced. Berthelot disliked the Hungarians, and this could be felt equally in French diplomatic circles and even in Parisian high society.

France's Position during the First Visit

Once Karl had arrived in Hungary, the Swiss Foreign Ministry claimed that a few marshals,[652] among them Foch himself, had declared themselves "sympathiques à la restoration des Habsburg en Hongrie", but Louis Loucheur,[653] would be "un des adversaires irréductibles des Habsbourg" and that "aussi longtemps que Berthelot dirigera en fait la politique extérieure française,

---

650 Zeidler, Miklós, *A Monarchiától Trianonig egy Magyar Diplomata Szemével, Praznovszky Iván emlékezései*, Olvasó Sarok, Budapest, 2012, 71.
651 Ibid., 82
652 Among these generals and marshals was Franchet d'Espérey who headed the "Cercle Franchet d'Espérey", a society grouping royalists and Catholics that kept contact with Foch. Frachet d'Espèrey would have informed Karl that when he returned to Hungary, France would only protest and would avoid military intervention. ADMAE, Z Europe, Hongrie 34, 108–9 ff., Extrait du *Volksgazet* d'Anvers du 5 avril 1921. This is confirmed by a letter from Karl to René de Bourbon-Parme from June or July 1921, ADMAE, Z Europe, Hongrie 38, 225 f.
653 Loucheur was Clemenceau's chief advisor on economic affairs at the Paris Peace Conference. Minister of liberated regions in the (1921–1922) Briand government.

Chapter VI

il n'y aura rien de changé."[654] The well informed and highly concerned Swiss Foreign Ministry would add:

> Au récent Conseil des Ministres à Rambouillet, au moment du coup d'Etat, il fut décidé, dit-on, sous pression de MM. Millerand, Barthou[655] et Briand et malgré l'opposition de MM. Loucheur, Maginot et Marraud, de rappeler pour la forme le veto de l'Entente, mais de ne mobiliser aucuns soldats contre la Hongrie carliste et d'empêcher la Petite Entente de déclencher un conflit armé (?).[656]

As Karl was in Switzerland, that country had great interest in having inside information as to what the French government was planning relating to restoration. Millerand, the old supporter of the Danubian Confederation, now president of the Republic, as well as Briand did not want to go further than to make formal protestations. This report confirms Karl's own interpretation, which the latter gave to Horthy.

An interesting memoir by a French Jesuit also confirms this interpretation:

> Le prince [Elemér] Lonyay me raconte, un jour où nous parlions du roi Charles et de ses tentatives de restauration, tenir personnellement du ministre de Suisse en Hongrie en 1921 que M. Fouché, ministre de France lors de la tentative du roi Charles, avait en mains des lettres du gouvernement français l'accréditant auprès du gouvernement du roi

---

[654] "[...] sympathetic to the restoration of the Habsburgs in Hungary [...] for as long as Berthelot will in fact direct French foreign policy, nothing will have changed." Documents diplomatiques suisses 1848–1945, no. 8, doc. 66, 196–97. La Division des Affaires étrangères du Département politique aux Légations de Suisse, Berne, April 12, 1922.

[655] Jean-Louis Barthou was one of Briand's main supporters in his plan to set up a Danubian Confederation. Ádám, *Little Entente*, 130.

[656] "At the recent Meeting of the Ministers at Rambouillet, at the moment of the coup d'état, it was presumably decided, under the pressure of MM. Millerand, Barthou, and Briand, and in spite of the opposition of MM. Loucheur, Maginot, and Marraud, to recall pro forma the veto of the Entente, but not to mobilise any soldiers against pro-Karl Hungary, and to prevent the Little Entente from launching an armed conflict (?)." Documents diplomatiques suisses 1848–1945, no. 8, doc. 66, 196–97. La Division des Affaires étrangères du Département politique aux Légations de Suisse, Bern, April 12, 1922. A British Foreign Office document confirms that if restoration was a success, France would not intervene. NA, FO 371 C6817/180/21, Lindley, High Commissioner to Austria, to Curzon, Vienna, April 1, 1921.

Charles, dont il aurait pu faire immédiatement usage en cas de succès. Le prince Lonyay ayant fait l'incrédule, le ministre de Suisse lui affirma de la façon la plus formelle avoir personnellement vu ces lettres entre les mains de M. Fouché [sic].[657]

But the most puzzling of the sources are the words of Berthelot, who was known to be pro-Czech and was already a high ranking member of the Quai d'Orsay in 1917.[658] Berthelot demanded that Karl depart, but he emphasised that there would be only formal protestations if Karl were to try to reconquer the throne. He said that France's interests lay not in the Habsburgs but in Karl's restoration in Hungary, because in that way it would be possible to realise it also in Austria, and that would hinder Austria's attachment to Germany. He continued by saying: "It is France's eminent interest that the territorially and demographically reduced Germany does not find compensation in the Anschluss of Austria and it is impossible to avoid it in another way."[659] Berthelot said that it was, however, impossible to support this plan, because it had to be subordinated to the Little Entente's interests. France would not send one soldier against Hungary nor would Britain, but France thought it good to have Karl removed because of the little Entente and its intentions. In other words, Berthelot had expressed France's interest in the restoration but claimed it was impossible at this point, given that Horthy had refused to give the throne back.

British sources show that Lord Hardinge, British minister to Paris, had set up private inquiries to find out the truth about Briand's support. If it was

---

[657] "Prince Lonyay tells me, one day when we were speaking of King Charles and his efforts at restoration, drawing personally from the minister of Switzerland in Hungary in 1921, that M. Fouché, minister of France at the time of King Charles' attempt, had in his hands letters from the French government accrediting him to the government of King Charles, of which he could have made immediate use in the case of success. Prince Lonyay having feigned disbelief, the minister of Switzerland affirmed for him in the most formal of fashions that he had personally seen these letters in the hands of M. Fouché." Archives des Jésuites de Vanves, Papier Delattre SDE 120 Cahier 9, 100–1. Lonyay was the second spouse of Princesse Stéphanie of Belgium, widow of the crown prince, Archduke Rudolf, who died in Mayerling.

[658] He was the one who placed a passage in the peace conditions, demanded by Beneš, concerning the liberation of the Italians, Slavs, Romanians and Czechs from foreign domination, exposed in a note to Wilson of January 10, 1917. Beneš, E., *My War Memoirs*, London, 1928, 144; Bogdan, *op. cit.*, 351.

[659] Ormos, *Soha*, 48.

obvious that France's Catholic and monarchist milieu was supportive, it also became clear to Hardinge that Briand "was not entirely ignorant of what was in progress", as he had been in contact with three of Karl's agents—not named, but likely Windischgraetz, Sixte and most probably Seeholzer or Strutt. Eventually, President Poincaré told Briand that, when president of the Republic, he had given his word to the Italians that France would not support Karl or any other member of his family. "Since that interview, Briand has told all his friends that he never gave any encouragements to the adventure."[660]

After analysing all these sources, one can only conclude that Briand had indeed made promises; and as he was not the only diplomat who favoured the return of Karl to Hungary, among them Berthelot himself, it is safe to say that in 1921 the Quai d'Orsay would have preferred a Danubian confederation between Hungary and Austria to Horthy's regime—whose entourage had been corresponding with Ludendorff[661]—supported by Britain.[662]

There remains the question of why Briand did not support the king once he was in Hungary. To this question one can give the following interpretation. Since no support was to be forthcoming before a *fait accompli*, and as upon the king's arrival, Horthy did not return the throne, questioned Briand's unofficial support, asked Fouchet about it, and eventually did not keep it secret, hope for Briand's support was doomed. Briand had already put himself in a more than uncomfortable position in the Lancken affair during the war, after which he was accused of being a traitor. Briand could not risk his position a second time if this plan did not go smoothly. He did keep his word to Karl, since he even left unanswered the telegrams from his diplomats in Central and South-Eastern Europe who were asking for instructions following reports "suggesting that Briand had not objected to the return of Charles" and no *démenti* of the Quai d'Orsay was issued in the press. Briand broke his silence only on March 30, after his meeting with Poincaré.[663]

---

660 The meeting with Poincaré was probably on March 29 or 30. NA, FO 371 C8422/180/21, Hardinge to Curzon Paris, April 23, 1921.
661 Ludendorff was plotting with Hitler to bring the Weimar Republic down.
662 Ádám, *Little Entente*, 97.
663 Ibid., 131–32.

After the First Attempt

The first return attempt in April 1921 gave Horthy's "free elector" entourage, led by Gyula Gömbös, an opening to develop more efficient anti-legitimist propaganda by affirming that the king had endangered the country by his visit. This was only half true. Even though Czechoslovakia and the SHS Kingdom were very irritated and sent an ultimatum to the Hungarian government, only after Karl had left Hungary, there was no true military menace, as Britain and France were holding back their allies. Not to mention that Romania, not following its allies with the ultimatum, officially joined the Little Entente only after Karl's first return to Hungary.[664]

Within the officer corps the visit had a negative effect and brought about the loss of power of the legitimists. The new national government had attracted k.u.k. officers because they were better prepared than the Hungarian national army, the Honvéd. In 1920, the commander of the new Royal Hungarian Army and many other k.u.k. officers were dismissed by Horthy because they were considered unreliable since they were legitimists. One has to consider that King Karl's attempts had put many officers in a dilemma, since they had had to take an oath first to the king, when they became officers, and then to Horthy.[665]

Luckily for the legitimists, politics did not follow the propaganda of Horthy's entourage. A new prime minister, Count István Bethlen,[666] was nominated due to the ambiguous position of Count Teleki in the events.[667] Nevertheless, Bethlen was ready to build his new governing party with the legitimist party, Andrássy's *KNEP*. Bethlen envisioned a long-term restoration. He asked the king to wait for the right moment, because he wanted to call him back after the consolidation of his new conservative regime.[668]

---

664 Ibid., 124–26.
665 Horthy was also ordering the disbandment of the pro-legitimist, Major Ostenburg's gendarmerie battalion, which was a threat to himself and was to be incorporated into the units of the more controllable National Army. Brook-Shepherd, *The Last Habsburg*, 283.
666 Bethlen had proven to be probably the brightest Hungarian politician of the interwar period.
667 Teleki knew that the king was in Hungary from the moment of his arrival on Hungarian soil. He nevertheless did not announce the king's arrival to the regent, as agreed with Karl, leaving His Majesty make his surprise visit to Budapest.
668 Kardos, József, *Legitimizmus, Légitimista politikusok Magyaroszágon a két világháború között*, Korona, Budapest, 1998, 56–60.

Chapter VI

According to the royal couple's interpretation, after his spring misadventure Karl received new French emissaries, who told Karl that Briand was angry that the news of his support had spread. Karl explained that it was Horthy who leaked the information, and he told Briand that he was willing to try again.[669] According to Gusztáv Gratz, the Hungarian foreign minister during the first attempt, Karl had to move fast, because Briand was not certain to stay in government after the next elections and could not back Karl any longer.[670]

We have an account that says that one of these emissaries, Paul Deschanel's [671] private secretary during the war, brought an oral message from the French government and told Karl that "the French Government had been misled by the Karlists' own account of the feeling in Hungary and therefore been unable to support Charles in face of the evident opposition, but that he should not lose heart and might rely on the ultimate support of the French Government."[672]

But in this message, there was no mention of when Karl could return, since in March Horthy and his entourage had opposed returning the throne.

So a new plan was set up, but this time it was to be an armed coup. On October 17, the former French consul in Prague, a certain Frédéric Quitton de Saint Quentin—obviously a monarchist aristocrat—was received by a secret legitimist council in Sopron, in the presence of Duić, Dankl, and other prominent international legitimists. Quitton was said to declare at this meeting: "Although France has no knowledge of the monarchist movement in Central Europe, he [France] would nevertheless support it by every possible means."[673] This declaration was followed by laughter from the legitimist council. In other words, this French diplomat claimed that France was ready

---

669 Ibid., 280; Vivian, Herbert, *The Life of Emperor Karl of Austria*, Grayson, London, 1932, 243.
670 Gratz, Gusztáv, *Magyarország a két háború között*, Osiris, Budapest, 2001, 93.
671 President of the Republic (January–September 1921).
672 At least that was the information that Lieut.-Col. Cuninghame got from Hungarian legitimist Marquis Pallavicini, NA, FO 371 6103, 9781/180/21, Foreign Office Memorandum from Cadogan, London, May 11, 1921.
673 NA FO 371/6105/C20236, 185–88 ff., Intelligence Report, Col. Gosset, Chief of British Delegation, Inter-Allied Military Commission of Control for Hungary, to Director of Military Intelligence, War Office (onwards DMI), Budapest, October 21, 1921. It was considered important information, since it was sent to the British military attachés in Paris, Prague, Berlin, Bratislava and Vienna.

to support a movement it officially denied the existence of. To add to the intrigue, the British high commissioner in Budapest claimed that the French were supporting the movement financially and that it was the "'hangers-on' of 'Lyautey-Berthelot-Briand', nicknamed the 'Petite Duchesse' group set in Paris, who play about with Charles who are now supporting and also subscribing to this movement".[674] These notes show how British diplomats were still blaming the French for their intriguing behaviour in the region that the FO had already criticised during the peace talks with Hungary, though Briand's "wait and see" attitude was confirmed by many sources before Karl first failed attempt.

The Militarised Attempt

On October 20, King Karl and Queen Zita flew from Dübendorf near Zürich directly to western Hungary. However, the plot was not well organised and most of the Karlists were not even informed of his landing on that evening. The next day a train was organised for him to leave from Sopron and proceed towards Budapest, and at each stop of the royal train more garrisons joined his army. Karl managed to get to a town bordering Budapest, Budaörs, with an army of about 5,000 men; considering what was available in Hungary, this was a meaningful army. They were met by a few hundred armed Horthysts, some sources say there were about 2,000 at the end, some of them students from the Polytechnic University who had been gathered and armed by Gömbös.[675] Karl was eventually betrayed by one of his own commanders, General Pál Hegedüs. In order to avoid bloodshed in the ranks of the young students, Karl gave himself up. The response of the Little Entente to this second attempt was to mobilise both in Czechoslovakia and in the SHS kingdom.[676] Romania remained neutral because of a secret accord between Karl and King Ferdinand.[677]

---

674 NA, FO 371/5822/C13772, A-Johnson, High Commissioner, to Tufton, Budapest, June 27, 1921.
675 Ormos, *Soha*, 116; Ladányi, Andor, *Az egyetemi ifjúság az ellenforradalom első éveiben (1919–1921)*, Budapest, 1979, 212.
676 Ormos, *Soha*, 116–17. NA FO 371, 6109 89-91; ibid. 6111, 81–97, Clerk to Curzon, Prague, November 18–21, 1921.
677 Dugast-Rouillé, Michel, *Karl de Habsbourg*, Duclos, Paris, 1991, 247.

Chapter VI

The second return attempt had been particularly badly timed, since Bethlen—as a result of the agreement with Andrássy—was about to declare publicly his intention of calling King Karl back to Hungary. One day after Karl and Zita had flown into Hungary, Bethlen—unaware of the fact—gave his famous speech in Pécs (southern Hungary) in which he said, "once the *vis major* [revolutions, red and white terror] is over, the monarch will be obliged to take over his duties to rule". In other words, Karl's throne was guaranteed and an invitation to return was only a question of time.[678] At this moment it became clear that the Hungarian government was not talking about restoration, which had been a fact since the reestablishment of the monarchical system in 1920 and which was now confirmed by the prime minister, but more precisely of a return of the legitimate monarch.

Karl's accelerated return destroyed all hope of his return to the throne since it ended in a fiasco. After these events, Bethlen chose to unite with the Smallholders party, with anti-legitimist tendencies, and formed his governing party with them. Following this, the Habsburgs were dethroned by the Parliament on November 6, 1921, under pressure from the Entente.

In the western Part of Hungary, Transdanubia, the rural and town populations acclaimed King Karl when he arrived back in April and in October 1921, and soldiers joined the garrisons that marched with the king to take Budapest from Horthy, who resisted and refused to give the throne back. This was proof of the royal couple's immense popularity in western Hungary.

Concerning France's position during the second attempt, more caution has to be taken with Zita's claims, because this time neither the Quai d'Orsay nor Swiss diplomacy confirmed Briand's support or even neutrality.[679] In fact, Briand expressed his anger at Karl and opposed his second visit from the beginning. Karl had claimed yet again that he had the support of Briand. The latter pressed Hungary for Karl to be dethroned, though he did not want to see all Habsburgs excluded from the throne—this because Fouchet had informed Briand that the supporters of Archduke József

---

678 Kardos, *Legitimizmus*, 70.
679 There is a source which claims that Mr. Grant Smith, US high commissioner, would have told King Karl that it was time to return to Hungary. 7N Hongrie 2285, Rapport du 1 Décembre 1920.

in Parliament would turn against the Little Entente and would bring unrest to Hungary.[680]

But why did Karl think that Briand was still backing him and waiting for the *fait accompli*? As reported by Alphonse Dunant, the Swiss envoy to Paris, "Charles avait ici [Paris] des partisans dans les partis de droite."[681] As seen from British reports, French monarchists were still supporting him, among them some diplomats, but it appears that Seeholzer—who had special channels to the French Foreign Ministry—was not working for Karl anymore, and Karl's most devoted and reliable servant, Strutt, was not involved in bringing news from Paris anymore either. Finally, Sixte was invited to visit Berthelot, to whom he gave his word of honour that he had not been informed of the trip. Sixte declared that it was dangerous for his sister to take part in this adventure, and he agreed with Berthelot that this attempt had no chances of success.[682]

From the perspective of the international Legitimists' League—including its Austrian, Hungarian, Bavarian, Slovak and Croat members—the situation in Hungary had to be clarified in regard to tensions between the legitimists and the free electors before a coup could be undertaken. The operation originally planned for October 12 was therefore postponed for ten days to achieve this but also to take "steps to secure the cooperation of sympathetic elements in Bavaria, Croatia and Tyrol", and "arrangements were made to form military organisations among the various Monarchist groups".[683] Even though British intelligence considered that "the preparations of the coup were extensive",[684] the information regarding the agreement between Andrássy and Bethlen did not reach the right persons, such as Gratz, the former Hungarian foreign minister. Gratz was a pivotal person of the Karlist takeover, and action was therefore neither coordinated nor postponed in respect

---

680 Ádám, *Little Entente*, 165.
681 "Charles had supporters here among the right-wing parties." Archives fédérales suisses (henceforth AFS), BAR/E2300, Paris 74, Légation de Suisse au Département Politique Suisse, Paris, October 26, 1921.
682 Kovács, *op. cit.*, no. 249,777-8, Visite du Prince Sixte à M. Berthelot, Paris, October 23, 1921.
683 NA FO 371/6105/C20236, 185–88 ff., Intelligence Report, Col. Gosset to DMI, Budapest, October 21, 1921.
684 Ibid.

Chapter VI

to the results to be achieved by Andrássy.[685] When Andrássy was informed that the king had landed, he, too, said that no one had informed him that Karl would arrive one day before Bethlen's pro-legitimist speech.[686] Thus, there were two groups: the Karlists, including Gratz, who were ready for a putsch, and the more moderate legitimists, who wanted to achieve Karl's return to the throne of Hungary politically. In other words, Gratz had hidden the information of Karl's arrival, scheduled on October 20, from Andrássy, and the latter had not revealed the results of his most recent talks with Bethlen to Gratz on time.

The fate of the Karlists, but also of Andrássy, was that they were arrested after the coup backfired. They were condemned in court but pardoned by Horthy and soon released.[687] Following the Parliament's vote of the law of dethronement (November 6, 1921), the legitimists moved into the opposition. They followed—under the leadership of Andrássy until his resignation from politics in 1926—a Christian socialist policy, defended democratic rights, fought for universal suffrage and for a more socialist policy, including land reforms, which was surprising for a group of politicians including many landowning aristocrats. They stood up against the rise of National Socialism and extremisms and were much concerned about the German menace to Central Europe. Apponyi was more conciliatory with the government, continued his diplomatic services and represented Hungary at the League of Nations in Geneva. But he did not give up his legitimist feelings and agreed to preside over the Legitimist High Council, the most important organ of the legitimists.[688]

Gratz continued his career as a journalist and historian, got back into politics in the 1930s as a liberal politician, and as a member of Richard Coudenhove-Kalergi's Paneuropean Union he continued to fight for the idea of a Danubian Confederation. He also went on special diplomatic missions in order to promote Milan Hodža's (by then Czechoslovak prime minister)

---

685 Gratz, *Magyarország*, 102–3
686 Boroviczény, *op. cit.*, 225.
687 Ibid., 347–48, and document 4 (no page numbers).
688 Gergely, J., "A kereszténszocialisták politikai szerepe az elleforadalm első éveiben (1919–23)", *Századok*, no. 2, 1976, 255–56; Kardos, József, "Ifjabb Andrássy Gyula gróf utolsó évei", *Történelmi Szemle*, no. 3–4, 1994, 299–309; Csonka, *op. cit.*, 185.

Prague–Vienna–Budapest triangle, re-launching the idea of a smaller Danubian Confederation after the 1934 Anschluss attempt. In 1944, after the German occupation of Hungary, Gratz was deported to Mauthausen. He luckily survived and was liberated in spring 1945.[689]

The SHS Kingdom

Resistance Intensifies

The year 1920 ended with a general strike in Zagreb on December 30, and another strike was frustrated in Sarajevo by measures taken by the police.[690] Meanwhile, leading members of the Muslim community joined the opposition formed by Croats and Slovenes.[691]

The British Foreign Office was getting news that Radić's supporters were pro-Habsburg and was realising the importance of the anti-Serbian feeling in Croatia. Francis Oswald Lindley, the high commissioner in Belgrade, confirmed that there were doubts regarding the Slovenes' loyalty as well.[692]

This news was reinforced by Serb sources claiming that Radić's party was becoming more radical. In January 1921, a Serb newspaper published a secret letter from Vladimir Sachs, Frank's acolyte, to Maček, vice president of Radić's party, in which the former explained that he would not work with the Croat Committee (legitimist) anymore. Sachs and Frank had been in Fiume at least since autumn 1920 and working with D'Annunzio. Sachs thought that Duić, Sarkotić and Frank were not reliable people and that they only had 50 to 100 men in their legion, when they claimed to have thousands. Sachs claimed that Hungary gave only a little financial support to the Croat Committee and that Italy and the freemasons[693] had the means to support

---

689 Bécsi, Zoltán, "Les légitimistes hongrois et la question de l'Europe centrale (1929–38)", *Revue Européenne d'Histoire*, vol. 11, no. 3, 2004, 372–80.
690 NA FO 371/6193/C25, A. Young to Curzon, Belgrade, December 31, 1920.
691 NA FO 371/6193/C881, Belgrade, January 8, 1921, A. Young to Curzon.
692 As Lindley says, the Croats were "the stoutest of their [Habsburg] troops". NA FO 371/6193/C1314, Lindley to Curzon, Belgrade, January 13, 1921.
693 Freemasonry, as a progressive group, was considered anti-monarchist and republican.

the Slavs in the south and create a Croat republic, a Serb republic, a state of Montenegro and Albania. He also said that the form of these entities should be determined by the people. Maček would have asked Sachs's emissary for ammunition, information that was published after the emissary was arrested by the Serbs.[694]

Parallel to defamatory articles concerning the members of the Agrarian Party and the Party of Pure Rights, the Yugoslav administration made some arrests. Milan Accurti, former procurator, and Milan Šufflay, a professor of the University of Zagreb, were both arrested and accused of fomenting the separation of Croatia from the SHS State, with the support of the Hungarian army. This was revealed, again, through a confiscated secret letter addressed to a Hungarian military officer.[695]

These articles in the press and the arrests were a good propaganda instrument for the Serbs. The veracity of these letters might have been in question if Hungarian and Austrian sources did not confirm that the persons in question truly were involved in activities supporting the separation of Croatia from the rest of the SHS Kingdom, and they also confirm that Peasant Party leaders were implicated with the separatist groups. Yet, it was the timing for these arrests that had a propagandistic effect. The Serbs wanted to get rid of the anti-Yugoslav groups, and the likeliness of a Habsburg return in Hungary was growing.

According to Boroviczény, following the first return attempt, the Croat separatists informed the Hungarians that Croat and Slovene k. u. k. officers and politicians were still supportive of Karl, and had the king succeeded in his attempt, they would have proclaimed Croatia's separation from Serbia. Sarkotić's group of legitimist generals was continuing to prepare revolts in Croatia and Slovenia directed from the Austrian town of Graz. Radić, in Zagreb, was ready to take up arms against the Serb forces if they were to attack Hungary after Karl's victory in Budapest. He wanted to use this opportunity to detach his country from the Serb-directed kingdom and to create an independent Croat republic and even to join a Habsburg confederation centred in Budapest. However, only the return of the legitimate king of Hungary, who

---

694 NA FO 371/6193, 103–6 ff., A. Young to Curzon, Belgrade, February 4, 1921, Extract from the *Politika* of Belgrade of January 28, 1921.
695 NA FO 371/6193/c561, 83–86 ff., Young to Curzon, Belgrade, January 3, 1921.

already bore the crown of Saint Stephen, and the faithfulness of the Croats to him could bring Croatia back to Hungary, and the effect of extreme Hungarian chauvinism was a danger that could erase this attachment.[696]

Radić and the Vidovdan Constitution

Radić and his deputies refused to vote for the constitution and wanted to declare the independence of the Republic of Croatia within the borders of the SHS State during a meeting to be organised for May 16. The ban of Croatia, named Tomislav Tomljenović, summoned Radić to his office and forbade him to organise this meeting and proclaim independence.[697]

After the proclamation of the Vidovdan Constitution, Radić united with the Frankists within the "Croat lock"[698] and directed his protests against Belgrade and its lack of respect for Croatia's independence. He declared that the constitution "ne fut et ne sera jamais reconnue par le peuple Croate".[699] Radić also openly fustigated the Italian Fascists who were occupying Dalmatia.[700] Eventually, only 28 of 93 Croat MPs accepted centralism; all the others were against it.[701]

In the city council of Zagreb, of which he was member, Radić said that he would not take an oath on the constitution, since the only law "existante à ce sujet ordonnait de prêter serment au Habsburg roi de Hongrie."[702] Radić was more and more openly claiming his pre-1918 sympathies toward the Habsburgs in a provocative way.

---

696 Boroviczény, *op. cit.*, 152–53; *Horthy Titkos Iratai*, no. 4, 21–22.
697 ADMAE, Z Europe Yougoslavie 40, 200–221 ff., Clément-Simon à MAE, Belgrade, May 17, 1921. The French diplomat misspelled the ban as Lienavitch. In fact he was a Bunjevci (Catholic Serbs in Croatia and Vojvodina) from the Croatian town of Gospić.
698 Banac, *op. cit.*, 263.
699 "Never was and never will be acknowledged by the Croatian people." ADMAE, Z Europe, Yougoslavie 40, Clément Simon à Poincaré, Belgrade, March 3, 1922. This was a general movement in Croatia, even Ante Trumbic (1864–1938), the leading Croat in the Yugoslav Committee of London voted against the first constitution of Yugoslavia. Stallaerts, Robert, Jeannine Laurens, *Historical Dictionary of the Republic of Croatia*, Scarecrow Press, Inc., Lanham, MD, London, 1995, 234–35.
700 ADMAE, Z Europe, Yougoslavie 40, 259–62 ff. Consul de Zagreb à Prés. du Conseil, Belgrade, Nov. 15, 1922.
701 ADMAE, Z Europe Yougoslavie 40, 200–201 ff., , Clément-Simon à MAE Belgrade, May 17, 1921.
702 " […] on this subject ordered [that one] swear [allegiance] to the Habsburg king of Hungary." ADMAE, Z Europe, Yougoslavie 34, 198 f., Clément-Simon à Briand Belgrade, May 26, 1921.

Chapter VI

The Activation of the Legitimist Network

After the first failed return attempt, legitimist action was increasing, and preparations were being made for the next attempt. The Croat legitimists told Boroviczény that they were in possession of all the secrets of the Belgrade high command and they felt strong enough to realise Croatia's independence from Serbia if the SHS Kingdom were to start a war with Hungary. Once in Hungary, the king would be asked to go to the Danube–Drava frontier, ask Serbia if it wished to sign a peace agreement, and then wait to see if SHS Kingdom would accept or would attack. Since the Croats were expecting a mobilization, they would take this opportunity to declare the creation of the Croat army once the mobilization was realised.[703]

As British sources confirm, an international legitimist meeting was held in Szombathely at the Episcopal palace of the local bishop, Count Mikes. At this meeting the legitimist leader representing Hungary was Colonel Lehár. Representing Croatia there were, among others, Lieutenant Colonel Duić and Milan Accurti, who had been liberated by then from Serb custody. The bishop said that it would no longer be necessary to attempt a forceful return, as "it was now certain that Charles would return to Hungary in a legal and peaceful manner. The Government now intended to regulate the question of the Monarchy by constitutional means." Bishop Mikes was referring to the agreement made between Bethlen and Andrássy.[704]

The Croat representative, Duić, said that the uprising in Croatia would be on the day of King Alexander's return, October 25, the same day the legitimist conference in Graz was to be held: "In the case of such a rising in Croatia isolated action on the part of Hungary with regard to the return of Charles would be out of question." Duić was referring to the king's April visit and resistance shown by the Horthyists. He continued, saying that "the moment such a revolution broke out, Hungary would be bound to cooperate with the Croats. Risings would immediately follow in all the other countries of the old Monarchy and the 'King will no longer belong to Hungary alone

---

703 Boroviczény, op. cit., 178–79.
704 NA FO 371/6105/C20236, 185–88 ff. Intelligence Report, Col. Gosset to DMI Budapest, October 21, 1921.

but also to us.'" As the legitimists' preparatory meetings were to be held on the October 26 in Graz and 29 in Munich, the king was not awaited in Hungary before those two dates.[705] The aim of the revolts was to prevent mobilization in both the SHS Kingdom and Czechoslovakia.[706]

The other concern of the legitimists was the, by then forgotten, corridor between Czechoslovakia and the SHS Kingdom: "Hungarian propaganda was, at the same time, carried out amongst the Croatians with the object of demonstrating that the Little Entente's real aim as regards Western Hungary was to obtain a corridor between Czech-Slovakia and Yugo-Slavia and that should this object be effected their Croatian brothers in that area would suffer."[707]

The military preparation of the Croat separatists seemed well organised this time, but it is still difficult to imagine that the small Hungarian army and the Croat separatist troops in Hungary and in the SHS Kingdom could have stopped the (mainly Serb) Yugoslav army.

Yugoslav Mobilization

In the SHS Kingdom, the Serbs already had a consolidated army and represented a greater danger for Hungary. They had mobilised about 100,000 men to occupy Hungary. The mobilization continued even after King Karl had been arrested, because they were waiting for a good reason to occupy the northern part of Baranya county—which has remained Hungarian until today—and, which the Serbs considered to be a region that was unjustly held by vanquished Hungary. The Serb officers thought that Hungary was bellicose and well armed; they argued that Hungary could "put in the field 120,000 men", when its army was limited to 35,000 by the peace treaty. The British diplomats denied, categorically, this allegation.[708]

In the Croat part of the SHS Kingdom, instability ruled. Though the calling up of the reservists went well in general, there were some disturbances,

---

705 Ibid.
706 NA, FO 371/6111/C22064, "Recent Events in Hungary" by SIS (Secret Intelligence Service), November 21, 1921.
707 Ibid.
708 NA FO 371/6109, 89–91 ff., Lt.-Col. J.M. Blair, Ass. Mil. Attaché, to D.M.I, Belgrade, November 3, 1921.

which the governor's (ban) office in Zagreb claimed were "circulated by evilly disposed elements". Yet they nonetheless describe the unsuccessful disturbances, despite their lack of success. One of these was directed against recruitment in the Novska, Novigrad and Koprivnica districts by the Peasant Party leaders who asked the peasant population not to comply with the issued orders. The police arrested the offenders. During this period the leader of the Croat Block, Vratar, wished to "summon a Croat Assembly which would proclaim its severance from Serbia". In other districts, such as Dugoselo, members of the Peasant Party and Hungarian agitators "told the people that they should refuse to obey the call to arms and refuse to join the army, because all the Croat parties had to do this, and because King Charles was coming." Other similar cases were reported at Brukovljani and in Rugovica near Zagreb.[709]

It remains difficult to imagine how the separatists could have managed to stop the well-armed, numerous, Serb-directed army and turn against them.

Why did the Croat Separatist Plan Fail?

When in 1919 the Croat Committee approached the Hungarians, Hungary was still in a state of disorder and not yet consolidated. The anti-Habsburg elements were gaining influence and Hungary did not want to associate itself with Croatia if it meant that Hungary had to serve the "anti-Hungarian" or non-Hungarian interests of Karl; meaning that he had ambitions to become monarch elsewhere than Hungary. By mid-1921, it became obvious that both the Teleki government and that of his successor, Bethlen, were supporting the return of Karl as king but on the condition that Karl ask the Hungarian Parliament's permission if he was considering becoming monarch of another nation. Thus the concept of dualism, which implied that the monarch would also be head of state elsewhere, was an open question for the time being.[710] The efforts made by the ministry of minorities also made it clearer to both Croats and Slovaks that a legitimate Kingdom of Hungary would give

---

709 NA, FO 371/6111/C22140, Lt. Col. James Blair, Mil. Att. to Director of Mil. Int, Belgrade, November 15, 1921.
710 NA, FO 371/6111/C22064, "Recent Events in Hungary" by SIS (Secret Intelligence Service), November 21, 1921.

more than a Hungary governed by an elected national king, such as Horthy. But the failure of attempts to recover the throne sent a negative message to legitimist-separatist Croats, who gathered in the Frank and Radić parties. For those who were suspicious of the Hungarians, Karl's failures also meant that they could not see him become monarch in Vienna again, as Austria had refused restoration as well. When in October 1921 the Habsburg sympathisers discovered that Karl had given up, they stopped their preparations.[711]

Concerning Italy, the commitment signed in July 1919 with the Croat separatists was a durable one, and it was renewed on October 19, 1920, by the Fiume Command—now the Regency of the Cornaro—and it promised 20 million liras and 130,000 rifles; also, the list of Balkan allies had been enlarged with the separatists of Macedonia and Vojvodina. Throughout the summer of 1920 D'Annunzio and his associates had seriously been trying to find financial support for the Balkan uprisings but could only deliver smaller sums.[712] Eventually, the Balkan revolution had been compromised by the Treaty of Rapallo (1920) and by the lack of financial support and the retreat of the Italian government in its support for D'Annunzio. Since Italy had decided to get out of the game in 1921, D'Annunzio had not been able to provide the millions and the weapons needed for the uprising. Italy's interests were neither to support D'Annunzio nor to support, through the separatist Croats, a project involving the restoration of Karl, which it had always been the first to oppose.[713] To sum up, Hungary could not live up to its promises, and if Italy through D'Annunzio could not support it, it is obvious that the separatist project had no future.

The Fate of the Dramatis Personae

In 1925 Radić left the republican platform, which only confirms that a *modus vivendi* with Royal Serbia was a necessity after the death of King Karl. He remained the leader of the Croat opposition until his assassination in the Belgrade Parliament in 1928.

---

[711] Lehár, *op. cit.*, 48; Olivova, Vera, "Československá zahraniční politika a pokus o restauraci Habsburků v roce 1921" in *Československý časopis historický*, 4, 1959, 688–89.
[712] Ledeen, *op. cit.*, 184–85.
[713] Eventually, the Florence agreement of 1924 gave one harbour to Italy and one to the SHS Kingdom.

Chapter VI

Officers like Kvaternik and Duić participated briefly in the construction of Yugoslavia but soon understood the danger for Croatia in it. They started believing that they could choose the future of Croatia freely and had to conclude that the only way was resistance within and from abroad. The separatist camp (composed of Frank's and Radić's parties) grew from a minority in November 1918 to the most important anti-SHS military group and the largest coalition for independence by 1921.

The Croat Committee in Austria, led by General Sarkotić, was middle class, conservative and "reactionary" (in the literary sense of wishing for the return of a previous order) rather than revolutionary. Even though this group provided the initial means of communication between Ante Pavelić—later the Nazi leader of Croatia—and Fascist Italy as early as 1927, its impact was limited throughout the émigré period, as well as during the four years of Ustaša power under Nazi auspices in 1941–45. If Sarkotić was too closely identified with the old pre-1914 world to be part of it, he was too conservative to be fascist or extremist.[714] However, Slavko Kvaternik, though his wife was of Jewish origin, had an important role as a founder, with Pavelić, of the Ustaša movement and was minister of war and vice-Poglavnik (vice-Führer) in 1941 of Ante Pavelić's "Independent State of Croatia", a Nazi German puppet state. Duić also joined the Ustaša but was assassinated in 1934 in Graz and was not able to see the creation of the Ustaša state. The bitterness of their grievances against the Serbs had built up to a level of hate that radicalized some of these k.u.k. officers to become sympathisers of Nazism.[715]

Ivo Frank, the leader of the pro-Habsburg legitimists, who was often considered as a right radical, was much more moderate than was thought. He was upset by the fact that his nephew, Eugen Dido Kvaternik—the son of Slavko Kvaternik[716]—had been involved by Pavelić in the 1934 Marseilles assassinations of King Alexander I of Yugoslavia and the French foreign minister, Louis Barthou. In 1933, during a conference in Budapest on the

---

714 Trifkovic, Srdjan, "The First Yugoslavia and Origins of Croat Separatism", *East European Quarterly*, XXVI, no. 3, September 1992, 363. Richard Spence exaggerates Sarkotić's involvement regarding the Ustaša movement. Spence, "General Stephan Freiherr Sarkotić...", *op. cit.*, 147–55.
715 An in-depth analysis of the post-1920 careers of the Croatian members would be interesting in order to weigh the evolution of these former k.u.k. officers.
716 Slavko Kvaternik was Ivo Frank's brother-in-law.

necessity to create a Danubian Confederation, Frank openly expressed his fears about Germany and pan-Germanism, calling it a greater threat to Central Europe than pan-Slavism.[717] Frank died in exile in Budapest in 1939.

The truly pro-Habsburg and separatist Frankists were not only threatened by Serb dictatorship but also by the Ustaša regime that made martyrs of some of them, such as Manko Gagliardi, who was shot in 1942.

Czechoslovakia

Slovak Efforts

Hodža tried after the 1920 elections to offer a Slovak administrative autonomy and the formation of a Slovak union of counties that would have restored Slovakia's identity, at least partially. Hlinka still insisted on Slovak political autonomy, which Hodža neither wanted to nor could offer. This meant that Hlinka still would not give in to the Prague government.

As a result, the year 1921 was to be no calmer. By May the Slovak resistance was growing. Martin Mičura, the minister for the administration of Slovakia, alluded to renewed strong agitation against Czech officials in Slovakia.[718] Regarding Hlinka's international diplomacy, he was keeping up his relations with Hungarians, Poles and others who could help him separate from the Czechs. Juriga, Hlinka's acolyte, was setting up contacts with the Hungarian aristocracy.[719] Czechoslovak circles that wanted restoration were financing propaganda[720] as well as the Hungarians, who were still in close touch with the Slovak irredentists in Krakow. The Krakow Committee even planned to start a revolutionary movement once the harvest was gathered.[721]

---

717 Frank, Ivo, *A Revízió és Horvátország*, Erdélyi Férfiak Egyesülete, Budapest, 1933, 10.
718 NA, FO 371/5822/C9503, Clerk to Curzon, Prague, May 6, 1921.
719 Ibid.
720 NA, FO 371/5822/C18843, Slovakia, Summary for August 1921.
721 NA, FO 371/5822/C13772, A Johnson, High Commissioner, to Tufton, Budapest, June 27, 1921. It is confirmed by German reports that discussions were held in mid-January 1921 in Krakow on the new Hungarian–Polish coordination to attack Slovakia. Kirschbaum, *In Honour*, 84.

Chapter VI

As Clerk reported, the situation was moving from calm in the first half of June to agitated on June 27 when the Czech and Slovak Clerical parties amalgamated; both parties were aiming at decentralization.[722] By summer 1921 the Slovaks looked back to assess the results of all the promises made when the country was taken over by the Czechs, and the result was indeed negative.[723] By that time, the united Czech and Slovak Clerical Party had become the strongest in the House.[724]

The failure of Karl's first return attempt had an effect on Hlinka and his entourage (Juriga, Tománek), since they were cultivating hopes for Karl's return and believed that their autonomy could be guaranteed by the king. The fact that Horthy did not give the throne back was not a good sign for Hlinka, who had scorned Jehlička for not defending total autonomy—without Hungarian control—when the latter was negotiating with Horthy's Ministry of Minorities. The other bad sign was that the Bethlen government believed less in the Ministry of Minorities than had its predecessor.[725] Hence it is not surprising that given this uncertainty, Hlinka displayed loyalty to the Czechs at a well-attended Clerical Party meeting on October 17; not to mention that the ambitious priest had been promised the bishopric of Trnava or Nagyszombat (H) in return.[726]

During the same period, Jehlička and Unger—respectively the president and vice-president of the Slovak National Council stationed in Krakow—continued to ask for Polish as well as Hungarian support to achieve the independence of Slovakia under the protectorate of one or the other state. They suddenly took a big step by proclaiming the independence of Slovakia to the Slovak nation on May 25, 1921. Jehlička became president of the temporary government and Unger the vice-president and foreign minister. By then Beneš had made territorial concessions to Poland, since he felt that it was time to concede something to Poland in order to break it away from Hungary and promote the rapprochement with Czechoslovakia.[727]

---

722 NA, FO 371/5822/C15123, Clerk to Curzon, Prague, July 22, 1921.
723 NA, FO 371/5822/C17194, Slovakia, Summary for July 1921.
724 Ibid. Following the 1920 elections, Hlinka joined the People's Party (the party of Czech Catholics), led by Jan Sramek, in a parliamentary bloc, as both parties were against centralism and for Catholicism. Felak, *op. cit.*, 29.
725 Tilkovszky, *op. cit.*, 575, 582.
726 NA, FO 371/5823/C22435, Slovakia, Summary for October 1921.
727 Kovács, Endre, *Magyar-Lengyel kapcsolatok a két vilàghàború között*, Akadémia Kiadó, Budapest,

Unger turned to the Hungarian minister, Csekonics, to ask whether Hungary could recognise, officially or secretly, the temporary Slovak government as Hungary's official irredentist organ. Hungary as well as Poland distanced themselves from the Slovaks instead of supporting them as in the past. The Polish government went as far as to ban the Slovak National Committee of Krakow in June 1921.[728]

It is timely to ask why the separatist action did not happen. The answer requires summing up the above-mentioned factors. First, neither Poland nor Hungary continued to support the military enterprise of the Slovak separatists based in Poland and Hungary. Second, the legitimist offensive was badly coordinated, and many were not even informed of the surprise visit by Karl. Third, just a few miles from Budapest King Karl decided to call off the military coup and the separatist operations. Fourth, the Ministry for Minorities had changed its approach to the minority question. And, finally, Hungary was on the road to consolidation and would not take the risk of becoming a battleground again.

The Monarchist Threat in Prague

I have limited my research to the study of Slovakia, but in order to have a global view of what happened in Czechoslovakia, we have to look briefly at the problems in the capital, Prague.

The paranoia of the republicans towards crypto-monarchists was growing in Prague, and arrests of legitimists took place.[729] Even Prime Minister Kramář was at some point "believed to be flirting with the remnants of the Habsburgs and to desire a Catholic Danubian Monarchy" in spite of the fact that he was a hero of Czech independence and was jailed for two years by the

---

1971, 51; Michela, Miroslav, "Frantisek Jehlicska Politikai Pályafutása 1918–20-ban", *Pro Minoritate*, 2005, 41.

728 Kovács, Endre, *Magyar*, 52.

729 Twelve persons accused of fomenting a monarchist coup were arrested, which provoked considerable excitement. Among them were a number of officials of the National Defence Ministry, some women and Prince Friedrich and Prince Zdenko Lobkowitz. They were accused of giving or receiving money for the purpose of monarchical propaganda. They were released on September 25, 1920. BDFA, *op. cit.*, Doc. 16, 27–28.

Chapter VI

Austrians.[730] Kramář was a conservative; having inherited great wealth and being the owner of the *Norodni Listi* newspaper, he was considered a powerful and influential person having the Agrarians behind him.

The Czechs, who were still suspicious of France's "confederating" policy in Central Europe, were disturbed to see that Kramář was turning towards the French—"who appear to be making much of him"—as the British were supporting Masaryk.[731]

Sir George Clerk replied to these suppositions:

> There is possibly a feeling in this country that the revival in monarchism is more likely than the success of Bolshevism, but chiefly due to the general conviction, right or wrong, that the faults and failure of Bolshevism are now so thoroughly realised here that its adoption is even more improbable than the re-establishment of a Monarchy. To put it in another way, the numbers of those who hope for a monarchical restoration someday have remained constant, and have even received some show of addition from the growing chorus of discontent with the faulty administration of the present regime, while the numbers of those who looked to Bolshevism as a panacea of all ills has very noticeably diminished.
> Dr Kramar is in a sense re-actionary [sic], and might even be ready to welcome a King who would make him prime minister, but his supporters, the National Democrats [sic?] and some of the Moravian Agrarians, only follow him because of his ultra-nationalistic Czech attitude, while, as he probably realises, a monarchical restoration is scarcely possible without the help of the Deutsch-Böhmen, whose reward would be the end of Czech domination here. I have heard a report, for the accuracy of which I cannot vouch, that Dr Kramar, who was supposedly resting in the country, visited Switzerland this autumn, and saw Prince Sixtus of Burbon [sic?] -Parma, [...] but even if the story be true, I have no present reason to suppose that the cause of the Monarchy has been thereby advanced.

---

730 NA, FO 371 4721, 57 f., Political Report, Secret, SIS (Secret Intelligence Service), sent to FO and WO, Prague, November 3, 1920. Interesting to add that Kramář had earlier favoured a Romanov candidate for the Bohemian throne.
731 Ibid.

As regards Dr Kramar's preference for the French, this is entirely due to their Russian policy and especially their support of Baron Wrangel. Dr Kramer, whose wife is a Russian lady of great wealth, is a fanatical reactionary in Russian politics, and the ardour with which he preaches his doctrine has gone far to weaken his position in this country.[732]

Eight months later, in July 1921, a British report stated that the Czech (Bohemian) aristocracy was plotting against Masaryk;[733] though the British high commissioner in Prague would say about Karl: "There can be no doubt that he has given up all idea of regarding the Bohemian throne and that he is not behind any movement directed against the government in Prague."[734]

Czechoslovak Mobilization and the Danger of Implosion?

Beneš knew that his country was far from being consolidated, so he wanted to avoid the presence of Karl in the Danubian region, which would endanger the existence of Czechoslovakia.

Yet, in Czechoslovakia things were going wrong. It was said that the Czechoslovak monarchists had more than 10,000 weapons in their possession and that they had the Prague government's mobilization plans against Hungary.[735] They were also ready to destroy the railway going from the Czech capital to the Hungarian border. The legitimists planned that if the Czechoslovak army were to attack Hungary, the *Kaisertreu* recruits would pass, guns in hand, to the Hungarian legitimist troops.[736] Szabolcs de Va-

---

732 NA, FO 371/4721, 92–93 ff., Clerk to Curzon Prague, December 1, 1920.
733 NA, FO 371/5822/C17194, Summary for July.
734 NA, FO 371/ 4644, C10739, Prague, November 3, 1920, Lindley to Curzon.
735 L. Windischgraetz, *Ein Kaiser kämpft*,119; Vajay speaks of 18,000 weapons. Graduate Institute Archives Geneva, (henceforth GIIDS), Vajay, Szabolcs de, "L'aspect international des tentatives de la restauration Habsbourg en Hongrie mars-octobre 1921", Geneva, 1946, 172. These figures do not match the statistics published by Czechoslovakia in 1934. *Annuaire de Statistique de la République Tchécoslovaque*, Prague, 1934, 354, 339.
736 "Il était prévu qu'en cas de mobilisation, les fidèles de l'ex-Empereur se rendrait en masse sous les drapeaux, et en cas d'opérations militaires ils passeraient les armes en mains chez les Hongrois, comme l'ont fait pendant la Grande Guerre les Tchèques envoyés contre les Russes." (It was anticipated that, in the case of mobilization, those loyal to the ex-Emperor would gather en masse beneath the flags, and in the case of military operations they would deliver weapons into the hands of the Hungarians, as is done during the Great War, the Czechs sent out against the Russians. [syntax/

jay, the historian who was the first to study the papers of the Hungarian Foreign Ministry in the 1940s, says that Czechoslovak statistics for 1925 confirm that during the mobilization against Hungary in October 1921, 92 percent of the German recruits followed the order to mobilise, while only 42 percent of the Czechs and Moravians showed up.[737] In Vajay's interpretation, the Germans of Czechoslovakia were motivated not because they wanted to fight their former Habsburg emperor, which would be illogical for Germans, but because they were told to do so in order to desert and go over to the enemy. Other sources show that many thousands of Sudeten Germans fled across the border to Germany to avoid having to fight for a country they did not want to belong to.[738] The truth is to be found somewhere in the middle.

We know that only 76 percent of the recruits responded when they were mobilised to the Hungarian border.[739] Indeed, the 1922 Czechoslovak statistics show that of an army of 114,312 men, 23,645 were court-martialled, among whom only 6,316 were found not guilty. Among the condemned there were 102 officers and 2,492 NCOs (1 in 5 were court-martialled and 12 percent were condemned). The American legation confirmed that special courts were set up for this purpose that do not appear in Czechoslovak official statistics.[740]

There were also problems with the number of men that the Czech army counted. On October 26, the British legation sent information that divisions "will stretch out" along the Hungarian border.[741] A few days later, the British legation in Budapest would send a report stating the contrary, that the mobilization was a fiasco.[742] The British legation in Prague confirmed on November 2 that 350,000 men were mobilised.[743] Who was right?

---

grammar flawed in the original text]) Vajay bases this information on unpublished and published memoirs of diplomats such as Barcza ("Memoirs" and "Journals", Hoover Institution Archives) and Boroviczény. GIIDS, Vajay, *op. cit.*, 172.
737 Ibid.
738 J. Zorach, *op. cit.*, 182.
739 Ibid.
740 *Annuaire de Statistique de la République Tchécoslovaque*, Prague, 1934, 354, 339.
741 NA, FO 371/6106/C20522, 125 f., Clerk to Curzon, Prague, October 26, 1921.
742 NA, FO 371/6109/C21256, 58 f., Hohler to Curzon, Budapest, October 31, 1921.
743 NA, FO 371/6108/C21017, Clerk to Curzon, Prague, November 2, 1921.

If the unreliability of the army was a fact, then why did the British legation in Prague confirm that all was well? The explanation is as follows. In 1921, Beneš managed to make a lot of observers believe that the mobilizations went impeccably, and the British legation seemed to believe him. Magda Ádám has discovered that Beneš' misleading practices influenced the publication of official documents as well. The Czech documents published in the White Book on the attempts at restoration had been retouched before publication to give the impression that the Hungarian government was involved in the attempts.[744] Disinformation was systematic, since the official statistics show that there were 114,312 men in the Czechoslovak army from "1. VIII. 1921 to 31. I. 1922", whereas the incredible number of 350,000 was reported; and estimates went even higher, since the British legation would write on October 23: "Beneš told allied colleagues that mobilisation worked without a hitch and that there would be by tomorrow 400,000 men under arms."[745] A day earlier, on October 22, Beneš was saying to Clerk that in two to three days he would have 250,000 men under arms;[746] a difference of 150,000 men. It becomes obvious, after reading these lines, that there was much to question regarding the reliability of the mobilizations presented by Beneš to the British legation. The problem is in understanding whether a situation of total military chaos was reigning in Czechoslovakia or things were under control. The contradictory reports prove that Beneš bluffed about his incredible military potential in order to put pressure on the Entente to make it stop restoration in Hungary and have the whole Habsburg family dethroned. His aim was also to show the Entente that he would not hesitate to invade Hungary. The great number of court-martialled men shows that even if the situation was not chaotic, the disorders were important and Beneš had done as much as he could to dissimulate these facts by informing his allies that everything went smoothly.

Beneš knew that Czechoslovakia was far from being consolidated and that the removal of the Habsburgs was vital for the new so-claimed nation

---

744 Ádám, *Little Entente*, 158. Similar practises were possible in Hungary as well in the Hungarian White Book published on the same subject. Dugast-Rouillé, *op. cit.*, 261.
745 British Documents on Foreign Affairs, Part II, series F, vol. 1, 1919–1922, Doc. 223, 287.
746 NA, FO 371/6105/C20166, 137 f., Clerk to Curzon, Prague, October 21, 1921.

state. As a monarchist plot was also in preparation and 30 percent of the Czech army officers were unreliable, it is probable that an attack on Hungary would not have been a success and would have revealed many surprises for the Czech government—such as desertions and the formation of monarchist detachments that would have turned against the Republican army. One such detachment was under the direction of Prince Heinrich Beaufort-Spontin who was waiting for orders in Czechoslovakia during the October coup and who was called off by Karl when his coup failed.[747]

Eventually, reports concerning Slovakia did not show a good response to recruitment from the Slovaks: "The Slovaks have absolutely refused to join up and are now being more oppressed by the Czech military than before."[748]

Had the return attempt worked, the outcome would have been different for Czechoslovakia than for the SHS Kingdom. In Czechoslovakia great confusion would have prevailed and civil war might even have broken out; whereas the SHS Kingdom was well armed and ready to attack Hungary. There is little chance that the Allies would have been able to stop the conflict, as there were no important Entente forces in the region. Diplomacy alone would not have been enough to stop the Serb forces that were resolved to advance. The separatist plots, though this time apparently more organised, had fewer chances for success in the SHS Kingdom (thanks to Serb militarism) than in still-weak Czechoslovakia. Could the Entente exert the pressure needed to stop a war in Central Europe? Experience had proven that if the Entente asked the Little Entente countries for obedience, they usually obeyed. But a conflict involving the separation of Slovakia and Croatia from their new "nation states" was a much bigger issue than solely the Habsburg restoration.

Analysis of the political situation both in Croatia and Slovakia shows that certain ethnic groups either wanted to stay under Habsburg and Hungarian rule or decided, later on, that they had lived in comparatively better conditions under the Dual Monarchy. After 1918, the Habsburgs were still a potential threat for the Successor States, given that an exiled couple, Karl and

---

747 Lehár, "Egy", *op. cit.*, 48.
748 NA, FO 371/6109/C21256, 54–59 ff., Hohler to Curzon, Budapest, October 31, 1921.

Zita, were still capable of provoking great panic in the Little Entente—an alliance that was created to defend itself against Hungary and a modest but charismatic man called Karl. His son, Otto, was to haunt Beneš all through the 1930s and would be his most dreaded nightmare. Beneš is known to have said, "Hitler more than Habsburg", when speaking of the possible return of Archduke Otto to Austria, though he changed his tone towards the end of the 1930s.[749]

The future of the Autonomists

Hlinka—who was on the Slovak 1,000 crown note before the introduction of the Euro—is considered today as one of the fathers of Slovakia. In the words of Stanislav Kirschbaum, the famous Slovak historian, Hlinka was "a fiery speaker and consummate politician, he fought not only for the autonomy of Slovakia, but also for a democratic system, social justice and free enterprise, and opposed all socialist and communist theories and policies."[750]

Juriga was expelled from the Slovak People's Party and withdrew from politics.[751] Some members of the People's Party who flirted with Legitimism, became extremists, such as Professor Vojtech Tuka who became leader of the radical wing of the Hlinka Slovak People's Party and prime minister in 1939 after Jozef Tiso was summoned by Hitler to Berlin.[752] Jehlička, if not a moderate, proved to be a true fighter for Slovak autonomy.[753]

Fr. Juriga and Fr. Tománek had a row with Hlinka, who supported, at least at the beginning in 1928, Tuka when he was condemned for high treason by Prague. Both Juriga and Tománek supported a patriotic Czechoslovak line in the party. Juriga was put out of Hlinka's party in 1929, after which he created his own political party *Jurigova slovenská strana ľudová*, Juriga's Slovak People's Party. In other words, after the consolidation of the new state, some former au-

---

[749] Bécsi, Zoltan, "Les legitimists hongrois et la question de l'Europe centrale, 1929–1938", *European Review of History*, vol. 11. no. 3, 2004, 374.
[750] Kirschbaum, *Historical*, 71.
[751] Ibid., 86.
[752] Tuka was the first politician to submit an autonomy proposal for Slovakia to the Czechoslovak National Assembly in 1922. Kirschbaum, *Historical*, 175.
[753] Michela, *op. cit.*, 32–44.

tonomists supported Czechoslovakia. Hlinka was eventually put under pressure by the anti-Tuka group in his party and were able to get rid of Tuka in November 1929. The radicalization of Hlinka's party continued nevertheless. [754]

Quo Vadis Gallia?

A Contradictory Diplomacy

The study of French diplomacy in Central Europe reveals contradictory actions and individual decisions that mirror the competition of two different conceptions of Central Europe. For Fontenay, the minister to Belgrade, France had to support the little nations of the East to create an "alliance de revers" that would be devoted to it: "La Petite Entente sera, au contraire, entre nos mains, de part la volonté de ses auteurs, le plus bel instrument d'autorité dont nous disposerons dans l'Est de l'Europe, si toutefois nous n'en laissons échapper la direction."[755] Fontenay worked systematically against Millerand and Paléologue while actively supporting the creation of the Little Entente. After the departure of Fontenay, Louis Clément-Simon, the new minister, showed a more understanding attitude towards the Croat and Slovene grievances.[756] Clément-Simon claimed that a more advanced (obviously Western) civilization was brought to Croatia from Vienna and Budapest, and he recognised that the Austro-Hungarian administration was much better.[757]

He explained the tensions of the Croats and the Slovenes with the Serbs, but nothing shows that Clément-Simon or the Quai d'Orsay had been, in some way, supporting Croat and Slovene separatists. As French foreign policy was evolving towards accepting the Little Entente, there was no reason why it would do so.

---

754 Felak, James Ramon, *At the Price of the Republic: Hlinka's Slovak People's Party, 1929–1938*, University of Pittsburgh Press, Pittsburgh and London, 62–63.
755 "The Little Entente, by contrast, in our hands and given the willpower of its authors, will be the finest instrument of authority that we will have at our disposal in Eastern Europe, assuming however that we do not let its administration escape us." Pavlovic, *op. cit.*, 1.
756 ADMAE, Z Europe Yougoslavie 40, 208–10 ff., Clément-Simon à MAE, Belgrade, June 16, 1921.
757 ADMAE, Z Europe, Yougoslavie 48, 149 f., Clément-Simon à Briand, Belgrade, September 28, 1921.

The behaviour of Fontenay shows that differing conceptions regarding Central Europe occurred not only in the French army, especially in Czechoslovakia, but also were present in the Quai d'Orsay. The arrival of Briand to the Quai d'Orsay not only brought back the alternative of a Habsburg Monarchy but new tensions in the Quai d'Orsay.

Briand's Ambiguous Policy

Was French foreign policy conscious of the consequences of a plan to re-establish the Habsburgs in Hungary and eventually reunite the Successor States in a federation? We have shown that not only the Catholic monarchist milieu (Paléologue, Montille, Bainville, Franchet d'Espérey) and Millerand but also to a lesser extent Berthelot and even Clemenceau[758] were speculating on how to resurrect a form of Central European multinational state. As a result, we can claim that there was constancy in French foreign policy towards *Mitteleuropa*. This leads us to ask whether, if the return of Karl had been a success, would it have brought the end of the Versailles system that France had worked so hard to establish. Or if we go further in this logic, to ask whether Karl's return was not part of the new French alternative to the failed Versailles system of Clemenceau. Neither of these questions is correct. On the contrary, both the project of restoration and a Danubian Confederation were to be part of the Versailles system—though a slightly modified version of it, Versailles system bis for Central Europe—since they were both planned in order to avoid the Anschluss and German domination in Central Europe and since the Versailles system was obsessively directed against Germany and the Hohenzollerns. France's recurring Habsburg and Danubian Confederation ideas show that the Versailles system was not primarily directed against Austria, Hungary and the Habsburgs. In fact, the true alternative (the third and worst version of the Versailles system), which meant countering the fulfilment of French foreign policy, was created by Beneš and imposed on the Millerand government in the form of the Little Entente.

---

[758] Though not opposing the creation of Yugoslavia, Clemenceau would have preferred to keep Austro-Hungarian Yugoslavia as part of Austria (without the Habsburgs), maintaining, as a result, the latter as a multinational state in order to deter Germany from an Anschluss of Austria. Pavlovic, Vojislav, *op. cit.*, 3.

Chapter VI

On one hand, it is bewildering that in 1920 Millerand wanted to create a Danubian Confederation without giving Hungary the possibility of changing its borders and without acknowledging the acuteness of separatist feeling in Croatia and Slovakia. Further, it is as surprising to note that Briand was not only planning to restore Karl in Hungary but also to federate, eventually, Hungary with Austria under Karl[759] without paying much notice to the effects of such a decision on the Successor States. Was Briand willing to break up the Versailles system in order to take revenge on Beneš' creation of the Little Entente? Since there are no sources to prove that Briand was willing to change the borders of the Successor States or was willing to unite Austria with Hungary in anything other than their St. Germain and Trianon morphology, respectively, one can but question the logic of such a contradictory policy for Central Europe.

On the other hand, one has to admit that Briand took steps to deactivate the Slovak–Hungarian–Polish rapprochement by letting Count Csekonics know that there was no longer any question of realising the Polish–Hungary–Romanian federation.[760] After Hungary had been informed, France had to resolve the Polish–Czechoslovak conflict it had contributed to worsening by sponsoring the plan of the Polish–Hungarian–Romanian alliance. France sponsored a border settlement between Czechoslovakia and Poland. The Quai d'Orsay specified the importance of convincing Beneš of an accord on the Javorzina region (on the Polish–Slovak border) "dans un sens favorable à la Pologne".[761]

---

759 Ádám, *Little Entente*, 118.
760 "Me conformant aux intentions du Département [Quai d'Orsay], j'ai répondu [...] que la base de notre politique vis-à-vis de son pays était le traité de Trianon, et qu'il n'avait qu'à considérer un instant les stipulations de ce Traité pour se rendre compte de l'impossibilité d'une union polono-hongroise avec frontière commune, ainsi qu'il m'avait déclaré la désirer, sans violer les clauses attribuant la Ruthénie à l'Etat Tchéco-Slovaque." (Conforming myself to the intentions of the Department [Quai d'Orsay], I responded [...] that the foundation of our policies vis-à-vis his country was the Treaty of Trianon, and that he had only to consider for an instant the stipulations of this Treaty in order to realise the impossibility of a Polish-Hungarian union with a common frontier, in the manner in which he had stated to me that he desired it, without violating the clauses attributing Ruthenia to the Czechoslovak state.) ADMAE, Z Europe, Hongrie 48, 49–51 ff., Fouchet à Briand, Budapest, May 13, 1921.
761 "[...] in a manner favourable to Poland." *Documents Diplomatiques français*, t. II, 1921, I.E., Peter Lang, Bruxelles, 2005, doc. 357, 557, (doc. no. 240 du 16 août 1921, probably from Laroche.); The accord, eventually, was signed on November 6, and Bonnevay—interim minister of foreign affairs—would say: "Vous savez que le gouvernement français a favorisé de tout son pouvoir la conclusion de

On the southern front, since Rapallo, Italy, was less of a threat for the SHS Kingdom as the supporter of separatist groups, but considering that the Little Entente was now becoming France's ally, Briand opposed Italy's rapprochement with the Little Entente.[762] In other words, Briand took steps to consolidate the Successor States, and since he arrived at the Quai d'Orsay with Berthelot—the main supporter of the Little Entente—it is difficult to imagine that Briand would have encouraged the separatists of Croatia or Slovakia.

It remains a fact that the separatists were a real threat to the Successor States and Briand's discreet support for restoration of the Habsburg monarch remained explosive. What did Briand have in mind? Two possibilities can be assumed: either Briand ignored the separatist activity, or he did not take the threat seriously, which means that in both cases he did not correctly weigh the consequences of the return of Karl to Hungary. As opposed to this, British diplomacy was much better informed of what these consequences were to be, and its choice to support Horthy and its energetic action against Karl were not only a way of competing with France over Hungary but also to avoid having a new war in Central Europe.

---

cet accord, qu'il considère comme capital pour le maintien de la paix, et indispensable à la sécurité de la Pologne, qui ne pourrait faire face à l'Allemagne si elle n'était rassurée quant à l'attitude de la Tchéco-Slovaquie, dont le territoire lui offre en outre la seule voie sûre de transit pour son ravitaillement." (You know that the French government favoured with all its power the conclusion of this accord, which it considers as capital for the upholding of the peace, and indispensable to the security of Poland, which could not cope with Germany if it were not assured in terms of the attitude of Czechoslovakia, whose territory offers, furthermore, the sole sure transit route for maintaining its supplies.) Documents Diplomatiques française, t. II, 1921, I.E, 2005, doc. 357, 556–57, MAE à de Panafieu, Min. de France à Varsovie.Paris, November 14, 1921.

762 Italy was now in the process of a rapprochement with the SHS Kingdom as well as with Czechoslovakia, to which Romania was attached in a looser form. Ádám, *Little Entente*, 105. Boroviczény, the close supporter of Emperor Karl, described the relation of France and Italy relating to Central Europe in the following words: "Sous la direction de l'Italie, la rivale de la France, la Petite Entente a barré la route à la restauration de l'Empereur. Si l'on réussissait la restauration de l'Empereur, alors on les [les pays de la Petite Entente] priverait du seul point qui lie leurs intérêts entre eux, et ainsi disparaîtrait la raison d'être de leur alliance. L'Italie perdrait alors son influence sur le territoire de l'ancienne monarchie, et la France pourrait prendre sa place, pour la bonne raison que ce serait elle qui aurait réalisé la restauration." (Under the direction of Italy, the rival of France, the Little Entente barred the way to the restoration of the Emperor. If the restoration of the Emperor were successfully accomplished, this would then have deprived them [the countries of the Little Entente] of the sole issue that connects their mutual interests, and thus the raison d'être of their alliance would disappear. Italy would then lose its influence over the territory of the former monarchy, and France could lose its place, for the good reason that it would be France who would have realised the restoration.) Boroviczény, *op. cit.*, 88.

Chapter VI

If Briand was conscious of the danger of conflicts between Hungary and its Successor States when restoration took place, he could count on the influence of France on the Successor States to ensure obedience. He probably knew from earlier experience that the Entente could make itself respected and that, as in April 1921, it could call upon the Czechoslovak army not to attack Hungary. In other words, an explanation of this passive and secret support to Karl, with possibly explosive consequences, is that Briand had confidence in France's authority to maintain order in Central Europe. However, in October 1921 Beneš was more than resolute in his determination to act to stop the restoration in Hungary,[763] but he pretended to ignore the minority problem that raised its head during the mobilizations. Consequently, the second problem that was to be ignited by Karl's return was a conflict, or maybe even civil war, between separatists and their so-called nation states (Czechoslovakia and the SHS Kingdom). Briand did not seem to be specifically aware of this danger, and this last question therefore remains open. However, if he was aware, it was probably one of the reasons why he did not support Karl's second attempt.

The efforts of French policy in this direction continued even after the dethronement and Karl's death. France continued to sponsor federation plans. The first was the Tardieu plan for an economic Central European Union, which failed. After the first Anschluss attempt and the "Wacht am Brenner" (1934)—Mussolini's mobilization to the Italian–Austrian Brenner Pass—Leon Blum, the French prime minister in February 1937, sympathised with the idea of a restoration of Archduke Otto in Austria in order to avoid the Anschluss, and he even influenced the Little Entente to reconsider its position; but if Germany were to invade Austria, he would not go to war for Archduke Otto.[764] Finally, just after the war, Charles de Gaulle[765] wanted Pope Pius XII to help him establish a "Pan-Danubian

---

763 Since Czechoslovakia was in the process of consolidation, the elimination of the Habsburgs from Central Europe was a sine qua non condition to the survival of Czechoslovakia, which was still unstable due to the many factors presented in this work.
764 *Foreign Relations of the United States (FRUS)*, I, 1937, 1954, 54; Csonka, *op. cit.*, 164.
765 General de Gaulle was the leader of the French Government in exile "France Libre" based in London, then leader of liberated France in 1945, before being elected president of the French Republic in 1958.

Confederation" to roll back the Bolshevik menace and relaunch the idea of the *cordon sanitaire*.[766]

Danubian Confederation, King Karl and French Supporters

It is timely to weigh the true influence of three French personalities (Castellane, Bainville and Briand) and one foreign one (Karl I/IV) on French foreign policy in Central Europe. One thing is apparent: all four were quite similar in their arguments. Who inspired whom? Concerning Karl, it has to be pointed out that he was not a new Francophile but had been such at least since his coronation, when he started secret negotiations with France. The love he felt towards his Bourbon wife, his friendship with his brothers-in-law made him much more inclined towards France than Franz Joseph was. In other words, Karl chose the Entente against Germany at a very early stage, but his hands were tied due to his uncle's old alliance with Germany.

One can say that Castellane and Bainville were two royalists who were both supporting the re-creation of a Central European monarchy in order to tackle the problem of Germany. Knowing that Karl would still be very close to France after 1918, they were persuaded that his restoration would be one of the best deterrents against German domination in Europe. The suspended Emperor-King could become the element that could bring balance back to Central Europe. Castellane and Bainville were, therefore, in symbiosis with Karl's thoughts that were not only compatible with but instrumental to the policy that France was pursuing. The words of Wladimir d'Ormesson, then a young diplomat—later to become a member of the Académie française—exemplify quite well a sentiment that became generalised, if it was not already, after Karl's death in 1922:

> La plupart des français, devant les conséquences de la paix regrettent avec une amère anxiété la disparition de l'empire de Habsbourg. Ils se rappellent le mot célèbre: 'Si l'Autriche n'existait pas, il faudrait l'inventer',

---

[766] Based on American secret documents: Loftus, John, Mark Aarons, *The Unholy Trinity*, St. Martin's Griffin, New York, 1998, 54.

et devant le chaos russe et la toute puissance allemande, jamais ils n'ont mieux compris le sens politique de cette boutade.[767]

It appears that the reestablishment of the Habsburgs was vital for France in the opinion of many Frenchmen, and the steps taken in that direction by Paléologue and Briand exemplify well the concerns of many members of the Quai d'Orsay.

But how old was the idea that the greatest enemy of France was Germany? At least since 1870 France had considered Germany a greater enemy than Britain, and with the creation of the Entente in 1904 this became a fact. Austria, a lesser enemy in 1916, became a potential, but secret, ally when Emperor Karl made his separate peace proposals, at a moment when Austria was far from losing the war.[768] After the war it became clearer to many French statesmen that, with the peril of the Anschluss, those who defended the maintenance of Austria-Hungary were right, and French foreign policy would revert to an *Ersatz* of the Dual Monarchy, the project of a Danubian Confederation.

One could argue that writings were biased if coming from the pen of a French marquis like Castellane and a member of Action française such as Bainville or other nobles like Paléologue and Lazare de Montille. It cannot be argued, however, that Aristide Briand—first a radical socialist and then a republican—was biased when showing interest in Karl's plans during the wartime secret peace negotiations and probably even after the war.[769] The only explanation is that Briand was a *Realpolitiker* considering the interests of France when flirting with the idea of restoration.[770] There could also be a certain admiration or respect towards the Emperor-King's social ideas—lat-

---

[767] "Most French people, faced with the consequences of the peace, regret with bitter anxiety the disappearance of the Habsburg Empire. They recall the famous saying: 'If Austria did not exist, it would have to be invented,' and faced with the Russian chaos and the absolute power of Germany, they have never understood the political meaning of this joke better than now." Ormesson, Wladimir d', *Nos Illusions sur l'Europe Centrale*, Librairie Plon, Paris, 1922, 26. Wladimir d'Ormesson made a brilliant career, became ambassador to Romania and to the Holy See and was a member of the French Academy, like his nephew Jean d'Ormesson. In later years, his nephew became a friend of Otto de Habsburg, son and heir of Karl I.
[768] Bogdan, Henry, *Histoire des Habsbourg, Des origines à nos jours*, Perrin, Paris, 2002, 350–51.
[769] Ibid., 353–54.
[770] Suarez, *op.cit.*, 237–38; Windischgraetz, *Ein Kaiser kämpft*, 143, 158–59.

er expressed by a monarchist movement in Austria and Hungary as *Linksmonarchismus*.[771] The former Empress Zita contributed to an explanation of France's sympathies for Karl by saying that there were three groups of deputies that expressed sympathy for restoration:

> [...] some socialists who remembered the emperor's peace efforts; some nationalists who were appalled at the influence the new Czech leaders Beneš and Masaryk exerted over the Quai d'Orsay; and a section of the radicals who hated Horthy's military dictatorship and would have preferred to see a liberal monarchy in its place.[772]

And finally, the French general staff and most of the army's marshals and generals also favoured the cause, for example Lyautey, Franchet d'Espérey and even Foch.

Briand's approach, as well as the sympathy of the deputies mentioned above, nuances the importance of Catholic and Monarchist influence on French foreign policy. Three of these French personalities (Castellane, Bainville and Briand) had a clear strategy for how to deter Germany, and Karl was to become the key instrument of this project.

Eventually, Berthelot's puzzling remarks show that it was thought, even in the orthodox republican milieu, that it was advantageous to see Karl back on the throne, even if hardly possible. In other words, both royalist and republican circles supported it.[773] But one should not forget that if a Habsburg was to be used, it was only as an instrument to achieve the Danubian Confederation that was in the interest of France. Thus, for most of the French realist thinkers, it was neither sympathy towards the dynasty nor nostalgia towards its dual monarchy but truly Karl's usefulness for France's purposes that motivated the decision-makers of French foreign policy.

---

771 Windischgraetz, *Ein Kaiser kämpft*, 143. Documents on Karl's welfare state, Chapter 6, "Die Monarchie als Socialstaat", Feigl, *op. cit.*, 135–55. Otto, the first son of the emperor, continued the idea of a social monarchy in Austria, which was described as *Reformlegitimizmus* or *Linksmonarchismus* (Csonka, Emil, *Habsburg Otto*, Új Európa, Munich, 1972, 186).
772 Brook-Shepherd, *The Last Empress*, 256.
773 MNL K64, 3 cs., 1921-41-161, Práznovszky to Gratz. Paris, April 10, 1921.

Chapter VI

The French Plans in Light of Britain's Approach

As shown, the Quai d'Orsay and the French army were full of elements that were working against the government's policy. The British Foreign Office was much less fantasist and intriguing, yet its policy was not ideal and was eventually inefficient, as Robert Evans, the British specialist on Central Europe, explains:

> It is important to recognise the clear expectation of such people [such as Wickam-Steed and Seton-Watson] that the post-war settlement, through the League of Nations and the regional agreements, would establish (con)federal bodies in the eastern half of the continent. They could not conceive particularly of economic survival otherwise—just as, of course few liberals had thought that the war of 1914 could last so long in the context of Europe's advanced economic structures. In this they did see roughly eye-to-eye with British diplomats, who all urged some degree of federal co-operative organisation, as well as pressing the Successor States to accept the mediation of the League in certain sensitive matters, above all treatment of their minorities[...] But the results on the ground were more or less nil—and even the limitedly supranational initiatives which generated the "Czechoslovak" and "Yugoslav" experiments soon proved counter-productive. Arguably this failure of the post-war regimes, especially the most economically muscular and avowedly democratic Czechs, to respond to such promptings contributed in good measure as early as the mid-1920s to the British mood which made the Munich sell-out possible.[774]

Evans' words can only support the view that had the French managed to recreate the Danubian entity, the process that led to the falling apart of Czechoslovakia and Yugoslavia (which eventually happened from 1938 on) would have been accelerated, and France rather than Italy and Germany would have managed to create a Hungarian–Croatian–Slovakian and eventually also Austrian Confederation and secure its control of the region.

---

774 Evans, *op. cit.*, 12–13.

France's biggest mistake was not to have made the effort to execute its will. If defending France's geopolitical security in Europe was indeed so important, then France, as Europe's continental power (as opposed to Britain, which is an island), should have exerted greater pressure to create the Danubian Confederation and restore the Francophile Emperor-King. As we have seen, French foreign policy showed willingness to accept a restoration of the monarchy before World War II, once in Hungary (1920–21) and once in Austria before the Anschluss (1936–38), during the mandates of two left-wing prime ministers, Briand and Blum.[775] In both cases the aim was to create a Danubian Confederation and avoid the Anschluss, but neither of the two prime ministers exerted the necessary pressure to realise this aim: no threats of economic or military sanctions were made to those who opposed France's concept of Central Europe. The French governments did not bring their federalizing plans to fruition[776] and thus were not able to guarantee the security they believed they could maintain in Central Europe by virtue of the third choice, the "Versailles-Little Entente system", which failed.

---

775 Csonka, *op. cit.*, 164, 280. Let us not forget that there was also the Tardieu Plan for a Danubian Confederation.
776 Its members were never unanimous on the question.

Epilogue

Federalists and/or Legitimists?

After having gone through the activities and the political leanings of the different persons and groups considered to be federalists and/or legitimists, the reader might have the impression that these different groups and individuals were all federalist. In fact, they were heteroclite groups of malcontents frustrated with their post-war fate and describing themselves as autonomists, federalists, secessionists, independentists and at the same time, in some cases, Habsburg legitimists or with legitimist leanings, or just pro-Hungarians (a safer answer not involving pro or contra Habsburg positioning). In other words, many of them were just opportunists trying to get Hungary, or another country, to pay them as means of propaganda, as provocateurs or as agents setting up military resistance against Successor States, or by organising peaceful or more violent protests. The common denominator of these groups was that they all wanted to loosen the ties with their new nation state in some way or another. The aim for Hungary was to contribute to the destabilisation of the Successor States that had snatched immense chunks of its realm.

When discreetly stimulating resistance, Hungary was successful in making the Entente believe that they were not involved. Indeed, when the local press or civil servants of the Successor States denounced Habsburg or Hungarian activities against their state to the Entente, Paris or London would not once consider it as "fake news" intentioned to make the allies believe that the frustrated nationalities were plotting to make the new successor "nation states" fail. In fact, it was in many cases true.

For the Slovak and Croat malcontent groups and networks, the willingness of Hungary to finance their activities was a rich source of opportunity, and some of them asked for as much money as they could. The result, as we could see, was that not much happened, at least nothing really successful. Whether the success of King Karl's return attempts could have stimulated a successful outcome following all this Hungarian investment into separatist groups is open to speculation. It remains, however, clear that the turmoil created by a successful return of Karl would have favoured the aims of such groups, whoever they were. Eventually, not only did this situation not come into effect but it even consolidated the Successor States, as they were able to put enough pressure on the Entente to have the Habsburgs permanently dethroned in Hungary and to get both Britain and France to support the Little Entente as their useful ally.

The arrival of 1921 did not mean the end of Hungarian, and other malcontent states', support for separatist groups. The Hungarian and Italian support given to the terrorists of the 1934 Marseilles assassinations is proof of this.

The Radicalization of the Legitimists?

The charismatic leaders of Croatia and Slovakia, Radić and Hlinka, had much in common: both were arrested during elections, were counting on foreign support, were tending toward Legitimism and would have wanted a federalist solution, and died before seeing their countries achieve independence; and neither truly became a radical. They were patriots, maybe nationalists, but not radical nationalists. Neither Hlinka nor Radić can be considered to have been agents of Hungary or any other country, since their prime aim was to guarantee freedom and independence for their own countries. They were both arrested for having tried to defend their peoples' case at the Paris Peace Conference. Neither Slovakia nor Croatia was initially considered a vanquished nation of the war, but they were treated as such afterwards; just as the Hungarian delegation was practically under house arrest at a hotel in Neuilly-sur-Seine and was summoned to the meetings and the final signing of the peace treaty.

Among the Yugoslav countries, Croatia was not the only one obliged to comply. Montenegro, a free and sovereign state on the "good" side during the war, similarly tried to defend its case in Paris. Indeed, the last king went to Paris, where he was arrested in order not to delay the creation of Yugoslavia.

After analysing resistance in Czechoslovakia, Croatia and Hungary, it becomes clear that the lack of financial support after World War I and a badly organised opposition with many inefficient, unreliable and adventurist members resulted in unsuccessful actions. This would change dramatically during the 1930s, when the Janka Puszta[777] crisis proved that after many frustrated attempts the by then clearly radicalized nationalist and separatist movements had found support for their actions from malcontent countries. Italy and Germany, as the re-emerging powers of northern and southern Europe, had become the main sponsors of these movements, which were no longer fighting for autonomy but for total independence.

We have shown that the connexion between federalism and Legitimism was important in order to achieve federalist aims and to find an ally that would guarantee their independence or autonomy. They found this ally in a Hungary headed by the neutral Habsburg monarch. But we have also shown that some federalists turned to Italy, to Hungarian free electors or to Poland for help and protection. If there were legitimist monarchists such as Andrássy, Gratz or Ivo Frank who remained truly faithful to their king, there was also a large number of circumstantial legitimists or sympathisers, especially in Slovakia, such as Hlinka and Tuka (the latter flirted with all parties), or Ghilardi in Croatia. In the case of the latter group it was not the feeling of nostalgia—though there was some of that, too—that prevailed but the usefulness of Karl's return in view of the realisation of their common aim. Those of the most radical category—opportunists as well—would even join league with the devil in order to achieve their aims, for example, Tuka, the head of state of Nazi Germany's puppet state of Slovakia.

If it is clear that, in the period studied, federalists were not systematically legitimists, then most of the federalists conceived, at a certain moment in their political thinking, that their aim could well be realised through restora-

---

777 This was the Ustaša camp where people involved in the Marseilles assassinations got their training.

tion. Even the radical democrat Jászi and Austro-Marxist Renner conceived of a federalist Central Europe with the Habsburgs until the end of the war, but they did not wish to restore them after the break-up of the monarchy. Renner even tried to sponsor the idea of a Danubian Confederation again in July 1920.[778]

In addition to the true legitimists, many right radicals from Slovakia, Croatia and Hungary supported Karl, even though politically he was a moderate. Had Karl been able to take his throne back, he would have managed to attract radical groups, such as Croatian ones, to support his kingdom centred in Budapest. He was the unifying element that could, once in power, have disarmed the radicals and satisfied them with the autonomy and independence they were fighting for. This would have been possible, since the moderate Andrássy had agreed with the liberal-conservative Bethlen to bring the king back and consolidate Hungary as a Habsburg Kingdom. Given that Bethlen dissolved the extremist groups and brought Hungary into the League of Nations, without the Habsburgs eventually, he could have been the ideal prime minister to support Karl in his commitment to bring stability and satisfy the nationalist movements of Croatia and Slovakia that were evolving towards radicalization. In this case, the events of 1938, with the disintegration of Czechoslovakia and, maybe, of the SHS Kingdom, would have occurred earlier, but the radicalisation of nationalist groups that led to the Marseilles assassinations and the creation of Slovakia and Croatia under Nazi German patronage could have been avoided with a strong Central European union.

As for the presence of legitimist feeling in Slovakia and Croatia, it faded away with the end of the prospect of the return of Karl. The legitimist sentiment continued, nevertheless, to exist in Hungary and especially in Austria, where it was quite popular in regions such as Tyrol, and materialised in political parties. Especially after 1929, when the movement was reignited by the coming of age of Archduke Otto, it became, in both countries, a way to manifest resistance to Nazism and Anschluss. Legitimism became, therefore, an Austrian national antidote to Nazism and a means of resisting to it.

---

778 Chancellor Renner told Gratz that "[...] he never was a believer in the value of Austria's union with Germany. Although for tactical reasons he has repeatedly urged such a policy, he thinks that the establishment of a Danubian federation is still possible." Gratz, Minister for Foreign Affairs, to Teleki, Vienna, July 13, 1920, *PFRH*, v. 1, no. 447, 452–53.

Epilogue

Hungary

Hungary was a "historical nation" that partly gained back the independence it had lost at the battle of Mohács against the Ottoman Empire in 1526, thanks to the 1867 *Ausgleich*. Could the year 1918 have been a chance to regain complete independence for the whole of the Hungarian-inhabited regions (the Realm of Saint Stephen or greater Hungary)? It missed this opportunity because of a number of endogenous and exogenous factors. The exogenous factors were, first, that Hungary was on the defeated side in World War I and was to pay the consequences of its defeat in a way that did not respect the 1815 (Vienna Congress) tradition but that of *vae victis* instead; second, the communist takeover and installation of the commune by agents trained in Russia and led by Béla Kun; third, the conservative—semi-authoritarian but parliamentarian—regime of Miklós Horthy, supported by the Entente, was installed in Budapest.

The endogenous reasons were that after having declared the republic, Count Mihály Károlyi passed power to the Hungarian Bolsheviks and by doing so worsened Hungary's already "loser" situation vis a vis the victorious Entente and its allies. Whether or not he had a choice is another question, but his decision was still compromising for Hungary. Second was the negative and uncompromising approach of Hungary's conservative leadership—led by the legitimist Apponyi—to any modifications of its borders, which had already been modified de facto and confirmed de jure by the Trianon Treaty. As a man of the nineteenth century (the century of 1815), Apponyi could not accept that a sovereign "nation state", and one of the great and historical nations of Europe, could be so treated and carved up in such a devastating way. Hungary made the choice to pursue peaceful revisionist policy and join the malcontent camps of Italy and Austria in 1927.

If we add to this Hungary's pride in being a thousand-year-old nation and one of Europe's leading states until the end of the Middle Ages—a status it partly regained with the creation of Austria-Hungary—we can only draw the evident conclusion that Hungary had little alternative but to adhere to the forced itinerary it took during the interwar period. As Hungary's primary program was revision at all costs—except by military means once it joined the League of Nations—the idea of a Danubian Confederation was contrary to its aim. This did not mean that the Hungarian population was not mainly pro-Habsburg in 1921; but had the population grasped the true significance of Karl's program—the reunification of the nations of the Kingdom of Saint Stephen in an association of independent or semi-independent states—it probably would not have supported King Karl. The only accepting elements to a form of Danubian Confederation could be found among the legitimists led by the aulic aristocracy represented by Gyula Andrássy junior. They were probably the only group among which could be found those who would have accepted a post-Trianon Hungary associated on a confederal or federal basis to Slovakia and Croatia (and possibly Transylvania), instead of holding out for the revisionist plan of recuperating the detached regions to integrate them into a Hungarian nation-state.

In comparison, it is interesting to note that Croatia, which also claimed to be a "historical nation" (as opposed to the "non-historical" Serbia), would ask for the same: its recognition as an independent state with all its non-Croatian regions (Bosnia-Herzegovina).

Both Croatia and Slovakia claimed nothing less than that for which they had decided to join, respectively, Serbia and Czechoslovakia: federalism, if not outright independence. The non-acceptance of either of these forms by the new *Herrenvölker,* respectively the Serbs and the Czechs, and their claim that they were one people with their newly-attached "partners", would fatally bring the Croats and the Slovaks into the arms of the same group of malcontents as the Hungarians, the leadership of which was held first by Fascist Italy and then Nazi Germany.

The Hungarian government's approach to these former regions was different in both cases. It was looking at reintegrating Slovakia into Hungary as strongly as it could, whereas Hungary was open to a federal type of alliance with Croatia—a country with which it had been in *Personalunion* under the Crown of Saint Stephen since 1102. Before the war, Hungary wanted to avoid transforming its state internally into a federation and continued this policy after the war when negotiating with the Slovaks. The only step was the possibility of granting autonomy to Slovakia, which was supported by the legitimists. Though it was not a proposal to create a federation, it was already a big step for a nation that considered the Realm of Saint Stephen as a nation-state, and a first step in the direction of federalism. In fact, the same process of building a Danubian Confederation crystallised around Hungary could only have been possible with states that were not originally part of the Realm of Saint Stephen, such as Croatia, an associate realm. A further confederation with the Czechs, former members of Cisleithania, could only have been possible if they had left Slovakia, entirely or maybe partly, to Hungary.

This also means that the Paléologue Plan of a Danubian Confederation—in its maximal form—implied concessions from the Successor States to Hungary. In other words the maximal plan would have been composed of a confederation of the six Successor States of the Dual Monarchy, with Hungary being granted border modifications to recover some of its Magyar populations living in Slovakia, but also Romania and the SHS Kingdom.

The minimal version implied that Hungary or Poland would occupy Slovakia—involving the destruction of Czechoslovakia—bridging Hungary to Poland and creating an autonomous Slovak region. If Croatia had joined Hungary—already federated to Poland—in the form of a confederation, federation or *Personalunion*, with the military help of Hungary and Italy, it would have created the sea-to-sea *cordon sanitaire* (Baltic to Adriatic) or Intermarium that was already planned by the maximal version. These rearrangements probably would have caused fierce resistance from Czechoslovakia and the SHS Kingdom, but the adventure would have likely been worth a try for the security of France as well as of the whole Central European region. A solution that would have been forced on the republican Czechoslovaks and the pro-Karađorđević Yugoslavs but welcomed by the larger (Croat and Slovak) and smaller (Hungarian, Bosnian Muslim, Ruthenian etc.) minorities of the Successor States who were mostly for independence, autonomy or federalism.

Hungary, Karl and France

Apart from the element of tradition in the Hungarian population's relation to the dynasty, the Hungarian national elites, since 1867, had considered the Habsburgs as a necessary evil that they had gotten used to and started to respect, and eventually, in some cases, even to venerate. The fact that Hungary reverted to monarchism in 1920 shows that the Hungarian nation was not made up of republicans. When the Károlyi government declared Hungary a republic, it done so mainly to separate Hungary from Austria and get a better peace deal. It was an act of disengagement from Austria and Germany, its old allies. When the Treaty of Trianon was signed, the number of true- and traditionally legitimist persons was augmented by legitimist sympathisers who saw in the return of Karl a possibility to reunite the lands of the Kingdom of Saint Stephen. The bulk of the Hungarian people followed the interests of their country and not the legal concept of a legitimism that was to become a notion of political combativeness only in 1921, when armed conflict between legitimist and pro-Horthysts occurred.

In other words, if, by recalling the king, Hungary's policy was to restore the country's integrity, then France's was to use Karl's return to create the Danubian Confederation. The instrument was the same, but the expected result different. But what did the king have to say to his being instrumentalised? Karl would have preferred the con/federal solution in Greater Hungary as well as in his other former lands, but as Hungary had not made this concession in 1916, at his coronation, and after the war had resisted giving a truly federal form to Hungary, it is difficult to imagine that the country would later have conceded expected reform to its non-Magyar ethnic groups. The failure of the French plans, as well as the secret Hungarian plan of devolution of powers to the Slovaks and Croats, was the result of the contrary nature, in their aims, of both plans, which led instead to the establishment of the Little Entente.

By not being willing to respond to Hungary's true need (border corrections), and by giving the impression that it would respond to Hungary's conditions, France sent the wrong message to Prague. The reason for this ambiguous policy is to be found in France's earlier wartime policy. France had to pay the price for its policy (and of that of its allies) of alliance with the Republican Czecho-Slovaks, Romania, Italy and Serbia—all of which joined the Allies during the war. France's alliance was needed in order to vanquish its enemies, yet it hindered France's freedom of action in its policies after the war. In other words, France's dilemma was whether it would be faithful to its wartime promises or put the stability of Europe ahead of them. The Millerand administration chose to subordinate security to its promises, and since those who advocated that the Little Entente would be a sufficient guarantee of security got it wrong, France and the whole of Europe would suffer the consequences less than twenty years later. Even though the maximal or minimal Paléologue Plan would also have its group of malcontents, it was a better solution for Central Europe than a third version of the Versailles System—the first one being Clemenceau's and the second Paléologue's—with a Little Entente cutting the region into two groups: victors and losers of the war.

The Failed States of Yugoslavia and Czechoslovakia

The root of Croat-Serb conflict at the beginning of the twentieth century was a combination of two factors of instability: an endogenous and an exogenous one. The endogenous one was the existing nationality problem caused by the rise of national identity and nationalisms that appeared all around Europe in the nineteenth century and pushed the Croats to strengthen their position within the Habsburg Monarchy by heading the Yugoslav movement within the borders of Austria-Hungary. To the east, Serbia—which had liberated itself from Ottoman rule in the nineteenth century—was experiencing a renewal of its national consciousness and had the same aim as Croatia, except that it wanted to push to the west and lead the Southern Slavs of the Habsburg Monarchy as well. The exogenous factor was the involvement of the Entente in 1918 in support of the creation of Yugoslavia, under the primacy of the Kingdom of Serbia, and encompassing all of the Southern Slavs. This would be done without consulting the peoples by plebiscites to determine whether they wanted to be part of a federal state, be independent, or belong to the new nation state of Yugoslavia. If it is true that the instability was there before 1918, the fact that the Entente gave its benediction to the new state, which created a Serb-led Yugoslav dictatorship in 1929, could only aggravate dissension among the nationalities.

As a result, we can say that the main feature of the nineteenth- and twentieth-century history of the Yugoslav area is the confrontation of Serb and Croat identities, in the Austro-Hungarian frame as well as in the Serb-dominated Yugoslavian ones. The consequence of such a multi-secular division is that a country uniting Croatia and Serbia went against common sense. After a stormy 70-year experience—with the interval of Nazi occupation—the new, composite and artificial state could only lead to failure and to a break-up process that ended in 2006 with the proclamation of the independence of Montenegro and the still-debatable independence of Kosovo in 2008.

My perspective on Czechoslovakia is less severe, but with Slovakian national identity increasing, the days of its existence were being counted down. As there was no room for reconciliation between Prague and Budapest, if the former did not give some territories back to Hungary, the solution was an alliance of Hungary with the Slovaks, which was accepted by the first Teleki government and could have meant a more satisfied and stable Slovakia had the victorious powers accepted this alliance at Trianon. This hypothetical stability can of course be questioned, but what we know as fact is that Hungary would continue its revisionist policy and would look for the support first of Italy and then of Germany leading eventually to the return of southern Slovakia and the Sub Carpathian region of Czechoslovakia to Hungary in 1938.

As the SHS Kingdom, similarly to Czechoslovakia, refused border modifications to the advantage of Hungary, the same process of federalism was possible between Hungary and the separatist Croats as an *ersatz* to the cul-de-sac witnessed with the Serbs. With this core to start with, the process of reconstructing a multinational Danubian entity would have been possible later on, since Austria's position towards Germany had evolved by the 1930s and it was now looking for allies to avoid the Anschluss by restoring the Habsburgs.[779] In other words, the likelihood of such a confederation was increasing after Hitler ascended to power in Germany. Naturally this project would have necessitated border modifications, without which it was a non-starter for Hungary. For Czechoslovakia, under Beneš, it was the prospect of the Habsburgs in Hungary or Austria which was a non-starter. In terms of security, a Danubian Confederation was a consolidation project that looked well into the future, since it was a concept similar to the Visegrad Group

---

779 Schuschnigg, Kurt, *Austrian Requiem*, Victor Gollancz Ltd, London, 1947, 101, 165.

(Hungary, Poland, Slovakia and Czech Republic) of today or to a smaller form of European Union. The problem was that the "nation-states" of 1920–1921 were not yet ready for a multinational Central European Union.

Not allowing federalization brought both Czechoslovakia and Yugoslavia towards the radicalization of malcontent and frustrated nationalities, but the roots of both Czechoslovakia's and Yugoslavia's failure are to be found in their DNA of 1918.

Hungary had wrongly chosen the French unitary nation-state model, meaning forced assimilation of other nationalities through language during the Ausgleich. It was now both Yugoslavia and Czechoslovakia that chose to recreate this failed model. They pushed both Croats and Slovaks towards virulent nationalism and into the arms of Hitler, resulting in the pro-Nazi puppet states of "independent" Croatia and Slovakia. After World War II, the reconstructed version of these two states would reappear under communist rule. Even if Czechoslovakia had benefited from a better, but short lived, consolidation during the interwar period, the cement in both cases was dictatorship and not democracy after 1945.

Since the nineteenth century the nationalities of Central Europe had been in a period of national emancipation that was in a much calmer phase before 1914, but which was reignited by the Great War. This phase continued until the end of the war and could not be cooled down without living up to the promise of Wilsonian self-determination. Given that the Successor States did not make a sufficient effort in this direction, the nationalist movements would obviously continue their work to liberate themselves and would not refrain from getting the support of as many states and organisations as they could win over to their cause. The most significant example is the support given to weaken Yugoslavia and indirectly assassinate King Alexander. Not only were Italy, Germany and Hungary involved with their support of the Ustašas, but Bulgaria was supporting the Macedonian separatists and Albania the Kosovo Albanians.

When observing post-1945 cases, where terrorism (kidnapping, assassinations, bombs) was also used as means to exert pressure, the outcome was more autonomy: South Tyrol autonomous region, IRA in Northern Ireland, the Quebec Liberation Front or even in peaceful Switzerland where the

French-speaking Jura region was granted a canton following a few terrorist actions in 1972. Experience shows that not much can be done other than to negotiate with these centrifugal forces, because sooner or later the outcome is violence and eventually a negotiated peace with the granting of special status and a devolution of some kind.

The Continuation of a School of Thought

In the introduction I mentioned François Fejtö's statement that the war started as a conventional one and finished as an ideological one because of the influence of the anti-clerical and uncompromisingly zealous republican elements in their fight against the Catholic monarchy. Fejtö shows that Beneš and Masaryk were instrumental in bringing down Austria-Hungary and had convinced the Entente of this necessity. However, it has to be taken into consideration that republicans such as Millerand and Briand, and to a certain extent Clemenceau, thought that Austria had to be maintained as a confederation of successor nations to avoid the Anschluss. In other words, no matter how strong the hatred of the clerical monarchy, the French heads of government all thought—at a certain point in time—that it was in the interest of France to maintain its existence. This, of course, doesn't mean that left wing and radical republican parties and political pressure groups, which had a significant influence on public opinion, were not lending a hand to achieve its destruction. And it should not be forgotten that the American support of its destruction through Wilson's Fourteen Points—unwilling support, since the USA wished at first only to federalise the Dual Monarchy—was an involvement in European affairs with a new ideology, a sort of new human rights of peoples, that went against the integrity of multinational empires but also against the concept of sovereignty of European nation states composed of different ethnic groups. This could have been applied to the federal state of Switzerland, had it not been a neutral state for centuries, considering it as a nation, on the basis that the German-, French- and Italian-speaking populations should be attached to Germany, France or Italy respectively.

This ideology of willing or forced self-determination of peoples that contributed to the destruction of the Habsburg Monarchy was an element of external interference into the internal organisation of the sovereign Dual Monarchy. This involvement changed the war aims in such a way that they became transformational. As a result, the war itself turned ideological, ending with the destruction of Austria-Hungary together with its structure and regime. Instead of concentrating solely on Austria-Hungary's defeat, its internal nationality problems were stimulated and encouraged by the Allies and eventually written down as peace conditions by Wilson and his European allies. It was a transformation that was forced on a sovereign entity, which was a new way of ending war in European history. It did have a slight similarity with the treaties of Westphalia though, because the peace that ended the Thirty Years War did reinforce the internal sovereignty of the member states, but it did not destroy the Holy Roman Empire.

What was certain was that the territory of the old Habsburg Monarchy in October–November 1918 could never be the same again: but that did not mean that the Habsburg Monarchy was ruled out in all parts and lands of Austria-Hungary. In 1919, the restoration of the pre-war regime in Hungary entailed that the monarchy only be suspended during the Republic and Republic of Councils. As shown in earlier chapters, had it not been for strongly punitive policies in both Czechoslovakia and the SHS Kingdom—supported by the Entente through its inaction—against federalists or separatists and independentists, these groups could have changed the map. Thus, in November 1918, the dice had not yet been thrown, because the secessionist elements were not sure of their allegiances and to which Successor State they wanted to belong; this was even more true in Croatia than in Slovakia. In the case of Croatia in less than a few months and in the case of Slovakia in less than three years the majority of the population voted for parties whose leadership considered as a possible option being reattached to the Habsburg Monarchy (Croatia preferring Vienna to Budapest) in the form of a con/federal entity. It is precisely for that reason that a plebiscite was not permitted in either of these regions. In the only place where one was performed, in Hungary, in the town of Sopron, the mostly Germanophone population voted for attachment to Hungary rather than to Austria. It was obviously a risky option to let peoples chose their future home country because the outcome could be different than previously planned.

After 1918, the existence of a growing group of separatists from the SHS Kingdom and Czechoslovakia demonstrated that the survival or re-emergence of the Habsburg Monarchy, as a con/federation, was still a possible option, and it was the Successor States that outlawed this alternative more than France or Britain. The process of federalization belatedly initiated by Karl and so strongly desired by Wilson produced multinational "nation-states" instead of provoking recognition of all the different nationalities of Austria-Hungary. Indeed, the successor "nation-states" forbade smaller ethnic groups from achieving autonomy or federalism, either with them or with a reduced Hungary.

Having concluded that some nations of the old Dual Monarchy did not want to be completely separated from it and that France was morally supportive of the idea of its survival, I will be bold enough to claim that the Habsburg Monarchy (in its limited Hungarian form) did not entirely disappear in November 1918 but rather in November 1921. The latter was the date when the law of dethronement was voted by the Hungarian Parliament under foreign pressure, as the decision to allow Karl back on his Hungarian throne most probably would have caused a reorganisation of the map of Central Europe to the advantage of the dynasty and Hungary, thus creating grounds for the Danubian Confederation under French patronage.

What we have seen all through this book is the persistence of a certain idea of a Central Europe that wanted to maintain the multinational heritage of the Habsburg Monarchy but eventually transformed it into an idea of the future; a form of a union of sovereign nation states.

In 1918, the belated process of federalization of Cisleithania initiated by the emperor as well as the post-war Danubian Confederation plans had been the distant results of the natural process of independence initiated in 1848 and stopped due to Austrian neo-absolutism. The *Ausgleich*, as the consequence of the battle of Sadowa, had resulted in applying the wrong solution to an empire that was not only multinational in Cisleithania but also in Transleithania. The Deákian concept of a French-type Hungarian unitary nation-state was the wrong solution for dealing with a country which, since the end of Ottoman rule, had been progressively inhabited by more non-Magyar "minorities" than Magyars. At the beginning of the age of nationalism (nineteenth century), the different ethnic groups of both Austria and

Hungary were developing their own national identities and were claiming their autonomy, some within and others outside of the empire. Thus there were two possible options for the Habsburgs: to recognise none of the nations as states (which they could hardly afford to do with respect to Hungary) or to recognise all of them as autonomous nations and thus accept decentralization and federalization of the whole of their empire. Instead of that, only Hungary had been granted the privilege of becoming a separate state in *Personalunion* with Austria, which would undoubtedly lead others to make a claim for the same treatment. In other words, after 1848, dynasticism—which allowed for the possibility of neo-absolutism—had to be replaced by the idea of multinational federalism. The problem was that the decentralizing process, which had been progressing in Cisleithania since 1867, did not evolve in the nation-state of Hungary.[780] Even after 1918, while falling apart, Hungary did not make the necessary effort to offer a federal solution to the nationalities of Greater Hungary.

After Hungary lost its king in 1922 and was unable to make the multinational inheritance of the Habsburgs its own, Austria took over with a precursory idea and understood the full meaning of its multinational calling. The same year as the death of Emperor-King Karl, an Austrian count, Richard Coudenhove-Kalergi, published his first article on the idea of Paneuropa. In 1923, he published his book *Paneuropa*, on a United States of Europe, and in 1926 the Paneuropean Movement was founded in Vienna, with its headquarters—an irony of history or a premeditated decision?—in that city's *Hofburg* (Imperial Palace). Its first president, the chancellor of the Republic of Austria, Ignaz Seipel, would express the view that the future capital of the United States of Europe would be Vienna, and that this city, and the Austrian people, would continue their historical, multinational and "imperial" calling as the new centre of a united Europe.[781] Since Coudenhove-Kalergi was one of the initiators of the European idea and was largely responsible

---

[780] Article 19 of the Constitution of 1867 states: "All peoples of the Empire are equal and that each people has the right to keep and cultivate its nationality and language." Humbert-Knittel, Geneviève, "De l'égalité des nationalités au droit des minorités nationales", in Reffet, Michel, ed., *L'Autriche et l'Idée d'Europe*, Editions Universitaires de Dijon, Dijon, 1997, 321.

[781] Saint-Gilles, Anne-Marie, *La "Paneurope". Un débat d'idées dans l'entre-deux-guerres*, Presses de l'Université de Paris-Sorbonne, Paris, 2003, 280–85.

for inspiring Aristide Briand—who joined the Paneuropa Union very early—to give his 1929 speech on a European Federation in Geneva, it can be said that Austria had taken the lead in showing the way to a united Europe.[782] In a Europe of nation-states, Austria, with the Paneuropa Movement, tried to inspire the continent to become a large multinational union, just as the Habsburg Empire had been as a multinational state. In a way, Austria can claim that the European Union is the heir to the Dual Monarchy's and the Danubian Confederation's concept of multinationality, even if the Europe it envisioned would eventually not be centred in Vienna.

After the end of Communism in Europe, it was common motivations that could attract Central European states to join the EU: a common economic interest and a willingness to be part of Western Europe and to leave the Balkanised Ostblock or "kidnapped West". The mere existence of the European Union, enlarged to include Romania and Croatia, shows that the idea of a multinational Danubian Confederation was a vision of the future. With the incorporation of these two states into the EU, practically all of Hungary's pre-1918 territories (except the Sub-Carpathian region and Vojvodina) are within the EU. Hungary is now more able to solve its external Hungarian minority problem, since borders are eroding in the Schengen Zone. The next phase is trans-border regions, where ethnic nationalities can reunite. Both the EU and the Visegrad Group have made it possible to pacify the region and have facilitated economic and cultural projects between states that were at odds with each other in the twentieth century. The once-forbidden con/federalist projects have provided the inspiration for a successful and peaceful Central Europe.

---

782 Chabot, Jean-Luc, *Aux origines intellectuelles de l'Union européenne, L'idéee d'Europe unie de 1919 à 1939*, Presses Universitaires de Grenoble, Grenoble, 2005, 43–50. Nurdin, Jean, "Coudenhove-Kalergi et le Mouvement Paneuropéen", in Reffet, Michel, ed., *op. cit.*, 273–77.

Postface

The years 2004, 2007 and 2013 have marked great expectations and events: the European Union admitted eleven new Central and Eastern European—formerly *Ostblock*—states, seven of which, and a fraction of Ukraine (Galicia-Bukovina and Subcarpathia), were part of the Austro-Hungarian Empire and consequently of Western Europe. It has been, therefore, highly topical to treat a subject such as this. If in future years it is to be hoped that Serbia, Bosnia-Herzegovina and Ukraine will join the EU, then all regions that had been separated from the former Central European Empire will be reunited with the Europe they belonged to and were, partially or entirely, part of at the beginning of the twentieth century.

These three years also brought many other hints to justify even further the topicality of this work. One of which was Pope John Paul II's decision to beatify the last Emperor-King of Austria-Hungary, Karl of Habsburg-Lorraine in 2004—more than eighty years since the events described. The passage of so much time also meant that unpublished sources that had been under embargo became accessible, enabling the readers of this book to discover the Danubian Confederation project of the first and foremost person concerned with this vast region: Karl of Austria-Hungary.

After 1918, Central Europe was rearranged with new borders, and brand-new Successor States, claiming to be nation states, were created. A process of fractioning instead of uniting made Central Europe vulnerable to German or Soviet imperialism. And, as the long and terrible twentieth century proved, they could not survive the weight of history. The aim of my research was to discover the alternative to the status quo confirmed by the peace treaties of suburban Paris and also the resurgence of the nineteenth-century idea of a Danubian Confederation and its supporters after World War I. The study of this alternative makes a great deal of sense, as history also deals with political plans that were not realised, plans that can contribute to understand many contemporary problems of the region.

It is a great privilege to write these lines in Coppet (Lake Geneva, Switzerland), just a few yards from the castle of Mme de Staël (born Germaine Necker). It was the meeting point of the great political *penseurs* of the time, and Mme de Staël remained there until she was able to go back to Paris after the fall of Napoléon. Coppet is only a few miles from Prangins, where Emperor-King Karl spent two years in exile before returning, unsuccessfully, to Hungary to reclaim his throne. At the other end of the lake in Clarens one can see the wonderful "Villa Karma", by the avant-garde Austrian architect Adolf Loos, where Prince Lajos Windischgraetz resided during the same period. History breathes in every corner of this region of natural beauty, dissidence and exiles. Where could one find a better place for inspiration?

Coppet, November 3, 2018, the day of 100th anniversary the Austro-Hungarian Armistice at Villa Giusti ending World War 1.

Bibliography

1. Sources

1.1. Archives

AUSTRIA

OESTERREICHISCHES STAATSARCHIV
NPA, Budesministerium für Heereswesen
    -Abteilung 2, Zahl 1700:
        Königreich S.H.S 1920–1921
        Tschekoslowakei 1920–1921
        Ungarn 1920–1921

Nachlässe und Sammlungen:
    -B 1521, Stevo Duić
    -B 132, Stephan Sarkotić.
    -B 1514/4 Duić Mario

Liasse Personalia:
    -Katon (K) 424 Stevo Duić
    -K 425 Ivo Frank
    -K 427 Karl I
    -K 453 Karl Werkmann
    -K 456 Donauföderation
    -K 427 Habsburg (general)
    -K 762 Ivo Frank

FRANCE

ARCHIVES DU MINISTÈRE DES AFFAIRES ÉTRANGÈRES, QUAI D'ORSAY (ADMAE)
Correspondance Politique et Commerciales
    Z Europe:
    -Autriche 41
    -Hongrie 6, 42, 44–49, 58, 60, 65

Bibliography

-Tchécoslovaquie 34–35, 44–46
-Yougoslavie 24, 32, 40–42, 48, 54, 62–65

ARCHIVES NATIONALES DE FRANCE (ANF)
-Fonds Alexandre Millerand

SERVICE HISTORIQUE DE L'ARMÉE DE TERRE (SHAT):
-Fonds Foch, 1K
-7N Hongrie 2885, 2886, 2988
-7N Tchécoslovaquie 3094, 3104, 3105, 3109, 3111
-7N Yougoslavie 3197, 3200

GREAT BRITAIN

NATIONAL ARCHIVES (NA), FOREIGN OFFICE (FO) 371 (FOREIGN CORRESPONDENCE):
FO 380/22 (Legation to the Holy See)
FO 371/3529 (Hungary)
FO 371/3533 (Hungary)
FO 371, 4644 (Austria)
FO 371/4650 (Austria)
FO 371/4714 (Austria)
FO 371/4721 (Czechoslovakia)
FO 371/5822 (Czechoslovakia)
FO 371/5823 (Czechoslovakia)
FO 371/5827 (Czechoslovakia)
FO 371/5829 (Czechoslovakia)
FO 371/5830 (Czechoslovakia)
FO 371/5831 (Czechoslovakia)
FO 371/5832 (Czechoslovakia)
FO 371/5833 (Czechoslovakia)
FO 371/6102 (Hungary)
FO 371/6105 (Hungary)
FO 371/6106 (Hungary)
FO 371/6107 (Hungary)
FO 371/6108 (Hungary)
FO 371/6109 (Hungary)
FO 371/6111 (Hungary)
FO 371/6193 (SHS Kingdom)
FO 371/6194 (SHS Kingdom)
FO 371/6195 (SHS Kingdom)

OXFORD BODLEIAN LIBRARY
Manuscript Department (MS)

Bibliography

Oppenheimer Papers
C.A. Macartney Papers
Rumbold Papers

SSEES (SCHOOL OF EAST EUROPEAN AND SLAVONIC STUDIES) ARCHIVES, LONDON
Seton-Watson Papers (SEW) 10/2/1

HUNGARY

MAGYAR NEMZETI LEVÉLTÁR (HUNGARIAN NATIONAL ARCHIVES), (MNL):
Hungarian Foreign Office papers:
-K58 Minister's cabinet
-K64 Foreign Ministry's Political department's special paper.
-K26, K27, Proceedings of the Council of Ministers
-Oszkár de Charmant Fonds

HUNGARIAN ACADEMY OF SCIENCES, ARCHIVES OF THE INSTITUTE
OF HISTORICAL STUDIES (TTI), BUDAPEST:
-Gratz, Gusztáv, *Erinnerungen*, 1946, (manuscript).

SWITZERLAND

ARCHIVES NATIONALS SUISSE, (SWISS NATIONAL ARCHIVES)
Département des Affaires Etrangères:
-BAR/E2300 Paris 74

GRADUATE INSTITUTE OF GENEVA LIBRARY (ARCHIVES)
(Unpublished thesis)
Vajay, Szabolcs de, *L'aspect international des tentatives de la restauration Habsbourg en Hongrie mars-octobre 1921*, 1946.

UNITED STATES OF AMERICA

HOOVER INSTITUTION ARCHIVES, STANFORD UNIVERSITY, CALIFORNIA:
-Barcza, György papers
-Osusky, Stefan papers
-Scitovsky, Tibor papers

VATICAN CITY

ARCHIVIO DELLA SACRA CONGREGAZIONE PER GLI AFFARI ECCLESIASTICI STRAORDINARI (STATE SECRETARIAT ARCHIVES)
-AE, Austria 525, 526

1.2. Primary Print Sources

Diplomatic Papers

(BDFA) British Documents on Foreign Affairs, Reports and papers from the Foreign Office Confidential print, Part II, series F (Europe 1919–1939), Vol. 13, University Publications of America, London, 1993.

(DBFP) Documents on British Foreign Policy, Series I and IA, HMSO, London, 1934.

(DDF) Documents diplomatiques français, série 2, Ministère de Affaires étrangères, Paris, 1963–.

(DDS) Documents diplomatiques suisses 1848-1945, Vol. 8. Benteli Verlag, Bern, 1988.

(DGFP) Documents on German Foreign Policy 1918-1945, series C+D, Government Printing Office, Washington, D.C., 1945–.

(DFBC) Litván, György, Ádám, Magda (ed.), *Documents Diplomatiques français sur l'histoire du bassin des Carpates, 1918–1932*, Akadémia, Budapest, vol. 1–3, 1993–.

(FRUS), Foreign Relations of the United States, 1937, Vol. 1, Government Printing Office, Washington, D.C., 1980.

(PFRH) Deák, Francis, Ujváry, Dezsö, eds., *Papers and Documents Relating to the Foreign Relations of Hungary*, v. I: 1919–1920, v. II: 1921, Royal Hungarian Ministry of Foreign Affairs, Budapest, 1939.

Other Published Papers

Feigl, Erich (Herg.), *Kaiser Karl, Persönliche Aufzeichnungen, Zeugniss und Dokumente*, Amalthea, Wien, 1984.

The Hungarian Question in the British Parliament: Speeches, questions and answers thereto in the House of Lords and the House of Commons from 1919 to 1930, Grant Richards, London, 1933.

Gergely, Jenö, Ferenc Glatz, Ferenc Pölöskei (ed.), *Magyarországi pártprogramok 1919–1944*, Kossuth Kiadó, Budapest, 1991.

Kardos, József, *A Legitimizmus alternatívái Magyarországon (1918–1946)*, Korona, Budapest, 1996.

Kazimirović, Vasa, *NDH u svetlu nemačkih dokumenata i dnevnika Gleza fon Horstenau 1941–1944*, Nova knjiga, Beograd, 1987.

Kerekes, Lajos, *Allianz Hitler-Horthy-Mussolini: Dokumente zur Ungarischen Aussenpolitik (1933–1944)*, Akadémia, Budapest, 1966.

Kovács, Elisabeth, *Untergang oder Rettung der Monarchie*, t. II Documenten, Böhlau Verlag, Wien, 2004.

A Magyar Békétárgyalások, Jelentés, vol. I–II, Magyar Kir. Külügyminisztérium, Budapest, 1920.

Memoirs

Andrássy, Gyula Gróf, *Diplomácia és világháború*, Göncöl-Primusz, Budapest, 1990.

Auer, Pál, *Egy fél évszázad*, Occidental Press, Washington D.C., 1977.

Barcza, György, *Diplomata emlékeim*, Európa, Budapest, 1994.
Boroviczény, Aladár, *A Király és Kormányzója* (translated from *Der König und sein Reichverweser* [1924]), Europa, Budapest, 1993.
Castellane, Boni de, *L'art d'etre pauvre*, Les éditions Du Crès et Cie, Paris, 1925.
Eckhardt, Tibor, *Regicide at Marseille, Recollections of Eckhardt Tibor*, The American Hungarian Library and Historical Society, New York, 1964.
Giuriati, Giovanni, *Con D'Annunzio e Millo in difesa dell'Adriatico*, G.C. Sansoni, Florence, 1954.
Glaise-Horstenau, Edmund von, *Die Katastrophe, Die Zertrümmerung Österreich-Ungarns und das Werden der Nachfolgestaaten*, Amalthea, Zürich, Leipzig, Vienna, 1929.
Habsbourg, Otto de, *Mémoires d'Europe. Entretiens avec J.-P. Picaper*, Criterion, Paris, 1994.
Habsburg, Otto, *Isten akaratából*, Corvina, Budapest, 1991.
Hardinge, Lord, *Old Diplomacy*, John Murray, London, 1947.
Herczeg, Ferenc, *Hüvösvölgy*, Szépirodalmi Könyvkiadó, Budapest, 1993.
Hodža, Milan, *Federation in Central Europe*, Jarrolds, London, 1942.
Horthy, Miklós, *Emlékirataim* [1953], Europa, Budapest, 1990.
Jászi, Oszkár, *Magyar Kálvária, Magyar Föltámadás*, Bécsi Mayar Kiadó, Vienna, 1920.
Jehlička, Francis, *Father Hlinka's Struggle for Slovak Freedom, Reminiscences of Professor Francis Jehlička*, The Slovak Council, London, 1938.
Lehár, Antal, *Egy katonatiszt naplója 1919-1921*, in *Historia*, no. 11, História Alapítvány, Budapest, 1993.
Polzer-Hoditz, Arthur Graf, *Kaiser Karl. Aus den Erinnerungen eines Kabinettschefs*, Wien–Zürich, 1929.
Schuschnigg, Kurt, *Austrian Requiem*, Victor Gollancz Ltd, London, 1947.
Shvoy, Kálmán, *Titkos naplója és emlékirata 1918-1945*, Kossuth, Budapest, 1983.
Stomm, Marcel, *Emlékiratok*, Magyar Hirlap, Budapest, 1990.
Szemere, Pál, Erich Czech, *Habsburgs Weg von Wilhelm zu Briand*, (Die Memoiren des Gräfen Tomas Erdödy), Wien, 1931.
Windischgraetz, Ludwig, *Ein Kaiser kämpft für die Freiheit*, Verlag Herold, Wien, 1957.
----, *Mémoires*, Paris, Payot, 1923.
----, *My Adventures and Misadventures*, Barrie and Rockliff, Cop., London, 1966.
----, *Vom Roten zum Schwarzen Prinzen, Mein Kampf gegen das k.u.k. System*, Berlin, Verlag Ullstein, Wien, 1920.
Zeidler, Miklós, *A Monarchiától Trianonig egy Magyar Diplomata Szemével, Praznovszky Iván emlékezései*, Olvasó Sarok, Budapest, 2012.

1.3. Theses

Bátonyi, Gábor, Britain and Central Europe 1918-1932, Oxford, 1985.
 (Bod MS. D.Phil. C.11019)
Vajay, Szabolcs de, L'aspect international des tentatives de la restauration Habsbourg en Hongrie mars-octobre 1921, HEI Geneva, 1946.

Bibliography

2. Works

2.1. Books

Annuaire de Statistique de la République tchécoslovaque, Prague, 1934.

Ádám, Magda, *Little Entente and Europe (1920-1929)*, Akadémia Kiadó, Budapest, 1993.

Adler, Jasna, *L'Union Forcée: La Croatie et la Création de l'Etat Yougoslave (1918)*, Georg, Geneva, 1997.

Arday, Lajos, *Térkép csata után: Magyarország a Brit külpolitikában 1918-19*, Magvető, Budapest, 1990.

Andrássy, Gyula, *Miskolci programbeszéd*, the author, Budapest, 1920.

Balla, Tibor, *A Nagy Háború osztrák-magyar tábornokai: Tábornagyok, vezérezredesek, gyalogsági és lovassági tábornokok, táborszernagyok*, A Hadtörténeti Intézet és Múzeum Könyvtár, Budapest, 2010.

Banac, Ivo, *The National Question in Yugoslavia*, Ithaca-London, Cornell University Press, 1988.

Bangha, Ernő, *A Magyar Királyi Testőrség 1920-1944* (The Royal Hungarian Lifeguards), Europa, Budapest, 1990.

Bainville, Jacques, *Les conséquences politiques de la paix*, Librairie Arthème Fayard, Paris, 1920.

----, *Les conséquences politiques de la paix*, and (in the same book) Keynes, J.M., *Les conséquences économiques de la paix*, Gallimard, Paris, 2002.

Bátonyi, Gábor, *Britain and Central Europe, 1918-1933*, Clarendon Press, Oxford, 1999.

Bauer, Ernst, *L'Ultimo Palladino del'Impero*, Triest Libri, Trieste, 1989.

Biondich, Mark, *Stjepan Radić, the Croat Peasant Party, and the Politics of Mass Mobilization, 1904-1928*, University of Toronto Press, Toronto, 2000.

Béhar, Pierre, *Vestiges d'Empire, La décomposition de l'Europe centrale et balkanique*, Editions Desjonquères, Paris, 1999.

Benda, Kálmán, *Magyarország Történeti Kronológiája* (Chronology of Hungarian history), no. III, Akadémia, Budapest, 1983.

Bérenger, Jean, *Histoire de l'Empire des Habsburg, 1273-1918*, Fayard, Paris, 1993.

Bethlen, Count Stephen, *The Treaty of Trianon and European Peace*, Longmans, Green and Co., London, 1934.

Bled, Jean-Paul, *François-Ferdinand d'Autriche*, Tallandier, Paris, 2012.

----, *L'Agonie d'une monarchie: Autriche-Hongrie, 1914-1920*, Tallandier, Paris, 2014.

Bogdan, Henry, *Histoire des Habsbourg, Des origines à nos jours*, Perrin, Paris 2002.

Boia, Eugene, *Romania's Diplomatic Relations with Yugoslavia in the Interwar Period, 1919-1941*, East European Monographs, Columbia University Press, New York, 1993.

Boniface, Pascal (ed.), *Lexique des Relations internationales*, Ellipses, Paris, 1995.

Borbándi, Gyula, *Magyar politikai pályaképek 1938-1948*, Európa, Budapest, 1997.

Boros, Ferenc, *Magyar csehszlovák kapcsolatok 1918-1921-ben*, Akadémia, Budapest, 1970.

----, *Hongrois et Slovaques*, Press Publica, Budapest, 2002.

Brook-Shepherd, Gordon, *The Last Habsburg*, Weidenfeld-Nicolson, London, 1968.

Bibliography

----, *The Last Empress: The Life and Times of Zita of Austria-Hungary, 1892–1889*. Harper-Collins, London, 1991.

Broucek, Peter, *Karl I. (IV.), Der politische Weg des letzten Herrschers der Donaumonarchie*, Böhlau, Vienna, 1997.

Carmi, Ozer, *La Grande Bretagne et la Petite Entente*, Librairie Droz, Geneva, 1972.

Cartledge, Bryan, *Károlyi and Bethlen, Hungary: The Peace Conferences of 1919–23 and Their Aftermarth*, Haus Histories, London, 2009.

Castellan, Georges, *Histoire des peuples d'Europe centrale*, Fayard, Paris, 1994.

Chabot, Jean-Luc, *Aux origines intellectuelles de l'Union européenne, L'idéee d'Europe unie de 1919 à 1939*, Presses Universitaires de Grenoble, Grenoble, 2005.

Chaigneau, Pascal (ed.), *Dictionnaire des relations internationales*, Ed. Economico, Paris, 1998.

Csonka, Emil, *Habsburg Ottó, Egy különös sors története*, Új Európa, Munich, 1972.

Deák, István, *Beyond Nationalism, A Social and Political History of the Habsburg Officer Corps, 1848–1918*, Oxford University Press, New York–Oxford, 1990.

Dickes, Christophe (ed.), *Jacques Bainville, L'Europe d'entre deux guerres 1919–1936*, Godefroy de Bouillon, Paris, 1996.

Dikés, Charles, *Jacques Bainville. Les lois de la politique étrangère*, Bernand Giovanangeli, Paris, 2008.

Dombrády Lóránd, *A legfelsőbb Hadúr és Hadserege*, Zrinyi, Budapest, 1990.

----, *Katonapolitika és Hadsereg*, Ister, Budapest, 2001.

Droz, Jacques, *L'Europe centrale et l'évolution historique de la "Mitteleuropa"*, Payot, Paris, 1960.

Durandin, Catherine, *Histoire de la nation roumaine*, Complexe, Brussels, 1994.

Dugast-Rouillé, Michel, *Karl de Habsbourg*, Duclos, Paris, 1991.

Duroselle, Jean-Baptiste (ed.), *La Politique étrangère et ses fondements*, Paris, 1954.

Evans, R.J.W, "Great Britain and East-Central Europe, 1908–48: A Study in Perceptions", *The First Masaryk Lecture*, Kings College, London, 2001.

Fischer-Galati, Stephen, *Twentieth Century Rumania*, Columbia University Press, New York, 1991.

Fejtö, François, *Requiem pour un empire défunt*, Point Seuil, Paris, 1993.

Felak, James Ramon, *"At the Price of the Republic" Hlinka's Slovak People's Party 1929–1938*, University of Pittsburgh Press, Pittsburgh and London, 1994.

Fiziker, Róbert, *Habsburg kontra Hitler, Legitimisták az Anschluss ellen, az önálló Austriáért*, Gondolat, Budapest, 2010.

Frank, Ivo, *A revízió és Horvátország*, Erdélyi Férfiak Egyesülete, Budapest, 1933.

Ferguson, Niall (ed.), *Virtual History, Alternatives and Counterfactuals* [1997], Penguin Books, London, 2011.

Gergely, Jenő, *Gömbös Gyula*, Vince Kiadó, Budapest, 2001.

----, *A kereszténysocializmus Magyarországon 1924–1944* (Christian-socialism in Hungary), Typovent Kiadó, Gödöllö, 1993.

Glatz, Ferenc, *Minorities in East-Central Europe, Historical Analysis and a Policy Proposal*, Europa Institute, Budapest, 1993.

----, *A kisebbségek kérdése Közép Európában tegnap és ma*, Historia Plusz, Budapest, 1992.

Gobron, Gabriel, *La Hongrie mystérieuse*, no pub., Paris, 1933.

Bibliography

Goldstein, E., *Winning the Peace, British Diplomatic Strategy, Peace Planning, and the Paris Peace Conference, 1916–1920*, Clarendon Press, Oxford, 1991.
Gratz, Gusztáv, *Magyarország a két világháború között*, Osiris, Budapest, 2001.
Griger, Miklós, *A Legitimizmus és a Magyar Feltámadás. Aktuális-e a királykérdés?*, Budapest, 1936.
Grumel-Jacquignon, François, *La Yougoslavie dans la stratégie française de l'Entre-deux-Guerres (1918–1935), Aux origines du mythe serbe en France*, Peter Lang, Bern, 1999.
Guerri, Giordano Bruno, *D'Annunzio*, Oscar Mondadori, Milan, 2008.
Gulick, Karl A., *Austria: from Habsburg to Hitler* [1948], II, University of California Press, Berkeley, Los Angeles, London, 1980.
Heimann, Mary, *Czechoslovakia, The State that Failed*, Yale University Press, New Haven, London, 2009.
Horel, Catherine, *L'Admiral Horthy: le régent de Hongrie*, Perrin, Paris, 2014.
Ignotus, P., *Hungary*, E. Benn, London, 1972.
Iordache, Nicolae, *La Petite Entente et l'Europe*, IUHEI, Geneva, 1977.
Jászi, Oszkár, *A Monarchia Jövöje* [1918], Akv-Maecenas, Budapest, 1988.
----, *The Dissolution of the Habsburg Monarchy*, University of Chicago Press, Chicago, 1929.
----, *Magyar Kálvária Magyar Föltámadás*, Magyar Hirlap, Budapest, 1989.
Jehlička, Franz Rudolf, *Une étape du calvaire slovaque: le procès Tuka, 1929–1930*, Argo, Paris, 1930.
----, *Revizió és a Szlovákok*, Erdélyi Férfiak Egyesülete, Budapest, 1933.
----, *André Hlinka à la Conférence de Paix*, no pub., Geneva, 1938.
Jelinek, Yeshayahu, *The Parish Republic: Hlinka's Slovak People's Party 1939–1945*, Columbia University, New York, 1976.
Judson, Pieter M., *The Habsburg Empire. A New History*, The Belknap Press of the Harvard University Press, Cambridge MA, London, 2016.
Juhász, Gyula, *Hungarian Foreign Policy 1919–1945*, Akadémia, Budapest, 1979.
----, *Magyarorszag külpolitikája 1919–1945*, Kossuth, Budapest, 1987.
Kalhous, Rudolf, *Budováni armády*, Melantrich, Prague, 1936.
Kann, Robert, *A History of the Habsburg Empire, A study of integration and disintegration*, Octagon Books, New York, 1973.
Kardos, József, *A szentkorona-tan története 1919–1944*, Akadémia Kiadó, Budapest, 1985.
----, *Legitimizmus,Legitimista politikusok Magyarországon a két világháború között*, Korona Kiadó, Budapest, 1998.
Keylor, William R., *Jacques Bainville and the Renaissance of Royalist History in the Twentieth-Century France*, Louisiana State University Press, Baton Rouge, London, 1979.
Király, Béla K., Peter Pastor, Ivan Sanders, (Eds.), *Essays on World War I: Total War and Peacemaking, A Case Study on Trianon*, Brooklyn College Press, distributed by Columbia University Press, New York, 1982.
Ki-Kicsoda? Kortársak lexikona, Béta Irodalmi RT, Budapest, no date.
Kirschbaum, Stanislav J., *A History of Slovakia: The Struggle for Survival*, Macmillan Press, London, 1995.
----, *Historical Dictionary of Slovakia*, Scarecrow Press, Lanham and London, 1999.

Bibliography

----, (ed.), *Slovak Politics, Essays on Slovak History in Honour of Joseph M. Kirschbaum*, Slovak Institute, Cleveland, Rome, 1983.

Kiss, Gy. Csaba, *Közép Európa, nemzetek, kissebségek*, Pesti Szalon, Budapest, 1993.

Kovac, Dusan, *Szlovákia Története*, Kalligram, Pozsony-Bratislava, 2001.

Kovács, Endre, *Magyar-Lengyel kapcsolatok a két világháború között*, Akadémia Kiadó, Budapest, 1971.

Ladányi, Andor, *Az egyetemi ifjúság az ellenforradalom első éveiben (1919–1921)*, Akadémia Kiadó, Budapest, 1979.

Lampe, John, R., *Yugoslavia as History, Twice there Was a Country*, Cambridge University Press, New York, 1969.

Latour, Francis, *La papauté et les problèmes de la paix pendant la première guerre mondiale*, L'Harmattan, Paris, 1996.

Ledeen, Michael Arthur, *The First Duce, D'Annunzio at Fiume*, Johns Hopkins University Press, Baltimore, London, 1977.

----, *D'Annunzio: The First Duce* [2002], Transaction Publishers, New Bruskwick, London, 2009

Liebich, André, André Reszler, *L'Europe centrale et ses minorités*, IUHEI-PUF, Geneva, Paris, 1993.

Loftus, John, Mark Aarons, *The Unholy Trinity*, St. Martin's Griffin, New York, 1998.

Lukacs, John, *The Great Powers and Eastern Europe*, American Book Company, New York, 1953.

Macartney, Carlile Aymler, *Hungary and her Successors 1919–1937*, Oxford University Press, New York, 1937.

----, *The Danubian Basin*, Clarendon Press, Oxford, 1939.

Macmillan, Margaret, *Paris 1919: Six Months that Changed the World*, Random House, New York, 2007.

Magaš, Branka, *Croatia through History, The Making of a European State*, SAQI, London, 2007.

Mágocsi, Paul Robert, *The Shaping of a National Identity, Subcarpathian Rus 1848–1948*, Harvard Univerity Press, Cambridge, MA, 1978.

Mamatey, Victor S., Radomir Luza, *A History of the Czechoslovak Republic*, Princeton University Press, Princeton, NJ, 1973.

Matsch, Ervin, *Der Auswärtige Dienst von Oesterreich (-Ungarn), 1720–1920*, Vienna, 1986.

Mension-Rigau, Eric, *Boni de Castellane*, Perrin, Paris, 2008.

Montador, Jean, ed., *Jacques Bainville, Historien de l'Avenir*, France Empire, Paris, 1984.

Mousset, Albert, *La Petite Entente*, Paris, 1923.

Nagy, Zsuzsa, L., *A Szabadkőművesség a XX. Században* (Free Masonry in the XXth century), Kossuth, Budapest, 1977.

Ormesson, Wladimir d', *Nos Illusions sur l'Europe Centrale*, Librairie Plon, Paris, 1922.

Ormos, Mária, *From Padua to the Trianon 1918–1920*, Akadémia, Budapest, 1920.

----, *"Soha amig élek!" Az utolsó korónás Habsburg puccskisérletei 1921-ben*, Pannonia, Pécs, 1990.

----, *Hungary in the Age of the Two World Wars 1914–1945*, East European Monographs No. 723, Atlantic Research and Publications, Inc., Highland Lakes, NJ, 2007.

Pastor, Peter, ed., *Revolutions and Interventions in Hungary and its Neighbour States, 1918–1921*, East European Monographs, Columbia University, New York, 1988.

Bibliography

Pethő, Sándor, *A Magyar Capitoliumon, A magyar királyeszme a Duna völgyében*, Gellért Kiadó, Budapest, 1932.

----, *Magunk Útján*, Deák Ferenc Tarsaság, Budapest, 1937.

Pierré-Caps, Stéphane, *La Multination, l'avenir des minorités en Europe Centrale*, Odile Jacob, Paris, 1995.

Popély, Gyula, *Felvidék 1914–1920*, Magyar Napló, Budapest, 2010.

Prazmowska, Anita, J., *Eastern Europe and the Origins of the Second World War*, St. Martin's Press, New York, 2000.

Ránki, György, (ed.), *Magyarország Története, 1918–1919*, vol. 8/1, Akadémia, Budapest.

Ránki, György, *Economy and Foreign Policy: The Struggle of the Great Powers for Hegemony in the Danubian Valley*, Atlantic Reasearch and Publications, Inc., Highland Lakes, NJ, 1983.

Renner, Karl, *La Nation, Mythe et Réalité* [1964], Presse Universitaire de Nancy, Nancy, 1998.

Renouvier, Charles, *L'Uchronie, l'Utopie dans l'histoire*, Bureau de la Critique philosophique, Paris, 1876.

Reisner, Ferenc, *Csernoch János hercegprimás és IV Károly*, Márton Áron Kiadó, Budapest, 1991.

Renouvin, Pierre, *Histoire des Relations Internationales*, t. IV, Paris 1953–58.

Rieder, Heinz, *Kaiser Karl. Der Letzte Monarch Österreich-Ungarns 1887–1822*, Callwey Edition, Munich, 1981.

Romsics, István, *Bethlen Istvan*, Magyarságkutató Intézet, Budapest, 1991.

----, *The Dismantling of Historic Hungary: The Peace Treaty of Trianon, 1920*, Social Sciences Monographs, Boulder, CO, 2002,

Rothwell, V.H., *British War Aims and Peace Diplomacy, 1914–1918*, Oxford University Press, Oxford, 1971.

Rothschild, Joseph, *East Central Europe between the two World Wars* [1974], University of Washington Press, Seattle, 1992.

Saint-Gille, Anne-Marie, *La "Paneurope" Un débat d'idées dans l'entre-deux-guerres*, Presses de l'Université de Paris-Sorbonne, Paris, 2003.

Saint-Ouen, François, *Le Fédéralisme*, Infolio éditions, Gollion (CH).

Sakmyster, Thomas L., *Hungary, the Great Prowers, and the Danubian Crisis 1936–1939*, University of Georgia Press, Athens, GA, 1980.

Sked, Alan, *The Decline and Fall of the Habsburg Empire 1815–1918*, Longman, London, 1989.

Snyder, Timothy, *The Red Prince, The fall of a dynasty and the rise of modern Europe*, The Bodley Head, London, 2008.

Somogyi, István, *Hartensteinről Funchalig: egy királydráma története hiteles adatok nyomán*, the author, Budapest, 1936.

Soutou, Georges-Henri, "1918 le basculement vers une Europe de Etats Nations", in *La Tchécolslovaquie sismographie de l'Europe au XX siècle*, Instiut d'Etudes slaves, Paris, 2009.

Steier, Lajos, *Felsömagyarország és a revizió*, Magyar Férfiak Egyesülete, Budapest, 1933.

Stallaerts, Robert, Jeannine Laurens, *Historical Dictionary of the Republic of Croatia*, Scarecrow Press, Inc., Lanham, MD., London, 1995,

Suarez, Georges, *Briand*, vol. 5–6, Plon, Paris, 1938–52.

Sulyok, Dezsö, *A Magyar Tragédia*, I, Newark, NJ, 1954.

Swanson, John C., *The Remnants of the Habsburg Monarchy: The Shaping of Modern Austria and Hungary 1918-1922*, East European Monographs, Boulder, CO, 2001.
Szarka, László, *A Szlovákok Története*, Bereményi Kiadó, Budapest, 1993.
Szilassy, Sándor, *Revolutionary Hungary 1818-1921*, Danubian Press, Inc., Astor Park, FL, 1971.
Tanner, Markus, *Croatia, a Nation Forged in War*, Yale University Press, New Haven-London, 1997.
Thurnig-Nitter, G., *Die Tschecoslovakische Legion in Russland*, Wiesbaden, 1970.
Tisseyre, Charles, *Une erreur diplomatique: la Hongrie mutilée*, Mercure, Paris, 1922.
Toma, Peter A., Dusan Kovac, *Slovakia, from Samos to Dzurinda*, Hoover Inst. Press, Stanford, CA, 2001.
Valiani, Leo, *The End of Austria-Hungary: The definitive account of the collapse of a great Empire*, Secker and Warburg, London, 1973.
Vivian, Herbert, *The Life of Emperor Karl of Austria*, Grayson, London, 1932.
Wandycz, Piotr S., *France and Her Eastern Allies 1919-1925, French-Czechoslovak-Polish Relations from the Paris Peace Conference to Locarno*, University of Minnesota Press, Minneapolis, 1962.
Werkmann, Karl von, *Le calvaire d'un empereur*, Ed. Payot, Paris, 1924.
Wierer, Rudolf, *Der Föderalismus im Donauraum*, Verlag Hermann Böhlaus, Graz, Cologne, 1960.
Zeman, Zbynek, Antonin Klimek, *The Life of Edvard Beneš 1884-1948*, Clarendon Press, Oxford, 1997.
Zsiga, Tibor, *Horthy ellen a királyért*, Gondolat, Budapest, 1989.
----, *Burgenland oder Westungarn*, Burgenländisch-Ungarischer Kulturverein, Oberwart, 1991.

2.2. Articles, book chapters

Ablonczy Balázs, "A magyar reviziós politika szlovák ágensei a két világháboru között", *Nyombiztositás*, Pozsony-Bratislava, Kalligram, 2011, 69-87.
Ádám, Magda, "Confédération ou Petite Entente", *Acta Historica*, no. 25, 1979, 61-113.
Andrássy, Gy., "La Hongrie et la Paix", *La revue politique internationale*, vol. XI, no. 36, 1919.
----, "National Self-Determination", *La revue politique internationale*, vol. IX, no. 37-38, 1919, 180-188.
Angyal, Béla: A csehszlovákiai magyarság anyaországi támogatása a két világháború között. (Financial support from the motherland for the Hungarians in interwar Czechoslovakia), *Régió*, no. 3, 2000, 133-178.
Bainville, Jacques, "Le règne et les idées de Karl I, empereur d'Autriche", *La Revue universelle*, III/14, 1920.
Bécsi, Zoltán, "Les légitimistes hongrois et la question de l'Europe centrale (1929-38)", *Revue Européenne d'Histoire*, vol. 11, no. 3, 2004, 365-382.
Bled, Jean-Paul, "Avant-propos", *Revue d'Europe centrale*, no. 1, 1993.
----, "L'Autriche-Hongrie: un modèle de pluralisme national?", in Liebich, A., A. Reszler, eds., *L'Europe centrale et ces minorités*, Paris, 1993, 25-35.

Bibliography

Cisek, Janusz, "The Beginnings of Joseph Beck's Diplomatic Career: The Origins of his Diplomatic Mission to Admiral Horthy in October 1920", *East European Quarterly*, XXVII, no 1, March 1993, 129–140.

Diószegi, István, "A revizió büvöletében, Külpolitikai alternativák Trianon után", *Rubicon*, no. 9–10, 1999, 13–15.

Farkas, Márton, "Az Osztrák-Magyar Monarchia megmentésének kísérletei és a páduai fegyverszünet", *Századok*, 1976, 306–346.

Feketené Cselényi Zsuzanna, "Magyarország Területi Épségének Védelmi Ligája megalakulásának körülményei és tevékenysége", *Egri Ho Shi Minh Tanárképző Föiskola Közleményei*, XVII. Eger, 1984, 101–112.

Ferencuhova, Bohumila, "La Tchécoslovaquie et le Plan Tardieu", *Revue d'Europe Centrale*, Strasbourg, Centre d'Etudes Germaniques, no. 2, 1997, 15–30.

----, "La vision slovaque des relations entre la France et la Petite Entente (1918–1925)", *Nations, Cultures et sociétés d'Europe centrale au XIX et XX siècles, Mélanges offerts au Professeur Bernard Michel*, Paris, Publications de la Sorbonne, 2006, 83–109.

Forst de Battaglia, Otto, "Restauration der Habsburger", *Europäische Gespräch: Hamburger Monatshefte für auswärtige Politik*, year VIII, no. 11, 1930, 5–7.

Foster, Alan, J., "Britain and East Central Europe 1918–1948", in *Mitteleuropa History and Prospects* (ed. Peter Stirk), Edinburgh University Press, 1994, 112–115.

Gergely, J., "A keresztényszocialisták politikai szerepe az ellenforradalom első éveiben (1919–23)", *Századok*, no. 2, 1976, 225–273.

Gratz, Gusztáv, "Le légitimisme hongrois", *Nouvelle Revue de Hongrie*, June 1936.

Graydon A. Jr, "Austria-Hungary", in Richard F. Hamilton, Holger H. Herwig (eds.), *The Origins of World War I*, Cambridge University Press, Cambridge, 2003, 112–149.

Hajdu, Tibor, "Mozgástér és kényszerpálya: Horthy-korszak", *Rubicon*, no. 4–5, 1998, 39–44.

Hamard, Bruno, "L'idée révisioniste dans la diplomatie hongroise de l'Entre-deux-guerres, le cas du comte Albert Apponyi, représentant du Royaume de Hongrie à la SDN", in Rohr, J. and B. Hamard, eds., *La faillite de la paix en Europe centrale, Le révisionnisme hongrois et ses conscéquences (1918–1939)*, Vécu Contemporain, 1996.

Hanák, Péter, "Oszkár Jászi's Danubian Patriotism", *Hungarian Studies Review*, 18 (1–2), 1991, 11–16.

----, "Egy szétört régió nyomorusága", *Rubicon*, no. 9–10, Budapest, 1999, 6–9.

Hinteregger, Robert, "Abwehrmassnahmen an der untersteierischen Grenzen 1918/19", *Zeitschrift des Historischen Vereins fur Steiermark*, 66, 1975.

Horel, Catherine, "La Hongrie et la France en 1934: des positions inconciliables", *Revue d'Europe Centrale*, Strasbourg, Centre d'Etudes Germaniques, no. 2, 1999, 132–145.

Humbert-Knitel, Geneviève, "De l'égalité des nationalités au droit des minorités nationales", in *L'Autriche et l'Idée d'Europe*, ed. Reffet, Michel, Editions Universitaires de Dijon, 1997, 317–333.

Janco, Anton, "La France et la création de l'armée tchécoslovaque", in *Le rôle de la France dans la création de l'Etat Tchécoslovaque (1918)*, 1993.

Janek, István, František Jehlička: szlovák hazafi vagy Budapest ügynöke?, ÚJ SZÓ ONLINE, January 17, 2016. https://ujszo.com/panorama/frantisek-jehlicka-szlovak-hazafi-vagy-budapest-ugynoke (01.03.2019)

Bibliography

Jeszenszky, Géza, "A Dunai államszövetség eszméje Nagy-Britanniában és az Egyesült Államokban az I. világháború alatt", in Romsics, Ignác (ed.) *Magyarország és a nagyhatalmak a 20. Században*, Teleki László Alapítvány, Budapest, 1995, 49–65.

Kardos, József, "Ifjabb Andrássy Gyula gróf utolsó évei", *Történelmi Szemle*, no. 3–4, 1994, 299–309.

Kende, János, "Horthy tisztek a kommün vörös hadseregében", in Halmos, Ferenc (ed.), *Száz Rejtély a Magyar Történelemből*, Gesta, Budapest, 1999.

Kerekes, Lajos, "Az Anschluss és a Dunai Konföderáció 'Alternativája' Otto Bauer Külpolitikájában 1918–1919-ben", *Történelmi Szemle*, 14 (3–4), 1971, 442–464.

Kilinger, William, "Antonio Grossich e la nascita dei movimenti nazionali a Fiume", *Quaderni*, Volume XII, Centro ricerche storiche Rovigno, 1999, 115–146.

Kovac, Dusan, "L'année 1918 dans l'histoire slovaque", in *La Tchécoslovaquie sismographe de l'Europe au XXe siècle*, Institut d'Etudes slaves de Paris, 2009, 43–52.

Laroche, Louis-Pierre, "L'Affaire Dutasta: Les dernières conversations diplomatique pour sauver l'Empires des Habsbourg", in *Revue d'Histoire diplomatique*, Editions A. Pedone, Paris, 1994.

Litván, György, "Jászi's Viennese Years: Building Contacts with the Democratic Left in the Successor States", *Hungarian Studies Review*, no. 18, 1991, 43–51.

Meunier, Fabrice, 1996, "Le Traité de Trianon à l'origine du révisionnisme hongrois", in Rohr, J. and B. Hamard (eds.), *La faillite de la paix en Europe centrale, Le révisionnisme hongrois et ses conséquences (1918–1939)*, 1996.

Michela, Miroslav, "František Jehlička politikai pálfordulatai 1918–20-ban", *Pro Minoritate*, 2005, 32–44.

Olivova, Vera, "Ceskoslovenska zahranicni politika a pokus o restauraci Habsburkou v roce 1921", *Ceskoslovensky casopis historicky*, 4, 1959, 675–698.

Ormos, Mária, "A Briand-terv és Magyarország", *Rubicon*, no. 5–6, 1997, 69–70.

Pallai, László, "A Páneurópai-mozgalom", *Rubicon*, no. 5–6, 1997.

Massagrande, Danilo L., "Un tentativo di restaurazione asburgica nel 1919 (dalle Carte di alessandro Casati)", *Politico*, 39 (3), 1974, 497–512.

Nurdin, Jean, "Coudenhove-Kalergi et le Mouvement Paneuropéen", in *L'Autriche et l'Idée d'Europe*, Reffet, Michel, ed., Editions Universitaires de Dijon, Dijon, 1997, 273–279.

Reszler, André, "Un grand libéral centralisateur hongrois, le baron Eötvös", in *Etudes Danubiennes*, vol. IX, no. 2, 1995.

Schönborn, Card. Christoph, "Carlo d'Austria: Imperatore et Re", *L'Osservatore Romano*, Supplemento, no. 229, Domenica 3 Ottobre 2004.

Simon, Attila, "Legionárius telepitések a két háború között", *Századok*, no. 68, 2004, 1361–1380.

Soutou, Georges-Henri, "L'imperialisme du pauvre: La politique economique du gouvernement francais en Europe centrale et orientale de 1918 a 1929", *Relations internationales*, No. 7, 1976, 219–239.

Spence, Richard B., "General Stephan Freiherr Sarkotić von Lovcen and Croatian Nationalism", *Canadian Review of Studies in Nationalism*, 17 (1–2), 1990, 147–155.

Szabó, Miklós, "Trianon multja és jelene", *Rubicon*, no. 9–10, 1999, 10–13.

Trifkovic, Srdjan, "The first Yugoslavia and origins of Croatian Separatism", *East European Quarterly*, XXVI, no. 3, 1992.

Tilkovszky Loránt, "Területi integritás és területi autonómia: A magyar kormány 1920. évi felvidéki szlovák autonomia-terve", *Századok*, no. 3, Budapest, 2000, 555–596.

Zeidler Miklós, "A Magyar Reviziós Liga, Trianontól Rothermere-ig", *Századok*, no. 2, 1997, 303–352.

Zorach, Jonathan, "The Nationalities Problem in the Czechoslovak Army", *East Central Europe*, vol. 5, no. 2, 1978, 169–181.

Zsuppan, F.T, "The Hungarian Red Army as Seen through British Eyes", in Pastor (ed.), *Revolutions and Interventions in Hungary and Its Neighbour States, 1918–19*, War and Society in Central Eastern Europe 20, New York, 1988, 89–104.

Index

Accurti, Milan, 230, 232
Ádám, Magda, 98, 101, 102, 213, 243
Adler, Jasna, 53, 141
Albert of Habsburg-Teschen, 35
Allizé, Henri, 212
Almond, Mark, 9
Andrássy, Gyula, Count, 29, 30, 32, 33, 36, 37, 114, 115, 202, 208, 223, 226–28, 232, 259, 260, 262
Apponyi, Albert, Count, 18, 19, 30, 99, 125, 126, 128, 196, 202, 208, 228, 261
Arthur, Duke of Connaught, Prince, 35

Badoglio, Pietro, 168
Bainville, Jacques, 75n191, 89–93, 110–11n288, 112n292, 113, 247, 251–53
Balfour Arthur (Lord Balfour), 68
Banac, Ivo, 53, 148n391, 156, 169
Barthou, Jean-Louis, 220, 236
Battaglia Forst, Otto, de, 31
Batthyány, Tivadar, Count, 29
Bauer, Otto, 52, 75, 78
Beaufort-Spontin, Heinrich, Prince, 244
Béhar, Pierre, 8
Benedict XV, Pope, 41, 42, 44, 48, 55, 81
Beneš, Edvard, 104, 111, 117, 119, 120, 171, 173, 175, 180, 189, 204, 214, 218, 221n658, 238, 241, 243, 245, 247–50, 253, 266, 268
Beniczky, Ödön, 31
Bérard, Léon, 92
Berchtold, Leopold, Count, 30, 57n132,
Bérenger, Jean, 8
Berthelot, Philippe, 92, 109, 116, 117, 125–27, 136, 212, 214, 219, 220n654, 221, 222, 225, 227, 247, 249, 253
Beskyd, Antonij, 175n495

Bethlen, István, Count, 25, 28, 118, 202, 223, 226–28, 234, 238, 260
Bismarck, Otto von, 71
Bled, Jean-Paul, ix, 16
Bleyer, Jakab, 193, 194, 196n585, 200
Borghese, Livio Giuseppe, Prince, 147
Bornemisza, Julius, 31
Boroviczény, Aladár, 147, 181, 230, 232, 249n761
Bourbon-Parma, Sixte, de, 32, 57, 213
Bourbon-Parma, Xavier, de, 57, 213
Briand, Aristide, 32, 87, 92, 116, 121, 211–22, 224–27, 247–55, 268, 272
Bridges, Tom, 63
Brodmann, Willibald, 155
Brook-Shepherd, Gordon, 63, 215
Buré, Emile, 92

Cadogan, Sir Alexander, 77–79
Cambon, Jules, 213
Campbell, Ronald, 68 n.173, 69, 118 n.306
Castellane, Boni (Boniface) de, Marquis, 65–83, 90, 93, 101, 109, 110n288, 119, 121n319, 251–53
Cecil, Robert, 58n137
Clemenceau, Georges, 8, 32, 57, 62, 81–83, 87, 91, 98, 124, 136, 139, 152n408, 213, 215, 219n653, 247, 265, 268
Clément-Simon, Louis, 246
Clerk, Sir George, 88, 119, 190, 199, 238, 240, 243
Cochin, Denys, 92
Coudenhove-Kalergi, Richard, Count, 58n137, 228, 271, 272
Crowe, Sir Eyre, 59, 76, 79
Curzon, George Nathaniel (Lord Curzon), 62, 63n157, 66, 68, 69, 76, 125

Index

Czartoryski, Adam, Prince, 15, 97
Czernin, Ottokar, 38, 82, 215
Csáky, István, 95

D'Annunzio, Gabriele, 14, 147, 154n415, 154n417, 168, 169, 229, 235
Daeschner, Émile, 120
de Gaulle, Charles, 250
Deák, Ferenc, 18
Deschanel, Paul, 98, 224
Duić, Stjepan (Stevo), 145, 147n387, 150–533, 157, 224, 229, 232, 236
Dunant, Alphonse, 227
Dutasta, Paul, 8, 82n212
Dvorčák, Viktor, 174, 176, 181, 196, 201–3, 207, 208

Eötvös, József, Baron, 16–18
Esterházy, Ferenc, Count, 30
Esterházy, Móric, Count, 28
Evans, R.J.W., ix, 58n138, 254

Fejtö, François, 7, 8, 268
Felak, James, 184
Ferguson, Niall, 9
Foch, Ferdinand, 116, 173, 219
Fontenay, Joseph de, 137, 157, 159, 161, 162, 165–67, 169, 246, 247
Forgách, János, Count, 57, 124
Franchet d'Espérey, Louis, 28, 139, 173, 219n652, 247, 253
Francis I, 21, 35n75
Frank, Ivo, 138, 145–48, 151, 153–55, 168, 229, 236, 237, 259
Frank, Josip, 137, 138, 144, 145
Franz Ferdinand, Archduke, 18, 39, 65, 67, 82, 135n348, 137, 158
Franz Joseph, I, 13, 16, 20, 21, 39, 251
Frigyes (Frederic) of Habsburg-Teschen, Archduke, 35

Gagliardi, Emmanuel, 145, 155
Gagliardi, Manko, 237

Gamelin, Maurice, 116
Garami, Ernő, 29
Gasparri, Pietro, 50, 52, 63
George V, King, 60
George, Lloyd, 119, 125–27
Ghilardi, Leon de, 148–50, 152, 153, 168, 259
Giuriati, Giovanni, 154, 169
Gosling, Cecil, 187
Gould, Anna, 65
Gömbös, Gyula, 29, 35, 74, 149, 150, 223, 225
Gratz, Gusztáv, 28, 224, 227–29, 259
Graziani, Rodolfo, 114
Grossich, Antonio, 14
Guernier, Charles, 107

Haguenin, François-Émile, 83, 85
Halmos, Károly, 110n288
Hardinge, Charles (Lord Hardinge), 57, 59, 60n147, 65–68, 79, 221, 222
Henrys, Paul, 139, 174
Hevesy, Pál, 95
Hlinka, Andrej, 178–86, 192, 196, 199–204, 208, 237, 238, 245, 246, 258, 259
Hodža, Milan, 172–79, 228, 237
Hohler, Thomas, 36, 38n84, 118
Horthy de Nagybánya, Miklós, 6, 13, 14, 24, 25, 34, 36–38, 69, 73, 74, 87n224, 96n246, 104, 118, 151, 193, 200, 217, 218, 220–26, 228, 235, 238, 249, 253, 261, 264
Horvat, Aleksandar, 133
Host-Venturi, Giovanni, 154
Hoyos, Alexander, Count, 57n132
Huszár, Károly, 193, 196

Ionescu, Take, 119, 120, 204
Jászi, Oszkár, 7, 17, 18, 33, 172, 175–77, 192, 260
Jehlička, František, xi, 179–82, 185, 194, 196, 199, 200, 202, 203, 205, 207, 208, 238, 245
Jelinek, Yeshayahu, 185
Joffre, Joseph, 119

Index

John Paul II, Pope, 273
József, Archduke, 34, 35, 36n77, 101, 171, 226
Judson, Pieter, 7
Juriga, Ferdiš (Ferdinand), 182, 185, 186, 237, 238, 245

Wilhelm II, Emperor, 21, 60
Kann, Robert, 4, 7, 11, 12
Kardos, József, 23n44
Karl, Charles, Károly (Karl I in Austria, Károly IV in Hungary), xi, 1n1, 2, 4–6, 10–12, 21, 22, 25, 26, 29, 31, 32, 34–42, 44–54, 56, 57, 60–68, 70, 72, 73, 78, 80–89, 91, 97, 101, 114, 115, 121n319, 124, 129, 132–34, 140, 145, 147, 158, 159, 170, 171, 181, 182, 190, 198, 211–28, 230, 233–35, 238, 239, 241, 244, 245, 247–53, 258–60, 262, 264, 270, 271, 273, 274
Károlyi, Gyula, Count, 29
Károlyi, Mihály, Count, 28, 29, 31, 35, 171, 261
Kirschbaum, Stanislav, 207, 245
Kissinger, Henry, 130
Kleindin, Imre, 149, 150
Klobularic, Benno von, 145, 146, 153
Kmoško, Michal, 194, 199, 200, 202, 203, 207, 208
Kossuth, Lajos, 15–17
Kramář, Karel, 239–41
Kremmer, Rodolph, 31
Kun, Béla, 28, 29, 31, 124, 152, 192, 261
Kvaternik, Eugen Dido, 236
Kvaternik, Slavko, 138–40, 150, 152, 236
Lammasch, Heinrich, 60
Lancken, Baron, 213, 222
Laroche, Jules, 212, 248n760
Leeper, Allen, 126
Lefevre-Pontalis, Eugène, 116
Lehár, Antal, 38, 232
Lindley, Francis Oswald, 229
Lipostyak (Liposcak), Anton, 152
Lobkowitz, Friedrich, Prince, 239n728
Lobkowitz, Zdenko, Prince, 239n728
Lónyay, Elemér, Prince, 220, 221

Lyon-Dalberg-Acton, Richard (Lord Acton), 64
Lorenz of Habsburg-Lorraine, Archduke, ix
Loucheur, Louis, 219, 220
Lovcen, Stephan Freiherr Sarkotić von, 137
Lubomirski, Ladislas, Prince, 64
Ludwig, Karl, 39
Lyautey, Hubert, 213, 216, 225, 253

Maček, Vladko, 157, 159, 162, 229, 230
Maglione, Luigi, 61
Maria Theresia, Queen, 23, 73n180
Marie-Antoinette, Queen, 122
Masaryk, Tomáš Garrigue, 8, 175n495, 177, 178n510, 180, 182, 206, 240, 241, 253, 268
Mension-Rigau, Eric, 68n173, 81
Meštrović, Ivan, 131n336
Mičura, Martin, 237
Mihailović, Antun, 133n339
Millerand, Alexandre, 98, 100, 101, 107, 108, 112, 114, 115, 117, 121, 125–27, 197, 216, 220, 246–48, 265, 268
Millo, Enrico, 168
Mittelhauser, Eugène, 115, 116, 205
Montgomery-Cuninghame, Thomas, 63
Montille, Lazare de, 107, 247, 252
Musulin, Sándor, Baron, 30

Namier, Lewis, 59, 60n147
Napoleon I, 20n41, 91, 274
Napoleon III, 91
Napoleon family, 61
Necker, Germaine (Mme de Staël), 274
Nitti, Francesco, 125–27, 147

Oppenheimer, Francis, 59, 60
d'Ormesson, Jean, 252n766
Ormesson, Wladimir, d', 251, 252n766
Otto, Archduke, 22, 27, 75n189, 245, 250, 260

Paléologue, Maurice, 87, 92, 93, 98, 99, 101, 102, 104–12, 117, 118, 121, 126, 127, 216, 219, 246, 247, 252, 263, 265

Index

Pallavicini, György, Marquis, 28
Pašić, Nicola, 137
Pavelić, Ante, 138n358, 236
Pazman, Josip, 144, 162, 169
Pejačević, Teodor, 157, 167
Pellé, Maurice, 115, 116
Peretti della Rocca, Emmanuel, 212
Pethő, Sándor, 27
Petričević, Niko, 145
Pichon, Stéphen, 136, 139, 152, 173, 174
Piffl, Friedrich Gustav, 44
Plamenatz, Jovan, 154
Poincaré, Raymond, 45–46n106, 65, 81, 83, 92, 93, 98, 213, 222
Popovici, Aurel, 18
Práznovszky, Iván, 148–50
Prebeg, Valdimir, 144, 162, 169
Pribičević, Milan, 141, 146
Pribičević, Svetozar, 134, 136, 144, 146

Quitton de Saint Quentin, Frédéric, 224

Ráday, Gedeon, Count, 29
Radić, Stepan, 137n351, 140, 144, 145, 151, 155–62, 164–69, 229–31, 235, 236, 258
Ránki, György, 111
Rašin, Alois, 188
Rattigan, Frank, 120
Rauch, Pavao, 157
Renner, Karl, 17, 18, 29, 38, 198, 260
Renouvier, Charles, 9
Rudolph of Habsburg-Lorraine, Archduke, 9, 39
Rumbold, Sir Horace, 31, 58
Wittelsbach, Ruprecht, Prince, 87n223, 114, 115
Sachs, Vladimir, 145, 146, 154, 229, 230
Saint Stephen, 24, 25, 36, 134, 154, 176, 193, 194, 217, 231, 261–64
Salis, John de, Count, 62–64, 150
Sándor, Anna-Mária, ix
Sarkotić von Lovcen, Stephan Freiherr, 137
Schmidt, Harry, 30

Seeholzer, Heinrich, 65, 68, 83, 85, 211, 212, 222, 227
Seitz, Karl, 50
Seton-Watson, Hugh, 70
Seton-Watson, R. W., 58, 59, 70, 178, 199, 254
Sforza, Carlo, 147, 168
Sigray, Antal, Count, 28, 38
Sked, Alan, 7
Škrlec, Ivan, 157
Soutou, Henri, 75n191
Šrobár, Vavro, 178, 179, 182, 183, 185, 186, 192, 197
Stipetić, Wilhelm, 145
Strutt, Edward, 60, 63, 216, 222, 227
Šufflay, Milan, 230
Supilo, Franco, 131n336
Szilassy, Gyula, Baron, 30, 82, 83, 95, 96
Szmrecsányi, György, 28, 145

Talleyrand-Périgord, Charles-Maurice de, 93
Tardieu, André, 55, 56, 152, 250, 255n774
Teleki, László, Count, 15
Teleki, Pál, Count, 25, 37, 95, 223, 234, 266
Thwaites, William, 63
Tiso, Jozef, 185, 245
Tisseyre, Charles, 107
Tisza, István, Count, 20, 40
Tomljenović, Tomislav, 231
Trumbić, Ante, 131n336, 136, 231n698
Tuka, Vojtech, 185, 245, 246, 259

Unger, František/Ferenc, 200, 203, 204, 238, 239
Vajay, Szabolcs de, 242
Valfré di Bonzo, Teodoro, 50
Vályi, Félix, 30, 32
Vaux, Leon de, 30
Vázsonyi, Vilmos, 26, 29, 30
Veitsberger, Andreas, Baron, 31
Villani di Castello-Pillonico, Frigyes, Baron, 153n410

Index

Villani di Castello-Pillonico, Lajos, Baron, 153n410
Vix, Fernand, 173, 174

Wandycz, Piotr, 97, 98
Weber, Erich, 27
Wekerle, Sándor, 133, 134
Werbőczy, István, 24n45
Wickham Steed, Henry, 58, 81, 124

Wilson, Woodrow, 11, 12, 33, 93, 125, 129, 132–34, 159, 161, 175n495, 268–70
Windischgraetz, Lajos, Prince, ix, 29, 30, 157, 181, 214, 215n640, 222, 274
Wrangel, Pyotr, Baron, 69, 241

Žatkovyč, Gregory, 175n495
Zita, Empress, 50, 51n118, 60, 147n385, 215, 216, 225, 226, 245, 253